Insights into Second Language Reading

THE CAMBRIDGE APPLIED LINGUISTICS SERIES

Series editors: Michael H. Long and Jack C. Richards

This series presents the findings of work in applied linguistics that are of direct relevance to language teaching and learning and of particular interest to applied linguists, researchers, language teachers, and teacher trainers.

Recent publications in this series:

Insights into Second Language Reading

A Cross-Linguistic Approach

Keiko Koda

Carnegie Mellon University

PUBLISHED BY THE PRESS SYNDICATE OF THE UNIVERSITY OF CAMBRIDGE
The Pitt Building, Trumpington Street, Cambridge, United Kingdom

CAMBRIDGE UNIVERSITY PRESS
The Edinburgh Building, Cambridge CB2 2RU, UK
40 West 20th Street, New York, NY 10011-4211, USA
477 Williamstown Road, Port Melbourne, VIC 3207, Australia
Ruiz de Alarcón 13, 28014 Madrid, Spain
Nautica Building, The Water Club, Beach Road, Granger Bay,
8005 Cape Town, South Africa

http://www.cambridge.org

First published 2005

Printed in the United States of America

Typeface Sabon 10.5/12 pt.   *System* LATEX 2_ε [TB]

A catalog record for this book is available from the British Library.

Library of Congress Cataloging in Publication Data
Koda, Keiko, 1954–
Insights into second language reading : a cross-linguistic approach / Keiko Koda.
    p. cm. – (Cambridge applied linguistics series)
    Includes bibliographical references and index.
    ISBN 0-521-83662-X (HB) – ISBN 0-521-54513-7 (pbk.)
    1. Language and languages – Study and teaching. 2. Reading.
I. Title. II. Series.
P53.75.K63 2004
407–dc22   2004040399

ISBN 0 521 83662 X hardback
ISBN 0 521 54513 7 paperback

Contents

Tables and figures

Tables

Figures

Series editors' preface

In *Insights into Second Language Reading: A Cross-Linguistic Approach*, Professor Keiko Koda provides a comprehensive, psycholinguistically oriented introduction to the cross-linguistic study of reading in a second language (L2). Her goal is to establish a clear conceptual foundation for research on L2 reading competence (as distinct from necessary, but insufficient, general L2 linguistic proficiency) and its acquisition within well-defined, empirically testable frameworks. The main focus is cognitively mature adults literate in their L1, but research on other kinds of readers (young children, etc.) is also covered where appropriate. Both L1 and L2 reading research are reviewed with a view to differentiating the two processes, distinguishing between (notably, orthographic and phonological) knowledge, on the one hand, and skills in each, on the other, and identifying needed work on individual differences in L2 reading.

Part I provides an overview of the volume, before covering theoretical underpinnings for conceptualizing and analyzing L2 reading competence. Part II consists of six chapters treating the components of reading ability: word recognition, vocabulary knowledge (both how this helps reading and how reading helps build vocabulary), intraword awareness and word-knowledge development, information integration in sentence processing, discourse processing (including the role of coherence, inference, and background knowledge in comprehension), and narrative and expository text structures and comprehension. Part III pulls things together, highlighting connections among the components in a holistic portrayal of reading. Chapter 9 deals with individual differences (what characteristics define good and bad readers), and Chapter 10 focuses on the role of metacognitive processes in strategic reading. Finally, in Part IV, Chapter 11 covers the assessment of L2 reading, and Chapter 12 reviews research on the reading instruction and makes suggestions for pedagogy.

Understanding Second Language Reading: A Cross-Linguistic Approach is one of the most comprehensive treatments of L2 reading available. It is a fine addition to the *Cambridge Applied Linguistics Series* and will assuredly be very useful to all those engaged in teaching and research in what has become an area of such major importance in applied linguistics.

Michael H. Long
Jack C. Richards

Foreword

For the past three decades, second language (L2) reading has attracted unprecedented research attention. A multitude of studies have sought ways to identify the factors either promoting or impeding effective reading in a second language. As the field expanded, the research focus progressively shifted from merely describing what L2 readers could or could not do to explaining the basis of their behavior. Currently, the conceptual trends in L2 research tend to lean toward first language (L1) reading theories. Although, to be sure, L1 constructs are the logical point of departure in pursuing new lines of inquiry, the "borrowed" research paradigms to date have not spawned viable L2 reading models. To achieve a clear understanding of L2 reading's unique nature, we need coherent frameworks through which L2 data can first be analyzed and then synthesized into functional theoretical explorations.

Toward this end, *Insights into Second Language Reading* stems from in-depth analyses of the multiple dimensions of L2 reading. Reading is a multifaceted, complex construct in that it involves a number of component operations, each dependent on a wide range of competencies. Obviously, the complexity increases in L2 reading since, by definition, it involves more than one language. The ultimate goal of the analyses is to lay a conceptual foundation for building serviceable models of L2 reading capable of delineating how L1 and L2 reading theories must differ. Three specific objectives guided the pursuit: (1) providing detailed descriptions of the processing components inherent in L2 reading; (2) applying cross-linguistic analyses of research-based insights, derived primarily from monolingual studies; and (3) exploring potential new directions for expanding current research paradigms. It is to be hoped that, collectively, the analyses will establish a platform for enhancing effective L2 reading instruction. To wit, a shrewder grasp of the complexities governing effective L2 reading should enable L2 teachers to adapt their instruction to the diverse needs of individual learners, and thereby achieve greater instructional quality.

My interests in the integration of reading and L2 acquisition were formed in my graduate school days at the University of Illinois. I am deeply indebted to Muriel Saville-Troike, Gary Cziko, David Pearson, and George McConkie – all profound mentors – whose work and guidance helped mold my research directions. My thanks are also owed to Dick Anderson, Bill Nagy, and Chuck Perfetti, who not only were generous in sharing their thoughts but were wonderfully adept at triggering insights. Their noteworthy work inspired me to address, in various ways, how insights are best uncovered.

Many others provided support and encouragement for this book. At the inception, Barry McLaughlin helped shape the overall approaches. Through skillfully worded probing, Dick Tucker generated continuous forward momentum and steered me in the right directions. I also owe a large debt to Bill Grabe, whose wisdom, experience, and broad knowledge helped me separate the wheat from the chaff. I am grateful to many colleagues with whom I collaborated during the book's evolution for their assistance and support: Annette Zehler, Hirofumi Saito, Mike Fender, Min Wang, Chin-Lung Yang, Chiou-lan Chern, Etsuko Takahashi, and Sufumi So. I also was privileged to work with an ETS NEW TOEFL reading team, including Mary Enright, Bill Grabe, Pat Mulkahy-Ernt, and Mary Schedl, for many thought-provoking discussions on reading assessment. A distinguished professor, when asked to what he attributed his high achievements, said, "I had smart graduate students." I have somewhat the same feeling. My thanks go to a number of graduate students who worked with me on the various research projects discussed in this volume for their contributions and assistance: Margaret Chang, Dan Dewey, Muljani Dojomiharudojo, Hisae Fujiwara, Bonnie Gairns, Megumi Hamada, Yoshiko Mori, Eunyoung Park, and Yukiko Wada.

The project has been partially supported by an IAS/Mellon Fellowship from the National Foreign Language Center (NFLC). I am grateful to Richard Brecht at the NFLC for providing the opportunity to work intensely on cross-linguistic issues in lexical knowledge development. The work there helped me to think through many of the critical issues explored in various chapters. I also need to express appreciation to students in the L2 reading seminar in the past year: Patti Spinner, Jenee Wright, Javier Coronado-Aliegro, and Marina Saiz, in particular, for allowing me to field-test the volume and for sharing their candid reactions. Hisae Fujiwara did incredible work on the References. Continuous encouragement from Mike Long, a series editor, and support and guidance from Julia Hough, Commissioning Editor at Cambridge, greatly facilitated the overcoming of many impediments.

Finally, but importantly, Lou Rubin deserves my deepest gratitude for all he has done in tolerating my crisis moments and for providing me with time, encouragement, criticism, and assistance as my first reader and critic. Without his support, the book would not have come to life.

Acknowledgments

Appreciation is expressed for permission to reprint the following works:

Chapter 4 – Table 4.1. What is involved in knowing a word. Nation, I. S. P. 2001. *Learning vocabulary in another language.* © Cambridge University Press, page 27.

Chapter 4 – Figure 4.1. The bilingual interactive activation model. Dijkstra, T., & van Heuven, W. J. B. 1998. The BIA model and bilingual word recognition. © Erlbaum, page 200.

Chapter 5 – Table 5.1. Relationships among words, characters, and radicals. Koda, K. 2000. Cross-linguistic variations in L2 morphological awareness. *Applied Psycholinguistics, 21.* © Cambridge University Press, page 303.

Chapter 6 – Table 6.1. Cross-linguistic variations in cue selection in actor assignment. Bates, E., & MacWhinney, B. 1989. Functionalism and the competition model. © Cambridge University Press, pages 44–45.

Chapter 8 – Figure 8.1. Causal-chain (top) and causal-network (bottom) representations of the sample narrative. Van den Broeak, P. 1994. Comprehension and memory of narrative texts. © Academic Press, pages 543, 545.

Chapter 9 – Table 9.1. Component skills assessment battery. Carr, T. H., Brown, T. L., Vavrus, L. G., & Evans, M. A. 1990. Cognitive skill maps and cognitive skill profiles: Componential analysis of individual differences in children's reading efficiency. © Cambridge University Press, page 13.

Chapter 9 – Figure 9.1. Model of the information-processing structure of the reading system to guide component skills analysis. Carr, T. H., Brown, T. L., Vavrus, L. G., & Evans, M. A. 1990. Cognitive skill maps and cognitive skill profiles: Componential analysis of individual differences in children's reading efficiency. © Academic Press, page 8.

Chapter 9 – Figure 9.2. Cognitive skills map of individual differences in reading performance. Carr, T. H., Brown, T. L., Vavrus, L. G., & Evans, M. A. 1990. Cognitive skill maps and cognitive skill profiles: Componential analysis of individual differences in children's reading efficiency. © Academic Press, page 27.

Chapter 9 – Figure 9.3. Schematic representation of the relationship between lower-level and higher-level language-processing skills. Nassaji, H., & Geva, E. 1999. The contribution of phonological and orthographic processing skills to adult ESL reading: Evidence from native speakers of Farsi. *Applied Psycholinguistics, 20.* © Cambridge University Press, page 259.

Chapter 10 – Table 10.1. Categories of processing strategies. Anderson, N. J. 1991. Individual differences in strategy use in second language reading and testing. *Modern Language Journal, 75*, p. 463.

Chapter 10 – Table 10.2. A classification of different types of verbalization procedures. Ericsson, K. A., & Simon, H. A. 1984. *Protocol analysis: Verbal reports as data.* © MIT Press, page 12.

Chapter 11 – Table 11.1. Reading levels associated with text types and processing skills. Lee, J. F., & Musumeci, D. 1988. On hierarchies of reading skills and text types. *Modern Language Journal, 72*, p. 174.

PART I

THEORETICAL FOUNDATIONS

1 Introduction

The rapid internationalization of business and industry, together with a sustained immigration influx, has resulted in an unprecedented interest in enhancing second language (L2) learning. In seeking better approaches to second language teaching, as well as L2 subject-matter instruction, applied linguistics has witnessed major advances in both theory and practice. As a consequence, research on L2 reading, a recognized area of applied linguistics, also has made impressive gains in quality and quantity.

As the title *Insights into Second Language Reading* implies, this book's intent is not a simple review but an effort to establish a foundation for expanding current L2 reading research within well-defined frameworks, and to establish a research base that can facilitate productive innovations in second language reading instruction. These objectives have been approached through a series of analyses: synthesizing ongoing issues in first language (L1) reading literature; examining possible implications of L1 research for conceptualizing L2 reading competence and its acquisition; exploring means of incorporating established L1 research paradigms in empirical examinations of L2 reading; and identifying troublesome gaps in L2 reading research. Because, by definition, learning to read a second language involves two or more languages, the analyses are cross-linguistic, exploring both L1 and L2 characteristics as possible sources of individual differences in L2 reading development.

Although the book is not designed as a classroom teaching manual, basic principles for translating research into practice, and pedagogical implications of research findings, are included. Descriptions of L2 reading processes are incorporated under the assumption that a clear understanding of the multiple complexities inherent in L2 reading development will enable language teachers to identify the range of difficulties L2 learners are likely to encounter in learning to read in a new language, discriminate potential sources of learning difficulties more precisely, and restructure instruction in beneficial ways. Conceivably, a

3

broader pathways to reading mastery in a new language will also be useful in tailoring pedagogical strategies to accommodate the varying needs of individual learners.

Basic concepts and constructs

Although studies on L2 reading have expanded considerably, only recently has serious attention been given to the mechanisms governing knowledge increase and performance effectiveness. The newer theoretical ground, moreover, has evolved largely from implications derived from L1 studies. Although this was a logical point of departure, "borrowed" research paradigms do not seem capable of capturing the unique attributes of L2 reading. Because L1 and L2 reading differ fundamentally, when L1 precepts are extrapolated without due regard for the requirements stemming from these differences, conceptual oversights may occur, and subsequent applications to practice could be weakened.

Logic suggests that in-depth analyses of the complexities associated with L2 reading should help determine where its theories must depart from accepted L1 constructs and – even more critically – pinpoint new research objectives. Both L2 learning and reading are complex, multidimensional constructs, and their respective research literature reflects a broad base of interdisciplinary perspectives. It should be noted, however, that in this book, the primary orientation is psycholinguistic. This is in no way meant to diminish the merits of other perspectives; rather, it is simply a matter of focus. To illustrate the psycholinguistic frame of reference in the analyses, the main concepts and constructs are briefly defined.

The nature of reading competence

Reading competence is perhaps the most fundamental construct in reading research. The term *competence* is used inclusively throughout the book in reference to linguistic knowledge, processing skills, and cognitive abilities. Reading competence and reading ability, moreover, are used interchangeably. Conceptualized in several different ways, diverse definitions exist, but all stem from the same basic assumption that successful comprehension emerges from the integrative interaction of derived text information and preexisting reader knowledge. Put simply, comprehension occurs when the reader extracts and integrates various information from the text and combines it with what is already known. Each of these operations is generally used to define reading competence, although from different perspectives.

The cognitive view, as an illustration, posits that reader–text interaction can be subdivided into three processing clusters. First, in *decoding*, linguistic information is extracted directly from print. Next, in *text-information building*, extracted ideas are integrated to uncover text meanings. Finally, in *situation-model construction*, the amalgamated text information is synthesized with prior knowledge (e.g., Carpenter, Miyake, & Just, 1994; Kintsch, 1998; Miller, 1988; Perfetti, 1994). Thus, in this view, reading success is governed by three competency groups: visual information extraction, incremental information integration, and text-meaning and prior-knowledge consolidation. Traditionally, reading research has pursued individual competencies within each cluster, giving little attention to their functional, as well as developmental, interconnections.

From a developmental perspective, Gough and his associates (Gough & Tunmer, 1986; Hoover & Gough, 1990) suggest a different way of defining reading competence. Their contention is that, although learning to read entails the mastery of two basic operations – decoding and comprehension – they do not develop in parallel. Both reading and listening share similar processing requirements, and children amass comprehension skills in the course of oral language development. By the time they begin to read, therefore, their listening comprehension ability, in most instances, is already well developed. In principle, children should be able to transfer their oral comprehension ability to reading, but in actuality, they cannot do so until they attain sufficient decoding efficiency. However, decoding, unlike comprehension, does not evolve as a corollary of speech, thus requiring substantial print-information processing experience. Lacking decoding competence, children have insufficient information to construct text meaning. And, in the absence of automaticity, the attention required for decoding substantially detracts from what otherwise would be available for comprehension. Thus, decoding creates a threshold for exploiting the comprehension competence children bring to their reading acquisition processes.

Reasoning from a functional perspective, Carver (1990, 1997, 2000) proposes yet another way of conceptualizing reading competence. He believes the purposes for which texts are read determine the manner in which their information is processed. He describes five reading "gears," serving disparate purposes, on a continuum of cognitive complexity. Consider, for example, three goals in text reading: locating lexical information (scanning), detecting main ideas (basic comprehension), and acquiring new concepts (learning). Cognitively, reading for lexical information is the least challenging, involving simple lexical access. Reading for basic comprehension is somewhat more taxing because it necessitates, beyond lexical access, syntactic analysis for information integration. Acquiring new concepts in learning, is the most demanding of the three. According to Carver, processing requirements increase as the "reading gear" shifts upward – and, as a consequence of greater task complexity, the reading rate decreases. Hence, he concludes that indices of comprehension success vary in accordance with reading purposes. In the less demanding, lower reading gears (scanning and skimming), competence implies speedy information extraction. In the higher gears, however, accurate and complete text understanding is more important than speed. The clear implication is that why, and how, texts are read must be considered in determining reading competence.

To sum up, then, reading competence can be defined from multiple perspectives. The cognitive view, reflecting the interactive nature of reading, emphasizes three operations as the critical core of competence: decoding, text-meaning construction, and assimilation with prior knowledge. The developmental perspective, in contrast, highlights sequential mastery of two operations – decoding and comprehension – and their functional interdependence. The reading gear theory, moreover, suggests a third factor, reading purpose, to be incorporated in defining the core construct.

In exploring L2 reading development, these diverse perspectives also need to be incorporated. Clarifying the construct's multilayered complexities is essential for two reasons. Because L2 literacy learning commences at various ages and under diverse circumstances, we can reasonably assume that considerable variances exist in prior literacy-learning experience. Without a reliable basis for determining what has been mastered in L1, empirical examination of its influence on L2 reading behaviors is not possible. In addition, the manner and rate of L2 reading development also are likely to differ among learners because L2 reading instruction begins at different points in their L2 development. Hence, without a precise construct definition, L2 reading competence cannot be differentiated from L2 linguistic proficiency. Lacking a fine-tuned description of the progressive stages of L2 reading acquisition, tracing developmental changes at a given point in time is also prohibitive.

Defining L2 readers

The term *L2 reading* covers a broad span, and its use is excessively general, often overlooking important differentiation, which has strong impacts on how learning to read proceeds in a second language. For example, there are several distinct L2 reader populations, including preschool children without prior literacy experience, school-aged children with disparate L1 literacy experience, adult learners literate in their L1, and adult learners nonliterate in their L1. L2 linguistic knowledge is a common variable in each of these groups, but the developmental profiles may deviate in three critical dimensions: L1 literacy, cognitive maturity, and conceptual sophistication. Each of these categories interacts with contextual variations relating to where, how, and why L2 literacy is being pursued. For example, the learning experience of six-year-old native Chinese-speaking children, acquiring reading skills in English as a second language in an American public school, is strikingly different from that of native English-speaking students taking an elementary Chinese course, to fulfill a foreign language requirement, in an American university.

Logically, an essential first step in gaining a clear understanding of L2 reading development is to determine the particular learning characteristics of the specific group involved. Similarly, in considering research implications for L2 reading instruction, it is equally imperative to clarify the nature of the target L2 readers. In the interest of clarity, it is important to note that in the subsequent chapters, "L2 readers" generally refers to cognitively mature individuals already literate in their respective first languages learning to read a second language. Other L2 reader cohorts are described separately wherever pertinent.

Differentiating L1 and L2 reading

Once a target L2 reader population has been defined, differences between L1 and L2 reading can be determined. In the focal group used for this volume – literate adult L2 learners – three major distinctions separate the two. Unlike beginning L1 readers, L2 learners can draw on their prior literacy experience, which potentially provides substantial facilitation. In addition, beginning L1 readers, through oral communication, have already established a basic linguistic foundation by the time formal literacy training commences. In contrast, L2 reading instruction, more often than not, begins before sufficient L2 linguistic knowledge has been acquired. Hence, the initial focus in literacy training necessarily differs. Whereas L1 instruction emphasizes decoding to enable children to link print with oral vocabulary, L2 instruction focuses on linguistic foundation building. Further, as indicated earlier, L1 reading assumes that information processing occurs in a single language, whereas L2 reading necessitates dual-language involvement – another factor separating L1 and L2 reading.

In view of these distinctions, it is obvious that L2 research must go beyond the standard array of variables essential in L1 reading and emphasize the specific constituents that define L2 reading competence. In particular, serious attention should be given to the special conditions associated with the preceding three factors – prior literacy experience, limited linguistic sophistication, and dual-language involvement – because collectively they form a base from which to further probe L2 reading issues. Research agendas, as an illustration, can be generated simply by converting well-established L1 reading suppositions into questions incorporating L2 points of view. For example, one of the fundamental premises underlying contemporary reading theories is that text understanding results from the integrative interaction of textual information and preexisting reader knowledge. Inasmuch as L2 readers have prior literacy experience, the premise can be turned into a question: In what ways does L1 reading experience affect integrative interaction in L2 reading? An additional question could be derived from the same premise, based on another L2-specific factor, limited linguistic sophistication: What are the impacts of L2 proficiency on integrative interaction during reading comprehension? With respect to dual-language involvement, a third question might be, What are the minimal L1 and L2 competency requirements necessary for integrative interaction to occur during L2 reading? Strategies of this sort are, in essence, simply a matter of utilizing what we know about L1 reading to elucidate what we do not know about L2 reading.

In view of the complexities inherent in reading competence, numerous research questions could be formulated by evaluating the validity of L1 reading principles on L2 issues – from L2 vantage points. In short, L1 reading research has yielded a number of significant insights. A clearer understanding of L2 reading, however, cannot be attained by simply extrapolating L1 percepts – both conceptual and methodological – without due regard for the dominant factors characterizing L2 reading.

Principal approaches

The benefits of cross-linguistic analyses

Potential variations in L2 processing behaviors – stemming from L1 properties – also should be central in L2 reading research. The importance is manifested in the growing interest in cross-linguistic variances in language acquisition and processing. Child-language studies demonstrate that children are sensitized to the particular features of their native languages relatively early. Such linguistic conditioning not only channels subsequent language development but also molds the cognitive procedures accommodating its structural and functional peculiarities. Experimental studies with skilled readers have repeatedly shown that information-processing procedures at various processing levels – word recognition, sentence parsing, and discourse processing – systematically differ across languages (e.g., Katz & Frost, 1992; Mazuka & Itoh, 1995; Saito, Masuda, & Kawakami, 1999; Taft & Zhu, 1995; Vaid, 1995).

Curiously, cross-linguistic variance, despite its centrality, has attracted relatively little attention among L2 reading researchers, although interest is mounting. The neglect may have been attributable, in part, to the heavy reliance on L1 theories, without essential allowances for important L1–L2 distinctions. L1 research concerns are restricted to monolingual processing, and consequent cross-linguistic issues are beyond its scope. Given that two or more bodies of linguistic knowledge – together with their corresponding processing skills – are involved in L2 reading, it is doubtful whether a comprehensive understanding of its anatomy can be achieved through investigations of its monolingual perspectives alone. Ideally, L2 research should address learners' L1 and L2 processing experiences in tandem, examining their probable interplay as well as subsequent conjoint impacts on L2 reading development. The central assumption underlying the cross-linguistic approach is that L1 experience embeds habits of mind, instilling specific processing mechanisms, which frequently kick in during L2 reading. Diversity in L1 experience, therefore, can induce *qualitative* procedural differences, whereas variances in L2 experience may yield *quantitative* efficiency differences. As a consequence, inferences about L2 reading competence – based solely on either qualitative or quantitative performance differences – often are inadequate and misleading. Cross-linguistic analyses can illuminate the subtle ways in which L1 and L2 experiences meld and interface during L2 reading development. Presumably, the resulting insights derived from such bifocal analyses may explain competency differences among L2 readers with substantially greater precision.

Advantages of competency dissection

To recapitulate, reading involves continual extraction and incremental integration of text information. Successful comprehension, therefore, depends on both linguistic knowledge and the skills to utilize the knowledge for text-meaning construction. Theories of L2 reading, therefore, should elucidate the specific knowledge and processing skills that underlie successful comprehension in a given language. Linguistic knowledge and its corresponding processing skills do not, of necessity, develop concomitantly. As a result, it is important to treat knowledge and knowledge use as separate constructs, and to devise procedures for assessing them independently.

In L1 research, this distinction is widely recognized. For example, empirical evidence confirms that decoding efficiency varies considerably among beginning L1 readers who have attained normal oral language development (e.g., Perfetti, 1985; Stanovich, 1991). The findings make it plain that oral vocabulary knowledge does not automatically equate with an ability to recognize it in print. Although both are essential in efficient information processing, knowing something and knowing how to use it effectively are discrete capabilities. The implication of these competency distinctions is clear. Because processing inefficiency can be attributable to either a lack of relevant knowledge or underdeveloped usage skill, or both, without fine-tuned component analyses, it is difficult to determine the precise root of the problem. However, this differentiation has not been fully acknowledged in L2 reading research, resulting in the widespread but erroneous belief that processing skills improve automatically as a byproduct of increased linguistic knowledge.

L1 reading studies also suggest that two forms of linguistic knowledge – orthographic and phonological – independently influence English decoding efficiency (e.g., Barker, Torgesen, & Wagner, 1992; Stanovich, 2000; Stanovich & West, 1989). Inasmuch as the two do not develop concomitantly with other aspects of linguistic knowledge (e.g., Gough & Tunmer, 1986), we cannot simply assume that all beginning readers have acquired the requisite knowledge at the time they begin learning to read. Even if they have, there is no assurance that they will master the complementary skills to use the knowledge during decoding. The knowledge–skill distinction is particularly critical, because linguistic knowledge varies widely among L2 learners.

In sum, four major assumptions support the importance of competency dissection: Linguistic knowledge and language processing skills are related but distinct competencies; discrete aspects of linguistic knowledge contribute disparately to comprehension; linguistic knowledge is a necessary but insufficient condition for efficient text-information processing; and requisite linguistic knowledge, as well as its corresponding processing skills differs across languages. For these reasons, to the extent possible, a clear distinction has been made between linguistic knowledge and processing skills, in the subsequent analyses of L2 reading competence.

General organization

This volume's primary objectives are to establish a foundation for expanding current L2 reading research by reexamining accepted L1 reading concepts from L2 points of view and, in so doing, to uncover new research agendas particularly relevant to L2 reading development. To achieve these goals, the major component operations in reading were subjected to sequential analyses, including syntheses of existing L1 reading literature, summaries of L1 research implications, explorations of L1 and L2 research integration, and suggestions for future L2 research agendas. The theoretical underpinnings used in conceptualizing and analyzing L2 reading competence are described in Chapter 2. Thereafter, the content is organized, first, according to processing components, and second, by major research issues.

The six chapters in Part II examine the component competencies essential to reading comprehension, illustrating within each how text information is extracted, integrated, and understood. Chapter 3 deals with word recognition, explaining its function and procedure in the context of reading. Chapter 4 delineates the symbiotic relationship between vocabulary and reading comprehension, incorporating an in-depth analysis of the nature and acquisition of word-meaning knowledge. Chapter 5 explores the parameters of intraword awareness and their relation to lexical learning and processing, explaining the facilitative benefits of such awareness in word-knowledge development through reading. Next, the processes involved in intrasentential information integration are described. Chapter 6 begins with an analysis of the linguistic sensitivity underlying sentence processing and then progresses to an examination of its relationship to performance variation. Research on discourse processing – how text is progressively reconstructed in the reader's mind – is summarized in Chapter 7. The chapter also deals with text coherence building and inference, as well as the contributions of background knowledge to text comprehension. Chapter 8 clarifies the impacts of text-structure variables on discourse processing by reviewing the distinct properties of narrative and expository texts.

In the interest of a balanced view, Part III presents a holistic portrayal of reading, emphasizing the interconnections of components described in the previous chapters. Chapter 9 focuses on individual differences in reading acquisition and performance. Using systematic comparisons of processing behaviors among good and poor readers, it considers the cognitive and linguistic requirements for proficient reading as well as their comparative effect on performance variations. Chapter 10 examines the nature of strategic reading, elaborating on the role of metacognition as an oversight mechanism regulating cognitive resources during comprehension.

Part IV touches on pedagogical issues, highlighting principles incorporating theory into practice. Chapter 11 discusses contradictory views on reading, laying out their implications for comprehension assessment. Finally, Chapter 12 offers a compendium of research findings that bear directly on L2 reading instruction and describes basic principles and processes for designing research-based instructional interventions.

2 *Theoretical underpinnings*

To accomplish the book's major intent – analyzing accepted L1 reading concepts from L2 points of view – it would be advantageous to describe the theoretical foundations of the issues examined. A sensible beginning would be transfer theory, because cross-linguistic interactions are central to L2 processing as an important basis for examining reading behavior variations. As the basic cognitive mechanism explaining skills acquisition and performance improvement, a consideration of the connectionist theorem affords a useful groundwork. What is commonly referred to as the component skills approach constitutes a means of contrasting the competency components and their relative impacts on L2 reading efficiency. Finally, three additional formulations, each of which helps conceptualize L2 reading ability differences, are described.

Cross-language reading skills transfer

Language transfer has long been a central concern among L2 researchers. As an outgrowth of the contrastive analysis (CA) hypothesis, transfer concepts were widely endorsed in the 1950s and 1960s. Their basic hypothesis, a derivative of behaviorism, contends that the principal barriers to L2 learning stem from interference factors spawned by previous language-learning experience. In more recent contentions, however, language learning is viewed as continuous hypothesis formation and verification, based on available linguistic input. This view makes completely different assumptions about the effects of previous language-learning experience – namely, providing facilitation by creating an essential basis for establishing an additional linguistic system. The current shifts in transfer research have materialized during this compelling transition in language-learning theories.

A good number of studies have shown that various aspects of L1 capabilities are transferred during L2 production and interpretation: morphosyntax (e.g., Hakuta, 1976; Hancin & Nagy, 1994; Kilborn

13

& Ito, 1989; Sasaki, 1991, 1993), phonology (Gundel & Tarone, 1983; Hancin-Bhatt & Bhatt, 1997), pragmatics (e.g., Rutherford, 1983; Yanco, 1985), metalinguistic awareness (Durgunoglu, Nagy, & Hancin, 1993; Koda, 1998, 1999, 2000b), and communicative strategies (e.g., Cohen, Olshtain, & Rosenstein, 1986; Irujo, 1986; Olshtain, 1983; Scarcella, 1983). In light of these findings, it seems reasonable to assume that many reading skills developed in one language can be applied to another. Oddly, despite its significance, it is only recently that reading skills transfer has attracted serious research attention. During its relatively brief history, the research has been heavily dominated by two major perspectives: the presupposition that reading procedures are universal across languages, and the conviction that reading necessitates language-specific processes.

The early transfer research was bound by the former universal framework, focusing on two fundamental issues: the interrelationship between L1 and L2 reading competence (e.g., Cummins, 1979, 1991; Cummins, Swain, Nakajima, Handscombe, & Green, 1981; Legarretta, 1979; Skutnabb-Kangass & Toukomaa, 1976; Troike, 1978), and the conditions inhibiting, or facilitating, reading skills transfer (e.g., Clarke, 1980; Devine, 1987, 1988). Heavily influenced by top-down conceptualization, the universal view was governed by three intrinsic premises: Reading success depends on conceptual processing and strategic manipulations (e.g., using background knowledge in forming anticipatory hypotheses about immediately ensuing text and confirming them through subsequent information); such competencies do not vary from language to language; and, therefore, the more transfer, the easier and better L2 comprehension. In short, the universal perspective, as Goodman (1973) put it, treats reading as a "psycholinguistic guessing game," relegating information extraction and integration skills to peripheral. As a result, scant attention was given to processing components and their transfer in these early studies.

More recently, however, controversy regarding the universality of language acquisition and processing has increased greatly. Experimental psychologists now routinely challenge language-processing theories based on data obtained exclusively from English-speaking participants. Cross-linguistic studies on sentence processing, for example, consistently show that the cognitive procedures involved in sentence comprehension and production are heavily constrained by the particular syntactic properties inherent in each language (e.g., Bates & MacWhinney, 1989; Bates, McNew, MacWhinney, Devescovi, & Smith, 1982; Kail, 1989). Similarly, child-language studies indicate that children cannot deal efficiently with linguistic forms that violate the prototypical sentence structure in their primary language (e.g., Berman, 1986; Hakuta, 1982; Slobin, 1985; Slobin & Bever, 1982). Second language acquisition (SLA) investigations, moreover, affirm that the linguistic conditioning generated by L1 linguistic features not only influences L2 acquisition (e.g., Flynn, 1987a, 1989; Gass, 1989; Gass & Schachter, 1989; Phinney, 1987; White, 1989) but also constrains the cognitive procedures used in L2 processing (e.g., Kilborn & Ito, 1989; Koda, 1992; McDonald, 1987; Sasaki, 1991, 1993). In brief, information-processing procedures vary systematically across languages, at least to the extent that the morphosyntactic features essential to sentence comprehension and production deviate.

The language-specific perspective of reading transfer emerged from the cross-linguistic research. In contrast to the universal position, it stresses the language-processing competencies essential to text-meaning construction, including decoding, morphological analyses, syntactic parsing, and discourse processing. An increasing number of studies have examined the extent and manner in which L1 processing skills are incorporated in L2 processing (e.g., Green & Meara, 1987; Hancin & Nagy, 1994; Juffs, 1998; Koda, 1990b, 2000; Wang, Koda, & Perfetti, 2003). Three major issues within the language-specific stance are central to the current research scene: possible developmental changes in the use of transferred skills during L2 processing (McDonald, 1987; Sasaki, 1993), L2 reading facilitation brought about through transferred skills (e.g., Koda, 1989, 1998), and the effects of L1 and L2 distance on L2 reading skills development (e.g., Muljani, Koda, & Moates, 1998).

In essence, the language-specific view contends that learners with different L1 backgrounds deploy different cognitive tactics during L2 reading – a contention self-evidently contrasting sharply with the inferences stemming from the universal framework. In the interests of both scholarship and practice, it would be useful to resolve this seeming contradiction. Although the points of view appear contradictory, when reasoned through their deeper implications they may, in actuality, be complementary. Because reading involves both text-information processing and conceptual manipulations, we can postulate that whereas the former is language-specific, the latter is not. Rather than favoring one perspective over the other, we would do better to investigate reading transfer from both vantage points.

Still, it is important to be clear about the base assumptions underlying each view, because the two perspectives generate completely different research agendas and outcome predictions. For example, when competency invariance is presumed across languages, it would be logical to expect that transferred skills facilitate L2 reading comprehension. This, in turn, would suggest that research should focus on the disparate forces affecting reading-skills transfer from one language to another, including, for example, reader-related variables (e.g., age, motivation, L2 linguistic knowledge, L1 reading competence) and contextual elements (e.g., degree of environmental support, instructional objectives, and L2 teaching methods). However, when aspects of text-information processing are thought to be language specific, future investigations logically should center on differences in the requisite cognitive, linguistic, and metalinguistic competencies underlying comprehension in the languages involved. Detailed cross-linguistic analyses, therefore, are imperative. Approached from both these diametric positions, transfer research could yield enlightening accounts of prior literacy effects on L2 reading development.

Connectionist accounts of skills acquisition

A viable theory – variably referred to as connectionism, associative networks, or parallel distributed processing – has recently evolved, offering strong promise for the clarification of the mechanisms central to language learning and processing. Based on computer simulations of human cognition, connectionist models postulate that performance improvement can be explained through the cumulative upgrading and adjusting of connections among processing units in associative networks. The theory assumes that computational models effectively can simulate the ways in which people learn, through gradual transitions from vagueness to clarity, uncertainty to certainty, and deliberation to automaticity (e.g., Bereiter, 1991; Lee & Gasser, 1992).

Bereiter (1991) suggests that simulation models consist of networks containing large numbers of neuron-like units, interlinked via connections, that, through cumulative experience, progressively strengthen. As the network is "trained," each connection gradually adjusts and readjusts until the desired outputs are derived from particular connection patterns. Over repeated practice, involving thousands of trials, the network gradually assimilates the structural regularities inherent in the inputs. Thus, in McClelland and Rumelhart's words, "information processing is thought of as the process whereby patterns of activation are formed over the units through their excitatory and inhibitory interactions" (1985, p. 159).

Connectionist models have several definitive characteristics. First, prescriptive rules are not assigned on the assumption that approximations of rule-based behavior can transpire without explicit rule specifications. Second, *parallel architecture*, postulating simultaneous activation of multiple processors, is used – in sharp contrast to the prespecified processing sequence presumed in many other processing models. Third, knowledge is distributed over network units rather than represented as symbolic entities in their entirety. In contrast to nonconnectionist models of language learning/processing, as an illustration, connectionist models do not presuppose that words are stored in the mind in their entirety. Rather, what are stored are activation patterns of letter sequences. For instance, when readers see the letter *t*, appearing at the first position in a word, the letter most likely to be activated is *h*, simply because the probability that *t* will be followed by *h* is fifty times higher than that for any other letter (Adams, 1990). Similarly, the interletter linkage, once established, activates a subsequent connection between *h* and *e*, eventually resulting in speedy, effortless access to the lexical entity "the" in its entirety. To reiterate, the connectionist rubric holds that what are learned and stored are not symbolic representations, such as words, but rather activation patterns of interconnected units, which form desired outputs.

Using the connectionist theorem, MacWhinney and Bates (1989) developed the competition model, describing the central mechanism for sentence processing. Under the functionalist premises, the model construes language processing as mappings between linguistic forms and their corresponding functions. As a consequence, language acquisition is seen as a process of internalizing such form–function relationships implicit in linguistic input. *Forms* refers to surface linguistic elements, such as preverbal positioning, subject–verb agreement, case-marking devices, and so on, all of which are mapped onto meaning-making functions, such as agency, causer, and topicality. In the model, language acquisition is regarded as a process of internalizing probabilities of form–function co-occurrences. The dominant empirical claim, in fact, is that cue strength, defined as "actual usage of particular forms for a given function during comprehension and production" in adult native speakers, is directly proportional to cue validity, referring to "relative frequency of the forms used to express the function" (MacWhinney, 1992).

Connectionist views of skills acquisition have several important implications for L2 reading development. The conception of experience-based learning not only provides theoretical justification for incorporating L1–L2 distance as a main factor explaining L2 processing efficiency variance, but also establishes empirical procedures for gauging the distance effects on L2 reading development. Because similar processing requirements necessitate little additional "experience" in the new language, linguistic distance could well serve as a powerful basis for predicting precisely how developmental rates are likely to vary among L2 readers with different L1 backgrounds. Moreover, as suggested earlier, the rationale of probabilistic learning implies that processing competence is shaped through cumulative experience with the target language. Logically, then, the resulting skills should reflect the language's structural and functional properties, suggesting that between any given languages, by analyzing these properties, we should be able to pinpoint cross-linguistic variations in the capabilities underlying information processing.

In the connectionist rubric, moreover, processing automaticity is interpreted as the effortless, nondeliberate retrieval of specific activation patterns previously stored in memory (Logan, 1988). As such, it spawns yet another implication for L2 research. Inasmuch as nondeliberate activation occurs, irrespective of the learner's intention, well-developed L1 mapping procedures are likely to be activated by L2 input – regardless of L1–L2 typological distance. In fact, automatic activation of well-rehearsed L1 procedures during L2 lexical processing has been reported in bilingual experiments (e.g., Dijkstra, Van Jaarsveld, & Ten Brinke, 1998; Van Heuven, Dijkstra, & Grainger, 1998). The connectionist conception of automaticity thus establishes an empirical basis for predicting procedural variations stemming from L1 skill activation among L2 readers with diverse backgrounds.

In sum, the connectionist theorem offers clear starting points from which several critical questions in L2 information processing can be addressed. Toward this end, the following premises establish a platform from which L2 reading competence and its development are conceptualized and analyzed:

- Linguistic processing requires an ability to map between language forms and their corresponding functions.
- Processing competence evolves through progressive print-processing experience in the target language.
- Once established, form–function mapping procedures are activated automatically irrespective of the learner's intention.

In addition, it is important to note that connectionist accounts are based on the premise that language's structural regularities are accessible in input, which are internalized when associations among sets of a finite number of features are established. Therefore, their adequacy likely is limited to operations dealing with featural information. Many researchers believe that pattern-association accounts do not provide adequate explanations either of how abstract linguistic knowledge is acquired (because it is not reflected in input) or of how conceptual manipulations develop (because they do not entail feature mappings).

Competency dissection: Component skills approaches

The component skills approach, proposed by Carr and Levy (1990), is widely used by L1 reading researchers to examine both individual variations and developmental differences in reading competence. Its major objective is to identify the cognitive skills underlying reading and, in so doing, to compare their relative contributions to performance. Several fundamental suppositions underlie this method (Carr, Brown, Vavrus, & Evans, 1990). Reading, for example, is the product of a complex information-processing system, involving a constellation of closely related mental operations. Each operation is theoretically distinct and empirically separable, serving an identifiable function. These skill components interactively facilitate perception, comprehension, and memory of visually presented language. According to the researchers, the approach attempts to illuminate the full scope of cognitive skills underlying reading by distinguishing the following:

- the set of mental operations involved in any given performance
- the organization of the operations and the pattern of information flow among them
- the means by which the system of operations is controlled and coordinated, including the stimulus conditions, strategies, and capacity demands associated with effective performance; and
- parameters of the system – of its individual operations, its organizations, and its controls – whose variation is responsible for individual and developmental differences in the system's overall effectiveness and efficiency. (Carr et al., 1990, p. 3)

The approach offers definitive advantages over single-factor theories, in which a particular skill deficit is often treated as a single source of reading difficulty. Implications from single-focus studies are somewhat limited, because the component competencies are closely interrelated and a deficiency in one skill can create problems in others. It may be shortsighted, therefore, to disentangle interconnected competencies inherent in complex cognitive tasks such as reading by examining single skills in isolation. Without a clear understanding of the multilayered relationships among component skills, accurate identification of the sources of reading impediments is highly unlikely. Moreover, a sense of their functional interdependence, although labor-intensive, is critical in tracing their continuously shifting interconnections and interactions.

Because of its multiple-skills orientation, the component approach is particularly well suited for assessing L2 reading development – especially when multiple-skills analyses are used in examining reading skills transfer. Regrettably, however, little is known about either the beneficial conditions promoting transfer or the specific skills most likely to transfer. Because L2 readers vary in L1 reading ability, L2 proficiency, and similarity in L1 and L2 "learning-to-read" experiences, we cannot assume that transfer occurs in the same manner, either across all skills or among all L2 readers. Systematic competency categorizations could enable us to identify the cognitive and linguistic variables advancing skills transfer, as well as to distinguish transferable from nontransferable skills.

The component approach, moreover, aids in determining the requisite skills for reading proficiency in any given language. The distinction is critical for two reasons: (1) Although mastery of component competencies varies from reader to reader, it is unlikely that the variations in all skills are uniformly responsible for reading ability differences; and (2) as has been noted, languages contrast in the ways they represent functionally significant elements in their writing systems. Required competencies, therefore, are likely to vary across languages. By comparing the relative impacts of disparate skills on reading efficiency in L1 and L2, the approach permits empirical validations of cross-linguistic variations in the requisite competencies for reading acquisition. Further, competency comparisons of skilled and less skilled L2 readers may enable us to classify common deficiencies and limitations characterizing poor L2 readers.

Of greatest importance, however, the component approach provides a reliable means of analyzing cross-linguistic interactions between L2 input and transferred L1 skills. Two-way comparisons of reading behaviors, one concerning intra-individual differences in reading L1 and L2 and the other relating to performance variations across distinct L1 groups learning to read the same target language, will make it possible to estimate probable interplay between L1 and L2 processing experiences in L2 reading skills development. Such multidimensional analyses should allow us to draw more valid inferences about the complexity associated with dual-language processing.

Conceptualizing L2 reading competence differences

When reading in an unfamiliar language, even accomplished readers commonly function like novices, exhibiting many of the same problems as unskilled readers. Nevertheless, they exhibit a range of individual differences, a phenomenon that has created a long-standing debate over possible variables responsible. Two competing theoretical formulations – one dealing with developmental interdependence and the other concerning linguistic threshold – commonly are used to explain the phenomenon. Alderson (1984) advocated systematic examinations of reading competency differences and is widely credited with posing a celebrated question: "Is second language reading a language problem or a reading problem?" Despite its seeming simplicity, the query penetrates the actual core of the issue and has prompted a number of studies. Two primary hypotheses, and their variants, stem from Alderson's question:

• Poor reading in a foreign language is due to poor reading ability in the first language. Poor first-language readers will read poorly in the foreign language and good first-language readers will read well in the foreign language.
• Poor reading in a foreign language is due to inadequate knowledge of the target language.

At least two modifications are possible:

• Poor foreign language reading is due to incorrect strategies for reading that foreign language, strategies which differ from the strategies for reading the native language.
• Poor foreign language reading is due to reading strategies in the first language not being employed in the foreign language, due to inadequate knowledge of foreign language. Good first-language readers will read well in the foreign language once they have passed a threshold of foreign language ability. (1984, p. 4)

In his conjectures, Alderson identifies two significant variables, L1 reading ability and L2 proficiency, as the principal factors accounting for L2 reading ability variance. Two well-known theoretical constructs underlie his speculations. The first hypothesis, "developmental interdependence" (Cummins, 1979, 1986), suggests that L1 reading ability is the major factor in L2 reading development; the second hypothesis, "linguistic threshold" (Clarke, 1980; Yorio, 1971), underscores the importance of L2 knowledge as the dominant source of performance variance. From a somewhat different, developmental, perspective, the "simple view of reading" (Gough & Tunmer, 1986; Hoover & Gough, 1990) contends that decoding competence is yet another significant factor explaining reading ability differences. Although the postulation focuses on beginning L1 readers, it also bears directly on L2 reading development, because the fundamental competency elements – decoding and comprehension – are the same in L1 and L2 reading. The following implications arising from the three theoretical formulations are worthy of consideration.

L1 reading ability: The developmental interdependence hypothesis

In a series of influential papers, Cummins (1979, 1984, 1991) proposed what he calls the "developmental interdependence hypothesis," contending that the forms and levels of L2 competence that bilingual children attain are determined largely by the prior L1 capability they developed before intensive L2 exposure occurs. He argues that communication demands vary on two continua – cognitive complexity and contextual support – each of which imposes different requisites. The competency essential for highly contextualized communication – as in casual face-to-face conversation on familiar topics, for example – differs considerably from that necessitated in reading cognitively demanding contents devoid of non-linguistic contextual embellishment. According to Cummins, whereas context-embedded communication skills are relatively easy to master, the acquisition of decontextualized communication competence is considerably more difficult, requiring not only basic linguistic knowledge but also a sufficient cognitive foundation for manipulating information without supporting frames of reference. Cummins maintains, however, that the latter competence, once developed in a primary language, serves as a base for dealing with similar decontextualized, cognitively complex communication in a second language. In the absence of this competence, even though "learning to read" may be possible, "reading to learn" is formidable. The main contention, in short, is that L2 reading success depends heavily on previously acquired L1 literacy competence.

Several research lines provide further empirical support for such developmental interdependence. Evaluation studies in bilingual education, for example, demonstrate that L1 and L2 reading abilities correlate highly among school-aged English learners (e.g., Cummins, 1979, 1986, 1991; Cummins & Mulcahy, 1978; Legarretta, 1979; Troike, 1978). Similarly, investigations comparing age differences in L2 academic achievement indicate a positive connection between learners' age and their L2 reading proficiency (e.g., Skutnabb-Kangass & Toukomaa, 1976; Snow & Hoefnagel-Hohle, 1978; Cummins et al., 1981). Older students, presumably with greater L1 literacy experience, develop L2 reading competence more quickly than younger learners.

Cummins's developmental interdependence hypothesis helps explain why some learners successfully achieve a full range of L2 linguistic capabilities and others do not. Its scope, however, is limited to young learners whose L1 literacy is still emerging. Whether L1 ability has a similar effect on the reading development of already literate adult L2 learners remains open to question. To date, L2 studies have yielded somewhat conflicting results. Earlier work linked many L2 reading problems to limited L1 ability (e.g., Coady, 1979; Rigg, 1977), but more recent research consistently shows that, although the advantages of L1 ability are observable, their magnitude, compared with L2 knowledge, is somewhat limited (Bernhardt & Kamil, 1995; Bossers, 1991; Carrell, 1991), suggesting that connections between L1 and L2 reading capabilities are not as straightforward as was previously presumed. Further analysis, consequently, is needed to unfold the precise ways in which L1 reading competence facilitates L2 reading mastery. Although metalinguistic awareness is a strong predictor of reading success among novice L1 readers, for example, it may not differentiate metalinguistically sophisticated adult L2 learners. L1 conceptual capabilities, on the other hand, may become increasingly significant as text content becomes more abstract and complex. In essence, disparate variables give rise to individual differences at initial "learning to read" stages and later "reading to learn" stages. Because facilitation benefits derived from L1 reading experience seemingly vary among L2 learners at continuous developmental stages, analyzing their points of progression may afford better ways of identifying L1 reading factors that bolster L2 reading development. Much might be gained, obviously, if new research could bring additional light to bear on these issues.

L2 proficiency: The linguistic threshold hypothesis

The conviction that L2 proficiency is a vital prerequisite to efficient L2 reading is widely accepted. Clarke's short-circuit hypothesis (1980), for example, argues that "limited control over the language 'short-circuits' the good reader's system causing him/her to revert to poor reader strategies when confronted with a difficult or confusing task in the second language" (1988, p. 120). Similarly, Yorio (1971) maintains that "the guessing or predicting ability necessary to pick up the correct cues is hindered by the imperfect knowledge of the language" (p. 108). Recent empirical studies, in addition, further demonstrate that L2 knowledge, in point of fact, explains 30% to 40% of L2 reading variance (e.g., Bernhardt & Kamil, 1995; Bossers, 1991; Carrell, 1991). Put bluntly, limited L2 knowledge inhibits L2 learners from using their previously acquired L1 skills.

Although empirical data generally support the need for proposing minimum proficiency requirements for L2 text comprehension, little is known about what might constitute sensible linguistic thresholds. Reading and L2 proficiency are both complex constructs, but the research on their interrelationship has been restricted to so narrow a range of capability components that there is serious danger of overgeneralization. In most studies, for example, both constructs are operationalized unidimensionally: L2 proficiency is often operationalized as knowledge of vocabulary and/or grammar, and reading is construed as an ability to understand major text ideas. Moreover, as noted earlier, each reading subcomponent necessitates its own set of linguistic competencies. Decoding, for example, requires orthographic and phonological knowledge (e.g., Stanovich, 1991; Vellutino et al., 1996), but sentence processing relies on a grasp of morphosyntactic structures (e.g., Bates & MacWhinney, 1989; Berman, 1986). Therefore, it seems essential for ensuring "linguistic threshold" research to incorporate more finely grained analyses to identify specific L2 linguistic requirements for individual reading competency components.

Several other factors also could be addressed. Reading modes, as a case in point, are potentially significant because they alter the nature and degree of L2 linguistic sophistication necessary for successful text comprehension. As suggested in Chapter 1, texts can be grasped, although in different ways, through diverse modes – for example, scanning, skimming, comprehending, and learning – depending on reader purposes (Carver, 2000). Each mode entails distinct processing requirements, utilizing different cognitive and linguistic capabilities. Directly addressing this issue, Taillefer (1996) demonstrated that L2 proficiency becomes progressively more significant in successful text comprehension performance as task demands increase.

Because L2 reading involves various combinations of languages, sharing their structural and functional properties in varying degrees, L1 and L2 distance in virtually all aspects of linguistic elements also needs to be considered as another potential factor determining requisite L2 proficiency. Assuming that shared structural properties impose similar processing demands, it is highly likely that different degrees of L2 processing experience are necessitated in acquiring needed L2 competency components among readers with related and unrelated L1 backgrounds.

Decoding as a source of individual differences: Simple view of reading

As described earlier, the "simple view of reading" (Gough & Tunmer, 1986; Hoover & Gough, 1990) suggests that visual-information extraction is central to efficient reading. The researchers maintain that decoding efficiency is essential for young L1 readers to take advantage of the comprehension skills they have previously acquired through oral language development. Because decoding is unique to visual communication, its acquisition depends entirely on reading experience. However, because children vary widely in their reading experiences, both before and after reading instruction begins, considerable individual differences exist in the rate at which decoding competence matures. Varying rates of decoding development, in turn, explain the disparate degrees to which children exploit their listening comprehension ability during reading at a given point in time. Decoding efficiency, therefore, is largely responsible for early reading achievement among beginning L1 readers.

The critical question in L2 research is whether a similar developmental relationship exists among L2 readers. Considering that inefficient decoding is a prominent characteristic among less competent L2 readers (e.g., Oller, 1972; Oller & Tullius, 1973), and also that decoding accounts for a moderate, but significant, portion of L2 reading variance (e.g., Koda, 1993; Nassaji & Geva, 1999), decoding efficiency clearly is a strong predictor of L2 reading performance. Still, several other factors should be considered, because, unlike L1 reading, decoding and oral language comprehension develop simultaneously among most L2 readers. In all probability, therefore, the two are indirectly related to L2 reading ability through their common denominator, L2 proficiency, at least in their initial stages.

Moreover, empirical findings suggest that L2 decoding efficiency, in part, is determined by L1–L2 orthographic distance (e.g., Koda, 2000b; Muljani et al., 1998). A developmental lag in decoding efficiency among L2 learners with unrelated L1 backgrounds thus would hardly be surprising. L2 decoding progress therefore could be predicted by different factors among L2 readers with diverse L1 backgrounds. L2 proficiency, for example, may be a better predictor of L2 decoding efficiency among learners with dissimilar L1 orthographic backgrounds. L1 decoding competence, in contrast, is likely to be a strong factor in discriminating high- and low-efficiency L2 decoders with similar L1 backgrounds.

By way of summation, the formulations above clearly demonstrate that three distinct constructs – L1 reading, L2 proficiency, and L2 decoding – significantly contribute to successful L2 reading comprehension, as well as suggest that their individual differences collectively explain L2 reading competence variance.

PART II

ESSENTIAL COMPONENTS

3 Word recognition

Word recognition refers to the processes of extracting lexical information from graphic displays of words. Individual words are critical building blocks in text-meaning construction, and efficiency in converting graphic symbols into sound, or meaning, information is indispensable in comprehension. Consequently, how this competence develops is a chief concern among researchers. Word recognition has attracted the attention of psychologists as well, because words are the ideal unit for analysis in the study of cognition. Words can readily be segmented into their constituents at multiple levels – such as graphemes, phonemes, and morphemes – and therefore allow systematic investigations of how language is represented in the mind (Balota, 1994). A multitude of studies with both children and adults have tackled the core issue in word recognition: how information, "packaged" in a word, is perceived, extracted, sorted, and retrieved.

Building on the accumulated findings from L1 word-recognition research, this chapter explores systematic variations in visual-information extraction among L1 and L2 readers. By way of background, the chapter begins with an explanation of how word-recognition efficiency facilitates text comprehension. Three component operations are described: orthographic, phonological, and semantic processing. Then, using subsequent cross-linguistic comparisons of word-recognition procedures as a footing, major characteristics of word-recognition behaviors among L2 readers are discussed. Although the terms *word recognition* and *decoding* are often used interchangeably in other chapters, here, word recognition refers to the processes of obtaining words' sounds and meanings, and decoding deals specifically with the extraction of phonological information.

Roles of word recognition in reading comprehension

Changing views

L1 reading research has undergone dramatic changes in the way word-recognition function in comprehension is conceptualized. Supported by a large body of empirical studies, the prevailing current view treats efficient visual-information processing as one of the vital competencies for successful comprehension (National Reading Panel, 2000; Snow, Burns, & Griffin, 1998). Among researchers, however, the view is far from unanimous. In top-down conceptualization, for example, reading is seen as a "psycholinguistic guessing game" (Goodman, 1973), where the reader's primary task is to generate hypotheses about the forthcoming content of the text. Text information, in this interpretation, seems only to confirm the hypotheses. In short, the source for text-meaning construction is the stored knowledge in the reader's own mind. Reflecting the strong predominance of this view in the 1970s and early 1980s, word recognition received limited attention in reading research.

Nonetheless, the tide turned. Subsequent research provided little support for the top-down claims, and emphasis on information-extraction competencies returned. Eye-movement studies, for example, repeatedly show that virtually every content word receives direct visual fixation (Balota, Pollasek, & Rayner, 1985; Just & Carpenter, 1980, 1987), and the absence of even a single letter can be disruptive, heavily diminishing reading efficiency (e.g., McConkie & Zola, 1981; Rayner & Bertera, 1979). Contrary to the earlier predictions of the top-down conceptualization, the newer findings clearly showed that most text words are thoroughly processed during reading. Moreover, developmental studies uniformly demonstrated that poor readers have difficulty in deriving information from print, and deficient word recognition is directly linked to poor comprehension (e.g., Perfetti, 1985; Stanovich, 1988). Given the heavy reliance on textual information, in lieu of prior knowledge, these findings are hardly surprising. A likely scenario depicting a cumulative downslide among poor readers would be as follows: Because of difficulty in print-information extraction, poor decoders become increasingly frustrated with reading. With sustained frustration, reading becomes anything but rewarding, further discouraging voluntary reading. In the absence of adequate reading practice, word-recognition skills remain underdeveloped, and poor comprehension continues. Moreover, with limited text understanding, conceptual growth is seriously restricted. The plausibility of such a scenario is supported by longitudinal studies demonstrating that first-year decoding performance is a powerful predictor of subsequent reading achievement (e.g., Juel, 1988; Juel, Griffith, & Gough, 1986). Put succinctly, inefficient word recognition takes long-term tolls, directly and indirectly, on the acquisition of reading competence.

Word-recognition efficiency and successful comprehension

Several areas of research help clarify how word-recognition efficiency promotes comprehension. To begin with, reading comprehension necessitates the construction of textual meaning. In contrast to writing, however, where the writer is relatively free from creative constraints, the reader is restricted to textual information. If, for example, the reader forms an interpretation unjustified by the text – however plausible – the comprehension is hardly successful. Visual sampling skills are required to extract sufficient information for text-meaning construction. The process, obviously, is seriously impaired when the extracted information is either insufficient or inaccurate. It is important to note, moreover, that local (word-level) and global (context-level) processing are highly interactive, and success at both levels is mutually enhancing. At the same time, although visual-information extraction is essential for context building, individual words derive their precise meanings from the context in which they appear. If the reader does not grasp the preceding context, therefore, finely tuned word-meaning selection is hardly possible.

An additional explanation stems from limitations of working-memory capacity. A principal hurdle in complex cognitive activities, such as reading, is that the number of mental resources that can be simultaneously activated in working memory is limited (e.g., Daneman, 1991; Daneman & Carpenter, 1980, 1983; LaBerge & Samuels, 1974; Schneider & Shiffrin, 1977). In reading, however, interlinked processing components must be simultaneously activated. To accomplish this within the capacity limitations, however, several components must become automated. Because word recognition involves the extraction, rather than the construction, of information, automaticity can be relatively easily achieved in this operation (e.g., Adams, 1994; LaBerge & Samuels, 1974; Perfetti & Lesgold, 1977, 1979). By reducing the processing load in working memory, automated word recognition facilitates conceptual manipulations of the extracted information.

Component processes

As suggested earlier, word recognition involves two major operations: obtaining a word's meaning and extracting its sound. Consequently, it is important to be clear about two related, but distinct, processes – phonological decoding and semantic access. And, because both are activated through visual input and achieved via an analysis of graphic symbols, orthographic processing itself needs to be clarified.

Orthographic processing

Fluent reading requires rapid and effortless access to word meanings. It may seem that good readers recognize many words instantly and access their meanings and sounds without letter-by-letter processing. In actuality, however, word-recognition studies have repeatedly confirmed that skilled readers are, through automaticity, capable of analyzing and manipulating word-internal elements, such as letters and letter clusters (e.g., Ehri, 1998; Shankweiler & Liberman, 1972). Competent readers, furthermore, are adept at pronouncing both individual letters and nonsense letter strings (e.g., Hogaboam & Perfetti, 1978; Siegel & Ryan, 1988; Wagner, Torgesen, & Rashotte, 1994). In essence, what seems like seamless performance is not attributable to whole-word retrievals, but rather to children's accumulated knowledge of their writing system, sound–symbol relationships in particular (e.g., Adams, 1990; Ehri, 1994, 1998; Seidenberg & McClelland, 1989). Thus, orthographic knowledge is responsible for facile extraction of lexical information from print. To develop word-recognition competence, children must first become aware that written symbols correspond to speech units, and then learn the specific ways in which symbols are combined to represent spoken words. Orthographic knowledge, once acquired, becomes a powerful mnemonic device that "bonds the written forms of specific words to their pronunciation in memory" (Ehri, 1998, p. 15).

Within connectionist premises, Seidenberg and McClelland (1989) explain how orthographic knowledge develops in native English speakers. They define English orthographic knowledge as "an elaborate matrix of correlations among letter patterns, phonemes, syllables, and morphemes" (p. 525), contending that its acquisition involves forming interletter associations through cumulative exposure to visual word input. The more frequently a letter sequence pattern is experienced, the stronger the associated connections. Ultimately, it is this connection strength that engenders fluent recognition performance. Consequently, processing competence can be described as the degree to which interletter associations are internalized. As Ellis (2002) puts it, performance efficiency is directly tied to input frequency and practice.

Phonological processing

Although the most widely recognized objective of word recognition is retrieving context-appropriate word meanings, many theorists contend that phonological decoding – the processes involved in accessing, storing, and manipulating phonological information (Torgesen & Burgess, 1998) – is as important as semantic access. Studies consistently document that poor readers uniformly are handicapped in a wide variety of phonological tasks. Their deficiencies, moreover, tend to be "domain-specific, longitudinally predictive, and not primarily attributable to non-phonological factors – such as general intelligence, semantic, or visual processing" (Share & Stanovich, 1995, p. 9). Ability to obtain phonological information is vital to successful comprehension, and in all probability is causally related to reading proficiency. One might wonder why phonology is critical in silent reading, where overt vocalization is not required. The best answer, perhaps, lies in the ways phonology facilitates comprehension.

The predominant function of phonological codes is to enhance information storage in working memory (e.g., Kleiman, 1975; Levy, 1975). According to Gathecole and Baddeley (1993), the phonological loop – a major component of working memory – mediates the formation and retention of phonological representations. Its specific contribution derives from the capacity to maintain durable representations in working memory, which thereafter can be referenced and cross-referenced with existing knowledge in long-term memory. Competence in converting visual input into its phonological form, therefore, is vital in both new word learning and unfamiliar-word recognition.

Another function of phonological codes is affording quick access to oral vocabulary in lexical memory because it is stored in phonological forms. The ability to convert graphic symbols into a word's speech sound enhances efficient lexical-information access in long-term memory. Because a primary task in learning to read is linking visual word labels to oral vocabulary, decoding competence is pivotal in early reading development. Ability to pronounce printed words is, in fact, regarded as a powerful predictor of reading success among primary grade children (Bowers, Golden, Kennedy, & Young, 1994; Share & Stanovich, 1995; Torgesen & Burgess, 1998; Wagner, Torgesen, & Rashotte, 1994).

It should be observed, moreover, that the benefits of decoding competence are not restricted to either English or alphabetic languages in general. Cross-linguistic studies repeatedly suggest that phonological decoding also is important in nonalphabetic languages such as

Japanese and Chinese (e.g., Perfetti & Zhang, 1995; Sasanuma, 1984; Tzeng & Wang, 1983). Phonological skill deficits, in addition, are a common attribute of weak readers in typologically diverse languages, including Arabic (e.g., Abu Rabia, 1995), Portuguese (Da Fontoura & Siegel, 1995), Chinese (e.g., So & Siegel, 1997; Zhang & Perfetti, 1993), and Japanese (Kuhara-Kojima, Hatano, Saito, & Haebara, 1996). Working-memory experiments also show that phonological transformation is more efficacious than visual encoding in retaining visually presented information in working memory among native Chinese readers (e.g., Mou & Anderson, 1981; Yik, 1978; Zhang & Simon, 1985). All in all, it seems reasonable to conclude that phonological decoding is perhaps the most indispensable competence for reading acquisition in all languages.

Semantic processing

Retrievals of context-appropriate word meanings are pivotal in text-meaning construction. The nature of word-meaning knowledge and its relationship to comprehension are discussed in Chapter 4, but the observations here focus on contextual constraints on semantic-information processing during word recognition. Words derive their precise meanings from the context in which they appear; semantic processing necessitates an ability to integrate lexical and contextual information. Consider the following sentences: "I deposited three checks at the bank" and "I ran along the bank." Competent English readers will neither become confused nor misinterpret the sentences, simply because they recognize that *bank* has multiple meanings, and they are capable of deciding which meaning to apply in each sentence. Obviously, in both sentences, what aids "meaning selection" is context. By restricting the word's semantic possibilities, the context helps the reader decide which of the two meanings is congruent with the evolving interpretation of the sentence. Such selection, more or less, is operative in any word – even those lacking clearly distinguishable multiple meanings (e.g., Adams, 1990; Nagy, 1997). The word *Japan*, for instance, is likely to trigger very different images in a discussion of international trade and one on martial arts. The extent to which subtle differences in a word's meaning is captured often determines the preciseness of the resulting text representation.

There is, however, a long-standing controversy among reading researchers as to how contextual constraints facilitate semantic processing. In the approach described above, context constrains the semantic possibilities of a word, thus simplifying decisions about its appropriate meaning. In this approach, the contextual facilitation is assumed to occur *after* the word's semantic information has been accessed. In an opposing view, context facilitation is thought to occur *before* the semantic information is retrieved. Put another way, if the preceding context imposes sufficient semantic constraints, the less-relevant meanings of the forthcoming word are not likely to be activated. Should this be the case, meaning selection is an optional process, necessitated only when contextual constraints are insufficient.

The empirical evidence heavily favors the former, demonstrating that all of a word's known meanings are activated by its orthographic input, even when the context imposes strong constraints (e.g., Seidenberg, Tanenhaus, Leiman, & Bienkowski, 1982). It is also worth observing that word-recognition performance among less-skilled readers is affected by context to a far greater extent than among skilled readers (e.g., Allington & Fleming, 1978; Biemiller, 1979; Becker, 1985; Perfetti, 1985; Stanovich, 1988) and that contextual effects on word-meaning retrievals decrease as reading proficiency improves (e.g., Becker, 1985; Pring & Snowling, 1986; Stanovich, 1986). Seen as a whole, these findings indicate that contextual reliance is a strategy that poor readers lean on to compensate for their underdeveloped visual-information sampling skills. The self-evident inference of these findings is that successful semantic processing depends on both efficient access to stored word information and contextually appropriate meaning selections.

Cross-linguistic variations in word recognition

Before considering cross-linguistic variations in word recognition, it is necessary to acknowledge that multiple methods are used by single readers as well as among different readers within the same language. Ehri (1998) maintains there are five ways of reading words in English:

- assembling letters into a blend of sounds
- pronouncing and blending familiar spelling patterns
- retrieving sight words from memory
- analogizing to words already known by sight
- using context cues to predict words. (p. 7)

She believes that children learn to use all five methods as they develop reading proficiency. Good readers are adept in all five, and are capable of selecting the best suited to a given situation. Thus, diversity in approach is associated with neither developmental stages nor reading ability differences. Assuming that multiple methods are also available in other languages, cross-linguistic variations are likely to be observable in the methods themselves, as well as in particular preferences.

Inasmuch as specific procedures result from print-processing experience in accommodating the unique properties of a writing system, a description of their variations may be worthwhile.

Writing systems differ on two dimensions: orthographic representation and depth. Orthographic representation refers to the linguistic unit each graphic symbol denotes. For example, in alphabetic systems, such as English and Spanish, each letter represents a phoneme – either a single consonant or a vowel. Although Korean Hangul is also alphabetic, it requires the assembly of individual symbols into syllable blocks, which in turn constitute basic graphic elements for forming words (Taylor & Taylor, 1995). In logography, such as Chinese characters and Japanese Kanji, in contrast, each symbol maps onto a morpheme – the single functionally identifiable unit in the composition of words. For example, one character corresponds to a free morpheme, say, "sky," embodying the word's sound and meaning. Lexical information thus is assigned holistically to a single graphic symbol.

The second dimension, orthographic depth, refers to the degree of regularity in symbol–sound correspondences. In *shallow* orthographies, the symbol–sound relationships are highly regular, and thus transparent. In Spanish and Serbo-Croatian, for example, each letter corresponds to one phoneme, constituting a phonologically regular system with a highly consistent and reliable set of grapheme-to-phoneme correspondences. English orthography, in contrast, is characterized as a phonologically *deep* system – that is, while governed by phonemic constraints, it tends to preserve morphological information at the expense of phonological transparency. Reflecting this tendency, many spelling irregularities in English are more readily explained by morphological rather than phonemic constructions. To illustrate, the past tense morpheme *-ed* is pronounced in three different ways, as in *talked*, *visited*, and *called*. Hence, preserving the grapheme *-ed* to exhibit its underlying morphological information creates a violation of one-to-one sound–symbol correspondences.

To explain how orthographic depth affects phonological decoding across writing systems, Katz and Frost (1992) proposed the orthographic depth hypothesis (ODH). According to the ODH, in shallow (transparent) orthographies, phonological information is assembled primarily through letter-by-letter, symbol-to-sound, translation. Conversely, in deep (less transparent) orthographies, phonological information is obtained after a word has been identified, based on the stored knowledge of the word. The major contention here is that orthographic depth is directly related to the degree that phonological decoding necessitates lexical information. Transparent sound–symbol relationships in shallow orthographies allow rule-based computational procedures. Therefore, their decoding is not dependent on particular word information retrieved from lexical memory. In support of this contention, Frost, Katz, and Bentin (1987) successfully demonstrated the differential impacts of word frequency on word naming speed in three writing systems with varying orthographic depths: unvoweled Hebrew (deepest), English (deep), and Serbo-Croatian (shallow). Naming is the commonly used technique to measure decoding efficiency, where participants are asked to pronounce visually presented words or nonsense letter strings. Frost et al. (1987) reported that Hebrew readers were most seriously affected by word frequency, followed by English and Serbo-Croatian readers. The differential impacts of frequency highlight varying extents to which readers rely on lexical information during phonological processing in the three writing systems.

Supporting evidence is also available from experimental and clinical studies of Japanese readers. The multiple orthographies in Japanese (logographic Kanji and syllabic Kana), for example, allow comparisons of processing mechanisms individuals use in the two scripts. Experimental studies have indicated that phonological interference has differential effects in Kanji and Kana processing (Saito, 1981; Saito, Inoue, & Nomura, 1979). Mann (1985) also found that recall of Kanji words correlated with both linguistic (spoken nonsense words) and nonlinguistic (visual nonsense designs) memory, while recall of alphabetic (English) and syllabary (Kana) words related only to linguistic memory. Further, clinical observations revealed that two kinds of Japanese aphasic patients, with either a Kana or a Kanji impairment, have lesions in different areas of the brain (e.g., Hayashi, Ulatowska, & Sasanuma, 1985; Sasanuma, 1975, 1984). Collectively, these findings provide solid empirical reinforcement for the postulation that reading a particular writing system entails a command of the cognitive mechanisms specifically designed for dealing with its structural and representational properties.

Factors affecting L2 word recognition

Word recognition, despite its significance, has received scant attention in L2 research. Two primary factors seem to contribute to the data shortfall. First, in the 1970s and 1980s, top-down conceptualization dominated L2 reading research (Bernhardt, 1991). In the top-down framework, as observed earlier, reading is defined as "an active process in which the reader produces hypotheses about the message of the text, then samples textual cues to confirm or reject those hypotheses" (Clarke, 1980, p. 204). In this approach, as noted in the preceding chapters, word-recognition skills received minimal research priority. Second, in the L2 research, linguistic knowledge and language-processing skills are not always clearly distinguished (Bialystock, 1988, 2001; Sharwood Smith, 1991). As a result, L2 proficiency often is equated with L2 linguistic knowledge. Because reading efficiency generally increases as L2 proficiency improves, it is often assumed that reading skills – word recognition, in particular – automatically develop as by-products of increased L2 linguistic knowledge. Nonetheless, there is no theoretical basis to uphold such an assumption. Similarly, on empirical grounds, there is no real support for the presumption that word-recognition skills are the automatic outcome of increased linguistic knowledge. As discussed earlier, considerable individual differences in L1 word-recognition skills among children with normally developed oral language competence attest to the inadequacy of linguistic knowledge as the sole foundation for subsequent processing-skills acquisition.

In L2, oral language competence varies widely among learners when they begin learning to read. The liabilities of limited linguistic knowledge on processing behaviors are an important issue in L2 word recognition research. Moreover, L2 readers have prior print processing experience in their L1. L1 influences are another concern in this research. What complicates the matter, moreover, is L1–L2 distance, because similarity between the two languages may determine the degree of facilitation brought about by L1 experience. Much current research on L2 word recognition has been shaped by these factors (accumulated L2 knowledge, L1 reading ability, and L1–L2 distance) surrounding the prior experiences of L2 learners.

Word recognition among high- and low-proficiency L2 learners

A major factor differentiating novice L1 and L2 readers is their linguistic foundation formed through preceding oral language development. To review, a primary task in L1 learning to read is connecting acquired oral vocabulary with its visual forms. In L2 learning, however, oral language and literacy competencies develop, in most instances, simultaneously. Skills acquisition, therefore, must occur while linguistic sophistication is still limited. The question, then, is how such limitation affects recognition performance. One way of seeking an answer is to compare the processing behaviors of high- and low-proficiency readers. Because reading is often subsumed as an integral aspect of general language proficiency, it should be noted that, in the subsequent discussion, the label "high/low proficiency" refers to L2 proficiency bearing directly on reading ability.

A notable variation has been observed in visual-information extraction efficiency among high- and low-proficiency readers. Low-proficiency readers are invariably slower and less accurate in a variety of word-recognition tasks (e.g., Favreau & Segalowitz, 1982; Haynes & Carr, 1990; Macnamara, 1970), including word and letter naming, lexical decision (determining whether a given letter string is a real word), and visual matching (judging whether two words, presented together or sequentially, are identical). Similarly, inverse correlations have been reported between L2 proficiency and eye-movement efficiency indices, such as fixation frequency and duration (e.g., Oller, 1972; Oller & Tullius, 1973; Saito, 1989). It seems that inefficient word recognition is common among low-proficiency readers irrespective of their L1 backgrounds.

Another group of studies, contrasting reading strategies across proficiency levels, also confirmed that low-proficiency readers are more heavily involved in word-level than in discourse-level processing (e.g., Cziko, 1980; Horiba, 1990). They rely on a word's graphic cues rather than its semantic information (Chamot & El-Dinary, 1999; Clarke, 1980). As a result, they engage in conceptual manipulations, such as hypothesizing and predicting, to a lesser extent than their high-proficiency counterparts (e.g., Chamot & El-Dinary, 1999; Anderson, 1991). Low-proficiency learners as well are less sensitive to syntactic and contextual constraints than their high-proficiency counterparts (Cziko, 1980; Hatch, Polin, & Part, 1974). Consolidated, these findings create a picture remarkably similar to that depicting poor L1 readers – namely, with seriously restricted word-recognition skills, low-proficiency readers expend considerable time and energy in their visual-information sampling, which, in turn, severely constrains their ability to use multiple information sources.

In a further sequence of studies, Segalowitz and his associates (Favreau & Segalowitz, 1982, 1983; Segalowitz, 1986; Segalowitz, Poulsen, & Komoda, 1991) determined that word-recognition speed varied considerably among otherwise fluent bilingual speakers. More critically, the observed recognition efficiency differences were directly attributable to their reading performance. These findings corroborate those from L1 studies, again suggesting that oral language competence in itself does not guarantee processing-skills acquisition. The implication is significant: Word-recognition skills and oral language proficiency do not necessitate the same underlying competencies and thus develop independently through separate mechanisms. The acquisition of one, therefore, does not ensure that of the other. The contention has been further buttressed by recent longitudinal studies with school-aged L2 learners, showing no systematic relationships in a second language between oral language proficiency and word reading ability (August, Calderon, & Carlo, 2000, 2001; Durgunoglu et al., 1993; Gholamain & Geva, 1999).

Impacts of dual-language involvement on L2 word recognition

Inasmuch as L2 readers already are literate, we can logically assume that L2 word recognition skills emerge from print-processing experience in two languages. The issue, then, is how, and to what extent, their L1 and L2 experiences conjointly affect the formation of L2 word recognition competence. Based on the connectionist principle of experience-based learning, the straightforward conjecture would be that differences in L2 print experience account for processing efficiency variance. And because processing skills transfer across languages, we can further surmise that the degrees of facilitation that derive from transferred L1 competencies will vary to the extent the two languages share similar properties. When learning to read a typologically similar L2, transferred skills can be used with minimal modifications and require little additional print experience in the new language. When the two languages are dissimilar, however, L1 skills must undergo considerable modifications through L2 print-processing experience. Further, knowing that properties of writing systems differ across languages, we can also presume that the use of transferred skills invokes procedural variation in processing behaviors. Once again, under the connectionist premise, we can further postulate that transferred competencies continue to mature, through cumulative L2 processing experience, in order to accommodate the idiosyncrasies of the L2 writing system.

These hypotheses suggest three possible ways in which L1 and L2 experiences shape L2 word-recognition competence. One possibility could be that L2 processing experience simply has a greater impact. If this is the case, procedural variations attributable to L1 experience eventually should disappear. Thus, there would be no long-term L1 influences on L2 processing procedures. In addition, we can further anticipate that facilitation benefits stemming from L1–L2 orthographic similarity are observable only until sufficient L2 print experience is accumulated, but not thereafter. A second projection might be that L1 processing experience continues to have the greater impact. Under this circumstance, qualitative differences stemming from L1 experience are not likely to disappear, and we can expect that the performance efficiency of L2 learners with dissimilar L1 backgrounds always will lag behind those with similar backgrounds. The third scenario suggests that L2 learners from unrelated L1 backgrounds would increase processing efficiency through the use of transferred L1 skills. In this event, the resulting competence would systematically vary across cohorts with diverse backgrounds – but the distance effect on processing efficiency might not be evident. Obviously, if we knew which of the three possibilities would most accurately predict performance variations among L2 learners, we could deal with individual learning problems with far greater precision. In the sections that follow, these hypothetical predictions are examined through the lens of L2 word-recognition studies.

Studies on L2 word recognition

L2 experience impacts

Although the causal connection between processing experience and efficiency in itself is hardly surprising, little is known about which specific capabilities are critically affected by experience – and how. Of late, however, L2 studies have begun to shed light on L2 performance variance attributable to target-language experience. In an investigation of visual-information processing, Haynes and Carr (1990) compared visual matching performance among three groups of participants: novice and experienced Taiwanese college students learning English, and a group of native English speakers. Participants were presented with a sequence of letter-string pairs one at a time and asked to determine whether the two strings in each pair were identical. Three types of letter strings were used: real English words, pseudo-English words (nonsense, but orthographically legal, letter strings); and non-words (orthographically illegal letter strings). The results showed a clear contrast between L1 and L2 participants. The L1 group's performance was roughly parallel in the pseudo and realword conditions, while both L2 groups declined considerably in the pseudoword condition. The poorer performance on pseudowords was taken as an indication that what separates L1 and L2 learners is sensitivity to the constraints on letter combination patterns. This in turn implies that the amount of processing experience directly contributes to the acquisition of the highly abstract knowledge of the target language's writing system.

Segalowitz and Segalowitz (1993), working from a different vantage point, tackled the development of automaticity, a central concern in processing efficiency. They used a lexical-decision task to compare word-recognition speed and variability among high- and low-efficiency Francophone learners of English at a Canadian university. Not surprisingly, high-efficiency participants were faster and more stable than their low-efficiency counterparts, thus confirming that processing speed and variability are reliable indicators of processing competence. Interestingly, however, performance speed and stability both improved on repetitious items, but the variability differences among high- and low-efficiency participants were greater than the proportional reduction attributable to the variance in speed. The researchers contended that processing efficiency can be achieved not by simply increasing the speed of individual processing components, but rather by eliminating some of the inefficient, thus cognitively resource-demanding, components. Their dominant conclusion was that although performance improvement can be explained in part by a gradual increase in performance speed and stability, attainment of automaticity may, in addition, involve the internal reorganization of procedural components. Whether variations in L2 experience entirely explain performance variance in L2 word recognition, it is clear that they do have significant consequences.

L1 and L2 distance impacts

L1–L2 orthographic distance constitutes another significant factor explaining quantitative variations in L2 word recognition. Cross-linguistic research on L2 learners with divergent L1 orthographic backgrounds repeatedly attests to the faster and more accurate recognition performance among those with related L1 orthographic backgrounds (e.g., Akamatsu, 1999; Fender, 2003; Green & Meara, 1987; Koda, 1988, 1989; Muljani et al., 1998). Koda (1989), for example, analyzed orthographic distance effects on word-recognition development and their relation to text comprehension among L2 learners of Japanese with logographic and alphabetic L1 backgrounds. Her word-recognition measures included syllabary letter naming (indicating the pronunciation of individual syllabary symbols), syllabary word identification (providing English translations of words written in a syllabary script), and Kanji word identification (providing English translations of given Kanji characters). The comprehension battery consisted of sentence completion, multiple-choice main-idea detection, and cloze (fill-in blanks to complete a paragraph-length text). As expected, the logographic L1 group outperformed their alphabetic counterparts in all measures. All word-recognition measures correlated positively, although to varying degrees, with comprehension indices. An analysis of longitudinal data, moreover, showed that, while the initial group differences in simpler tasks, such as word identification and sentence completion, remained constant over time, the performance gap widened considerably on more complex tasks, requiring information syntheses and manipulations. Collectively, these findings seem to suggest that shared orthographic knowledge provides long-term facilitation in L2 reading development, first by promoting mastery of L2 visual-information sampling skills and then facilitating information integration from multiple sources.

The critical questions as to what extent and how L1 and L2 orthographic similarities facilitate L2 word recognition still remain. Muljani and colleagues (1998) shed significant light on the issue, by comparing lexical-decision performance among ESL learners with related (Indonesian: Roman alphabetic) and unrelated (Chinese: logographic) L1 orthographic backgrounds. The researchers manipulated two word-related variables: frequency and structural consistency. Structural consistency has to do with whether the syllable structures of the target words were permissible in both English and Indonesian (consistent) or only in English (inconsistent). Because Chinese does not use the Roman alphabet, the variable was predicted to have no impact on their performance. Although Indonesian participants outperformed the Chinese across all conditions, structural consistency differentially affected the two groups. Items with consistent syllable structures benefited lexical judgment performance among Indonesian but not among Chinese participants. Interestingly, however, the performance difference between the groups was far less pronounced on items whose syllable structures were not shared with the Indonesians. The researchers surmised that the performance superiority was attributable to the accelerated efficiency stemming from the common processing requirements shared by the two alphabetic languages. L1-based facilitation thus occurs only where L1 and L2 processing demands are identical, but the benefits do not automatically transfer to other subcomponent processes where L1 and L2 pose disparate requirements. In sum, typological distance not only explains overall performance differences among learners with related and unrelated L1 backgrounds, but it also underscores the ways L1 experience facilitates L2 lexical processing.

L1 experience impacts

Inasmuch as reading skills transfer transpires in various aspects of L2 reading (e.g., Gass & Selinker, 1983; Kellerman & Sharwood Smith, 1986), a logical assumption would be that L2 readers bring their L1 knowledge and its corresponding processing skills to their L2 word-recognition processing. A string of experimental studies have shown that L2 learners utilize clearly identifiable L1 processing devices during L2 word recognition (e.g., Brown & Haynes, 1985; Gairns, 1992; Green & Meara, 1987; Koda 1989, 1990b; Ryan & Meara, 1991).

Using what is known as a letter-search task, for example, Green and Meara (1987) compared visual scanning strategies among three groups of ESL learners with contrasting L1 orthographic backgrounds: Roman alphabetic (Spanish), non-Roman alphabetic (Arabic), and nonalphabetic (Chinese). Participants in the experiment were first shown a target symbol (either an alphabetic letter or a logographic character), which was immediately followed by a five-symbol string. The task was simply to determine whether the target symbol appeared in the string. Different writing systems have different ways of displaying their graphic symbols, and readers gradually evolve distinct strategies for scanning visual input, such as left-to-right "sweeping" in English, as opposed to right-to-left in Arabic. The task was designed to capture such scanning predilections. The rationale was that a target symbol is detected more rapidly when it appears at "premier" locations where readers normally direct their attention. The groups' response patterns varied systematically in their L1s, suggesting, as predicted, that distinct scanning strategies are used in typologically diverse writing systems. Further, in performing the task in English, all L2 participants demonstrated a strong tendency to rely on search strategies very similar to those used in their respective L1s. The researchers accordingly concluded that L1 writing systems have deep, lasting effects on the ways L2 visual input is processed.

In a subsequent experiment, using a visual-matching task, determining physical similarities, Ryan and Meara (1991) compared the ability to detect missing vowels among Arabic and non-Arabic ESL learners. Participants were first presented with a ten-letter high-frequency English word (e.g., *department* or *revolution*), and then with either a repetition of the same word or a slightly altered letter string created by deletion of a single vowel (*dpartment* or *revoltion*). The task was merely to judge whether the items in the two consecutive presentations were identical. Arabic participants were considerably slower and less accurate than non-Arabic ESL learners. The researchers attributed the efficiency differences to Arabic-speaking ESL learners' lack of sensitivity to vowel absence because, in their words, "modern Arabic writing does not normally represent short vowels" (p. 533). The findings thus further corroborate the earlier contention that L1 orthography has a long-term impact on L2 processing.

Additional evidence of cross-language transfer lies in research investigating phonological processing. Koda (1990b), for example, compared the phonological decoding procedures of ESL learners with alphabetic (Arabic and Spanish) and logographic (Japanese) L1 backgrounds. Participants read two linguistically matched texts (one describing a variety of cocktails and the other depicting different types of fish) in two phonological conditions, accessible versus inaccessible. In the phonologically accessible condition, nonsense, but pronounceable, letter strings (e.g., *mermo*) were used as names for either the cocktails or the fish described. In the phonologically inaccessible condition, Sanskrit symbols were inserted as names of the items depicted. Because the participants did not know how to pronounce these symbols, they served as phonologically inaccessible elements. The alphabetic ESL readers were seriously impaired by the Sanskrit symbols, but they had virtually no effect on the logographic participants' reading performance. The contrast definitely indicated that L2 learners use qualitatively different procedures for phonological decoding in L2 text-information processing. Again, the findings confirm Green and Meara's and Koda's conclusion that L2 learners with various L1 orthographic backgrounds use distinct processing skills.

Analogous results also were obtained through a cross-linguistic experiment involving logographic (Chinese) and non-Roman alphabetic (Arabic) ESL learners (Gairns, 1992). Under two forced-choice conditions (orthographic and phonological), lexical-decision performance between the two ESL groups was compared. In the orthographic condition, participants were presented with two phonologically identical letter strings (e.g., *snow* and *snoe*) and asked to determine which of the two was a real English word. In the phonological condition, contrastingly, the task was to choose which of two orthographically legal letter strings (e.g., *rane*, *tane*) sounded like a real English word. She found, first, that both groups did better when orthographic rather than phonological information was available, and, second, that the performance of Chinese participants declined far more sharply than that of Arabic learners when orthographic cues were unavailable. The clear implication is that the extent to which phonological and orthographic cues are used differs widely among ESL learners with contrasting L1 backgrounds. The fact that alphabetic L1 readers depend on phonological information to a much greater degree than logographic L1 readers provides still further support for the L1 orthographic influence on L2 word recognition.

Approaching from another perspective, Brown and Haynes (1985) examined the effects of L1 reading experience on L2 component skills development among Arabic, Spanish, and Japanese ESL learners.

Although the Japanese participants were superior to other groups in visual discrimination, the superiority vanished in decoding, requiring symbol-to-sound translation, further confirming the significant force L1 experience exerts on L2 processing capabilities. Interestingly, they also found that listening and reading comprehension abilities correlated differently among logographic (Japanese) and alphabetic (Arabic and Spanish) groups. Although reading and listening skills were closely related among Arabic and Spanish participants, the correlation was negligible with their Japanese counterparts, suggesting that L1 orthographic experience may interact with the cognitive and linguistic requirements of some processing tasks.

To summarize, cross-linguistic comparisons of L2 word recognition collectively demonstrate that L1 orthographic experience has long-lasting, clearly detectable impacts on L2 lexical processing, further implying that L1 processing experience is a major source of performance variations among L2 learners. All in all, L2 research provides evidence that both L1 and L2 processing experiences affect L2 word recognition development, but little is known about their relative contributions to the shaping of L2 processing competencies. It is premature to draw any valid inferences about which of the three possibilities described earlier best projects accurate pictures of longitudinal L1 and L2 impacts, but in view of the observed dual-language involvement, it may be fruitful to concentrate on long-term developmental changes in the manner and extent to which L1 and L2 processing experiences coalesce in forming L2 word-recognition skills.

Summary and future research suggestions

The importance of word recognition is widely acknowledged among L1 reading researchers. Four conclusions can be drawn, with reasonable certainty, from a significant body of research: Phonological skills have a direct, and seemingly causal, relationship with reading ability; knowledge of letter patterns and their linkages to sounds facilitates rapid automatic word recognition; such knowledge evolves gradually through cumulative print-processing experience; and limited word-recognition skills tend to induce overreliance on context.

Stimulated, perhaps, by these conclusions from L1 research, word recognition among L2 readers has just begun to attract serious research attention. Although still limited, empirical examinations have yielded some promising insights. Studies investigating L2 proficiency effects, for example, consistently suggest that inefficient visual-information sampling is a dominant characteristic among low-proficiency L2 learners. Other studies of L1–L2 distance suggest that L1-based facilitation occurs only in those operations where L1 and L2 pose identical processing requirements. The data on cross-language transfer, moreover, have provided evidence that L2 learners use qualitatively diverse procedures. Such diversity generally is consistent with the procedural variations predicted based on L1 writing system properties.

In light of the centrality of dual-language involvement in L2 reading, two directions appear to hold strong potential for expanding current research on L2 word recognition. Although existing research traces the effects of both L1 and L2 processing experiences, little is known about how the two interface. Because transferred skills lead to procedural variations, linguistic factors, known to affect lexical-information extraction in a target language, are likely to induce diverse influences on L2 learners with various L1 backgrounds. New research, therefore, would do well to focus on the cross-linguistic alliance that may transpire in L2 reading development. Current studies make it plain that no aspects of performance variance can be entirely explained by either L1 or L2 variables alone, and it will be essential to examine quantitative and qualitative variations in L2 word recognition in tandem. Only through such multilayered analyses can we access useful insights with which to guide further theoretical refinements.

With regard to the second direction, demonstrated L1–L2 distance effects suggest another possible approach to extending word-recognition research: the longitudinal tracing of facilitation brought about through transferred L1 competencies. Existing transfer studies focus on empirical demonstrations of L1 processing procedures used in L2 word recognition. Little is known, however, about the relative extent to which transferred skills facilitate L2 reading acquisition across various L1 groups. The question is important, because there is good reason to believe that the degrees of facilitation vary in direct proportion to the similarity in processing requirements that the L1 and L2 writing systems mandate. To date, only a handful of studies on record have directly addressed L1–L2 distance effects on L2 reading development. It would be of considerable advantage if more research could be aimed at clarifying variations in sustained L1-based facilitation, prompted by L1–L2 typological distance, in L2 reading skills development.

4   *Vocabulary knowledge*

Successful comprehension is heavily dependent on knowledge of individual word meanings. The widely recognized relationship between vocabulary and reading comprehension attests to the crucial role word knowledge plays in text understanding among both L1 and L2 readers (e.g., Alderson & Urquhart, 1985; Anderson & Freebody, 1983; Carrell, 1988; Carroll, 1971; Davis, 1968; Koda, 1988; Qian, 1999). What is less well understood is that there is also a reverse relationship – that is, vocabulary learning and processing are equally dependent on comprehension. Inasmuch as multiple meanings often are associated with a particular word, its precise meaning is determined in large part by the context in which it appears. Moreover, such meanings are closely linked with the reader's real-life experience. What is triggered by individual words, therefore, may go well beyond dictionary definitions. The word *house*, for example, can evoke all the different images of houses that readers have actually encountered, ranging from a large mansion to a decrepit shack with a leaking roof. Selecting the particular meaning best fitting the emerging text interpretation is vital to accurate content understanding.

Vocabulary processing during reading necessitates interrelated processing skills, including constructing a context, accessing stored information through visual word displays, selecting a relevant meaning based on contextual information, and evaluating the appropriateness of the chosen meaning in subsequent sentences. Despite their potential impact on both theory and practice, relatively restricted attention in L2 research has been given to the ways in which vocabulary and comprehension mutually enhance operations and development. This chapter concentrates on cross-examinations of their interplay by analyzing what it means to know a word, how the knowledge contributes to comprehension, how it is acquired through reading, and how the vocabulary and reading relationship may vary among L1 and L2 readers.

Vocabulary knowledge and comprehension

Research consistently demonstrates that vocabulary knowledge correlates more highly with reading comprehension than other factors, including morphosyntactic knowledge (e.g., Koda, 1989; Qian, 1999; Ulijin & Sirother, 1990) and reading strategies (e.g., Haynes & Baker, 1993). Despite overwhelming evidence of their strong connection, however, there is little consensus as to the exact reciprocation between the two. Vocabulary traditionally has been viewed as the dominant enabling factor. A more recent view, however, propounds a two-way reciprocal affiliation where the two are mutually interdependent during their development.

Anderson and Freebody (1983), for example, evaluated two contrasting hypotheses: instrumental and knowledge. The instrumental hypothesis assumes a direct causal link between vocabulary and comprehension, contending that knowledge of word meanings facilitates comprehension. Conversely, the knowledge hypothesis presumes an indirect relationship between the two, contending that their tie is correlational, linked through a third construct, background knowledge. Ruddel (1994) also compared alternative explanations of their connection. First, overall vocabulary knowledge is a reliable indicator of the probable percentage of known text words. The postulation clearly rests on the same underlying assumption as in Anderson and Freebody's instrumental hypothesis that the proportion of known text words is the decisive factor in determining the degree of text comprehension. A second explanation is based on the premise that vocabulary size mirrors conceptual knowledge. Once readers have real-world experience, their text understanding is substantially enhanced. The supposition stems from the same logic underlying the knowledge hypothesis. A third explanation suggests that general verbal ability is a common bond between the two because both depend on similar processing competencies. A fourth postulation contends that vocabulary knowledge is the natural by-product of reading experience. The logic is straightforward: the more reading, the more opportunities to encounter new words as well as to learn them from context. Obviously, their relationship is anything but simple.

Furthermore, a meta-analysis of L1 vocabulary studies (Stahl & Fairbanks, 1986) offers little support for the commonplace assumption that vocabulary knowledge is the dominant factor promoting reading comprehension. Their analysis demonstrated that the conjecture was unduly simplistic. Vocabulary instruction, for example, which only provides definitions of new words, has a limited impact on overall comprehension improvement. The pre-teaching of specific text-related vocabulary items, moreover, is not uniformly effective in increasing subsequent text comprehension. To gain a better understanding of the relationship between vocabulary and comprehension, it is necessary to first clarify what it means to know a word.

Nature of vocabulary knowledge

It has long been recognized that word knowledge is multifaceted. Although central to this knowledge is a word's meaning information, syntactic and grammatical properties are also important in conceptualizing what it means to know a word. The sections below discuss various dimensions of word knowledge.

Knowing word meanings

Anderson and Nagy (1991) described two dimensions of word-meaning knowledge: denotation and connotation. In their view, denotation refers to the total range of entities that can be associated with a word. Connotation, on the other hand, implies rule distinctions determining whether the referent of a word – for example, a particular action, object, or property – belongs to a particular semantic category, which establishes its denotation. If, for example, *cat* constitutes a given denotation, some rule or algorithm must be used to distinguish between specific cats with different characteristics (Persian, Siamese, Cheshire, and so on), as well as to distinguish cats from other similar-looking animals. In this sense, word-meaning knowledge is closely intertwined with real-world experience, whether direct or vicarious. Knowledge, obviously, is cumulative, evolving through repeated encounters with a particular object, event, or attribute in particular situations. For example, the meaning of *doggie* initially can be limited to a particular pet in a child's family and later expanded, through further exposure, to a variety of dogs in different circumstances (e.g., Adams, 1990; Clark & Clark, 1977; Hintzman, 1986). On the other hand, in a child's mind, *doggie* initially could refer to all four-legged animals, and this overextended meaning could later be modified once the child can distinguish dogs from other animals. Aitchison (1994), in fact, likens L1 vocabulary acquisition among children as performing three interrelated but distinct tasks: labeling (what concept is signaled by the word), packaging (what items are included in this concept), and network building (what other words also are used to convey this or related concepts).

Inasmuch as individuals' real-life experiences vary, it seems rational to assume that the entities constituting a word's *denotation* also differ widely. For instance, because words are used to communicate, the writer must make a priori judgments about what a specific word will mean to the reader. Effective writers use the right word in the right context by making reasonably accurate assumptions about the reader's background knowledge. In contrast, word *connotations*, in Anderson and Nagy's definition, once formulated, may vary from reader to reader, to a lesser extent. Connotations, therefore, provide a stable base of word meanings.

These two dimensions of word-meaning knowledge help explain how, and to what degree, constructed text meanings can vary among individual readers. Similarly, Anderson and Nagy's conception of connotation also clarifies how conceptually mature L2 readers benefit from dictionary use in learning new words to a much greater extent than L1 children. In sum, word-meaning knowledge, in its broad sense, is far more complex, structurally and conceptually, than what is captured in definitions, and its acquisition requires far more than establishing definition–form associations.

Knowing a word's properties

Although there is a general consensus that other dimensions of word knowledge also are essential for reading comprehension, less agreement exists about how non-meaning aspects of the knowledge can be categorized. Nation (2001), for example, divided knowledge dimensions into three major categories: form, meaning, and use. As shown in Table 4.1, the "form" category includes knowledge of the word's spoken and written forms, as well as parts. The "use" category, conversely, entails understanding of the word's collocational behavior (knowing which words co-occur with the word – *auspicious*, for example, collocates with *event*), grammatical functions, and usage constraints (where, when, and how often the word can appear). His "meaning" category, similar to Anderson and Nagy's distinction above, involves knowledge of the connection between the word's form and meaning, as well as the relationship between the concept represented and its referents. Also, there are other ways of dissecting knowledge dimensions. From a pedagogical viewpoint, Graves (1986) suggested three: learning new concepts, learning new labels for known concepts, and bringing words into students' productive use. Drum and Konopak (1987), on the other hand, distinguished various states of "knowing" a word: recognizing the word aurally; its meaning, but not its form; and partial meaning or a different meaning.

Table 4.1. *What is involved in knowing a word (reprinted from I. S. P. Nation, 2001, p. 27)*

Form			
Spoken	R	What does the word sound like?	
	P	How is the word pronounced?	
Written	R	What does the word look like?	
	P	How is the word written and spelled?	
Word parts	R	What parts are recognisable in this word?	
	P	What word parts are needed to express the meaning?	
Meaning			
Form and	R	What meaning does this word form signal?	
meaning	P	What word form can be used to express this meaning?	
Concept and	R	What is included in the concept?	
referents	P	What items can the concept refer to?	
Associations	R	What other words does this make us think of?	
	P	What other words could we use instead of this one?	
Use			
Grammatical	R	In what patterns does the word occur?	
functions	P	In what patterns must we use this word?	
Collocations	R	What words or types of words occur with this one?	
	P	What words or types of words must we use with this one?	
Constraints	R	Where, when, and how often would we expect to meet	
on use (register,		this word?	
frequency)	P	Where, when, and how often can we use this word?	

Note: In column 3, R = receptive knowledge, P = productive knowledge.

These distinctions are important because aspects of word knowledge are relatively independent and therefore are acquired at various rates, as well as in different sequences (Durso & Shore, 1998; Nagy & Scott, 2000). Studies involving adult L2 learners, in fact, show that possessing one knowledge aspect does not guarantee the acquisition of others (Laufer & Patribakht, 1998; Schmitt, 1998). Acquisition modes also are likely to differ among different facets of word knowledge. Ellis (1994) maintained that word forms and meanings entail contrasting modes of learning: word-form knowledge is acquired primarily through implicit learning, whereas meaning understanding necessitates more explicit, conscious, learning. Ellis believes that implicit learning requires attention to the stimulus, but not any particular conscious operations. Therefore, it is strongly affected by input frequency. In contrast, explicit learning, because it involves searching and applying rules, is seriously influenced by both amount of attention and quality of mental operations.

Nation (2001) emphasizes that grammatical and phonological properties are essential for language processing. Building on Levelt's speech-production model (1989), Nation explained that the processes involved in converting preverbal message segments, or fragmented thoughts, into internal speech plans are lexically driven. What this implies is that the grammar, morphology, and phonology of the intended message are determined by the particular words chosen. Knowledge of a word's morphosyntactic properties is thus equally critical to its semantic information in language production, and, by logical extension, comprehension. Considering its extensive dimensions, it is reasonable to assume that the full spectrum of vocabulary knowledge develops only through repeated encounters with words in diverse contexts. Consequently, the following section deals with research on vocabulary learning in context.

Learning words from context

Most L1-speaking children are capable of learning words rapidly and effectively. They not only encounter vast numbers of words during their school years but also retain many of them (e.g., Anderson & Nagy, 1991). Nagy and Anderson (1984) estimate that native English-speaking children encounter roughly 88,000 distinct word families during their school years. Similarly, the average fifth grader confronts almost 10,000 unknown words a year (Anderson & Freebody, 1983). Even more impressively, vocabulary growth between the third and ninth grades, calculated from various estimations of absolute vocabulary size, ranges from 2,000 to 3,000 words a year (Nagy & Herman, 1987), suggesting that children learn, on average, roughly every fourth word they encounter in various contexts.

Given the magnitude of this achievement, it is unrealistic to assume that the gains result from explicit vocabulary instruction. Classroom surveys, in fact, reveal that the number of vocabulary words taught is, at best, a few hundred a year (Durkin, 1979; Roser & Juel, 1982). Durkin (1979) found that in the 4,469 minutes of reading instruction she observed, only 19 were devoted to explicit vocabulary instruction, and a miniscule 4 minutes were given to a review of the instructed vocabulary. Based on these and similar findings, Nagy, Herman, and Anderson (1985) argue that "incidental learning from context during free reading is the major mode of vocabulary acquisition during the school years, and the volume of experience with written language, interacting with reading comprehension ability, is the major determinant of vocabulary growth" (p. 234).

These findings have straightforward implications: Repeated exposure to a large volume of words in print is essential to acquiring academic vocabulary, and developing skills for learning new words from context is equally imperative. Tenth percentile students, in fact, read 1/200th as much per year as ninetieth percentile students (Nagy, Anderson, & Herman, 1987). Increased reading, moreover, opens several additional windows for developing vocabulary knowledge through extensive reading: providing more opportunities for encountering unknown words, extracting partial information from those words, and deriving lexical inferences from other available sources.

To summarize, as a multifaceted construct, word knowledge should be conceived in terms of its distinct aspects. Although its facets are likely to be functionally independent, little has been explored about how they enhance diverse operations in text-meaning construction. Similarly, limited information is available on possible ways reading skills contribute to word-knowledge development. Currently, vocabulary researchers focus mainly on how diverse aspects of the knowledge are learned and assessed, whereas reading researchers emphasize how a single aspect of the knowledge – word definitions – relates to comprehension. Given this multitude of complexity surrounding vocabulary knowledge and comprehension ability, it would be useful to clarify diverse ways in which the two mutually enhance each other.

Conceptions of vocabulary knowledge in L2 studies

Interest in L2 vocabulary has increased sharply over the last two decades. Traditionally, viewed as a building block for achieving target-language proficiency, vocabulary was introduced in the L2 classroom primarily to facilitate the teaching of other skills (Zimmerman, 1997). As a result, L2 vocabulary research has focused almost exclusively on the words that should be incorporated in instruction, together with their related teaching methods. Only recently has a refined approach to L2 vocabulary knowledge begun to attract serious attention (e.g., Henriksen, 1999; Swan, 1997). Conceptualization of vocabulary knowledge in the L2 research context follows.

Research on L2 vocabulary learning

One way of analyzing how vocabulary knowledge is conceived is to canvas what is regarded as the desired outcomes of vocabulary learning, because, in most instances, the anticipated ends determine the means. A growing number of studies have assessed different ways to enhance word learning. The key word *mnemonic* is one such technique that has been extensively studied. A key word is a familiar, concrete term that bears a phonological resemblance to a salient part of the target word to be memorized. For example, the English word *carline*, whose meaning is *old woman*, can be encoded in memory by using the key word *car* together with an associative image: an *old woman* driving a *car* (Pressley, Levin, & McDaniel, 1987). Many believe the method accelerates learning and boosts immediate recall of newly learned vocabulary (e.g., Ellis & Beaton, 1993; Hulstijin, 1997; Levin, Levin, Glashman, & Nordwall, 1992; Pressley et al., 1987; Wang, Thomas, & Ouellette, 1992).

Other researchers have looked into the benefits of using bilingual dictionaries and text glossaries in new-word learning during reading. Although the empirical findings generally do not attest to the usefulness of dictionary use in word learning among young L1 readers (e.g., McKeown, Beck, Omanson, & Pople, 1985; Miller & Gildea, 1987), L2 studies have yielded conflicting results. Bensoussan, Sim, and Weiss (1984), for example, determined that reading comprehension among advanced ESL readers is largely unaffected by the absence or the presence of dictionaries. Knight (1994), however, reported that second-year college Spanish students learned more words and achieved higher comprehension scores when a bilingual dictionary was available during reading. Further, incidental word learning during L2 reading has also been studied extensively. The empirical findings consistently suggest that adult L2 learners do acquire a relatively small, but significant, number of words as a by-product of reading (e.g., Dupuy & Krashen, 1993; Fraser, 1999; Paribakht & Wesche, 1997, 1999; Pitts, White, & Krashen, 1989).

All in all, vocabulary learning research addresses a broad span of issues, ranging from learning enhancement to information retention and lexical scaffolding. Irrespective of the study objectives, however, L2 word knowledge is almost uniformly conceptualized as readily accessible definitional information. In sum, vocabulary learning is operationalized explicitly and implicitly as a process of connecting L2 visual forms with their meanings via definitions in L1, L2, or both.

Research on L2 vocabulary assessment

Another way of scrutinizing conceptions of vocabulary knowledge in the L2 context is to identify the specific competencies measured in widely used vocabulary tests specifically designed for L2 learners. Based on their essential functions, the current L2 vocabulary measures used in research and instruction can be classified into three major categories: assessing vocabulary as an integral aspect of general L2 proficiency, estimating vocabulary size (number of words known), and measuring vocabulary depth (how well they know each word).

The first category, frequently incorporated in traditional psychometric L2 proficiency tests, is designed to yield an index of learners' overall linguistic knowledge. Simple multiple-choice formats – including synonym substitution, translation matching, and definition completion – are commonly employed in these tests. The underlying assumption is that because words are meaningful structural units, test performance can be interpreted as a reliable indicator of both structural and semantic aspects of L2 knowledge (Read, 1997). Inasmuch as performances on these tests generally correlate highly with other language skills, the conventional multiple-choice format, because of its ease of use, is broadly accepted, with little attention to what is measured. In reality, the multiple-choice tests merely determine whether learners possess the definitional information of sampled words at the point of testing.

The second category, vocabulary size, provides numerical estimates of words known. Size tests typically use simple, easy-to-administer, checklist formats. Meara and associates (Meara, 1996; Meara & Jones, 1988, 1990), as a case in point, devised a computerized Eurocentres' Vocabulary Size Test. The test consists of real-word samples selected from a wide range of frequency levels. Because the test utilizes a simple yes–no format, nonsense words also are incorporated to make appropriate adjustments for random guessing. Similarly, Nation's Vocabulary Levels Test (1990) comprises five groups, each consisting of 36 words sampled from five frequency levels. The task is to match words with their correct definitions. These and other size tests often are used in L2 classrooms as a quick, and easy tool for profiling students' vocabulary knowledge. Here again, vocabulary knowledge is measured through word definitions.

The third category, depth, assesses how well learners know each word. What is at stake is the quality, as opposed to size, of the knowledge. Consequently, in depth tests, vocabulary knowledge is viewed as a complex, multidimensional construct. Although a general consensus as to which specific dimensions to measure has yet to emerge, efforts to identify some of the critical components have been initiated. Richard (1976), for example, places heavy emphasis on linguistic, rather than conceptual, sophistication as the critical word-knowledge element among L2 learners. Similarly, Gass (1999) believes knowledge of a word's syntactic properties is vital for lexical processing during reading comprehension, because it provides useful guidance for identifying a word's grammatical categorization – for example, distinguishing adjectives from nouns – essential in phrase construction.

Both researchers have strong convictions that knowledge of a word's morphosyntactic properties is important, which is compatible, in fact, with a view commonly shared by L1 child-language researchers. L1 developmental studies verify that children's notion of grammatical categorization – that is, how words behave syntactically – facilitates their ability to form hypotheses about the possible meanings of unfamiliar words (e.g., Katz, Baker, & MacNamara, 1974; Naigles, 1990).

At present, a handful of vocabulary tests specifically designed to measure knowledge depth exist. Read (1993, 2000), for example, developed a procedure called Word Associates. Each set of items in the test consists of a target and an eight-word pool related to the target in one way or another. The task is to select four words out of the eight, representing particular relationships with the target – including paradigmatic (synonyms), syntagmatic (collocates), and analytic (sharing partial meaning with the target word). In this measure, the depth is seen as how extensively one knows a word through associations with other words.

Another depth measure developed by Paribakht and Wesche (1993, 1997) is the Vocabulary Knowledge Scale (VKS). Vocabulary knowledge is assessed on a five-point scale based on learners' self-rated familiarity with words, ranging from "the word is familiar and I can use it in a sentence" to "the word is not familiar at all." Unlike Read's Word Associates, the VKS views knowledge depth as how well one knows a word, focusing on a developmental continuum ranging from receptive to productive competencies. Another advantage of the measure is that its gradation format allows test users to detect subtle changes in knowledge, even over a relatively brief period of time. The researchers affirm that the scale can capture the incremental nature of vocabulary knowledge because it treats the knowledge as a dynamic, continuously changing construct.

In an effort to clarify the mechanisms through which vocabulary knowledge expedites reading comprehension, Qian (1998) compared the relative impact of vocabulary size and depth on reading comprehension using Nation's Vocabulary Levels Test as a size measure and Read's Word Associates as a depth measure. The data showed that scores on the size and depth tests correlated highly; both scores also correlated significantly with reading comprehension. Although these results corroborate the findings from L1 and L2 vocabulary studies, reinforcing the close connection between word knowledge and comprehension, the implications of the high correlation between the two vocabulary tests are less clear. Is the correspondence simply an artifact of the testing procedures? Or does it suggest that those knowing more words also are likely to know them better?

To sum up, although the assessment research recognizes the multi-dimensionality of vocabulary knowledge, widely used vocabulary measures focus mainly on a single aspect of the knowledge – that is, definitional information. Other dimensions, however, are not addressed as systematically in current research. Consequently, implications of the high correlations among major vocabulary test scores are less than certain. Do they imply that distinct knowledge dimensions develop simultaneously among L2 learners, or do the measures simply tap the same underlying construct? Additional explorations of distinct L2 word-knowledge dimensions are desirable.

Vocabulary knowledge and comprehension among L2 learners

Thus far, little consensus in the L2 literature has been reached regarding what elements – beyond definitional information – should be considered in clarifying the relationship between vocabulary knowledge and comprehension among L2 readers. In an attempt to explore possible relationship variations in L1 and L2 reading, a recent controversy regarding the utility of vocabulary knowledge, acquired through two contrasting channels – decontextualized intentional learning and incidental learning from context – is examined in what follows.

The vocabulary-supports-comprehension view

The concept of vocabulary threshold – the boundary between having and not having sufficient knowledge – provides strong endorsement for the vocabulary-supports-comprehension view. Such a threshold has been tested by estimating the percentage of text vocabulary that must be known for text understanding. Hu and Nation (2000) compared effects of various text coverages (the proportion of known word tokens in a text), ranging from 80% to 100% on story comprehension among college ESL learners, with astonishing results. At 95% coverage (roughly one unknown word in every two text lines), some participants comprehended the text, but most did not. At the 80% level (roughly one unknown word in every five running words), none of the sample apprehended the text meaning. Clearly, for acceptable comprehension in unassisted reading, the majority of text words must be known. From their findings, the researchers speculated that adequate comprehension requires roughly 98% text-word coverage. This finding corroborates the estimated 99% coverage needed for pleasure reading among native English readers (Carver, 1994, 2000).

At least three factors support the usefulness of decontextualized word learning through associations. First, as repeatedly noted, cognitively mature L2 learners bring considerable conceptual knowledge to their reading processes. Known L1 equivalents, therefore, can be used to link unrecognized L2 lexical labels to existing conceptual insights. Paired word associations – through bilingual dictionaries, text glossaries, and similar aids – frequently afford L2 readers almost instant access to their stored knowledge base.

Second, incidental word learning depends heavily on readers' comprehension ability. But, unlike L1 readers, L2 learners often begin reading well before adequate oral proficiency has been attained. Therefore, they must develop reading skills and linguistic knowledge simultaneously in the target language. These circumstances create a learning paradox: To understand written texts, learners must have adequate vocabulary, but to build adequate vocabulary, they must have sufficient reading ability to use context as a clue to new words. The prevalent instructional approach is to equip learners with a core vocabulary of roughly two thousand high-frequency words in the target language (e.g., Laufer, 1997; Nation, 1990, 2001). The logic is straightforward: The core vocabulary accounts for roughly 80% of the words in most texts (Nation & Newton, 1997), and therefore the sooner these words are learned, the better L2 reading comprehension is expedited.

Third, it is commonly assumed that, when text content and presentation are inappropriate for learners' cognitive and linguistic capabilities, comprehension is impeded. Inasmuch as text vocabulary is largely responsible for content complexity, vocabulary limitations can give rise not only to inadequate comprehension, but also to frustration and slow progress in learning to read an unfamiliar language. When much of the text is unfamiliar, readers are likely to either give up or draw on their background knowledge – activated through a small collection of familiar words – in making sense of the text, rather than constructing its meaning from the information presented. Not only is this mode of comprehension likely to be inaccurate, but it also impedes learning new concepts through reading. Building the core vocabulary, therefore, should take primacy.

The mutual-dependency view

An increasing number of studies, as mentioned earlier, have demonstrated that L2 readers do learn vocabulary as a by-product of reading (e.g., Fraser, 1999; Gu & Johnson, 1996; Paribakht & Wesche, 1997, 1999). Convincing arguments for encouraging incidental word learning through extensive reading have been made. Many researchers, for instance, are convinced that connections between local (word-level) and global (text-level) understanding are bidirectional (e.g., Adams, 1994; Nagy, 1997). General semantic information from individual words is used to form a context, but the precise meaning of these words derives from the constructed context itself. For instance, while the generalized definitional meaning of the word *home* does not vary across contexts, it can evoke radically different images when it is used to describe the mansion of a millionaire as opposed to the make-do shelter where the homeless sleep. In this regard, all words are polysemic, and sense distinctions within a particular meaning develop through encounters with the word in diverse situations and thus are context dependent (e.g., Adams, 1990; Hintzman, 1986).

As a result, building vocabulary knowledge is a process of linking linguistic forms to a large amount of context-specific, experience-based information cumulatively acquired throughout the learners' life. Learning words consequently entails far more than memorizing new forms. Learners must sequentially develop the essential competencies for contextual word learning: recognizing that there are subtle differences in a word's meaning, understanding that word meanings are context dependent, extracting context-appropriate meanings from individual lexical items in connected texts, and linking new lexical information with preexisting conceptual knowledge. These competencies obviously cannot evolve from decontextualized associative word learning.

Learning new words, moreover, often requires the formulation of new concepts, even for cognitively mature adult L2 learners. Conceptual expansion through new-word learning entails progressive evolutions that go far beyond the form–definition linking. Sternberg (1987) identified several sequential operations: separating relevant from irrelevant text information for the purpose of inferring a meaning of an unknown word, combining relevant contextual cues to formulate a workable definition, and evaluating the hypothesized meaning against information from the subsequent context. Here again, acquisition of the skills for conceptual expansion through contextual word learning does not occur automatically, necessitating continuous training and practice.

Finally, text comprehension is not the by-product of stringing word beads together. To enrich text meaning, readers must read between the lines, integrating presented information with their prior knowledge. Knowing the definition of *subway*, for example, is not sufficient for understanding the sentence "She took off her diamond ring when she boarded the New York subway." Readers must also know the New York subway often has been associated with high crime rates.

Bridging inference of this sort requires an awareness of what is implied, and not merely individual word definitions.

Overall, the sharply divided conceptualizations of how vocabulary knowledge relates to comprehension give rise to skepticism over the adequacy of any single explanation of how stored lexical information enhances reading comprehension. It is important, however, to recognize that the two views – *vocabulary supports comprehension* and *mutual dependency* – are not mutually exclusive. The former emphasizes the significance of decontextualized word learning for short-term efficiency in building the core vocabulary. The latter, on the other hand, underscores the importance of self-regulated word-learning capabilities, promoting continual, long-term vocabulary expansion. Hence, conjointly, the two views explain how various learning modes contribute to word-knowledge development, as well as elucidate, in part, the different ways vocabulary knowledge and reading mutually affect one another.

Nature of vocabulary knowledge among L2 readers

To reiterate, the widespread view that vocabulary knowledge is synonymous with definitional information dominates, in many ways, current L2 vocabulary research. The resulting assumption is that L2 words evoke only fragments of the information encoded in L1 words. To wit, whereas an L1 word can give rise to images and emotions stemming from real-life experiences with its referents, its L2 equivalent may bring to mind only abstract generalizations of the word's allusion. Despite its significance, little is known about the fundamental distinctions between L1 and L2 word knowledge. In weighing such distinctions, two elements are essential: cross-cultural variations in word meanings and incongruity between conceptual and linguistic sophistication.

Cross-cultural variations in word meanings

Cross-linguistic studies suggest that the ways languages reflect reality vary from culture to culture; there is no exact one-to-one lexical correspondence across languages (e.g., Berlin & Kay, 1969; Schwanenflugel, Blout, & Lin, 1991; Wierzbicka, 1995). In Japanese, for example, two distinct words, *samui* and *tsumetai*, are used in place of the single word *cold* in English. *Samui* is used when referring to climate, as in "cold winter morning," and *tsumetai* is used when referring to temperature, as in "cold drink." Interestingly, *tsumetai* can be used figuratively to describe personality, as in "she is cold," but *samui* does not permit such figurative use.

There are more subtle, but equally definitive, word-meaning deviations. What each word – say, *cat* – means varies in accordance with the individual reader's experience with cats. As indicated earlier, competent writers are adept at making reasonably accurate assumptions about what meanings most readers, through experience, share in common. Based on their assumptions, they determine what elements should be explicit or remain unstated to convey their message effectively. Using the subway example again as an illustration, sophisticated writers would sense that most of their readers know that New York subways, because of the high crime rate, can be dangerous. They can then presume that a sentence such as "She clutched her purse firmly" will be understood by the reader without further explanation. This interpretation, however, may not be expected among readers from other cultures with little familiarity with New York subways. In Japan, for instance, subways are associated with crime to a far less extent. They are sometimes considered dangerous – not because of crimes, but because of earthquakes. The definitional meaning of *subway* does not differ in English and Japanese, but people's experiences with subways can vary considerably. Significantly, it is the latter, experience-related information that affects construal and interpretation during comprehension.

A third variable affecting word-meaning variation stems from cultural attitudes and beliefs. It has been argued, for example, that emotional concepts, as well as the linguistic means through which emotions are expressed, differ considerably across languages and cultures (e.g., Kitayama & Markus, 1994; Wierzbicka, 1995, 1999). Dewaele and Pavlenko (2002) contend that English and Russian systematically vary in the way emotions are conceptualized. In English, for example, emotions are taken as "passive states caused by external and/or past causes" (p. 285). The linguistic consequence of this view is apparent in the extensive use of adjectives in expressing emotions. In Russian, emotions are regarded as "inner activities in which one engages more or less voluntarily" (p. 285). As a result, verbs are predominantly used in Russian in describing emotions. The question in L2 research is whether differences in either the underlying conceptualization or its linguistic manifestations affect L2 text comprehension. Insofar as pioneer studies involving L2 learners with diverse cultural backgrounds demonstrate systematic patterns of L1 cultural effects on L2 speech perception (e.g., Graham, Hamblin, & Feldstein, 2001; Rintell, 1984), it would be productive to examine their implications for reading comprehension.

Gaps between vocabulary and conceptual knowledge

One of the major objectives in word learning is establishing connections among three lexical elements: meaning, symbol, and sound. In L1, children are expected to develop the skills for mapping familiar sounds and concepts onto graphic symbols. Conceptually mature L2 learners, however, are confronted with a fundamentally different objective from the very outset. In most instances, L2 learners are unfamiliar with word forms, both symbol and sound, but familiar with concepts through L1 words. Therefore, L2 word learning entails linking four, instead of three, lexical elements: symbol, sound, meaning, and L1 equivalent. Although in L1 vocabulary knowledge can be regarded as a reliable indicator of conceptual sophistication, the same is not necessarily true in L2. Hence, there is an apparent gap between word and conceptual knowledge among adult L2 learners.

The imbalance explains why definitions – core semantic information – provide a useful scaffolding for text comprehension among L2 readers. Using a bilingual dictionary, therefore, they can understand, though in varying degrees, L2 texts with a large proportion of unfamiliar words. Assisted reading, indisputably, is less than ideal. Looking up words can be disruptive in information integration during syntactic and discourse processing. Focusing on stringing L1 word definitions together may interfere with fathoming what is implied in statements. And comprehension is achieved only through L1 mediation; as a consequence, subtle cultural nuances can be lost during word-by-word translation. Hence, the knowledge imbalance among adult L2 learners may give rise to the possibility that the relationship between vocabulary and comprehension is mediated by different factors among L1 and L2 readers. Although conceptual knowledge is likely to be a strong mediator of the vocabulary–comprehension relationship among L1 readers, L2 proficiency may be a more significant mediating factor explaining the connection between the two among L2 readers. Here too, further explorations are possible in elucidating the extent and manner in which constructed text meanings differ among conceptually mature L2 learners with adequate L2 vocabulary knowledge and those dependent on external lexical scaffolding.

Dual-language lexical organization

The lexical organization of dual-language systems is a major issue in bilingual research. There is a long-standing debate among neurolinguists and psychologists over how L1 and L2 lexical information is stored in conjunction with conceptual knowledge. Whereas early studies focused on a composite of factors – age, learning context, and acquisition mode – affecting the extent to which L1 and L2 lexical knowledge are conjoined in conceptual storage (e.g., Albert & Obler, 1978; Ervin & Osgood, 1954; Jakobovits & Lambert, 1961; Lambert, 1969; Ruke-Dravina, 1971), more recent studies have focused on theory construction of bilingual lexical organization (e.g., Chen & Leung, 1989; Dijikstra & van Heuven, 1998; Kroll & Curley, 1988; Kroll & Sholl, 1992; Kroll & Sunderman, 2003; Potter, So, Von Eckardt, & Feldman, 1984). Insofar as the ways words' semantic information is extracted from dual-language lexicons bear directly on L2 text understanding, a brief overview of bilingual lexical organization research and its implications for L2 comprehension seems in order.

Bilingual research has yielded complex pictures of dual-language lexical organization by subjecting two competing models – word association and concept mediation – to stringent empirical examinations. The word-association model (presuming that L1 and L2 lexicons are linked directly through interlanguage word associations) postulates that conceptual information is accessed only through L1 words. In contrast, the concept-mediation model (presupposing that the two lexicons are linked indirectly through conceptual knowledge) posits direct access to conceptual storage in both L1 and L2. Hence, the two models, while both assuming separate, hierarchical representations for lexical and conceptual information, differ in one dimension – the manner in which L1 and L2 lexicons are connected (conceptually mediated versus directly linked through word associations).

Two tasks – picture naming and word translation – typically are used in this research. In picture naming, participants are shown a sequence of pictures and asked to indicate orally what they represent. The task involves three operations: identifying the object, accessing its meaning, and using the resulting information to search for the word representing the concept. Picture-naming speed, therefore, is taken as an indicator of efficiency in accessing lexical information from conceptual storage. In the translation task, participants are presented with a series of L2 words and asked to provide their translation equivalents orally. The logic of comparing reaction times in the two tasks is as follows: If L1 and L2 lexicons are conceptually mediated, the operations in the translation task should parallel the sequence required for picture naming. The concept-mediation model, therefore, predicts similar performance on the two tasks. If, however, dual-language lexical systems are connected through word associations without concept mediation, the translation task necessitates only a single step – that is, locating the L1 equivalent via word associations. Consequently, the word-association model predicts translation to be notably faster than picture naming.

Although initial results predominantly supported the concept-mediation model, by demonstrating similar processing performance in picture naming and translation (e.g., Potter et al., 1984), subsequent data produced somewhat conflicting results. By comparing beginning and advanced L2 learners, for example, Kroll and Curley (1988) found an interesting proficiency by task interaction. Although performance among advanced learners was virtually unaffected by task, beginning learners were far more efficient in translation than in picture naming. The researchers interpreted the results as indicating that L2 lexical processing is mediated by L1 until sufficient proficiency is attained. In a further study, Kroll and Sholl (1992) compared strength differences in L1 and L2 word associations by comparing efficiency in forward (from L1 to L2) and backward (from L2 to L1) translations. Superior performance was found in backward translation. They attributed the asymmetry to the stronger connections between L1 lexicon and conceptual knowledge, explaining that because L1 words afford easier access to meanings, they are likely to mediate semantic processing of L2 words, but the reverse is not likely during L1 lexical processing.

Consolidating these findings, Kroll and Stewart (1994) proposed a revised hierarchical model, a hybrid of the concept-mediation and word-association models, conjecturing that the strength of the connections between L1–L2 lexicons and concepts changes over time. The model assumes that both L1 and L2 words are linked to concepts, but initially the linkages are stronger for L1 than for L2. Therefore, meaning access in L2 is mediated by L1 words, creating stronger L2-to-L1 word associations among beginning learners. The connection strength between L2 words and concepts increases progressively over time, as L2 proficiency improves, allowing high-proficiency learners to access meanings directly during L2 lexical processing without L1 mediation.

These models presume some type of mechanism of controlling activation of information from either language. Such an assumption, however, is not entirely congruent with other models of bilingual lexical representations and processing. As a case in point, the bilingual interactive activation (BIA) model, proposed by Djikstra and van Heuven (1998), posits that the bilingual's lexicon is integrated across languages, claiming that lexical information in both languages is activated whenever the input shares features – visual, phonological, and semantic – with lexical alternatives in each of the languages involved (see Figure 4.1).

In fact, recent experimental studies have provided substantial support for the integrative lexical representation views (e.g., Brysbaert,

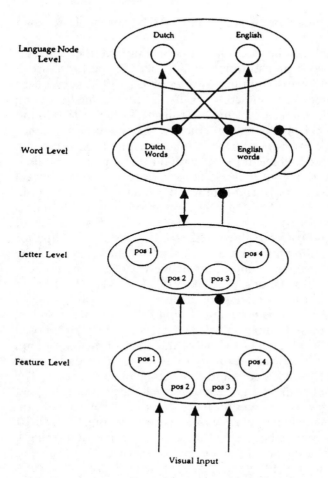

Figure 4.1   The bilingual interactive activation model (reprinted from T. Dijkstra & W. J. B. van Heuven, 1998, p. 200).

1998; Dijkstra et al., 1998; Van Heuven et al., 1998). Van Heuven et al. (1998), for example, demonstrated that L2 lexical-decision speed (time required for deciding whether a given letter string is a real word) among fluent Dutch–English bilinguals was influenced by both L1 and L2 words that are graphically similar (orthographic neighbors) to the target L2 word. The orthographic neighbor effect within a single language – the phenomenon wherein lexical-decision efficiency is affected by the number and frequency of the target word's orthographic neighbors – is well established in L1 word recognition research. Although Van Heuven et al.'s experiment involved bilingual participants, only one of their languages was required for task performance. Consequently, the observed cross-language effect was interpreted as suggesting that both languages are activated automatically during L2 lexical processing, regardless of either task requirements or learner intent.

From a different vantage point, Jiang (2002) also showed that L1 semantic information remains active during L2 lexical processing. Using semantic relatedness judgment, he compared rating patterns for two types of English word pairs among native English speakers and Chinese learners of English. The two word-pair types were those sharing the same translation equivalent in L1 (as in *problem* and *question*, which correspond to a single Chinese equivalent *wenti*, and those associated with two different L1 words (as in *interrupt* and *interfere*, translated into *daduan* and *ganrao*, respectively, in Chinese). Although relatedness ratings among native English speakers were virtually identical between the two types of pairs, L2 learners rated the *same* translation pairs more closely related than the *different* translation pairs. Jiang contends that the L2 lexicon integrates the established semantic content of their L1 equivalents, rather than creating new semantic specifications of its own. These findings also imply that the activation of L1 information is automatic, and therefore cannot be consciously controlled by the learner during L2 lexical processing.

The nonselective dual-language activation has significant implications for L2 text-information processing and subsequent comprehension. First, it renders strong support for the continuing role of L1 in L2 reading beyond initial learning phases. Although it is still unclear to what extent, and how, activated L1 information affects L2 text comprehension, the notion of dual-language activation hints at a strong possibility that both connotative and denotative word-meaning information, developed through L1, is likely to be incorporated in L2 text-meaning construction. Should this be the case, we can anticipate that the way L2 is learned – either through formal instruction within L1 linguistic/cultural milieu or through exposure and experience with the target language in L2 social context – bears directly on the extent to which L1-specific meaning information is integrated in L2 lexical entries even among advanced learners.

Second, nonselective dual-language activation provides a plausible explanation for L1–L2 orthographic distance effects on L2 word recognition efficiency. L2 learners' ease with visual-information extraction increases with degrees of similarity in L1 and L2 orthographic systems. L1 studies suggest that orthographic neighbors within a single language facilitate recognition efficiency for low-frequency words, although the neighbor size has little impact on high-frequency words (Andrews, 1992). Inasmuch as L2 words are predominantly unfamiliar, regardless of frequency, in the initial phases of L2 learning, L1 and L2 orthographic similarity – more specifically, the extent to which the two languages share cross-lingual homographs and cognates – should provide substantial facilitation in L2 word recognition. Orthographic distance thus can be a stronger predictor than frequency of word recognition efficiency, particularly among beginning L2 learners.

Given the complexity of the issues surrounding dual-language lexicons, one can conclude that the critical difficulty in this research is not simply to ascertain whether the two lexical systems are connected or integrated with conceptual knowledge, but rather to isolate the variables controlling the mechanisms through which lexical information is accessed across languages. All in all, it would be desirable to extend the current line of investigations by incorporating various types of word stimuli, especially verbs, because they contain qualitatively different information, as well as involving bilingual learners of languages with greater diversity employing typologically unrelated orthographies, such as Chinese and Arabic.

Summary and future research suggestions

This chapter has focused on the precise relationship between vocabulary knowledge and reading comprehension. The common assumption is that vocabulary knowledge engenders reading comprehension, but the close scrutiny described in this chapter makes it plain that the relationship is considerably more complex. Both necessitate similar competencies, and they also are functionally interdependent – that is, although knowledge of word meanings is essential to comprehension, vocabulary knowledge expands, in the main, through reading. What, then, might be said about their mutual developmental progression?

One way of conceptualizing their developmental interstices is to identify shared competencies underlying both reading and word-learning abilities. Lexical inference, as an example, is critical for successful comprehension and vocabulary building. It must be noted, however, that lexical inference also necessitates both vocabulary knowledge and comprehension capability. For instance, in determining what a word might mean in a particular context, learners must first formulate sentence-level understanding from linguistic cues, and then coalesce textual information with their own prior knowledge to reduce the semantic gap created by the unknown word. Functional interdependence of this sort clearly indicates that the acquisition of related competencies generates a series of symbiotic chains, so to speak, which reciprocally enhance their development and functionality.

Decoding efficiency – speed and accuracy in extracting lexical information from print – likely is another factor promoting both vocabulary acquisition and reading comprehension. As observed earlier, word learning can be conceived of as connection building among three lexical constituents: sound, symbol, and meaning. Once established, word knowledge can then be judged by the strength of these lexical links within a word. The stronger the connections, the more rapidly and accurately lexical information is accessed and retrieved. Effortless lexical information extraction, as discussed in Chapter 3, is also an essential requirement for reading comprehension. Hence, decoding efficiency is a partial, but significant, indicator of both vocabulary knowledge and reading proficiency.

Because of the dual-language involvement, moreover, additional fine dimensions must be incorporated in characterizing the vocabulary–comprehension relationship among L2 learners. A central factor in the complexity is cross-linguistic variations in a word's semantic content as well as the manner in which it is represented graphically. Despite the convincing empirical evidence on long-lasting L1 effects on L2 lexical learning and processing, there seems to be a considerable dearth of information as to what extent, and how, differences in L1 and L2 word-meaning knowledge affect L2 text comprehension. As a consequence of the gap between conceptual and linguistic knowledge among adult L2 learners, their text-meaning construction may be guided by both prior knowledge, reflecting their L1 real-life experience, and L1 vocabulary knowledge, mirroring the specific ways their L1 represents reality. Consequently, systematic analyses of L2 text representations constructed by L2 learners with diverse L1 backgrounds could shed substantial light on cross-linguistic variations in L2 text interpretation.

Finally, although reading and vocabulary knowledge are mutually interdependent, their functional relationship changes during the course of their evolution. In the earlier stages, for example, it is vocabulary knowledge that facilitates reading acquisition. In the later stages, however, vocabulary learning entails conceptual expansion. Learning to read familiar oral vocabulary necessitates connecting visual forms with already-known words. Learning conceptually unfamiliar words, on the other hand – beyond the connection making – demands additional linguistic and conceptual manipulations. To understand the concept represented by a new word, relevant information explaining its meaning must be accurately interpreted, and the newly acquired concept assimilated into the existing knowledge base. Reading ability, therefore, is the primary path to new-word learning.

Reading and word learning are coincidental. Each, in a sense, feeds the other. Given the reciprocal nature of their development, there may be considerable benefits in seeking better ways of promoting word-learning skills, in lieu of teaching the words themselves, simultaneously with reading comprehension. Because the vast majority of L1 academic words are learned incidentally, through reading, there can be little doubt that, during their school years, children develop their inherent heuristic capacity for self-teaching. Consequently, it would be extremely productive if research could uncover ways to capitalize on this heuristic capacity adult L2 learners likely have already developed in the L1 in their pursuit of vocabulary expansion in a new language.

5 Intraword awareness and word-knowledge development

Successful communication relies heavily on accumulated word knowledge. The research on record illuminates several key insights about its development. Word knowledge is formulated in specific contexts. Extracting lexical information from these contexts is in itself an acquired competence. Information extraction, moreover, is greatly expedited by an explicit understanding of a word's internal structure. Consequently, in-depth examinations of such structural awareness can point up the essential competencies underlying word-knowledge accretion through reading. The benefits of these examinations are further supported by the fact that languages differ in the way their elements are represented by the graphic symbols in their writing systems. Knowing that aspects of structural awareness particularly critical to word-knowledge development evolve through cumulative print-processing experience, there is good reason to believe that the nature of the awareness varies across writing systems. It seems reasonable to assume that systematic explorations of these variations should create a window for identifying cross-linguistic differences in the requisite capabilities for lexical learning and processing.

Thus, the primary aim of this chapter is to clarify the ways a writing system's properties relate to the nature of lexical competence in diverse languages. The chapter first reviews the roles of metalinguistic awareness in reading development. Using operational definitions of key concepts as a base, sequential analyses are applied to two typologically contrasting languages, English and Chinese. The intent is to illustrate, with step-by-step descriptions of the analyses, how cross-linguistic differences in the requisite structural awareness and resulting lexical competence can be identified. Empirical findings from recent L2 studies also are examined to evaluate the predictive validity of the hypothesized competence variations.

Metalinguistic awareness in early reading development

Metalinguisitc awareness is the ability to identify, analyze, and manipulate language forms. Multidimensional in nature, its disparate facets can be defined and measured in conjunction with various language features (e.g., Adams, 1990; Stahl & Murray, 1994; Yopp, 1988). Bialystok (2001) describes metalinguistic awareness as an explicit representation of "the abstract structure that organizes sets of linguistic rules without being directly instantiated in any of them" (p. 123). Although the understanding evolves through learning and using a particular language, metalinguistic awareness is distinct from linguistic knowledge in that it implies an understanding of language in its most general sense, independent of its specific details. For example, among English-speaking children, syntactic awareness reflects the realization that the order in which words are presented determines sentence meaning. An abstract notion of this sort contrasts with the more specific knowledge of canonical word order (subject-verb-object) in English sentences. Because of its generalized, abstract nature, metalinguistic awareness, once properly developed, is believed to regulate the perception and interpretation of linguistic input (Bialystok, 2001; Ellis, 2002; MacWhinney, 1987; Slobin, 1985), thereby guiding and facilitating both language learning and processing.

In recent times, interest in metalinguistic awareness has risen sharply among researchers. The general consensus is that learning to read is fundamentally metalinguistic, involving the recognition of functionally important elements of spoken language and their relation to the writing system, as well as the skills to map between the two (e.g., Fowler & Liberman, 1995; Goswami & Bryant, 1992; Nagy & Anderson, 1998). The facilitative benefits of metalinguistic awareness can be illustrated in two ways. First, for literacy learning to occur, children must understand that written symbols correspond to speech units. They then must learn what each symbol represents, as well as how it can be combined with others to form a word. Without these basic insights, written symbols are perceived as nonsense scribbles, and learning them is unduly dreary, because it seems useless and meaningless. Second, an understanding of the segmental nature of language promotes analytical approaches to word learning and processing, simply because the concept of segmentation bolsters the capacity for identifying the structure of words and their internal elements. Without analytical competence, the learner cannot extract partial information from a new string of symbols. In these circumstances, lexical processing becomes an all-or-nothing process, and reading capability is likely to be restricted to words previously encountered and remembered.

The roles of metalinguistic awareness in alphabetic literacy – English, in particular – have been extensively studied over the last two decades. As noted earlier, words denote both sound and meaning information, and many of the investigations have concentrated on the phonological and morphological aspects of the awareness. The research has led to the widely endorsed conviction that to master an alphabetic scrip, children not only must understand that words can be divided into sequences of phonemes (e.g., Liberman, Shankweiler, Fischer, & Carter, 1974; Liberman, Shankweiler, Liberman, Fischer, & Fowler, 1977; Liberman, Shankweiler, & Liberman, 1989) but also must acquire the ability to analyze a word's internal structure to break down its phonemic constituents (e.g., Blachman, 1991; Bradley, 1988).

In fact, a possible causal link between phonological awareness and reading acquisition has been suggested. Reading-development studies repeatedly illustrate that children's sensitivity to the segmental configuration of spoken sounds directly nurtures their capacity to read and spell, and also serves as a powerful predictor of reading success among early and middle grade students (e.g., Bryant, MacLean, & Bradley, 1990; Juel et al., 1986; Stahl & Murray, 1994; Stanovich, Cunningham, & Cramer, 1984; Yopp, 1988). Moreover, reading progress is significantly enhanced by phonological awareness training (e.g., Bradley & Bryant, 1991), further supporting the probability that phonological awareness is an enabling factor. Similarly, the contributions of morphological awareness in literacy acquisition also have been observed. Skilled readers are more sensitive to a word's morphological structure (e.g., Chilant & Caramazza, 1995; Fowler & Liberman, 1995; Stolz & Feldman, 1995; Taft, 1991; Taft & Zhu, 1995). Further, a close relationship has also been noted between morphological control and reading ability; less skilled readers commit far more errors of affix omissions in their writing and speaking (e.g., Duques, 1989; Rubin, 1991). In the same vein, the efficient use of morphological information during sentence comprehension distinguishes competent and less competent high school readers (e.g., Tyler & Nagy, 1989, 1990). In sum, the converging evidence makes it plain that multiple aspects of metalinguistic awareness cumulatively facilitate literacy learning throughout its various developmental stages.

Intraword awareness and lexical competence

Defining intraword awareness

Because both phonological and morphological awareness rely on the learner's sensitivity to words' internal elements, the term *intraword*

awareness (IA) in the following discussions refers to generalized metalinguistic insights specifically related to the capabilities underlying
lexical learning and processing. In its broadest sense, IA pertains to
the perception of a word's internal structure, as well as to an understanding of how a spoken word's internal elements relate to units of
graphic symbols. Thus, IA is a multidimensional construct, involving a
number of related, but distinguishable, core competency components –
to wit, understanding that words can be segmented into smaller, functionally identifiable elements; skill to map each functional element
onto units of graphic symbols; and abilities to manipulate (e.g., isolate, blend, and combine) segmental intraword information.

Operationalizing lexical competence

Lexical competence, in this frame of reference, pertains to the capabilities supporting and promoting word-knowledge expansion through
print. To reiterate, because the knowledge is multidimensional, evolving through diverse modes of learning, distinct capabilities presumably
underlie each mode. In intentional learning, for example, the objective
is to link three lexical elements – symbol, meaning, and sound – in the
words to be learned, as in, for example, memorizing word lists. This
mode, in all probability, necessitates two capabilities: linking words'
graphic features with their sound and meaning information, and encoding newly established linkages in lexical memory.

Incidental learning, in contrast, occurs as a by-product of other
activities, such as reading and studying. Encountering new words in
context obviously is a necessary precondition, and the ability to un-
ravel their meanings based on contextual information is also essential.
As a consequence, contextual lexical inference is central in incidental
word learning. It relies on three kinds of cues: word-internal elements;
contextual information, including syntactic, semantic, and pragmatic
constraints; and prior knowledge. It also mandates four operations:
identifying known elements within an unknown word, distinguishing relevant and irrelevant contextual information, combining word-
internal and contextual clues in formulating workable definitions, and
confirming their plausibility in subsequent contexts (Sternberg, 1987).

Word knowledge, moreover, develops incrementally through repeated exposures to words in various contexts. Because the knowledge
entails much more than definitions, complete understanding cannot be
attained until a word's new properties – whether functional, structural, or graphic – are recognized as such and incorporated into
lexical memory. For knowledge accretion to occur, therefore, lexical information, once encoded, must undergo repeated modification

and refinement. Three critical factors seemingly underlie incremental knowledge augmentation: recognizing a new word element associated with particular usage, establishing linkages between the word's graphic feature and its newly uncovered function, and incorporating the added information into stored knowledge.

In sum, word knowledge is acquired both intentionally and incidentally, progressively evolving through continuous expansion and refinement. Importantly, the disparate learning modes necessitate distinct capabilities. IA facilitation, consequently, should take diverse forms in word-knowledge accretion.

Roles of IA *in lexical learning*

The significance of IA in word-knowledge development can best be understood through its strong facilitative roles in analyzing and manipulating a word's internal elements. The schematic diagram in Figure 5.1 illustrates possible functional relationships between IA and lexical competence. The diverse ways in which IA enhances lexical learning and processing are described in the following sections.

Associative list learning

Associative learning, commonly used in L2 teaching, entails linking paired words. On the surface, the task may appear routine, simply establishing a single bond connecting the words' labels. Paired words, however, can be linked through multiple features: graphic, syntactic, and semantic (Voss, 1972). Consequently, variations in learning outcomes often can be explained by the quality and quantity of these linkages (Griffin & Harley, 1998). IA obviously offers substantial facilitation in analyzing the words' internal structure in order to identify possible links. Assuming that the more the linkages, the stronger the associations, analytical competence is vital. Moreover, newly encoded word information must be assimilated in existing lexical knowledge. Here, too, IA offers assistance in connecting new and stored word information.

Definition-based word learning

Intentional learning, as discussed in Chapter 4, involves the kind of definitional information typically found in dictionaries. Although such definitions convey explicit information about a word's meaning, they may offer virtually no clues to its usage (Nagy & Scott, 2000). As a result, a common problem among native English-speaking children is

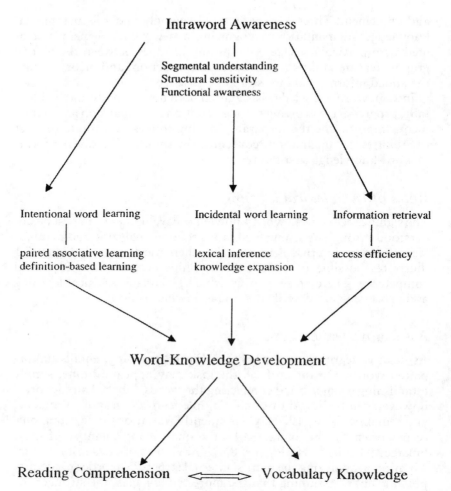

Intraword Awareness

Segmental understanding
Structural sensitivity
Functional awareness

Intentional word learning   Incidental word learning   Information retrieval

paired associative learning   lexical inference   access efficiency
definition-based learning   knowledge expansion

Word-Knowledge Development

Reading Comprehension ⟺ Vocabulary Knowledge

Figure 5.1   Role of IA in word-knowledge development.

the failure to recognize a word's proper usage because of excessive reliance on the single core-semantic aspect of its information (McKeown,
1993). Scott and Nagy (1997) contend that the observed deficiency is
attributable to insufficient sensitivity to a word's syntactic properties.
Even when syntactic clues are available in visual word displays, as
in "slow*ness*" and "slow*ly*," we cannot assume that children always
attend to the information. Theoretically, segmentation capability, the
core IA component, helps promote the awareness that an element of
a word's graphic presentation often conveys syntactic information.
In turn, such awareness enhances the fundamental conception that

words function in specific ways in sentences in accordance with their grammatical categories.

Lexical inference

Nagy and Anderson (1984) estimate that roughly 60% of the new words children encounter in printed school material are structurally transparent and morphologically complex words, such as *unhappiness* and *ladylike*. In principle, the meanings of at least half the new words could be deduced on the basis of their morphological constituents. In actuality, however, children, when confronted with new words during reading, do not always exploit the available morphological information. Contextual clues and background knowledge are both regarded as essential in lexical inference, but their contribution is limited to the formulation of a specific scenario, described in the text segment, where the word to be inferred appears (Nagy & Gentner, 1990). Such scenarios are helpful in forming workable hypotheses of what the word might mean, but they are too broad to provide sufficient semantic constraints. Hence, IA, by expediting intraword analysis and partial information extraction, plays a crucial role in reducing the large number of possibilities generated by context-based, top-down reasoning.

Knowledge incorporation and expansion

Word-knowledge development is incremental, evolving through "almost infinitesimally small steps" (Nagy & Scott, 2000). In addition to meaning information, as noted in Chapter 4, word knowledge includes an understanding of the relative frequency of a word in speech and print, syntactic and semantic constraints on its usage, its underlying form and possible derivations, various associations with other words, and so on. For lexical information to accumulate, subtle changes in a word's form and function must be recognized in the context of a given usage. It is in this process that IA offers substantial facilitation. The word *book*, for example, is likely to be interpreted initially as a noun. However, encountered in the sentence "The businessman booked a flight to Singapore," an opportunity to learn the word's other syntactic and semantic properties arises. The encounter itself, however, does not guarantee any modification of existing knowledge. The learner must recognize that *book* is used with the past tense marker *-ed*, and appears immediately after the initial noun phrase. On the basis of these observations, moreover, the learner must also be willing to extend the established knowledge of the word, and to explore its additional properties in conjunction with the new usage. If the learner lacks segmental understanding, new usage of a known word may go unnoticed.

In sum, intraword structural sensitivity is related directly, and perhaps causally, to lexical competence. By enabling intraword structural analysis and segmental information manipulation, IA invokes analytical approaches to lexical learning and processing. If a word is regarded as an indivisible whole, disallowing internal analysis, word learning is reduced simply to endless memorization.

Cross-linguistic analyses

Unlike L1 research, metalinguistic awareness has attracted limited attention among L2 researchers. Although systematic investigations currently are under way, IA research is still in its maturation stage and is likely to undergo further evolution. A meaningful research overview at this early juncture is simply prohibitive. However, in view of its promising potential, even at this early stage, it may be worthwhile to provide a glimpse of the emerging approach to illuminating cross-linguistic variations in lexical learning. The following sections illustrate the approach's rationale and procedures.

IA *as a cross-linguistic examination window*

IA offers several major advantages when cross-linguistic variations in lexical learning and processing among L2 learners are being probed. Because diverse aspects of IA make unique contributions to word-knowledge accretion; prior literacy experience can be translated into specific IA capabilities. This, in turn, creates a firm basis for predicting which capabilities are "transfer-ready" at a specific point in time among a particular age group of L2 readers. Because of its abstract nature, IA components, properly measured, should be less vulnerable to linguistic variables, such as frequency and visual/conceptual familiarity, than language-processing skills. Conceivably, then, it may yield a more stable picture of developing capabilities. In addition, inasmuch as IA competencies develop reciprocally through print-information processing experience (e.g., Bowey & Francis, 1991; Perfetti, Beck, Bell, & Hughes, 1987; Vellutino & Scanlon, 1987), they reflect the precise ways spoken-language elements are graphically represented in the writing system. Logic suggests, then, that the IA capabilities underlying lexical-competence development can be identified through prudent analysis of spoken-language elements, writing-system properties, and their relationships. Cross-linguistic comparisons of these relationships should yield significant insights into potential deviations in the requisite competencies for efficient lexical learning and processing.

Following this reasoning, if we want to identify cross-linguistic variations in requisite IA competencies in diverse languages, three sequential analyses are necessary: describing properties of the writing system in each; determining the IA capabilities – phonological and morphological awareness, in particular – necessitated for extracting lexical information from visual word displays; and comparing the mandatory IA competencies across languages. The following describes the analyses applied to two typologically contrasting languages, Chinese and English.

IA in Chinese
Writing system

According to Taylor and Taylor (1995), Mandarin, the national lingua franca used in China's schools as the language of instruction, has approximately 7,000 different morphemes and 400 syllables with four distinct tones, constituting 1,200 tone syllables. Generally, each graphic symbol (character) denotes a single morpheme, which in turn corresponds to one syllable. Because most single morphemes are used as words, one would expect that there are as many characters as words and morphemes. In actuality, however, roughly 6,000 characters are required for scholarly literacy, and 3,500 are designated as "modern Chinese characters for everyday use." During their 6 years of primary education, Chinese children are required to learn 2,834 characters through formal instruction. Hence, Chinese literacy demands a massive number of symbols, which, though visually far more complex than alphabetic letters, contain recurring internal elements. It is reasonable, therefore, to assume that IA plays an equally, if not more, significant role in character-knowledge development among logographic readers.

Characters are formed with radicals – that is, functionally identifiable, recurrent stroke patterns (e.g., Chen, Allport, & Marshall, 1996; Shu & Anderson, 1997). Many radicals are single-unit characters in themselves and are used both as independent words and as components in other characters. Some radicals, however, lack lexical status, serving only as character components. Although there are several character-formation procedures, semantic-phonetic compounding is by far the most dominant method used in the vast majority (80% to 90%) of multiple-unit characters (Zhang, 1994). The method

Figure 5.2   Basic structure of multiple-unit characters.

generally involves a nonlinear integration of two radicals, each conveying either phonetic or semantic information.

Of the approximately seven hundred phonetic radicals, many have lexical status, retaining both phonological and semantic representations. Their recognition, therefore, requires extracting phonological information from the radical, while disregarding its semantic information. In contrast, semantic radicals provide a guide to characters' meanings. For example, the meanings of characters containing the "water" radical generally relate to water in one way or another. To wit, the characters for 湖 (lake), 池 (pond), 洋 (ocean), 洪 (flood), 泳 (swim) all share the "water" radical. Roughly 140 semantic radicals are currently in use. The basic structure of the semantic-phonetic compound characters is shown in Figure 5.2.

Considering the functional salience of component radicals, it is legitimate to assume that competent character users usually are self-taught and gradually become aware of the specific role assigned to each radical. Indeed, recent studies demonstrate that skilled L1 logographic readers are sensitive to the functional properties of character components and process semantic and phonetic radicals differently (e.g., Chen & Allport, 1995; Leck, Weekes, & Chen, 1995). It has also been reported that children develop this sensitivity bit by bit during the first six years of schooling (e.g., Shu & Anderson, 1997).

Phonological awareness

Phonological information in Chinese is represented by a single graphemic unit. In a single-unit character, for example, the sound is holistically assigned to its grapheme. In a multiple-unit character containing more than one radical, however, the phonology generally is signaled by one of the internal elements – that is, a phonetic radical. Based on the locations where the radicals appear in a character, logographic readers must determine which radical provides the information.

Most phonetic radicals are independent, single-unit characters. In principle, therefore, the sound of the whole character can be accessed through its phonetic radical, but, in point of fact, fewer than half of multiple-unit characters share the same sound with their phonetic radicals. Estimates of the phonological consistency range from 37% to 39% (Perfetti, Zhang, & Berent, 1992; Zhou, 1978) to 42% (DeFrancis, 1989). Given these low consistency rates, the extent to which logographic readers utilize phonetic-radical information on a regular basis remains uncertain. It has been argued, for example, that phonological information in logography is obtained primarily through whole-character activation (e.g., Gleitman, 1985; Gleitman & Rozin, 1978). Nonetheless, well-controlled experimental studies repeatedly demonstrate that phonological information consistency strongly influences character-naming efficiency among native Japanese/Chinese readers (e.g., Peng, Yang, & Chen, 1994; Saito, Masuda, & Kawakami, 1999), suggesting that phonological processing may be guided by radical activation to a far greater extent than has been suspected.

Presumably, then, logographic readers need to understand that speech can be segmented into syllables and also that a change in the tone of a syllable leads to a change of its meaning. Chinese readers must also recognize that a distinct sound (usually a syllable) is holistically assigned to each single-unit character, whether it is used as an independent word or a component radical, and also know that, in a multiple-unit character, one of the internal elements conveys the phonological information of the character, realizing, at the same time, that not all phonetic radicals impart valid information. It is for these reasons that, in Chinese, phonological awareness implies an explicit understanding of these unique ways in which phonological information is conveyed through graphic symbols.

Table 5.1. *Relationships among words, characters, and radicals (reprinted from K. Koda, 2000, p. 303)*

Word type	Orthographic form	Morpheme components	Components function	Meaning
Single-unit/ single-character word	糸	–	–	thread
Multiple-unit/ single-character word	結	(radicals)		to unite
		糸	semantic information	things made out of thread or actions involving thread
		吉	phonetic information	–
Multiple character compound word	結婚	(characters)		marriage
		結	semantic/ phonetic information	to unite
		婚	semantic/ phonetic information	wedding

Morphological awareness

Semantic radicals are often equated with single morphemes because of their primary function – providing guides to character meanings (e.g., Nagy & Anderson, 1998; Packard, 2000; Shu & Anderson, 1997). Because characters holistically correspond with their meanings, they are also treated as equivalent to single morphemes (e.g., Taft & Zhu, 1995). Thus, in Chinese, morphemes are represented by both characters and radicals. Table 5.1. illustrates the ways morphological information is conveyed through various graphic elements.

As a consequence of the holistic and independent meaning–symbol association at each of the multiple representation levels (radical, character, and word), logic would imply that morphological processing, as in phonological decoding, requires parallel activation of character and radical information. A study (Zhou & Marslen-Wilson, 1994) notes that lexical-decision performance is facilitated, in varying degrees, by both word frequency and radical frequency, thus providing further support for the contention that logographic readers rely on both semantic-radical and whole-character information during lexical processing.

As already illustrated, semantic radicals in most instances convey the semantic category of the character meaning, as evident in the "water" radical. In this regard, semantic radicals serve as a form of category header or index to sort literally thousands of entries in character dictionaries. For this sorting system to work, however, certain conditions are mandatory. Each character, for instance, must have one, and only one, semantic radical. The semantic radicals, moreover, appear at designated locations within the character. These conditions obviously impose constraints on the way semantic radicals are incorporated in characters. Competent logographic readers, in all probability, progressively become aware of these constraints and develop a capacity to use them in facilitating semantic information processing during character recognition. It is hardly surprising, therefore, that studies involving Chinese children affirm that the ability to exploit semantic-radical information is directly associated with reading competence among logographic readers (Shu & Anderson, 1997; Shu, Anderson, & Zhang, 1995). Moreover, because the morpheme-grapheme connection is more fundamental than the phonology-grapheme linkage in the Chinese writing system, morphological awareness has been found to be a stronger predictor than phonological awareness of reading success among Chinese children (Li, Anderson, Nagy, & Zhang, 2002).

Nonetheless, it is also essential to underscore the functional limitations of semantic radicals, conveying information only partially related to character meanings. As a result, the substance of unknown characters cannot be elicited through semantic-radical information alone. Moreover, because other radicals supply no semantic clues whatsoever, it is highly improbable that whole-character meanings can be inferred only through the integration of partial radical information. Hence, constructing meaning from isolated characters is literally impossible. As a consequence, character inference necessitates extracting clues from character-external sources, such as neighboring characters, adjacent sentences, and contiguous paragraphs. Indeed, recent studies suggest that logographic readers, when encountering unknown characters in context, tend to infer meanings by combining semantic-radical and contextual information (e.g., Mori & Nagy, 1999; Shu, Anderson, & Zhang, 1995). Further, the relationship between semantic-radical information and whole-character meaning is not always obvious. For example, the "female" radical appears in the character for "son-in-law." In sum, semantic-radical information, while useful, does not create a solid basis for character inference. In addition, logographic readers need to understand how characters are combined to form compound words. Roughly two thirds of Chinese words are compounds consisting of two or more characters. Because each character in the compound generally makes a unique, independent contribution to the meaning and pronunciation of the entire word, the analysis, of necessity, involves radicals within each character – as well as the characters themselves as morphological components.

For these varied reasons, it seems legitimate to conclude that competent character users are aware that a single component of a character provides partial information on its meaning, and therefore characters with shared components generally are semantically related. However, they must also understand that semantic-radical information in itself is inadequate for character inference and that radical information is not always semantically consistent with the character meaning. Hence, recognizing these limitations of semantic radicals constitutes the core essence of morphological awareness in Chinese.

IA in English

Writing system

As noted in Chapter 3, although bound by phonemic constraints, English orthography is morphophonemic, having a tendency to preserve morphological information in its graphic representation. As a result, phonemic descriptions provide only partial accounts of English orthographic conventions. Distinctive orthographic patterns, for example, often help differentiate two morphemes sharing identical phonological representation, as in *threw* and *through*. On the other hand, shared morphemes can be represented by identical spellings, despite their distinct phonological status, as in *anxious/anxiety* and *electric/electricity*. Many English spelling irregularities thus are more readily explained by morphemic than by phonemic construction.

This being the case, it would be logical to presume a symbiotic relationship in which orthographic processing is heavily facilitated by morphological insights, and, at the same time, orthographic sophistication greatly enhances morphological processing. Studies testify that while an understanding of a word's morphological structure expedites reading and spelling development (e.g., Carlisle, 1988, 1995; Fowler & Liberman, 1995; Leong, 1989), spelling knowledge also promotes morphological analysis and decomposition (e.g., Derwing, Smith, & Wiebe, 1995).

Phonological awareness

It is generally accepted that phonological awareness is a by-product of the child's increasing understanding of the sound structure of spoken words (e.g., Stahl & Murray, 1994; Stanovich et al., 1984; Yopp, 1988). It involves a constellation of sequentially acquired abilities. Adams (1990), for example, describes five ability clusters: perceptual capability (remembering familiar rhymes), analytical perceptual capacity (recognizing and sorting patterns of rhymes and alliterations), intrasyllabic awareness (blending and splitting syllables), phonemic analysis (conducting full phonemic segmentation), and phonemic manipulation (regenerating words by deleting, inserting, or relocating phonemes). Similarly, by comparing the relative difficulty, reliability, and validity of ten frequently used phonological awareness measures, Yopp (1988) categorized two interrelated dimensions: simple awareness (recognizing intrasyllabic or onset-rime speech units) and compound awareness (analyzing and manipulating multiple phonemes).

These distinct awareness capacities, moreover, develop in disparate timetables. In a well-designed experiment, using a word-comparison task (determining whether orally presented paired words have any common sounds), Treiman and Zukowski (1991) found that pre-readers and beginning readers were equally adept in tasks involving both intrasyllabic and syllabic analysis, but they differed significantly in those requiring phonemic manipulation. While the achievement of beginning readers remained constant in tasks involving both syllable- and phoneme-level analysis, pre-readers' performance declined considerably in the phonemic task. The researchers concluded that pre-reading children have little difficulty distinguishing syllables and are capable of making phonological judgments based on the intrasyllabic, onset-rime distinction (the differentiation between the initial phoneme and the reminder within a syllable). Of greatest importance, children do not become capable of breaking intrasyllabic units into smaller, phonemic segments until they become independent readers. These findings clearly suggest that, whereas a basic understanding of the phonological structure of spoken words is a precursor of learning to read, more sophisticated awareness dimensions develop through print-information processing. Research on early spelling development also provides further support for such developmental interdependence by demonstrating that children are heavily dependent on spelling knowledge during phoneme counting tasks (e.g., Ehri, 1984;

Ehri & Wilce, 1980). Alphabetic literacy, in short, necessitates intraword phonological segmentation through sequential letter-pattern analysis and the integration of the segmental information. Hence, in alphabetic systems, phonological awareness presupposes an understanding of intrasyllabic speech units, ability to analyze and identify the intraword phonemic constituents, and efficiency in manipulating intraword segmental information.

Morphological awareness

The basic units of word formation and the principles governing their combination differ widely across languages. In concatenative languages, such as English, morphological formation generally entails the addition of affixes before or after base morphemes in a reasonably systematic and linear fashion. Three types of morphemes commonly are used in English: inflectional affixes, signaling grammatical information, such as tense and plurality; class-altering derivational affixes, deriving words by altering grammatical categories (*happy* → *happiness*); and class-maintaining derivational affixes, deriving words by changing meaning (e.g., *happy* → *unhappy*).

It is noteworthy that there is considerable variation in the systematicity with which spoken language elements correspond to their orthographic representations. Morpheme–grapheme relationships, for example, are relatively systematic in inflectional processes, where one-to-one correspondences are established between distinct grammatical functions (e.g., tense and plurality) and letter patterns (affixes) representing them. Contrastingly, derivational operations, where multiple forms correspond to multiple functions, entail complex many-to-many mappings. To illustrate, several forms are used to fulfill a single function, say, converting verbs into nouns (inform → informa*tion*; move → move*ment*; and arrive → arriv*al*). Conversely, a single form serves multiple functions, as in the case of the suffix -*al* used for verb-to-noun conversions (e.g., arrive → arriv*al*), as well as noun-to-adjective alterations (e.g., nation → nation*al*).

Still, despite various mapping complexities, empirical findings demonstrate that the ability to analyze words' morphological structures is a major factor in differentiating poor and good readers. As a case in point, skilled readers are adept at morphological analysis and decomposition (e.g., Stolz & Feldman, 1995). Recognition of multimorphemic, low-frequency words is enhanced by their high-frequency affixes (e.g., Katz, Rexer, & Lukatela, 1991; Kelliher & Henderson, 1990). Further, lexical decision is greatly facilitated when target words are preceded by presentation of their morphological relatives (e.g., Feldman & Bentin, 1994; Fowler, Napps, & Feldman, 1985). These findings confirm readers' consistent engagement in morphological decomposition during lexical processing, which in turn suggests that English morphological awareness comprises three essential competency components: sensitivity to the intraword morphological structure, ability to identify morphological constituents, and capacity to manipulate intraword morphological information.

Because of its complex mapping requirements, derivational information extraction requires two additional awareness components: syntactic and distributional (Tyler & Nagy, 1989, 1990). Syntactic awareness refers to the tacit knowledge that affixation alters grammatical categorization. To wit, a competent user of English understands that *generalize* is a verb by virtue of being suffixed with *-ize* and *generalization* is a noun because it is suffixed with *-tion*. Distributional awareness, in contrast, has to do with learners' sensitivity to the constraints on base-affix concatenation. They should know, for example, that the suffix *-able* can be used with verbs, but not nouns and adjectives – for example, whereas *scannable* looks plausible, *plainable* does not, even though neither appears in some English dictionaries.

Cross-linguistic variations

Because of the differences in the structural and functional properties of English and Chinese writing systems, the IA competencies underlying lexical processing vary in several important ways. First, whereas concatenative English generally affords reasonably systematic symbol-to-sound as well as symbol-to-morpheme mappings, the lack of formation systematicity in Chinese characters does not permit similar computational procedures. Second, individual intraword components, both phonological and morphological, collectively contribute to forming lexical information in English. Thus, intraword structural analysis is integral to lexical learning and processing. In logographic characters, however, a specific function is holistically assigned to each intraword element; that is, while the phonetic radical provides phonological information for the whole character, the semantic radical supplies a clue to the character's meaning. Therefore, visual identification of these radicals is essential for character information extraction. Third, because each graphic unit in English carries segmental phonological information, a linear assembly of the segments is vital in phonological decoding. Similarly, English morphemes are represented by letter clusters. Here again, sequential integration of segmental information is critical for morphological processing of English words. Inversely, Chinese lexical information is holistically and independently denoted in each graphic unit at both the character and radical levels. Character users, therefore, are required to attend to the whole character as well as its radical components through simultaneous information extraction rather than intraword analysis.

Development of IA among L2 learners

In view of the variations in the requisite IA capabilities, L2 research must address how, and in what degree, L1 IA affects the formation of L2 IA and subsequent L2 lexical-competence development. Consequently, three critical IA-related issues warrant consideration: cross-linguistic interactions in L2 lexical processing, prior literacy-experience contributions to L2 IA development, and IA contribution to biliteracy development among school-aged L2 learners.

Cross-linguistic interactions in L2 lexical processing

Knowing that L1 competencies transfer in L2 processing, irrespective of typological distance between the two languages, we can infer that L1 IA may serve as a filter through which L2 visual input is processed. Considering that the evolution of IA depends on print processing, L2 IA can be an amalgamated form resulting from cross-linguistic interactions between L1 IA and L2 visual input. Such interactions, through systematic comparisons of IA among L2 readers, are under way. Koda (1998), for example, describes a subtle, potentially significant, L1 influence on L2 phonological awareness among ESL readers with Chinese and Korean L1 backgrounds. Because intraword segmentation is central to phonological processing in alphabetic systems, but not mandatory in logographic orthographies, it was hypothesized that L1 alphabetic experience among Korean ESL learners would accelerate their acquisition of L2 IA, which in turn would enhance decoding performance. Two proficiency-matched ESL groups were compared in phonological awareness, decoding, and reading comprehension. Contrary to the predictions, the groups differed in neither phonological awareness nor decoding. However, there was a clear contrast in the extent the two variables related to reading comprehension. In the Korean data, both phonological awareness and decoding were closely interconnected with reading performance, but no direct relationships were observed among the three variables in the Chinese data. The contrast was interpreted as suggesting that L1–L2 processing requirement congruity does seem to induce a strong preference for particular processing procedures. However, the study did not confirm the predicted advantage for L2 IA formation among Korean ESL learners. Given that Korean uses a typologically congruent (alphabetic) yet unrelated (non-Roman) writing system, typological congruity alone may not be sufficient to achieve expected facilitation in L2 IA development.

In more recent studies, Koda and associates (Koda, 2000a, 2002; Koda, Takahashi, & Fender, 1998) compared the morphological awareness of adult Chinese and Korean L2 learners of English. Word formation is similar in Korean and English in that both entail the linear incorporation of affixes. Chinese character formation, contrastingly, involves placement of function-specific radicals. Hence, intraword segmentation and linear information integration are integral to morphological processing in English and Korean but not in Chinese. Based on the analysis, it was hypothesized that differential degrees of L1 and L2 morphological IA congruity affect L2 IA development. Specifically, Chinese ESL learners would be less sensitive to intraword structural variation, less efficient in morphological analysis, and less perceptive of the constraints on morpheme concatenation than their Korean counterparts. The hypothesis was tested through an online separability judgment task, in which participants were asked to determine whether presented words could be separated. Three types of words were used in the experiment: structurally salient words, consisting of prefixes and lexical stems (e.g., *in*-direct); structurally less-salient words, comprising prefixes and sublexical or Latinate stems (e.g., *in*-volve); and monomorphemic words sharing the same orthographic sequences as the prefixes used (e.g., *in*fant).

Virtually no difference existed between the two ESL groups in their sensitivity to intraword structural variation. However, as anticipated, Korean learners were considerably faster in all conditions. Notably, the groups' efficiency difference was far more pronounced with structurally less-salient and monomorphemic words, implying that ESL learners, regardless of their L1 backgrounds, benefit from structural salience and, more critically, that congruent L1 IA serves as a scaffolding for intraword analysis when the morphological structure of L2 words is less transparent. All in all, the predicted Korean superiority was apparent in some, but not all, aspects of L2 morphological awareness. Importantly, the aspects of L2 IA whose variance was not explained by L1 and L2: intraword structural congruity are directly linked to L2-specific features and thus critical to L2 morphological processing. Presumably, L2-specific IA aspects develop primarily through progressive experience with L2 lexical peculiarities and therefore are largely unaffected by L1 IA variance. Viewed collectively, these findings appear to suggest that L1 and L2 IA are both operative during L2 lexical processing, jointly impacting on L2 lexical-competence development.

Prior literacy-experience contributions to L2 IA development

Inasmuch as certain IA aspects are common across languages, once developed, they can provide substantial facilitation in the IA formation in another language. Metalinguistically trained adult L2 learners, consequently, should be adept at deducing how spoken-language elements are mapped onto graphic symbols in a new language. Studies on adult L2 learners of Japanese and Chinese offer some insights on the issue. With the growing interest in logographic literacy, an increasing number of studies addressing character-knowledge development among L2 learners of logographic languages have appeared. Their findings generally suggest that character-specific IA evolves relatively early among metalinguistically sophisticated learners, but, until then, their character learning can be characterized as unanalytical, all-or-nothing approaches. McGinnis's 1995 study on the self-perceived effectiveness of character-learning strategies, for example, concluded that beginning L2 learners of Chinese (CSL) regarded consistent practice and mnemonic devices as more useful than using component radicals in new character learning. Similarly, Everson (1998) found a high correlation between character naming (retrieving sounds) and identification (retrieving meanings) among first-year CSL learners. The same set of characters was used in both tasks. Because little performance variability was found in each stimulus item between the tasks, the strong correlation was interpreted as indicating that beginning CSL learners tend to obtain both phonological and semantic information through memory search rather than analysis.

Other studies, however, showed a sign of early IA development among L2 learners of Chinese and Japanese. In an instructional study, for example, Dwyer (1997) explored ways of facilitating Kanji learning among beginning learners of Japanese. His outcome demonstrated that systematic presentations of phonetic radicals, when introducing new characters, facilitated the mastery of Kanji pronunciations, and presenting a group of Kanji, devoid of common graphic elements, was beneficial in remembering character meanings. His results thus suggest that beginning learners use character components, or radicals, to learn and recall characters, supporting the conviction that sensitivity to a character's internal components among L2 learners evolves early in Kanji-knowledge development. Similarly, Ke (1998) found that, after a year of Chinese study, his college-level participants acquired a keen awareness of radicals' utility in building character knowledge and that such awareness was a direct corollary of their character-recognition ability. Through a systematic analysis of think-aloud protocols, Everson and Ke (1997) determined that, while intermediate learners depended on rote-memorization approaches to character identification, advanced learners were more analytic, invoking character segmentation and radical-information retrievals.

Working from a somewhat different base, Chern (1992), through graphic similarity judgment, compared perceptual sensitivity among L1 and L2 learners of Chinese. L1 readers concluded that paired characters were similar not only when they shared the same graphic component but also when they were placed in the same location. L2 learners, on the other hand, used a less-stringent criterion in determining similarity. They focused only on shared components, disregarding their locations. Inasmuch as radical positions signal the specific function assigned to them, the disparate sensitivity to radical locations among L1 and L2 participants clearly suggests that L2 learners have yet to learn the function-specific positional constraints on radical formation.

In a psycholinguistic experiment, Koda and Takahashi (2004) compared radical awareness among L1 and L2 Kanji users through semantic category judgment. In the experiment, participants were asked to decide whether a presented character (e.g., "lake") belonged to a specific semantic category (e.g., "body of water"). Their findings demonstrated that the groups benefited similarly from radicals when extracting semantic information from single-character words. However, the groups' responses differed when the characters and radicals provided incongruent information, as in the case of the "water" radical used in a character whose meaning had no relevance to "water." In short, occasionally, Kanji characters contain radicals that are invalid because they have no relevance to the character's meaning. Sophisticated readers detect the mismatch, but novices do not. Results clearly show this difference. While judgment speed among native Kanji users declined considerably, their accuracy rate remained the same, presumably because they took time to ascertain. Reaction times among L2 learners, in contrast, were minimally affected, but their error rates increased considerably, seemingly because they disregarded the incongruity. The findings thus indicate that L2 learners are sensitized to the basic function of semantic radicals and attentive to their information during Kanji processing. However, they still need to develop efficiency in detecting radical-information validity and selectivity in incorporating valid information during Kanji recognition.

In sum, studies involving L2 character users repeatedly suggest that adult learners of Japanese and Chinese progressively are sensitized to the functional and structural properties of character components and rely on this sensitivity both in learning new characters and in retrieving stored character information. Of greatest moment, such sensitivity, as predicted, readily develops with somewhat restricted character-learning experience (usually three hundred to five hundred characters) among metalinguistically adroit adult learners. This contrasts sharply with children learning to read Chinese as their L1, necessitating knowledge of roughly two thousand characters to develop similar IA insights (Shu & Anderson, 1999).

IA contribution to biliteracy development

In view of the irrefutable contributions of metalinguistic awareness to early L1 reading development, the consequential question is whether these contributions also occur among school-aged L2 learners. Presumably, young L2 learners are handicapped by a double bind. Generally, they lack adequate oral language command at the point when L2 literacy learning commences, and, unlike adult learners, they have limited prior literacy experience. Therefore, they must undertake the learning without benefit of either linguistic knowledge in the target language or print-processing competence developed in L1.

Because the primary objective in the initial learning-to-read phase is developing skills with which to map spoken-language elements onto graphic symbols, success in this phase largely depends on metalinguistic understanding of what is to be mapped. Young L2 learners, because of limited oral-communication experience, are likely to be less sensitive to the functionally significant linguistic elements. Conceivably, they may undertake the learning-to-read task without adequate knowledge of the actual elements to be mapped. Moreover, because of their limited prior literacy experience, we cannot assume that the children, unlike adult learners, have a clear conception of how print relates to speech. Therefore, L2 literacy development among young learners may take place with far weaker metalinguistic foundations than among adult learners. In the absence of basic understanding, linguistic knowledge, however developed, cannot automatically be used to decipher print information. Hence, linguistic knowledge alone may not be sufficient for literacy acquisition. Recent studies involving child L2 learners consistently demonstrate that oral language proficiency does not systematically relate to early reading success in a second language (e.g., August et al., 2000, 2001; Cormier & Kelson, 2000; Durgunoglu et al., 1993; Gholamain & Geva, 1999).

Are there, then, mechanisms to facilitate learning to read for these children seemingly having a dual handicap? One possibility is phonological awareness. The conviction that phonological awareness as a by-product of children's growing understanding of the segmental nature of speech precedes and supports initial reading acquisition, offers considerable promise. This fundamental realization, common across languages, serves as a basis for reading development in typologically diverse languages, including logographic Chinese (Ho & Bryant, 1999; Li et al., 2002). For this reason, the concept of phonological segmentation, once developed in one language, facilitates learning to read other languages, regardless of their orthographic typology. Research indicates that L1 phonological awareness is closely aligned with L2 decoding ability among school-aged learners of English with diverse L1 backgrounds (August et al., Carlo, 2000, 2001; Carlisle & Beeman, 2000; Durgunoglu, 1998; Durgunoglu et al., 1993; Gottardo, Siegel, Yan, & Wade-Woolley, 2001; Verhoeven, 2000) and also that L2 decoding efficiency is far more reliable than oral language proficiency in accounting for L2 reading performance variance (e.g., Geva, 1999; Geva & Siegel, 2000). These findings make it difficult to dispute that the early stages of L2 literacy development, as in L1 literacy, rely heavily on metalinguistic sensitivity in general and on phonological awareness in particular.

Summary and future research suggestions

To summarize, research on early reading development suggests that learning to read is fundamentally metalinguistic in that it involves understanding how functionally significant language units are mapped onto graphic symbols in the writing system. A large number of studies affirm that the concept of word segmentation enhances sensitivity to a word's internal structure, thereby assisting identification of the word's phonological and morphological constituents. Moreover, such sensitivity is a powerful predictor of successful early literacy acquisition. Intraword awareness (IA) refers to generalized metalinguistic insights, which are of fundamental importance in lexical learning and processing. The IA contribution can perhaps best be described as the essential facilitative agent in analyzing intraword elements as lexical information is elicited from the visual word display. Because of IA's evolution from print-processing experience, we can legitimately posit that IA capabilities are materially affected by the ways lexical information is represented in the writing system. It is conceivable, then, that the nature of IA varies across languages in direct proportion to the extent their writing systems' representational properties deviate.

Cross-linguistic variations obviously have major implications for L2 lexical development. There is much to suggest that L1 IA spawns the cultivation of L2 lexical competence in specific and measurable ways. Studies of adult L2 learners suggest that, while L2 print-processing experience is a primary force governing L2 IA development, L1 orthographic properties also have a continuing, clearly identifiable imprint on L2 IA formation. It has been suggested that L2 readers undergo much the same process as young L1 learners in developing lexical competence, progressing from a holistic method to more sophisticated, analytic approaches to lexical information extraction. Research on L2 learners of Japanese and Chinese, however, indicates that metalinguistically experienced adult learners acquire IA competence in a new language far more rapidly than beginning L1 readers. In fact, the current knowledge stockpile is beginning to indicate distinct ways in which L1 and L2 print-processing experiences specifically contribute to L2 IA development: L1 experience establishes the scaffolding for foundation building, and L2 input instills a linguistic base necessary in fine-tuning.

The cross-linguistic inquiries also offer strong indications that the IA framework can lead to promising new avenues for exploring lexical development in typologically diverse languages. Bolstered by further exploratory refinements, the ongoing conceptualization seemingly could shed useful insights on the aggregate IA sophistication stemming from the continuous conjoining of L1 and L2 processing experiences. By systematically comparing L2 IA among learners with diverse L1 orthographic backgrounds, as well as those with varying degrees of L2 print-processing experience, we might gain a clearer picture of the role L1 and L2 print-processing experience plays in L2 IA maturation and the consequent augmentation of L2 lexical competence.

Current theories about IA contribution to lexical competence by and large are based on correlational data, depicting patterns of corresponding variance between the two. However, IA and word knowledge are both multidimensional; hence, their relationship cannot be depicted simply by linking a single dimension of each construct. Moreover, the data are restrictive in that they tell us little about the specific facilitative impact of IA on word-knowledge development. Lexical learning, in addition, can transpire in several distinct modes entailing diverse sets of capabilities. IA facilitation, in sum, can be understood only through fine-grained, multifaceted analyses, incorporating component ability clusters in both IA and lexical competence. Further clarification of the aggregate effects of IA on lexical competence, coupled with their empirical validation, will not only eliminate some of the voids in the current conceptual foundation but also enlighten our investigative approaches to word-knowledge accretion through reading.

6 Information integration in sentence processing

The preceding chapters described the manner in which lexical information is learned, stored, and accessed during comprehension. Word identification, in itself, however, does not explain how meaning is constructed from visual input. Isolated words, for example, must be incrementally integrated into larger linguistic units – that is, phrases, clauses, and sentences – by incorporating their syntactic, semantic, and pragmatic information. Linguistic knowledge, therefore, is a major source of individual differences in sentence processing. Although texts vary considerably in their lexical and syntactic features, we have limited understanding of how the linguistic variables affect sentence comprehension. If some features have more impact on processing efficiency than others, we need to isolate them, disentangle their effects, and explore causal linkages with specific reading difficulties. Consequently, building on information extraction at the word level, this chapter explores information integration at the sentence level. After examining the relationship between linguistic variables and comprehension difficulty, by reviewing several models of sentence processing, it describes logical ways to compare processing procedures across typologically diverse languages. The implications of L1 research findings for L2 comprehension also are considered in a review of empirical studies on L2 sentence processing.

Linguistic complexity and comprehension difficulty

Linguistic determinants of text complexity

Whether systematicity exists in the relationship between syntactic features and comprehension problems has long received research attention. The resurrection of interest in the relationship has prompted major controversy between conventional views of text complexity and its automatic connection with reading difficulty. Traditionally, text complexity has been attributed to lexical and syntactic elements because of a belief that texts with large numbers of unfamiliar words and complex sentences are harder to understand. A major characteristic of readability formulas is their heavy reliance on quantitative indices – number and length – of linguistic features, such as words, prepositional phrases, and clauses. Based on the correlations between these indices and the reading scores of children using and liking the books, formulas for predicting scores – required to comprehend a given book – were devised. Two basic assumptions underscore the formulas: The length of each feature determines text complexity, which, in turn, constitutes a major source of reading difficulty.

Of late, however, both assumptions have been challenged on the grounds of their questionable legitimacy in relying heavily on quantitative indices in estimating either text complexity or reading difficulty. The skepticism has spurred a considerable effort to find more valid methods of gauging text complexity, particularly with respect to its relation to comprehension difficulty. Anderson and Davison (1988), for instance, note that two major lexical variables, word length and frequency, do not necessarily reflect the actual levels of difficulty readers encounter during comprehension. Although longer and unusual words generally are more difficult to process, many long words contain more than one semantic constituent, or morpheme, and therefore can be decomposed. Even when words as a whole are unknown, some of the word-internal elements are likely to be familiar. In fact, as noted in Chapter 5, more than half the English words in school texts are semantically transparent multimorphemic words – that is, either derivatives (*unhappiness*) or compounds (*firefighter*) (Nagy & Anderson, 1984). Thus, through morphological decomposition, readers have a good opportunity to infer meanings. In short, word length in itself is not a reliable indicator either of processing complexity or of comprehension difficulty.

Sentence length also is a quantitative variable presumed to evoke comprehension complications. The supposition is that because longer sentences are structurally more complex, they impose additional processing demands and difficulty. Although the correlation between syntactic complexity and sentence length generally is accepted, many scholars have raised questions about the presumed association between sentence length/complexity and reading difficulty. As a case in point, structural complexity typically stems from syntactic maneuvers, such as subordination. Because the motive behind such manipulation is to signal explicitly how internal clauses are semantically related, more often than not, it can enhance processing efficiency and consequent comprehension (e.g., Davison, Wilson, & Hermon, 1985). The facilitative potential becomes even more evident when clauses can be connected in more than one way, as in the following examples:

(1) I left the house. It was dark.
(2) I left the house because it was dark.
(3) After I left the house, it was dark.

The two simple sentences in (1) can be semantically integrated in two ways, as demonstrated in (2) and (3). Without subordination, the reader must determine the semantic connection of the internal clauses through contextual information and/or prior knowledge. Subordination entails connective devices and structural alteration, necessitating additional computation and temporary information storage. Therefore, structural complexity resulting from syntactic manipulations may correlate with processing demands, but it does not necessarily increase comprehension difficulty. It has been shown, in fact, that sentence length and complexity have little effect on comprehension performance among average seventh-grade students (Davison et al., 1985). Other studies also verify that native English readers, both children and adults, exhibit a strong preference for complex sentences conjoined with explicit connectives instead of loosely linked simple sentences (e.g., Irwin & Pulver, 1984; Pearson, 1975).

A similar tendency to favor syntactically complex sentences also is evident in planned spoken discourse (e.g., Berman, 1984; Biber, 1988; Chafe & Danielewicz, 1986). According to Biber (1988), syntactically complex constructions – relative clauses, for example – generally allow semantic elaboration under real-time processing constraints and, at the same time, provide relational information on how the semantic content can be integrated with the surrounding discourse. Seemingly, regardless of communication modality, syntactic maneuvers reflect the speaker's or writer's conscious effort to signal the logical connections between clauses. It seems reasonable, therefore, to conclude that neither syntactic complexity nor sentence length can automatically be linked with comprehension difficulty.

Syntactic knowledge as a source of comprehension difficulty

The contention that complexity is a major source of reading difficulty also has been scrutinized from a language-acquisition perspective. Heavily influenced by the linguistic theories emphasizing modular language organization, alternative approaches to studying language development have emerged. The modular position postulates that structural complexity has a minimal effect on children's syntactic knowledge because its acquisition is "pre-wired." Hence, it is irrational to attribute reading problems to syntactic-knowledge deficiency. Crain and Shankweiler (1988) examined two competing hypotheses explaining individual differences in early reading development: structural deficit hypothesis (SDH) and processing deficit hypothesis (PDH). SDH presumes that linguistic structures can be hierarchically ranked in terms of their syntactic complexity. Gradual stages of syntactic development, in strict accordance with their complexity ranking, is assumed. The hypothesis also entails two additional postulations: Individual differences in syntactic knowledge exist among beginning readers, and comprehension difficulty results from deficits in this knowledge – namely, insufficient understanding of the complex structures essential in sentence-meaning construction.

PDH, in contrast, presumes no association between reading problems and knowledge deficiency. Drawing on the concept of modular language organization, PDH posits that "the language module develops into a rich and intricate system of rules much more rapidly than many other cognitive structures because of its innately specified content" (Crain & Shankweiler, 1988, p. 173). Three premises are central in this formulation: Syntactic structures develop according to their own biological clock; syntactic complexity, because it is "pre-wired," has no impact on their acquisition; and much of the primary linguistic system already has been acquired before children begin learning to read. Consequently, PDH disputes any possibility that reading difficulty stems from a lack of syntactic knowledge. Empirical studies consistently demonstrate that children as young as age 3, can comprehend and reconstruct complex structures, such as restrictive relative clauses and subject–verb inversion in yes–no questions (e.g., Crain & Nakayama, 1987; Hamburger & Crain, 1982).

What, then, does explain comprehension difficulty among beginning readers? According to PDH, the answer lies in a limited ability to interface spoken language with its corresponding orthographic system. The view holds that reading problems occur when complex structures impose excessive demands on working memory. PDH thus predicts that, in lieu of syntactic knowledge, structural complexity and decoding ability affect working memory capacity, which in turn influences comprehension performance. Shankweiler and associates tested the prediction (Mann, Shankweiler, & Smith, 1984) in a series of studies, demonstrating that, in less-demanding postreading comprehension questions, third-grade participants' performance was affected only by syntactic complexity. In a more demanding rote-memorization task, however, sentence recall was influenced by both syntactic factors and decoding ability, suggesting that factors creating working-memory overload are a more likely explanation of sentence-processing performance variations. Similarly, other studies also showed that memory problems among poor readers arose when phonological conversion of verbal input was necessary (e.g., Katz, Shankweiler, & Liberman, 1981; Liberman, Mann, Shankweiler, & Werfelman, 1982; Stanovich, 2000), further reinforcing the contention that restrictions in using working-memory capacity are attributable to decoding inefficiency rather than insufficient syntactic knowledge.

Models of syntactic parsing

To recapitulate, sentence comprehension necessitates incremental integration of lexical information in such a way that the integrated "chunk" reflects the overall meaning of a given word string. The integration process, often referred to as *syntactic parsing*, involves two major operations: creating phrases through lexical-information integration, and assigning case roles to the created phrases. To wit, the sentence "Nancy tapped the man with the cane" is structurally ambiguous because it allows more than one interpretation of the cane holder. If the phrase "with the cane" is taken as a modifier of the verb "tapped," Nancy held the cane. If the phrase is interpreted to modify "the man," the cane was in his hand. Decisions about where to attach modifying phrases thus have major semantic consequences during sentence processing. Several distinct models delineating the basic mechanisms governing syntactic parsing are illustrated below. It should be noted, at the outset, however, that this research relies heavily on indirect procedures, because parsing occurs too rapidly to permit direct examinations. Natural languages are ambiguous. Therefore, in speculating about principles governing parsing behaviors, much of the exploration exploits inherent ambiguity.

Serial processing models

Serial processing models generally assume that parsing occurs sequentially, pursuing one interpretation at a time. Two fundamental principles are thought to regulate the parsing operations. The first, called *minimum attachment*, requires the parser to "attach incoming material into the phrase marker being constructed using the fewest nodes consistent with the well-formedness rules of the language under analysis" (Frazier, 1978, p. 24). To illustrate, in parsing the structurally ambiguous sentence "Nancy tapped the man with the cane," the minimum attachment principle dictates that the prepositional phrase "with the cane" be attached to the verb "tapped," endorsing the "Nancy as the cane holder" view. The attachment decision is explained by the assumption that this interpretation creates a simpler structure than the "the man as the cane holder" alternative.

The second principle, *late closure*, stipulates that the parser attaches "incoming material into the phrase or clause currently being parsed" (Frazier, 1978, p. 33). Frazier explains this principle through another structurally ambiguous sentence: "Because the boy left the room seemed empty." Because "left" can be used both as a transitive and an intransitive verb, the initial clause allows two interpretations: "Because the boy left the room" and "Because the boy left." The late closure principle designates that the phrase "the room" be the direct object of "left," so it can be incorporated in the currently open clause without initiating a new one. Based on this principle, we can anticipate that ambiguous sentences like the one above are likely to engender misinterpretation during initial analysis.

Both principles illustrate the major characteristic of the parser as a natural language processor – namely, having a strong tendency to integrate and interpret connected linguistic input prudently. Although subsequently supported by well-designed empirical studies (e.g., Ferreira & Clifton, 1986; Ferreira & Henderson, 1995; Frazier, 1990; Rainer, Carlson, & Frazier, 1983), the evidence is based on data obtained almost exclusively from L1 English speakers. At this point, whether the principles are similarly operative in other languages whose syntactic properties differ from those of English remains somewhat uncertain (e.g., Inoue & Fodor, 1995; Mazuka & Nagai, 1995).

Parallel processing models

Parallel processing models are based on a completely different premise – that all structural interpretations are formed concurrently and retained until the parser reaches a point of choice. For example, when processing "Because the boy left the room seemed empty," parallel models assume that the parser retains both of the two syntactically acceptable interpretations – "Because the boy left the room" and "Because the boy left" – until encountering the disambiguating word "seemed." Because of this all-inclusive property, reanalysis is not postulated in parallel models for syntactic disambiguation. The parallel parser is attractive because it supposedly computes all possible interpretations, and therefore, in theory, it does not miss the correct one. It is particularly appealing for use in head-final (or left-branching) languages, such as Japanese and Korean, where the central element of a phrase appears at the final position, following its complements. In head-final languages, therefore, sentences can be incessantly ambiguous to their end. Caution may be necessary, according to Inoue and Fodor (1995), because carrying out and retaining multiple interpretations can be extremely resource demanding. In other words, if presumed parsing operations exceed the normal working-memory capacity, the assumption that the parser is a natural language processor does not logically hold.

Minimum commitment models

Yet another class of models is somewhat of a hybrid of the two just described. Minimum commitment models call for neither full commitment to a single interpretation nor comprehensive analyses, positing instead that certain aspects of processing must be held in abeyance until the parser locates the information for resolving ambiguity. Although the models vary as to which specific elements should be suspended, it is generally held that smaller linguistic units, such as noun phrases and prepositional phrases, can be computed locally without suspension. What is most likely to be put on hold is the subsequent integration linking locally assembled units (e.g., Kennedy, Murray, Jennings, & Reid, 1989; Perfetti, 1990). Because parsing decisions are delayed until all necessary information is available, the minimum-commitment parser has a strong appeal for head-initial (or right-branching) languages, such as English and other European languages, where the central element of a phrase appears at the initial position, preceding its complement. Nonetheless, here again, the delay parser may be too labor intensive in head-final languages, because they demand many, and sometime lengthy, delays in parsing decisions until the sentence end (Mazuka, 1991).

Constraint-based models

Sentence processing is viewed very differently in constraint-based approaches (e.g., Bates & MacWhinney, 1989; MacDonald, Just, & Carpenter, 1992; McClelland, St. John, & Taraban, 1989; Tabossi, Spivey-Knowlton, McRae, & Tanenhaus, 1993). The models presume that varying constraints, both syntactic and nonsyntactic, constitute evidence supporting partially formed interpretations. For example, the competition model (Bates & MacWhinney, 1989) views the linguistic system as a set of correspondences between linguistic forms (i.e., available expressive devices) and their functions (i.e., meanings and intentions expressed). The model, as described in Chapter 2, assumes that language acquisition entails internalization of such form–function relationships implicit in linguistic input. Because these relationships do not always embody one-to-one correspondences, they are regarded as correlational tendencies rather than absolute rules. For example, in English, the function of agency (i.e., the perpetrator of the action) co-occurs with multiple linguistic forms, such as nominative case marking (e.g., use of "I" instead of "me"), subject–verb agreement (e.g., co-occurrence of "I" and "am"), and preverbal positioning (i.e., "I" appearing *before*, instead of *after*, the verb).

Hence, the model posits that the parser maps on many-to-many form-to-function correspondences, continuously updating its phrase assignments. To illustrate, in parsing "The cats are chasing the mouse," the initial noun phrase "the cats" is assigned to the agent role (or the sentence subject) because of its appearance before the verb. The fact that "the cats" refers to an animated entity also supports this assignment. The absence of conflict in subject–verb agreement further reinforces the initial parsing decision. Finally, when the noun phrase "the mouse" appears immediately after the verb phrase "are chasing," its syntactic and semantic confinement to the patient role (or the direct object) provides additional support for the assignment of "the cats" to the agent role. Clearly, in the model, parsing is seen as an incremental process of satisfying constraints. At each consecutive update, the initial parsing decision, if correct, is cumulatively strengthened. The model further presumes that alternative interpretations are active, although in varying degrees, depending on the relative strength of cues supporting them. Ambiguity resolution, therefore, is viewed as a processing outcome resulting from competitions among cues that engender conflicting interpretations, rather than from the parser making decisions based on fixed rules and principles. As a consequence, decision delays also are seen somewhat differently; that is, interruptions in "competition" results occur when parsing involves less common form–function correspondences, as well as when there are only weak constraints.

By way of summary, several distinct parsing models have been proposed in an attempt to explain incremental information integration during sentence processing. Although these models vary in their major contentions, they have a common goal: isolating the general properties of the parser as a natural language processor. As noted, however, most of the results, unfortunately, stem from a limited number of syntactic structures within a single language (e.g., Inoue & Fordor, 1995; Mazuka & Lust, 1990). Generalizations from highly restricted data can easily misconstrue the basic mechanisms involved. For this reason, increased attention of late has been given to cross-linguistic variations in sentence processing. The primary objectives have been twofold: distinguishing elements of the mechanism specific to one language from those reflecting more general principles, and, in so doing, identifying the fundamental principles regulating syntactic analysis in all languages (e.g., Carpenter, Miyake, & Just, 1995; Mitchell, 1994).

Cross-linguistic variations in sentence processing

Empirical research on sentence processing in languages other than English remains limited. The available data involve a handful of selective, primarily European, languages, including Dutch (e.g., Frazier & Flores d'Arcais, 1989), German (e.g., Bach, Brown, & Marslen-Wilson, 1986), Spanish (e.g., Cuetos & Mitchell, 1988), and Japanese (e.g., Inoue & Fodor, 1995; Mazuka, 1991, 2000; Sakamoto, 1995). Although it is generally believed that certain components of processing mechanisms are shared across languages, there is little agreement on which components are universal or how differences in syntactic structures can be accommodated within the existing frameworks. As a result, a sharp division among researchers emphasizing the universal aspects of parsing mechanisms and those focusing on language-specific components has developed.

A strong universal view has been advanced by Inoue and Fodor (1995), contending that the performance mechanisms for natural languages are likely to be universal because human language is innate. They argue that "whatever survival value may be gained by having innate linguistic knowledge would be wasted if extensive learning of performance systems were necessary before that knowledge could be put to practical use in talking and understanding" (p. 12). Under the premise that the human information processor, in the interest of parsimony, does not postpone the incorporation of incoming information, they propose a model featuring a nondelay serial parser. One of its notable attributes is a capability for online error correction; any parsing error resulting from initial misinterpretation can immediately be corrected, once detected, at virtually no cost. By using this capability, the researchers claim, the parser can operate in exactly the same way in typologically diverse languages, such as head-initial English and head-final Japanese, despite their contrasting syntactic features.

Others, however, contend that the major aspects of parsing are language-specific, arguing that any account of sentence processing must accommodate the structural peculiarities of a particular language (Cuetos & Mitchell, 1988; Weinberg, 1995; Mazuka, 2000). For example, Cuetos and Mitchell (1988) tested the applicability of the late-closure principle in Spanish. They found that in interpreting structurally ambiguous sentences, the dominant preference among native Spanish readers differed perceptively from that among English readers, thus casting serious doubt on the principle's universality. Similarly,

Mazuka and Itoh (1995) expressed strong skepticism about the universal view of the parsing mechanism, contending that, by and large, the specific grammar of a language determines whether a particular construction causes misinterpretation. Based on the contrasting features in the head placement in relation to its complements, the researchers believe that distinct parsing strategies are used among readers of typologically contrasting languages; for example, in head-final Japanese, parsing decisions remain tentative until the final word of the sentence is processed, whereas in head-initial English, the parser makes some early commitment about its structural interpretation.

Although the paucity of cross-linguistic data makes it difficult to identify the core principles governing syntactic parsing across languages, the competition model is a notable exception, yielding a sizable volume of empirical research involving a broad array of languages. As noted, the model is a particular instantiation of the general functionalist approach to language processing and acquisition (Bates & MacWhinney, 1987). Built around the fundamental functionalist premise that the "forms of natural languages are created, governed, constrained, acquired, and used in the service of communicative function" (MacWhinney, Bates, & Kliegl, 1984, p. 128), the model aims at explaining and predicting probabilistic differences in form–function mappings during sentence comprehension and production in typologically diverse languages.

Connections between units of external form and units of internal function constitute its core structure. In any given language, a variety of external units, such as pre- (or post)verbal positioning, subject–verb agreement, and case-marking inflections, coalesce to support decisions on case-role assignment. As a result, the competing and converging of simultaneously activated cues during parsing are regarded as the critical aspect of sentence processing. When various cues elicit conflicting information, the connection strength between the potential cues and the specific case role to be assigned essentially determine the competition winner for the final interpretation.

Currently, empirical investigations within the model have focused primarily on a single aspect of grammar, thematic-role assignment. Experimental procedures typically involve listening to a series of word strings and determining which word is the subject, or the "actor," of the sentence. In an early study, for example, Bates and associates (1982) compared the relative strength of syntactic (i.e., word order) and semantic (i.e., animacy) cues in guiding thematic interpretation among native speakers of two contrasting languages, English and Italian. Because the two languages differ in word-order rigidity, it was hypothesized that word order, in varying degrees, is used as a cue during syntactic processing; specifically, word order serves as the primary cue in rigidly ordered English, but it does not provide equally reliable information in loosely ordered Italian. The researchers found contrasting syntactic and semantic cue usage between the groups. As predicted, English-speaking participants relied more heavily on word order than on animacy, whereas their Italian counterparts made greater use of semantic cues. Their data thus suggest that contrasting cue usage is directly related to the dominant form–function mapping pattern of each language.

Table 6.1 summarizes competition model study results. The findings make it plain that different mapping procedures are used in typologically diverse languages and, more critically, that the procedural variations reflect differential correlational patterns between the external forms and internal functions across languages. This in turn implies that procedural preference can reliably be predicted from the relative strength of potential cues in a particular language.

Nonsyntactic factors constraining sentence processing

Although sentence processing models differ in important characteristics, they share a significant common feature: Sentence comprehension proceeds incrementally through initial analysis and subsequent adjustments. Given the online nature of information processing, it is reasonable to expect that syntactic parsing is equally, if not more heavily, constrained by nonsyntactic factors. Three major elements – local semantic property, discourse context, and working-memory capacity – serve as illustrations.

Local semantic property refers to the aspect of verb meaning directly associated with the argument structure – that is, how verbs are incorporated in particular sentence frames. For example, some verbs, like *give*, take two noun phrases as their direct and indirect objects, as in "The man gave *his wife a bouquet of roses*," whereas other verbs, such as *place*, are accompanied by a combination of a single noun phrase as the direct object and a prepositional phrase complement, as in "The man placed *his gloves on the chair*." Because verb knowledge typically includes the information specifying the type of argument structure in which the verb can be incorporated, we can hypothesize that the case-role assignment also is strongly affected by this knowledge (e.g., Ford, Bresnan, & Kaplan, 1982; Spivey-Knowlton, Tueswell, & Tanenhaus, 1994). Presumably, all possible usage forms for a particular verb are "tagged" in the order of their relative frequency. When a verb is processed, the argument structure associated with its most frequent usage form is most likely to be activated, biasing

Table 6.1. *Cross-linguistic variations in cue selection in actor assignment (reprinted from E. Bates, & B. MacWhinney, 1989, pp. 44–45)*

English
Adults: SVO > VOS, OSV > Animacy, Agreement > Stress, Topic
5–7:   SVO > Animacy > Agreement > NNV, VNN, Stress
Under 5:   SVO > Animacy > Stress, SOV, VSO > Agreement

Italian
Adults: SV Agreement > Clitic Agreement > Animacy > SVO > Stress, Topic
    (NNV, VNN interpretable only in combination with stress, clitics)
Under 7:   Animacy > SVO > SV Agreement > Clitic Agreement > SOV, VSO
    (no interactions of NNV, VNN with stress, clitics)

French
Adults: SV Agreement > Clitic Agreement > Animacy > SVO > Stress
Under 6:   SVO > Animacy > VSO, SOV (agreement not tested)

Spanish
Adults: Accusative preposition > SV Agreement > Clitic Agreement >
    Word order (animacy not tested)

German
Adults: Case > Agreement > Animacy > SOV, VSO, SVO

Dutch
Adults: Case > SVO > Animacy
Under 10:   SVO > Case > Animacy

Serbo-Croatian
Adults: Case > Agreement > Animacy > SVO, VSO, SOV
Under 5:   Animacy > Case > SVO, VSO, SOV > Agreement

Hungarian
Adults: Case > SV > Agreement > SVO, SOV > Animacy >
    V–O agreement
Under 3:   Animacy > Case > SVO > Stress (agreement not tested)

Turkish
Adults: Case > Animacy > Word Order
Under 2:   Case > Word Order (animacy not tested)

Hebrew
Adults: Case > Agreement > Order
Under 10:   Case > Order > Agreement

Warlpiri
Adults: Case > Animacy > Order
Under 5:   Animacy > Case > Order

Chinese
Adults: Animacy > SVO

Japanese
Adults: Case > Animacy > SOV

Note: S = subject, V = verb, O = object, N = noun.

subsequent parsing decisions. Although studies have shown that verbs' semantic properties have detectable impacts on sentence processing (e.g., Boland, Tanenhaus, & Garnsey, 1990; Ferreira & Henderson, 1990; Holmes, 1984; Mitchell & Holmes, 1985), whether such local constraints are strong enough to override the parser's initial interpretation, derived from the sentence's syntactic properties, remains a point of controversy.

Prior discourse context is also a nonsyntactic factor constraining syntactic parsing. The underlying presupposition is that the choice among alternative structural interpretations can be based on the degree to which a particular phrase attachment satisfies semantic constraints imposed by the prior discourse. Recall the example "Nancy tapped the man with the cane." If the prior context provides a unique antecedent for "the man," the noun phrase requires no further modification. Should this be the case, the unmodified noun-phrase interpretation, "Nancy used the cane when tapping the man," would prevail as the preferred option. If, on the other hand, more than one man was alluded to in the preceding context, there is an obvious need to specify which man is being referred to. Consequently, the noun-modifier version, "Nancy tapped the man who held the cane," would be a more likely choice.

A third type of constraint involves limited working-memory capacity. Because, as noted repeatedly, information processing is heavily constrained by working-memory capacity limitations, theories of language processing must factor in the restriction when weighing individual differences in sentence processing (e.g., Carpenter et al., 1994, 1995). In the syntactic domain, two major factors are known to strain working-memory capacity: structural complexity and ambiguity. Center-embedding clauses, such as "the student *that the teacher praised* scored perfect on the math test," serve as an example. Inasmuch as the embedding clause interrupts syntactic parsing of the main clause, its initial noun phrase "the student" must be retained in working memory until the embedded clause has been processed. Working-memory capacity, therefore, determines, at least in part, how well structurally complex sentences are understood. King and Just (1991), in fact, demonstrated that low-capacity readers' sentence comprehension was much more severely impaired by syntactic complexity than was that of high-capacity readers. A subsequent analysis of word-by-word reading times further revealed that low-capacity readers were considerably slower when critical syntactic information (i.e., the verb of the main clause "scored" in the example sentence above) became available. The researchers concluded that working-memory constraints become more evident when resources are depleted by increased processing demands, particularly among low-capacity readers.

Structural ambiguity by nature lends itself to multiple interpretations and is particularly vulnerable to working-memory limitations. Low-capacity readers, therefore, are likely to have greater difficulty coping with the demands of retaining multiple interpretations when processing structurally ambiguous sentences. The following examples, taken from a study by MacDonald and associates (1992), illustrate how structurally ambiguous sentences strain working-memory capacity.

(1) The experienced soldiers warned about the dangers before the midnight raid.
(2) The experienced soldiers warned about the dangers conducted the midnight raid.

In these sentences, punctuation was deliberately omitted to create structural ambiguity. Sentence (2) is initially ambiguous because it allows two interpretations: one taking the initial noun phrase "the experienced soldiers" as the agent/subject of the verb "warned"; and the other interpreting the same phrase as the patient/object of "warned" in a reduced relative clause construction. In processing this sentence, therefore, both interpretations must be retained in working memory until the disambiguating word "conducted" is encountered. MacDonald et al. (1992) hypothesized that working-memory capacity influences the text length over which readers can keep multiple interpretations in mind. They tested their hypothesis by comparing high- and low-capacity readers in word-by-word reading times and error rates when processing structurally ambiguous sentences, as in (2) above. Low-capacity readers were indeed handicapped, to a far greater extent than the high-capacity group, in ambiguity resolution during syntactic processing. Although different explanations have been set forth to interpret these and similar findings (e.g., MacDonald et al., 1992; Pearlmutter & MacDonald, 1995), what is indisputable is that working-memory capacity is a powerful predictor of performance differences in sentence comprehension.

Factors affecting L2 sentence processing

L1 research identifies a number of syntactic and nonsyntactic factors constraining sentence processing. Insofar as internal communicative functions are differentially conveyed by surface linguistic forms in different languages, L2 research, of necessity, incorporates additional factors directly associated with cross-linguistic variations in form–function relationships. What follows explores systematic means of extrapolating L1 research implications in studying L2 sentence comprehension – and, in so doing, highlights the unique characteristics of L2 readers' sentence-processing behaviors.

Linguistic complexity and comprehension difficulty among L2 readers

What constitutes linguistic complexity remains an ongoing debate in L2 research as well. To summarize the earlier discussion on L1 research, some theorists place heavy emphasis on quantitative factors (e.g., the number of words and phrases in a sentence) as reliable indicators of potential reading difficulty; others place greater weight on structural variables (e.g., syntactic ambiguity and opacity) as the predominant sources of comprehension problems associated with working-memory capacity limitations. The latter view regards quantitative indices simply as correlates of reading difficulty, disclaiming causal links between text length and comprehension difficulty. Further, increased text quantity and its resulting complexity often are taken as manifestations of linguistic elaboration, stemming from the author's effort to clarify the semantic relations among the sentence elements. This view, consequently, creates a seemingly paradoxical predicament: The longer the text, the easier it may be to comprehend. The significant question, then, is whether L2 readers benefit equally from linguistic augmentation and elaboration.

Several factors suggest that this may not be the case. Limited linguistic sophistication, for example, may prevent L2 readers from exploiting linguistic elaboration to the same extent as L1 readers. To benefit from the information provided by connective devices, the reader must have not only a sound grasp of their functions but also full understanding of the clauses to be connected. If what is to be connected, and in what way, is not clear to the reader, the relational information, however explicit, is unlikely to be incorporated in ongoing sentence interpretation. Presumably, elaborative linguistic elements are beneficial only when the reader has adequate command of the target language. Underdeveloped word-recognition skills, moreover, also may restrict the ability to capitalize linguistic elaboration. Inefficient decoding not only strains working-memory capacity but also, as described in Chapter 3, affects subsequent information integration. L2 decoding skills, therefore, can determine, to some degree, the extent to which linguistic elaboration is beneficial.

As a result, the facilitative assistance of linguistic elaboration in L2 sentence processing can be mediated by both L2 linguistic knowledge and decoding efficiency. Consequently, it is questionable whether, in the interest of elaboration, additional linguistic elements and increased complexity are uniformly helpful to L2 readers with different proficiency levels. It may well be, then, that quantitative indices are more reliable indicators of L2 rather than L1 comprehension difficulties, at least among low-proficiency learners. It should be noted, however, that the complexity–difficulty relationship, although initially manifest, may diminish as L2 proficiency increases. These speculations, obviously, offer promising future research possibilities in L2 sentence processing.

Syntactic factors contributing to L2 sentence-processing difficulty

L2 sentence comprehension, as observed, relies heavily on morphosyntactic knowledge. Hence, systematic examination of how limited-linguistic sophistication impedes L2 sentence processing remains a critical concern in L2 research. Berman (1984), for instance, identified two syntactic factors as major sources of L2 comprehension difficulty: violation of structural prototypicality and lack of structural transparency. She concluded that structural prototypicality is violated when "there is a conflict between the more basic ordering of semantic and syntactic relations and the surface form of sentences" (p. 140). To illustrate, in the passive construction in English, its surface form "object-verb-subject" does not conform to the prototypical syntactic ordering of "subject-verb-object" and therefore violates structural prototypicality. Structural conflicts of this sort clearly exert an additional burden on L2 learners with limited command of the target language.

Another source of difficulty, Berman contends, is structural opacity. The contention here is that some widely used cohesive devices in English, such as deletion and substitution, can obscure structural relationships among readers not yet familiar with the basic structural properties of the language, making case-role assignments difficult. Many L2 learners of English, for instance, have difficulty determining what the grammatical substitutes for repeated lexical items, as shown in the following examples:

(1) I told my sister how much I liked her *mug*. Next day, she bought *one* for me.
(2) He *washed* his car. So I *did* mine.

An absence of relative pronouns in reduced relative clauses also creates confusion by making the initial clause structurally ambiguous, as in "The members [who were] elected in the last board meeting are expected to take immediate actions." Cohesive signaling, moreover, is by no means universal across languages. When L2 devices are not prevalent in the L1, they too can create processing difficulty. Despite their pivotal relevance, however, these and other syntactic factors remain largely unexplored, particularly with respect to their collective impacts on L2 reading difficulty.

Dual-language effects on L2 sentence processing

Given the notable differences in form–function correspondence patterns across languages, one can readily speculate that such variation has a significant impact on L2 sentence processing. Because L1 form–function mapping procedures have largely become automated, we can expect that L1-specific patterns are activated involuntarily through L2 input, regardless of learner intent. Therefore, as in the case of L2 lexical-competence development, we can make a strong argument for L1–L2 cross-linguistic interactions, as well as for their conjoint influence on the formation of L2 sentence-processing procedures. However, this also imposes a mandate for further refinement of our conception of "language transfer."

Traditionally, in SLA research, "transfer" is interpreted as learners' reliance on their respective L1s. Krashen (1983) demonstrated how transfer "can be regarded as padding, or the result of falling back on old knowledge, the L1 rule, when new knowledge...is lacking" (p. 148). Gass and Selinker (1983) provided a similar, but somewhat more refined, view of the phenomenon: "the learner is transferring prior linguistic knowledge resulting in IL [inter language] forms which, when compared by the researchers to the target language norms, can be termed 'positive,' 'negative,' 'or neutral'" (p. 6). Moreover, Odlin (1989) reinforced the general thrust of this premise in stating that "transfer is the influence from similarities and differences between the target language and any other language that has been previously (and perhaps imperfectly) acquired" (p. 27). These views of transfer share two major assumptions: (1) What is "transferred" is linguistic knowledge; and (2) reliance on L1 knowledge is associated, more or less, with a premature grasp of the target language. Logic suggests, then, that the transfer of any particular aspect of L1 knowledge tends to cease when sufficient corresponding L2 knowledge has been acquired, and, more critically, that L2 competence variation among learners with diverse L1 backgrounds is generally minimal.

These convictions, although dominant in SLA research, are not uniformly accepted. Under the connectionist rubric, as observed earlier, language acquisition is regarded as the internalization of form–function relationships through cumulative processing experience. What is learned and stored, therefore, is not linguistic knowledge (grammatical rules, in specific) but rather patterns of activation linking particular linguistic forms with their corresponding functions. If, indeed, L1 procedures are activated by L2 input, language transfer should be viewed as a result of automatic L1 activation rather than as a compensating mechanism for limited L2 knowledge. With this supposition, a completely different set of predictions is possible: Transferred L1 procedures are involved across proficiency levels in all aspects of L2 processing. L2 sentence-processing procedures, as has been predicted in L2 word-recognition development, supposedly evolve from cumulative L2 processing experience through the use of automated L1 processing procedures. Presumably, systematic variations, arising from such cross-linguistic interplay, should become manifest in consequent L2 competence. The newer view of "transfer" thus offers entirely different conceptions of L1 influence on L2 processing-skills development.

Studies on L2 sentence processing

With the notable exception of research on thematic interpretation in the competition model, a dearth of empirical data hampers any systematic characterization of L2 sentence comprehension. The synthesis in the following sections summarizes disparate L2 sentence-processing studies on cross-linguistic transfer of syntactic processing, effects of L2 syntactic complexity, L1 influence on L2 verb-meaning acquisition, and effects of L2 syntactic modification on comprehension.

Cross-linguistic transfer of syntactic processing

The vast bulk of transfer research at the sentence level has occurred within the competition model arena. In the model, sentence processing, as indicated earlier, is credited with connecting linguistic forms and communicative functions. The underlying premise is that the acquisition of processing competence in a given language is heavily constrained by the language's particular form–function relationships. Presuming that the postulation extends to L2 mapping-skills development, the critical question is to what extent L1 structural properties affect the formation of L2 form–function mapping patterns. The question has prompted an impressive number of empirical studies.

McDonald (1987), for example, compared cue-usage patterns during a thematic-role assignment involving two groups of L2 learners – Dutch learners of English and American learners of Dutch – across three proficiency levels (novice, intermediate, and advanced). Her data demonstrated that both groups relied on the specific cues predominantly used in their respective L1s – word order by American learners and case inflections by Dutch learners. Interestingly, through increased proficiency, L2 learners' cue usage shifted from dominant L1 reliance to more native-like patterns. L1 English-speaking participants reduced their dependence on word order and, as proficiency levels rose, gradually increased their use of case inflections. Conversely, an opposite directional shift was observed among L1 Dutch participants. McDonald concluded that, with increased proficiency, L2 learners developed greater cue-strength sensitivity in the target language and gradually adapted their mapping procedures to L2 patterns.

Kilborn and Ito (1989) reported a series of studies involving adult L2 learners of two typologically diverse languages, Japanese and English. Their findings generally corroborated the McDonald study, further demonstrating that initial-response patterns among beginning L2 learners were more similar to their L1 than to L2 norms, regardless of the target language. Of particular interest, systematic differences also were observed among novice and advanced L2 learners. Whereas L1-based processing biases were observed across proficiency levels, advanced L2 learners progressively leaned toward cues typically used by native-speaking participants. Here again, the data implied a systematic developmental shift from L1 to L2 cue usage.

Harrington (1987) also examined cue-usage patterns among Japanese–English bilinguals. The study involved three groups of adult learners: Japanese learners of English, native speakers of Japanese, and native speakers of English. He found that, when assigning the thematic role in English sentences, cue-usage patterns among Japanese L2 learners matched those used by Japanese L1 speakers more closely than those common among native English speakers, further confirming L1 influence on L2 processing skills. Taken as a whole, these studies consistently suggest that L2 learners rely on case-signaling cues used in L1 sentence processing to a far greater extent than those in the target language, especially in early L2 learning stages.

Conflicting results, however, stem from other studies in the same conceptual rubric. Gass (1987), as a case in point, compared the relative use of two cue forms, syntactic and semantic, during L2 sentence processing among American learners of Italian and Italian learners of English. Whereas the predominant use of the semantic cue, supposedly manifesting L1 transfer, was observed among

Italian learners of English, transfer in the reverse direction was not apparent among L1 English speakers. Instead of the expected regression to the L1-based syntactic cues, they tended to rely on the semantic. Gass interpreted these results as an indication that crosslinguistic transfer does not transpire in bidirectional, symmetrical fashion, and concluded that L2 learners may seek solutions to processing conflicts in the workings of their native language, and, when prohibitive because of L1 and L2 syntactic incongruities, they revert to fundamental universal principles (e.g., using semantic cues) for resolution.

In a subsequent study, Sasaki (1991) contrasted cue-usage patterns among American learners of Japanese and Japanese learners of English in both their L1 and their L2. The results replicated the outcomes of the Gass study (1987), demonstrating that American learners of Japanese closely approximate the response patterns of native Japanese speakers, whereas Japanese learners of English are heavily dependent on their L1-based cues. Sasaki argues, consequently, that "transfer takes place only from a less syntax-centered language to one that is more so" (1991, p. 61). Obviously, the Gass and Sasaki studies both indicate that processing transfer may not be reciprocal in the two languages involved, as has been suggested in earlier investigations.

Finally, data from yet another study, involving adult L2 learners of Japanese, complicate circumstances even further (Koda, 1993). Because Japanese uses two linguistic devices, postpositional case-marking particles and word order, to signal case roles, the study compared relative reliance on each among L2 learners of Japanese with typologically diverse L1 backgrounds (Chinese, English, and Korean). Although the absence of the L2-specific cue – case-marking particles – seriously impaired the performance of all participants regardless of L1, absence of the other cue, word order, affected only those whose L1 used word order as the primary case-signaling cue (i.e., English). These findings seem to imply that L1 and L2 linguistic knowledge coalesces in complex interactions during L2 sentence processing, as has been observed in L2 lexical studies.

To summarize, then, the development of L2 sentence-processing competence involves complicated interplays among several critical variables, including universal principles, L1 mapping patterns, and L2 syntactic properties. Because empirical data to date are available only in limited syntactic features and a few target languages, little can be certain about either the specific effects of the variables involved or their interactions. More studies are needed to expand current findings to a greater range of syntactic features in a wider mix of languages. It is equally imperative to determine the extent to which findings from auditory sentence comprehension can be applied to visual-information processing.

Effects of L2 syntactic complexity

As an outgrowth of the modularity theory, it is commonly held that syntactic complexity in itself is an unlikely area of sentence-processing difficulty. Rather, the major L2 research concern is whether L1 and L2 syntactic knowledge develop in the same way. Although there is general consensus that L2 learners, like L1 child learners, have access to universal principles (e.g., Bley-Vroman, 1989; Flynn, 1987b; Flynn & Espinal, 1985; Gass & Schachter, 1989; Phinney, 1987; Rutherford, 1983; Schachter, 1988; White, 1989), how these principles are accessed remains a point of dispute. Indeed, if universal principles in one way or another are available to L2 learners, syntactic complexity should not provoke undue comprehension difficulty in L2 either.

In a well-controlled study, Juffs and Harrington (1996) tested this hypothesis with an online moving-window technique. This procedure makes it possible to measure word-by-word reading times by allowing experimenters to present the individual words in a sentence one at a time. Grammaticality-judgment performance was compared among Chinese-speaking adult ESL learners and native English speakers. L2 learners, though slower, achieved about the same accuracy level as L1 participants in rejecting ungrammatical sentences. The researchers interpreted these findings as an indication that L2 learners can detect violations of universal principles and therefore can access universal grammar (UG) principles during L2 sentence processing. Moreover, their word-by-word reaction times revealed that performance differences within each group related directly to the processing demands imposed by the various syntactic structures tested in the study. Their findings lend further support for the processing deficit hypothesis (Crain & Shankweiler, 1988) described earlier, making it plain that grammatical competence, in and of itself, is unlikely to create sentence-processing problems for L2 readers.

L1 influence on L2 verb-meaning acquisition

Other, nonsyntactic, factors also contribute to L2 sentence processing. Local semantic property – verb meaning, in particular – is one such factor. As noted earlier, a verb's semantic information restricts the type of sentence in which it can be incorporated. Presumably, the information plays a perceptible role in syntactic processing. Accordingly, a small but rapidly growing number of SLA researchers have focused on the acquisition of L2 verb knowledge, especially information regarding semantics–syntax correspondence, in typologically different target languages. Verb knowledge, in addition to its idiosyncratic meaning, entails information about specific ways aspects of verb meaning are expressed morphologically, as well as the particular manners in which syntax constrains verb meaning. The acquisition of this knowledge necessitates broad exposure not only to a wide variety of verbs, but also their disparate meaning aspects in relation to particular usage (Montrul, 2001). L2 input typically affords a limited range of exemplars, and it seems justifiable to assume that L2 input alone yields an insufficient basis for acquiring different aspects of L2 verb meaning. Should this be the case, it would be logical to hypothesize whether L1 knowledge can compensate for inadequate support from L2 input. Consequently, the major goal of this research is to determine the precise impact of L1 properties on L2 verb-knowledge formation.

In an initiatory study, Juffs (1998) posed two critical questions: Are L2 readers sensitive to local semantic constraints, and if so, are they capable of using this information in resolving syntactic ambiguity? By measuring word-by-word reading times among ESL learners from a variety of L1 backgrounds, he determined that L2 learners, regardless of their L1 experience, attended to the argument-structure properties of L2 verbs, using the resulting information in building, evaluating, and restructuring the syntactic structure of a sentence. The data showed considerable reaction-time differences among those with typologically similar and dissimilar L1 backgrounds, suggesting that, even among advanced learners, L1–L2 typological distance is a strong predictor of syntactic-processing efficiency. Ultimately, Juffs concluded that "adult ESL learners are influenced by typological properties of their L1s that are linked to L1 parsing strategies when processing ESL" (p. 107).

In a more recent study, Inagaki (2001) examined sensitivity to the syntactic properties of motion verbs among L2 learners of two contrasting target languages: English-speaking learners of Japanese and Japanese-speaking learners of English. English permits both manner-of-motion verbs (e.g., *walk* and *run*) and directed-motion verbs (e.g., *come* and *go*) in a prepositional goal phrase, as in "John walks/goes *to his office*," but Japanese only allows directed-motion verbs in a goal phrase. Based on this difference, Inagaki hypothesized that the acquisition difficulty of L2 syntactic structures for motion events varies among the two groups. Specifically, Japanese learners of English learn through input that manner-of-motion verbs appear with goal phrases, whereas L2 learners of Japanese have difficulty learning that manner-of-motion verbs cannot be used with goal phrases in Japanese, because nothing in the input indicates this to be prohibitive. Data from his grammaticality-judgment test yielded strong support for the hypothesis, showing that Japanese ESL learners accepted manner-of-motion verbs with goal phrases despite the fact that their L1 does not permit this construction. Moreover, American learners of Japanese also accepted – erroneously, in their case – the same construction in Japanese sentences, implying that when L2 input provides neither negative nor positive evidence for certain constructions, learners resort to their L1 knowledge. Therefore, Inagaki concluded that "L1 influence persists when an argument structure in the L2 constitutes a subset of its counterpart in the L1" (p. 153).

Based on similar logic, Montrul (2001) investigated the acquisition of verb meanings among L2 learners of Spanish and English. She contends that some classes of verbs share the same lexical meaning, accompanied by the same syntactic behavior, across languages, whereas others display different syntactic behavior from language to language, even though they share the same meaning. Her study focused on the latter. Agentive verbs serve as an example – a class of verbs appearing in the syntactic frame allowing only one (agent/subject) argument, such as *go* and *come* in English and Spanish. In English, agentive manner-of-motion verbs, such as *walk*, *march*, and *run*, also can occur in transitive sentences, expressing a causative meaning (i.e., the subject/agent causes the action to be executed by someone else), as in "Mary walked Bill to the bus stop." Unlike English, however, Spanish does not permit the transitive use of these verbs, despite their shared meaning in the intransitive usage. The issue, then, is how L2 learners determine which classes of verbs share similar syntactic behavior between languages and which do not. Montrul's analysis predicted that L2 learners tend to make overgeneralization errors (accepting ungrammatical forms) when a particular syntactic behavior (transitive alteration of agentive manner-of-motion verbs, in her study) is permitted in L1 but not in L2. Contrastingly, when a certain verb usage prohibited in the L1 is allowed in the L2, undergeneralization errors (rejecting grammatical forms) are likely to occur. The research tested these predictions by using the grammaticality-judgment test. Two groups of participants, Spanish-speaking learners of English and English-speaking learners of Spanish, were involved. The data confirmed the predictions, indicating that American learners of Spanish indeed committed overgeneralization errors when confronted with transitive alternation of agentive manner-of-motion verbs in Spanish sentences, whereas Spanish ESL learners made more undergeneralization errors in the same sentence forms in English. The findings corroborate those from the Juffs and Inagaki studies, suggesting that L1 structural properties constrain the acquisition of L2 verb meanings, thereby significantly affecting L2 syntactic processing.

Effects of L2 syntactic modification on comprehension

Input modification has long been a major concern in SLA research. Originating in speech modification, much of this research initially focused on listening comprehension, and later was extended to reading comprehension. Although modifications occur in virtually all facets of L2 input, the discussion here focuses on two specific input adjustments – syntactic and semantic – because both are directly relevant to sentence processing. Syntactic modifications can be characterized as using shorter sentences, adhering to canonical word order, marking of grammatical relations among sentence segments, and retaining linguistic elements that can be deleted (e.g., relative pronouns, as in "the members *who were* elected in the last meeting"). Semantic adjustments, in contrast, entail explicit signals of semantic connections, excessive lexical repetitions, and repeating noun and verb phrases instead of using grammatical substitutes. In addition, two kinds of functionally contrasting modifications – simplification and elaboration – should also be noted. Simplification aims at decreasing text-information quantity by reducing sentence length and structural complexity. Elaboration, on the other hand, involves making syntactic and semantic relations more explicit through linguistic devices. Contrary to simplification, therefore, input elaboration, as described earlier, typically results in longer, structurally more complex sentences.

The primary goal of this research is to determine whether, and in what ways, L2 learners benefit from input modifications. The general consensus is that modifications frequently are associated with improved comprehension (e.g., Berman, 1984; Chaudron, 1983; Kelch, 1985; Long, 1985), but simplification in itself does not always enhance comprehension gains (e.g., Chaudron & Richards, 1986; Pica, Doughty, & Young, 1986; Young, 1999). Berman (1984), for example, compared reading comprehension in modified and unmodified texts among Hebrew-speaking college-level learners of English. Her text modifications centered on increased referential clarity and structural transparency through the avoidance of grammatical substitutions for repeated lexical items, and the reduction of elliptical expressions and pronominalization. Using three types of comprehension questions (factual details, pronominal references, and global understanding), she demonstrated that reading a syntactically modified version improved performance in all three forms of questions. Because the original, unmodified, text provoked more errors on questions of specific local information, but not on those probing larger global content, Berman reasoned that "intra-sentential syntactic complexity might be more of an impediment to grasping specific details than to overall ideas" (p. 146).

Yano, Long and Ross (1994) found that simplification and elaboration differentially affect various aspects of text-information processing. The researchers compared the reading-comprehension facilitation benefits of the two forms of modification among college-level Japanese ESL learners. Their comprehension measure consisted of three kinds of questions, each of which could be answered through different forms of text-information processing, including surface linguistic analysis, intersentential synthesis, and inference. Their findings are illuminating. Although comprehension scores between the two types of text did not differ significantly, the two modification procedures had divergent effects on text-information processing. Simplification improved the extraction of text-explicit information, whereas elaboration engendered enhanced facilitation in apprehending text-implicit information. Yano et al. suggest that, although simplification and elaboration both enhance L2 reading comprehension, elaborative text modification "serves to provide semantic detail essential for second-language readers to make inferences about texts they read" (p. 214). In effect, they contend that elaboration can be a viable substitute for simplification.

Taken as a whole, the empirical findings favor input modifications largely because of their usefulness in assisting and promoting reading comprehension among L2 learners. Some caution should be exercised, nevertheless, because mixed results also have been reported in a fair number of other studies (e.g., Blau, 1982; Issidorides & Hulstijn, 1992; Parker & Chaudron, 1987; Speidel, Tharp, & Kobayashi, 1985; Ulijin & Strother, 1990). In view of its potentially significant contributions to better L2 comprehension and greater linguistic knowledge, additional research on input modifications would be highly desirable. Three critical issues in particular need further clarification. Because the magnitude of facilitation attributable to input modifications varies notably from study to study, a meta-analysis would be useful in teasing apart factors that intervene with modification effects on comprehension. Systematic explorations to elucidate possible developmental changes in the way modified input enhances comprehension would also be of benefit. Because simplification and elaboration affect text-information processing differently (e.g., Yano et al., 1994), it is highly improbable that they offer the same kind of assistance across proficiency levels in precisely the same way. Finally, much would be gained if instructional research could explore the conditions under which the potential benefit of input modification can be maximized. If, for example, the ultimate goal of L2 reading instruction is to enable students to cope with authentic texts by themselves, excessive or unduly prolonged use of modified input may be counterproductive by forestalling development of the essential skills necessary for disentangling surface linguistic elements during text-meaning construction.

Summary and future research suggestions

Incremental integration of lexical information obviously is central in sentence comprehension. Because the goal is to uncover the overall meaning of a given string of words, structural complexity is fertile ground for locating processing difficulties. The research corpus of L1 reading, however, suggests that a text's linguistic variables cannot automatically be linked to reading problems because word length, in itself, is not a reliable indicator of comprehension difficulty. Furthermore, inasmuch as increased sentence length and complexity often provide linguistic elaboration in explicating semantic relations among intersentential elements, once again, quantitative indices are not a reliable predictor of reading impediment. It is commonly held, moreover, that comprehension difficulty associated with syntactic complexity generally arises from a deficit in the decoding skills necessary for linking spoken language with its written forms rather than from a dearth of syntactic knowledge.

It is worth noting, perhaps, that the research on cross-linguistic variations in processing mechanisms, through which syntactic knowledge is utilized in sentence production and comprehension, is restricted in both scope and quantity. The one notable exception is the competition model, which has generated a large number of empirical explorations in a broad array of languages. Based on a functionalist approach to language acquisition and processing, the model aims at explaining and predicting probabilistic differences in the form–function mappings during sentence comprehension and production. Findings generally intimate that mapping procedures vary across languages, reflecting their differential mapping patterns.

Such cross-linguistic variations have significant implications for L2 sentence comprehension. Considerable research makes it plain that L2 sentence processing is heavily constrained by L1 morphosyntactic properties. However, these are not the only source of constraint. Other studies allude to additional factors influencing L2 syntactic behaviors, such as the L2 knowledge base, L1 and L2 typological distance, and universal principles. Although still inconclusive, some initial findings hint at the possibility that the L2 learner's procedural preference may shift from L1-based to more native-like patterns. Still other research supports the likelihood that input modifications facilitate L2 reading comprehension. Empirical findings generally verify the role of modified input as a facilitative device enhancing L2 reading comprehension. However, some studies yield mixed results, warranting caution in overgeneralizing the benefits of input modification across proficiency levels and instructional contexts.

L2 sentence-processing research covers a wide variety of issues stemming from diverse theoretical perspectives. These have given rise to a number of controversies, which may well receive attention on future research agendas directly relating to L2 reading comprehension. The following are illustrative: effects of L2 proficiency on procedural preferences, utilization of transferred skills, and effects of L1 and L2 typological distance. With respect to procedural preferences, the empirical findings remain inconclusive regarding developmental shifts (e.g., Kilborn & Ito, 1989; McDonald, 1987; Sasaki, 1993). Although it would be logical to postulate that processing procedures among L2 learners become increasingly native-like as proficiency improves, careful clarification is essential in determining what "shifting procedures" really means. Does the shift involve conscious decisions, particularly with respect to when to forego one procedural approach to adopt another? Or does it evolve as the natural consequence of increased L2 proficiency? Is it a continuous process of replacing one with the other over time, or does it take place abruptly once a certain level of L2 proficiency is reached? Scrutiny of this sort is vital because different ways of conceptualizing procedural shift entail very different investigations.

As for the specific contribution of transferred processing skills in L2 sentence comprehension, as referenced earlier, competition model studies suggest that transferred cue-usage patterns are a normal course of syntactic processing among L2 learners (e.g., Gass, 1987; Kilborn & Ito, 1989; Sasaki, 1991). Yet, little is known about the mechanisms and degree through which such L1-based procedures actually facilitate comprehension, especially when L1 and L2 are typologically dissimilar. Because knowledge of the L2 morphosyntactic features essential for intrasentential information integration is a major factor differentiating good from poor L2 readers (Koda, 1990a), and because L2 readers' information extraction patterns in a particular language systematically differ from those of L1 readers of the same language (e.g., Bernhardt, 1987; Hatch et al., 1974; Saito, 1989), plausibly, the defining characterization distinguishing the two is the ability to direct attention to the elements providing critical information for text-meaning construction. It follows, therefore, that learners with typologically similar L1 backgrounds have a better chance of identifying the ways essential information is conveyed by the surface linguistic forms. It is hoped that future research can illuminate the complex triple interactions among L1–L2 syntactic distance, L1 processing competence, and L2 proficiency.

A third possible agenda is the role of learner perception primarily in conjunction with L1 and L2 linguistic distance. Although distance effects on L2 learning are commonly noted across proficiency levels, little has been studied about the ways perceived distance affects L2 processing. Inasmuch as metacognitive operations, such as monitoring comprehension and using meaning-making strategies (e.g., translation) during L2 sentence comprehension, are under conscious control, distance perception presumably influences, to some degree, their activation and implementation. Kellerman (1983) contended that psychotypology, or perceived L1–L2 distance, controls, in large measure, the transferability of linguistic elements. Gass (1983) further noted that perceived salience partially governs cross-linguistic transfer. Because the activation of processing procedures is regulated, in part, by metacognitive processes (e.g., Baker & Brown, 1984; Miller, 1988), the perceived congruence of the two languages may be directly linked to the individual's procedural biases and preferences. Perhaps of greatest moment, however, systematic examinations of perceived L1–L2 linguistic distance compared with their actual distance may help considerably in locating missing pieces in the L2 learning puzzle.

7 *Discourse processing*

Text is not a sequential display of isolated words and sentences. Rather, it is visual communication transmitting the author's intended message. Text understanding, therefore, is the process of discerning the author's communicative intent. As Gray (1960) observed more than four decades ago, comprehension entails three major endeavors – reading *lines*, reading *between lines*, and reading *beyond lines* – going far beyond merely linking sentences. Research on discourse processing over the last 30 years has actively pursued efforts to unveil the processes through which "text" is progressively reconstructed in readers' minds based on the information retained in the "reconstructed text." The central research issues include how text information is represented in memory, how remembered information is organized, and the specific factors that influence the "reconstruction" process.

Using this extensive research as a base, this chapter explores its implications for L2 reading studies. Because of the unique characteristics of adult L2 readers, it is assumed that L1 and L2 text comprehension – both process and product – differ fundamentally. By systematically probing such differences, the intent is to lay foundations for developing viable models of L2 text comprehension and, in so doing, clarify further issues distinguishing L2 percepts from L1 theories. Toward that end, this chapter describes ongoing conceptualizations of discourse comprehension, with particular emphasis on two critical discourse-processing operations: text-coherence building through explicit connective devices and inferences. The unique factors affecting L2 text comprehension are then considered, and a review of L2 empirical studies is provided. Although two technical terms in this literature – *text* and *discourse* – have slightly different meanings, they are used interchangeably in this and subsequent chapters.

Building text representations

Models of text comprehension

Contemporary text-comprehension theories stem mainly from the increasingly intense interest in "meaningfulness" in language processing and learning. Early work by Bransford and associates (e.g., Bransford, 1983; Bransford, Barclay, & Franks, 1972; Bransford & Franks, 1972; Bransford & Johnson, 1972; Bransford & McCarrell, 1977), for example, illustrates the constructive nature of language processing. Under the premise that comprehension does not emerge from sequential concatenations of individual words and sentences, Bransford et al. set forth three compelling contentions based on their empirical observations. First, verbatim recall generally is more demanding than content-information retrieval, because readers typically encode the underlying meanings of text information, although not necessarily in their surface forms. Second, comprehension is an incremental process, involving the integration of information from different parts of a text. Third, the construction of text meaning requires a synthesis of explicitly stated text information as well as relevant knowledge stored in long-term memory.

Expanding these early insights, subsequent conceptualizations, collectively referred to as mental-model theories, helped in articulating how text information is represented in memory (e.g., Anderson, 1983; Johnson-Laird, 1983; van Dijk & Kintsch, 1983). For example, van Dijk and Kintsch (1983) identified three distinct levels of memory traces labeled as: *surface form*, *propositional textbase*, and *situation model*. In their theory, surface form corresponds to a sequence of syntactically, semantically, and pragmatically interpreted words. Propositional textbase, in contrast, refers to an interconnected network of semantic text information. The third representation level, situation model, denotes real-life situations described. Johnson-Laird (1983) also identified three levels of mental representations: *proposition*, *mental model*, and *image*. While proposition in his model is roughly equivalent to van Dijk and Kintsch's surface form, mental model parallels a combination of the textbase and situation model. Although image also partially overlaps with situation model, it specifically embodies a perceptual derivative, or picture, of the mental model from a particular viewpoint.

The basic assumption at the root of mental model theories is that what is formed in the reader's mind during comprehension goes well beyond the literal meaning of the explicit text statements, encapsulating real-world situations as the reader perceives them. Because these models, while differing in detail, share many common features, an illustrative portrayal of one may facilitate understanding of how the constructive nature of text comprehension is explicated in mental model theories. A description of a model proposed by Kintsch and his colleagues (e.g., Kintsch, 1988, 1992, 1994; Kintsch & Welsch, 1991; van Dijk & Kintsch, 1983) follows.

As already specified, the van Dijk/Kintsch model assumes that text information is represented in multiple levels, including surface linguistic forms, meaning-based propositional networks, and conceptually driven situation models. The basic unit of text representations is the proposition, defined as the smallest semantic element that logically can be falsified. To wit, although none of the lexical elements in "Orchids bloom forever" can be falsified, taken as a whole, the string becomes falsifiable. Each proposition contains a relational term, or predicate, and one or more arguments, in the form of either concepts or other propositions. To illustrate, the sentence "Bill bought a beautiful sweater" consists of two propositions: "Bill bought a sweater" and "The sweater is beautiful." To construct the meaning conveyed by a text, individual propositions, once computed, must be interlinked on the basis of argument overlap, or lexical repetition, as well as other clues signaling their semantic connections (e.g., Fletcher & Bloom, 1988; Kintsch, 1994; van Dijk & Kintsch, 1983). The two propositions just mentioned, for example, are linked through their shared argument, "sweater."

The propositional textbase, moreover, generally has a hierarchical structure. In the Kintsch model (Kintsch, 1994, 1998; van Dijk & Kintsch, 1983), for example, two levels of text structure, microstructure and macrostructure, are postulated. Whereas the microstructure lists text-based propositions (referred to as micropropositions), the macrostructure, containing summary propositions (referred to as macropropositions), organizes the micropropositions according to their relative relevance to the main text theme, and, in so doing, denotes the text's overall organizational structure. Whereas micropropositions are generated through analysis of the text's surface, macropropositions, independently of text analysis, are formed through completely different operations, utilizing reduction principles, or *summarization rules*. These principles include, for example, deletion (deleting unimportant propositions), generalization (replacing a string of propositions with a more general single proposition), and construction (generating synthesis propositions).

These rules repeatedly are applied to progressively shorten the number of macropropositions until the entire textbase is reduced to a single summary proposition, which manifests its core. Because of the essence-eliciting nature of their generation, macropropositions are more prominently represented in text memory. A number of experimental studies demonstrated that macropropositions were recalled more frequently than micropropositions, even when they shared the same semantic content (e.g., Kintsch & van Dijk, 1978; Singer, 1982). Kintsch (1998) contends that "for comprehension and memory, the gist of a text – expressed formally by the macrostructure – is usually what matters most" (p. 67).

The propositional textbase, however, does not provide adequate explanations of several well-established facts about comprehension. For example, it does not explain why the same text can produce diverse interpretations. As an illustration, the sentence "Jane behaves like Madonna" can evoke entirely different reactions. If the reader admires Madonna for who she is, and what she does, the statement is likely to be interpreted as a compliment, resulting in positive reactions toward Jane and her behavior. If, on the other hand, the reader disapproves of what Madonna represents, behaving like Madonna likely will be viewed negatively. Because the propositional content is identical, surface linguistic elements cannot account for variations in sentence interpretation.

In the same vein, textbases are incapable of explaining why texts often lose their central essence when translated into another language. As Hutchins (1980) noted, retaining propositional representations in itself does not guarantee successful translation, particularly when the languages represent different cultural assumptions and expectations. Such interpretive aspects of text comprehension are better represented in the situation model, where the basic premise is that readers use prior knowledge to concoct the physical situations conveyed by language. Therefore, unlike the propositional textbase, situation models differ from reader to reader at least to the degree that the readers' knowledge and experience vary.

The psychological reality of situation models repeatedly has been subjected to empirical examinations. An adroit experiment undertaken by Glenberg, Meyer, and Lindem (1987) is particularly noteworthy. The researchers showed two groups of readers slightly different versions of a story. Sentences (1) and (2) below distinguish the two:

(1) After doing a few warm-up exercises, John *put on* his sweatshirt and began jogging.
(2) After doing a few warm-up exercises, John *took off* his sweatshirt and began jogging.

Next, both groups read:

(3) John jogged halfway around the lake without too much difficulty.

If the textbase is converted into an appropriate, corresponding situation, after reading sentence (3), where John runs halfway around the lake, different mental images should emerge between the two groups of readers. The critical question, then, is whether, in the reader's mental image, the jogger is wearing his sweatshirt. Within the mental-model framework, we can postulate that the image created by those reading the first version should, in their "mind's eye," see the jogger wearing his sweatshirt; for those reading the second version, the sweatshirt has been left behind on the other side of the lake. Glenberg et al. confirmed these predictions by demonstrating that, when questioning whether the word *sweatshirt* appeared in the story, the group reading the first version responded far more quickly. This and similar studies make it plain that text representations contain much more than the information explicitly stated. Hence, text comprehension, beyond adequate language-processing skills, requires the ability to envision real-world situations inferred from the text statements.

Establishing text coherence

To recapitulate, text is not an amalgamation of randomly ordered sentences. It is organized in ways that facilitate its message transmission. To form coherent text representations, therefore, the reader must understand the specific ways *coherence relations* among text elements are signaled both explicitly and implicitly. Coherence relation, according to Sanders, Spooren, and Noordman (1992), refers to "the aspect of meaning of two or more discourse segments that cannot be described in terms of the meaning of the segments in isolation" (p. 2). For example, to recognize the two sentences "John wanted to send pictures to his friends via Internet. He bought a digital camera" as connected text elements, the reader must understand the meaning of each sentence, but also the underlying causal connection linking them. Hence, the successful incorporation of information on coherence relation makes the text meaning as a whole more than the sum of its parts.

A considerable number of studies, with both adults and children, have investigated individual differences in coherence awareness and its relation to text comprehension. The outcomes suggest that individual differences exist in knowledge of linguistic and similar discourse devices signaling text coherence (e.g., Danner, 1976; Garner, Alexander, Slater, Hare, Smith, & Reis, 1986), efforts to increase the structural salience of a text generally facilitate comprehension (e.g., Anderson & Davison, 1988; Beck & Dole, 1992), and explicit training on text coherence awareness frequently improves text comprehension and memory (e.g., Pearson & Fielding, 1991). Obviously, an understanding of text coherence and the ways it is conveyed is critical for successful text comprehension.

Several distinct methods – both explicit and implicit – are used to achieve text coherence. *Explicit methods* refers to identifiable text clues, including organizational conventions (e.g., paragraph formation, topic sentence placement, and similar graphic markers) as well as linguistic devices (e.g., connectives, co-references). *Implicit methods*, in contrast, implies conceptual manipulations – inference and reasoning, for example – to connect text elements.

Establishing coherence through explicit signals

A text's surface structure offers a variety of reliable clues signaling coherence relations among concepts intended by the author (Goldman & Rakestraw, 2000). Sequential ordering of text segments serves as one such clue. Readers form expectations that the sentence order within a paragraph, as well as paragraph order in the text, implies certain discourse functions. In English expositions, for example, main ideas tend to appear at the beginning of a segment, and the final segment typically summarizes the text content, leading to the resulting conclusions. Such organizational cues can provide substantial facilitation in identifying, reinforcing, and retaining a text's main points. Other devices available in text pages include section dividers (e.g., titles, headings, and subheadings) and text layout formats (e.g., indentation, centering, and underlining). Although the functions of these attention-drawing conventions may appear so obvious as to require no comment, not all readers either understand their implications or routinely pay attention to them.

Connectives are another explicit system conveying structural organization. Essentially, they are a specialized subgroup of linguistic cues whose main function is to express the underlying coherence relations. Four basic types have been identified (Halliday & Hasan, 1976): temporal (before, after), additive (and, in addition), causal (because, consequently), and adversative (however, nonetheless). By linking information appearing in two adjacent sentences, connectives directly contribute to local coherence building. Therefore, abilities to extract relational information from connectives and incorporate it in the emerging textbase are essential for successful comprehension.

Texts also use a variety of other devices that signal global coherence relations. They indicate, for example, how paragraphs relate to the main theme of the text and how ideas are linked across paragraphs. For example, relevance indicators (pointer words and phrases, such as "thus," "to reiterate," and "let me emphasize") help readers focus their attention on the information directly relevant to the major point. Summary indicators ("in sum," "by way of summary," and "in conclusion") alert readers that the designated content focuses on the main ideas of a paragraph, or even a longer segment. Enumerators (e.g., first, second, last), moreover, hint at the relationship of a particular discourse point to a global text organization, promoting comprehension by providing a structural frame for organizing text information. These devices are particularly useful when reading expository texts, because they indicate specific content for emphasizing, previewing, and summarizing (Lorch, 1989).

Co-reference is another system used to connect text elements between sentences. Halliday and Hasan (1976), in their time-honored book, explained co-reference as linguistic elements that can be interpreted only through references to other parts of the text. As a case in point, in the sentence "John broke it," the semantic content of the pronoun "it" cannot be resolved, because the sentence lacks specific reference information. In this regard, the sentence is ambiguous because there is no way to determine what John broke. Co-reference, because of its functional dependency on other text elements, prompts readers to look elsewhere, backward and forward, for interpretation. *Anaphoric* referential forms require rereading previous content for interpretation, as in the case of "*Jane* made a nice sweater because *she* wanted to surprise John on his birthday." In other words, the pronoun *she* can be understood only by a backward reference to *Jane*. In contrast, the interpretation of *cataphoric* forms necessitates looking forward in the text, as in the sentence "Because of *his* highly regarded work ethic, no one doubts that *John* can finish the project within two days."

Holliday and Hasan identified several distinct co-reference forms:

(1) Repeated form: the *Prime Minister* recorded her thanks to the Foreign secretary. The *Prime Minister* was most eloquent.
(2) Partially repeated from: *Dr E. C. R. Reeve* chaired the meeting. *Dr Reeve* invited Mr Phillips to report on the state of the gardens.
(3) Lexical replacement: *Ro's daughter* is ill again. *The child* is hardly ever well.
(4) Pronominal form: *Ro* said *she* would have to take Sophie to the doctor.
(5) Substituted form: Jules has *a birthday* next month. Elspetyh has *one* too.
(6) Ellipted form: Jules has *a birthday* next month. Elspetyh has too. (Halliday & Hasan, 1976, p. 143)

These forms constitute a referential hierarchy, because varying degrees of lexicality affect referential rigidity. As an illustration, lexicality ranges from full lexical forms, as in (1) through (3) above, to more attenuated forms, as in (4) through (6). According to Halliday and Hasan, lexically fuller forms are referentially more rigid. A proper noun, say "Nancy," generally refers to the same person throughout the text, but pronoun interpretations are more flexible because they change their referents from one context to another. The pronoun *she*, for example, can refer to any number of different females in a text.

Co-reference forms, moreover, differ in the degree to which their interpretation is constrained by the surrounding context (Garrod & Sanford, 1994). Compare the following sentences:

(1) Nancy ran into Jane and *Nancy* complained about a neighbor.
(2) Nancy ran into Jane and ϕ complained about a neighbor.
(3) Nancy ran into Jane and *she* complained about a neighbor.

The use of proper nouns generally reduces semantic ambiguity. In this regard, sentence (1) is semantically constrained, permitting only one interpretation. Using elliptical forms, as in sentence (2), imposes syntactic constraint – only Nancy could be the complainer. Sentence (3), however, allows either Nancy or Jane to be the referent of the pronoun *she*. Hence, pronoun interpretation is less constrained both syntactically and semantically. Moreover, various co-reference forms function differently in discourse. Whereas fuller lexical forms may initiate new referent relations, attenuated forms are restricted to already-established relationships. These differences explain their distinct usage. For example, lexical replacement commonly occurs without antecedents; pronoun usage is restricted by both semantic and syntactic constraints. The following example illustrates this point:

Mary likes to go to Valentino's for lunch. She fancies **the waiter** there. For dinner, she prefers Le Grand Bouffe, where the food is better but **the waiter/*he** is not nearly so handsome. (Garrod & Sanford, 1994, p. 678)

In this context, the pronoun *he* is unacceptable, because its interpretation is syntactically restricted to the waiter at Valentino's, but the semantic interpretation indicates that the Valentino's waiter is obviously a different person from the Le Grand Bouffe waiter.

In short, co-reference is a critical device for connecting text elements beyond sentence boundaries. Referential resolution, however, entails far more than simple mappings of anaphors onto their antecedents. Successful resolution necessitates, among other things, sensitivity to semantic and syntactic constraints, particularly when lexically attenuated forms are used as co-references.

Establishing coherence through inference

To recapitulate, constructing coherent textbases entails the integration of successive propositions into a meaningful whole. Texts, however, may not provide the necessary relational information for the required linking operations. Prior knowledge, therefore, must be activated to resolve relational gaps through inference. What, then, is *inference*? Several distinct definitions currently are in use: for example, "information that is activated during reading yet not explicitly stated in the text" (van den Broek, 1994, p. 556), "text base arguments and propositions that were not explicitly mentioned in a message" (Singer, 1994, p. 480), and "an inference represents encoded (non explicit) features of the meaning of a text" (McKoon & Ratcliff, 1989, p. 335). Seemingly, two common properties inherent in these definitions constitute the core essence of inference: An inference is information not explicitly stated in the text, and it arises from the need to mentally bridge voids in explicitly stated text elements. In sum, inference generation occurs in the normal course of reading and is an essential competence underlying text-meaning construction. However, the causal linkage between comprehension and inference is hardly one-directional, because the two are functionally interdependent.

Because text-information processing is constrained by restricted attentional capacity, it is generally assumed that only a subset of all possible inferences is generated during discourse comprehension. Questions then arise as to which specific types of inferences constitute the subset and how they contribute to text-meaning construction. Inasmuch as two dominant types of inferences – bridging and elaborative – have been the focus of intense scrutiny, they are briefly described in the following sections.

Bridging inferences

Bridging inferences occur automatically during the propositional analysis necessitated for establishing local coherence. In the following example, "The tooth was pulled painlessly. The dentist used a new method" (Singer, 1994, p. 487), no explicit cues indicate that the two sentences are related. Yet, it is not difficult to recognize them as connected. What links them, in this instance, is the realization that the tooth was pulled by the dentist. Obviously, the linking element stems from the reader's inference based on previous knowledge about tooth extraction.

The factor distinguishing those successful and unsuccessful in generating bridging inferences is the ability to recognize the underlying semantic connection between two seemingly unrelated statements. The following sentence sequences are illustrative:

(1) We got the beer out of the car. It was warm.
(2) We got the picnic supplies out of the car. The beer was warm.
     (Singer, 1994)

In sequence (1), interpreting the pronoun "It" is relatively simple, because its antecedent, "the beer," appears in the preceding sentence. In this case, coherence is established through co-reference resolution on the basis of explicitly stated information. In contrast, neither statement in sequence (2) provides any indication of their underlying semantic affiliation. Conjoining the sentences, therefore, is achieved through inferring an unstated element explaining their alliance – that is, "the beer" was part of the "picnic supplies." Without this inference, recognizing that picnic supplies and beer share the same referent is hardly attainable.

Bridging inferences also are necessary when identifying causal linkages among text statements. Because causal relations are fundamental in narrative texts, two particular kinds of causal connections, physical and psychological, have attracted serious research attention. For example:

(1) Kim pushed the wine glass accidentally. It broke into small
     pieces. (physical causation)
(2) Jane has a job interview today. She could not sleep at all last
     night. (psychological causation)

Here again, no explicit relational information is provided in either sequence. Therefore, if the sentences in each sequence are to be perceived as connected elements, their underlying relationships must be inferred. The linking operation in sequence (1), for example, depends on the realization that the wine glass was placed at the edge of something standing well above the floor, based on two pieces of explicitly stated information: that is, Kim pushed the glass, and it broke into small pieces. In sequence (2), the reader must perceive that the interview was very important for Jane. Thus, her strong desire to do well caused her to lose a good night's sleep. Hence, the primary step in making causal bridging inferences is to identify possible causal elements unstated in the text. Empirical studies, it should be noted, demonstrated that reading time for statements describing outcomes increases systematically as causal relatedness decreases (e.g., Keenan, Baillet, & Brown, 1984; Singer, Halldorson, Lear, & Andrusiak, 1992). This finding is of major significance in that it suggests that readers do indeed make causal inferences when reading sequential sentences and, even more critically, that the degree of causal relatedness seriously affects inference generation.

Elaborative inferences

Whereas bridging inferences are essential in propositional textbase construction, the other form, elaborative inferences, is necessary for situation model building. Unlike bridging inferences, elaborative inferences are not automatically generated as by-products of coherence building. Rather, their generation relies on the reader's intention to expand and elaborate on explicit text information. Successful inference generation, therefore, in large part can be predicted by the extent that content-relevant knowledge is readily available to the reader during text processing (Long, Seely, Oppy, & Golding, 1996). In narrative texts, for example, elaborative inferences can supply unstated intervening incidents that connect seemingly unrelated events. Narrative comprehension, therefore, can be described as the process of asking a series of "why" questions about story events, and elaborative inferences are analogous to answering those questions. Hence, elaborative inferences, although their generation may not be obligatory, contribute much to global semantic coherence and are integral in discourse comprehension.

Factors affecting inference generation

A long list of variables is known to affect inference generation during text processing. Because working memory affords the work space for mental computation and temporary storage of segmental information, the simultaneous presence of to-be-linked propositions in working memory is a critical condition for inference generation (e.g., Ehrlich & Johnson-Laird, 1982; Hayth-Roth & Thorndyke, 1979). Thus, the physical proximity of the concepts to be conjoined is a key factor affecting inference processing. When nonadjacent statements are to be linked through inference, additional conditions, such as the presence of unanticipated elements, become necessary. Causal-inference studies, for example, show that sentences containing surprises are more likely to remain active in working memory, beyond what immediately follows, and therefore facilitate inference generation even when the statements are not closely placed (e.g., Duffy, 1986; Fletcher & Bloom, 1988).

Text structure also affects inference generation. The specific ways text information is presented instigate particular processing procedures, requiring qualitatively different inferences (Singer, 1994). Perrig and Kintsch (1985), in fact, tested text-structure effects by comparing comprehension performance on two texts, describing a fictitious town in either survey or route formats. The survey text described the town from the perspective of an aerial observer looking down and using map positions, such as north and south. The route text provided equivalent information in the form of directions for driving through the town. After reading either the survey or the route text, participants took a sentence-verification test, in which they were asked to verify verbatim or inference statements. Performance was superior when inference sentences corresponded with the text version they read. Consequently, the researchers concluded that inference generation was closely tied to a situation model in the form of a mental map or the procedural representation of the town. Apparently, structure-specific processing requirements entail particular kinds of inferences, which then produce distinct situation models, highlighting different aspects of what is described.

Yet another discourse-related factor deals with the thematic status of individual text ideas (e.g., Cirilo, 1981; Fletcher & Bloom, 1988; Goetz, 1979; Walker & Meyer, 1980). Concepts in a text can be classified as either thematic or peripheral information, depending on their relevance to the text's main theme. Thematic information, because of its semantic centrality, is higher in the structural hierarchy of the textbase, as well as more strongly linked with other text elements. The thematic ideas, therefore, are likely to remain active in working memory longer than peripheral information, thus constituting stronger bases for inference generation.

In addition to discourse-related variables, reader characteristics have also been subjected to empirical examinations. Two reader-related factors in particular are widely regarded as essential for inference generation: working-memory capacity and background knowledge. Inasmuch as working memory is not a static entity, its capacity varies among individuals (e.g., Daneman & Carpenter, 1980, 1983). Considering the trade-off between the memory's dual functions – processing and storage – everything affecting propositional computation (lexical and syntactic knowledge, decoding efficiency, etc.) contributes to determining how much capacity is available for storage. Indeed, empirical evidence suggests that differences in working-memory capacity are directly associated with bridging-inference performance, particularly when the information to be linked appears in nonadjacent sentences (e.g., Daneman & Carpenter, 1980; Singer et al., 1992).

A second reader-related factor, background knowledge, was directly addressed in a well-known study by Anderson and associates (Anderson, Reynolds, Schallert, & Goetz, 1977). By comparing interpretations of the same text among two groups of college students, the researchers clearly demonstrated how readers' background knowledge alters text interpretation. A critical portion of the text they used for the study was as follows:

What bothered Spike most was being held, especially since the charge against him had been weak and the lock that held him was strong but he thought he could break it.

The two groups of students, one majoring in music and the other in physical education, made entirely different interpretations. Music students conjectured that Spike was a prisoner, planning to escape from a cell, whereas physical education majors were strongly inclined to picture him in a wrestling match, trying to escape his opponent's hold.

Singer (1994) offered a plausible explanation by describing precisely how background knowledge alters interpretations. As noted earlier, a major task in discourse processing lies in differentiating thematic from peripheral information. Because this process is dictated by readers' appraisals of the comparative significance of individual text ideas, what is considered thematic information is heavily prejudiced by their content knowledge. Consequently, the thematic/peripheral distinction varies across readers to the extent that their knowledge bases differ. Therefore, background knowledge strongly affects inference generation by influencing thematic status decisions. The place of reader knowledge in comprehension is discussed more fully in the sections that follow.

Functions of knowledge in text comprehension

It is plain that background knowledge influences all aspects of text-information processing. A simplistic explanation would suggest that a text is better understood when its content is familiar to the reader. An impressive body of research, however, demonstrates that the relationship between knowledge and comprehension is neither simple nor straightforward. Knowledge is not a unidimensional construct, and it contributes in multiple ways to discourse understanding. There is a general consensus that various aspects of knowledge differentially affect comprehension because of their distinct functions. Three specific aspects have been studied extensively: general, domain, and formal.

General knowledge of the world: Schema as structured knowledge

A schema is an abstract knowledge structure (Anderson & Pearson, 1984). It is abstract in that it does not detail individual instances.

Rather, it generalizes abstract information from a variety of instances. Schemas also are structured in that they denote the relationships among their component elements. Such structured understanding, according to Anderson and Pearson, provides conceptual scaffolding for organizing and interpreting newly encountered experiences. Dooling and Mullet (1973) moreover, demonstrated how text comprehension is guided by structured content knowledge. They devised a passage:

The procedure is actually quite simple. First, you arrange the items into different groups. Of course one pile may be sufficient depending on how much there is to do. If you have to go somewhere else due to lack of facilities that is the next step; otherwise, you are pretty well set. It is important not to overdo things. That is, it is better to do too few things at once than too many. In the short run this may not seem important but the whole procedure will seem complicated. Soon, however, it will become just another facet of life. It is difficult to foresee any end to the necessity for this task in the immediate future, but then, one never can tell. After the procedure is completed one arranges the materials into different groups again. Then they can be put into their appropriate places. Eventually they will be used once more and the whole cycle will then have to be repeated. However, that is part of life.

The passage contains many lexical items, such as "somewhere" and "facilities," whose interpretation is highly context-dependent. Because the passage does not provide sufficient information for disambiguating them, text comprehension is difficult. The availability of structured knowledge, or schema, should promote inferences that make semantic interpretation of the obscure words possible, thus facilitating comprehension. In the study, the researchers gave the title "Washing Clothes" to one group of participants before reading the passage and to another group after reading the passage. A third group did not receive the title. Post-reading recall data showed that the group made aware of the title before reading clearly outperformed the other two groups. Obviously, the title allowed activation of the "clothes-washing" schema, assisting readers in interpreting the obscure terms (e.g., "somewhere" referring to "laundromat" and "facilities" indicating "a washing machine and a dryer") by connecting text information and their real-life experience. When schema activation was blocked, however, readers were unable to make appropriate inferences about these terms solely on the basis of explicit text information, and, as a result, they remained ambiguous and semantically disconnected from the rest of the text. As Anderson and Pearson (1984) noted, "arbitrary information is a source of confusion, slow learning, slow processing, and unsatisfactory reasoning" (p. 286).

In the strongly affirmative version of schema theory, schemas and other structured knowledge, such as frames (Minsky, 1975), scripts (Schank & Abelson, 1977), and scenarios (Sanford & Garrod, 1981), are seen as cognitive control mechanisms, which regulate knowledge activation by filtering out inappropriate information. The schema is regarded as the element responsible for suppressing the activation of irrelevant information, predisposing the reader to interpret input in certain fixed ways. The theory thus attributes variations in text interpretation among readers with diverse backgrounds to this sort of top-down conceptualization.

Strong top-down explication is not universally accepted, however. Mental-model theories, described earlier, postulate different explanations for knowledge-activation patterns and their subsequent information elaboration. Kintsch (1994, 1998), for example, proposes the construction-integration model, positing that knowledge activation is "an uncontrolled, bottom-up process, determined only by the strength of the associations between items in long-term memory and the text" (1994, p. 733). Hence, the model renounces the possibility that cognitive structures, such as schematas, override explicit text information. Kintsch, in fact, contends that irrelevant information in memory is indeed activated by text input during propositional analysis, but is quickly deactivated when it fails to satisfy the constraints (e.g., syntactic, semantic, and pragmatic) imposed by the remainder of the text. The Kintsch model, consequently, offers a different explanation of why less-skilled readers are more susceptible to incomplete understanding and misinterpretation – namely, their textbase-construction (propositional computation and linking) skills are not sufficiently adequate to create the necessary constraints, thereby permitting irrelevant information to remain active during the integration process.

Domain knowledge

What is extracted from any given text can be predicted largely by the reader's knowledge of the content (Anderson & Pearson, 1984). The availability of a solid content-specific conceptual base is even more crucial in highly specialized texts, because other requisite competencies (e.g., IQ and verbal ability), as well as general background knowledge, do not adequately compensate for insufficient domain knowledge (e.g., Moravcsik & Kintsch, 1995; Recht & Leslie, 1988). Moravcsik and Kintsch (1995) compared the relative utility of three critical factors in text comprehension: clarity of text presentation, reading skills, and domain knowledge. All three variables were significantly related to recall of explicitly stated text information, but the regeneration of constructive/elaborative information was seriously impaired among those lacking in domain knowledge. The clear implication is that, while verbal skills and text clarity may be sufficient for analyzing surface text forms and generating propositions, they do not substitute for domain knowledge during situation-model building.

It is important to note that, in understanding the specific contribution of domain knowledge, there is a clear distinction between learning from a text and remembering its content. Kintsch (1998) contends that remembering entails the ability to reproduce the text verbatim or through summarization, whereas learning requires the capacity to use freshly acquired information productively in a new context. Remembering, therefore, necessitates building strong memory traces through the construction of multiple text representations. New insights derived from a text, however, cannot automatically be put to productive use until they are incorporated as an active component in the existing knowledge base. Patently, such conceptual assimilation is far easier when the reader has a well-established, content-specific knowledge base. This explains why domain experts are likely to extract more information, both new and old, than novice learners from any given text in their specialization.

Formal knowledge

As already noted, languages have built-in systems signaling a text's structural organization by indicating the interconnections among its components and their relative significance for meaning making. Over time, readers become sensitive to the specific ways content information is arranged to make the text a coherent whole. A knowledge of the specific devices used to achieve text coherence and structural organization is therefore pivotal. A large number of studies verify that text-structure knowledge greatly enhances text comprehension and memory. For example, stories are better remembered when they conform to the expected structure stemming from the goals and needs of particular protagonists (e.g., Mandler & Johnson, 1977; Stein & Glenn, 1979). During situation-model building, readers make extensive use of temporal and locative markers that signal the event structure (e.g., Haenggi, Gernsbacher, & Bollinger, 1993; Zwaan & Radvansky, 1998). Further, the availability of explicit linguistic devices marking the global structure of expository texts greatly improves recall performance (e.g., Meyer, Brandt, & Bluth, 1980). Similarly, departure from structural expectations seriously impairs text comprehension (e.g., Goldman, Cote, & Saul, 1995; Stein & Nezworski, 1978).

It should be noted, moreover, that structural organization varies widely across text genre, and, even more critically, that understanding such genre-specific structural properties is totally dependent on broad experience with diverse text types. Studies demonstrate that structural awareness correlates with amount of schooling (e.g., Danner, 1976; Garner et al., 1986), and explicit text-structure training improves text comprehension (e.g., Meyer et al., 1980; Pearson & Fielding, 1991). These findings suggest that, while text-structure awareness enhances discourse processing, its acquisition occurs only through formal training and substantial reading experience. Variance in text-structure knowledge across discourse genres is discussed further in the following chapter.

Factors affecting L2 discourse processing

In view of the numerous operations required for constructing mul-tilayered text representations, we can easily anticipate that, because of enlarged intricacies attributable to dual-language involvement and other unique L2 factors, L2 discourse processing is considerably more complex and demanding. This section explores impacts of L2-specific factors on two major discourse-processing operations: textbase construction and situation-model building.

L2 textbase construction

Construction of propositional textbases involves two major processes: propositional computation and coherence building. Because the former is achieved through analysis of the text's surface form, L2 linguistic sophistication – lexical and morphosyntactic knowledge, in particular – is a key factor determining its success. However, in addition to linguistic knowledge, the latter necessitates a functional grasp of discourse devices signaling local and global coherence. Although these basic requirements in themselves do not differ between L1 and L2 discourse processing, there is reason to believe that coherence building in L1 and L2 is facilitated by completely different variables. The discussion here focuses on L2-specific variables affecting L2 text-coherence building.

Explicit coherence markers – conjunctions and enumerators, for example – may function disparately in L1 and L2 text processing. If, like most other lexical items, these markers are learned through L2 definitions or L1 translations, their information is likely to be stored in the same way as other L2 content words. Because of the relatively small number of entities, however, as well as their repeated occurrences in and across texts, connective devices, conceivably, may be more firmly established in lexical memory and therefore more accessible than many content words. Should this be the case, it is probable that coherence markers can be used to compensate for limited lexical knowledge. If, for example, through repeated exposures, the reader knows the causal implication of *because*, the knowledge can be applied to constrain semantic possibilities of unfamiliar words in the sentence.

Also, referential resolution is, as noted repeatedly, a critical operation in local coherence building. However, identifying the correct antecedent of lexically attenuated forms (e.g., pronouns and ellipses) is not always easy, even for L1 readers. In L2 reading, cross-linguistic variations in referential expressions make this operation even more difficult. For example, languages differ in the possibilities they allow for subject ellipsis (Berman & Slobin, 1994). Subject ellipsis in the main clause, for example, is permitted in Spanish and Japanese, but not in English. Although the grammatical subject can be omitted in conjoined clauses in both English and Spanish, as in "Nancy ran into Jack and ϕ complained about a neighbor," different interpretations are required in the two languages when a third-person subject pronoun is added to a second clause. English permits such additions without any change in meaning, as in "Nancy ran into Jack and she (Nancy) complained about a neighbor." However, the equivalent construction in Spanish indicates a shift in subject, mandating the interpretation that someone else, other than Nancy, did the complaining. Conceivably, such variation in the syntax of subject expression, as well as other differences/preferences in referential forms, may have detectable impacts on both the efficiency and the manner in which lexically attenuated reference forms are interpreted during L2 text processing.

Finally, L1 literacy experience – more precisely, nonlinguistic aspects of L1 comprehension ability – constitutes yet another factor affecting L2 coherence building. For instance, lacking an adequate conception of "text coherence," readers can hardly be expected to engage in coherence building. Because such awareness develops only through repeated experience with connected texts, differences in L1 reading experience presumably can be a reliable predictor of the degree of attention given to text coherence during L2 reading comprehension. Moreover, many nonlinguistic skills developed in L1, such as distinguishing thematic and peripheral information and identifying underlying semantic relationships among propositions, should facilitate L2 coherence building, because these skills are not language specific – once developed in one language, they can, in principle, be applied to another. Little is known, however, about the extent to which L1 coherence-building skills are actually used during L2 text comprehension. Much could be gained by uncovering the necessary conditions under which non-language-specific L1 comprehension skills can be used in facilitating L2 textbase construction.

L2 situation-model building

Given the centrality of background knowledge in situation-model building, a natural assumption would be that L1 conceptual knowledge is a major source of individual differences in L2 text comprehension. The crucial questions, then, are to what extent and how. We could easily expect, for example, that L2 text comprehension can be aided to the extent that L1 knowledge is relevant and/or applicable to a particular situation depicted in an L2 text. It would then follow that L2 situation-model building may become progressively more difficult as the quantity of culture-specific information in a text increases. There are two ways that comprehension can be impaired when considerable cultural-specific knowledge is incorporated in a text. Because widely shared cultural information typically is not elucidated, if the reader does not possess the presumed knowledge, conceptual gaps are likely to occur. These gaps will leave large text segments semantically disconnected, and fragmented situation models may result. Another possible impediment is that L2 readers will draw on their L1 cultural knowledge to interpret unfamiliar elements they encounter in the text. Although this is a logical option for conceptually sophisticated L2 learners, conceptual adaptation could easily lead to misinterpretation, particularly when the two cultures have little in common.

Because the major characteristics of adult L2 readers include a reasonably solid conceptual base and limited L2 knowledge, top-down, conceptually driven processes presumably dominate L2 text processing, at least until adequate L2 knowledge develops. If valid, this supposition has two important implications. Adult L2 readers may be more susceptible than beginning L1 readers to misunderstanding and misinterpretation, simply because they rely more heavily on background knowledge than text information. At the same time, however, their reliance on conceptual knowledge can have a strong, facilitative impact in particular text genres, such as highly specialized texts requiring substantial domain knowledge. Multiple factors support the postulation. Although insufficient domain knowledge cannot be compensated for in specialized texts, such knowledge often offsets inadequate linguistic sophistication. Highly specialized texts generally are structured in a particular presentation format commonly accepted among domain specialists, and, as a consequence, their organization can be easily detected. Further, because special meanings often are assigned to technical terms, content understanding depends more heavily on knowledge of domain-specific jargon than on general vocabulary knowledge.

As a general rule, although L1 conceptual maturity can outweigh restricted L2 linguistic sophistication, when dealing with conceptually familiar texts, reliance on compensatory use of knowledge can have negative consequences. If readers engage in cursory top-down, conceptually driven processing, without sufficient attention to text information, their skills to extract and integrate linguistic (lexical and syntactic) information are not likely to improve. Moreover, when readers rely too heavily on prior knowledge, the resulting conceptions, reflecting what already is known, may not be what is intended in the text. And even more critically, if readers cannot detect such conceptual discrepancies, they may never acquire new insights from texts. Hence, learning through reading, a vital goal in academic pursuits, is not likely to occur.

Transfer of L1 skills during L2 text processing

Knowing that cross-linguistic transfer occurs in virtually every aspect of L2 processing, it seems logical to assume that transferred L1 competencies also play a role at the discourse level. Unlike decoding and syntactic parsing, however, many aspects of discourse processing are not automated. Therefore, we must anticipate substantially different L1 reading skills involvement. As a case in point, although automatic activation of L1 procedures may typify lower-level processing-skill transfer, the use of L1 skills cannot occur at this level in a similar mechanical fashion. Put simply, because much of L1 lower-level processing is automated, its activation likely is triggered by the L2 input regardless of the reader's intention. Discourse-level skills, in contrast, generally are poor candidates for automaticity, because many of the operations involve conceptual manipulations. Presumably, only a few higher-level L1 competencies are transferred via automatic activation. Text-structure knowledge could well be one such capacity. Because it is used in integrating partially assembled text information into global organizational frames, and because these frames generally are implicit in texts, it is logical to anticipate that well-established L1 structural expectations are likely to kick in and guide L2 coherence building. If this postulation is valid, an important implication results. Content misunderstanding and comprehension breakdowns still could occur with accurately computed propositions if they are improperly integrated, using incongruent L1 text-structure schemas. Comprehension problems, therefore, may continue even after high-level L2 lexical and morphosyntactic knowledge, essential in propositional computation, has been attained. In short, capability at one level does not obviate vulnerability at another. Additional impacts of L1 text-structure knowledge on L2 comprehension are discussed in Chapter 8.

Although processing transfer, presumably evolving from automatic L1 activation, plays a relatively minor role in L2 discourse processing, many useful L1 competencies can be brought into play at the reader's volition. In such intentional "borrowing," different factors influence both the extent and the utility of the L1 tactics used. For example, metacognitive awareness – that is, familiarity with one's cognitive-skills repertoire – provides a basis for determining which skills to invoke. Many so-called comprehension strategies, such as monitoring and repairing, are not language specific and therefore can be used with any language. But, because their implementation must be conscious rather than automatic, readers' awareness of their cognitive resources, as well as their intentions, should dictate which skills are activated. These possibilities are explored more fully in Chapter 10. Further research in unveiling the conditions fostering intentional transfer during L2 text comprehension is needed to determine how instruction and practice can maximize its utility.

Studies on L2 discourse comprehension

In view of the relatively brief history of L1 text-comprehension research, it is not surprising that only a handful of studies exploring mental representations among L2 readers are on record. In light of L2-specific factors, the formation of mental representations is likely to differ among L1 and L2 readers. Determining how L2 learners construe and recall text content, therefore, should have vital significance. An overview of two related lines of inquiry – issues regarding background knowledge and text coherence – are illustrative of current L2 text comprehension research.

Text representations among L2 readers

Initial attempts at seeking systematic approaches to examining text representations among L2 readers are under way. The basic issues at stake include how limited linguistic sophistication affects L2 mental representations, and whether L1 or L2 is predominantly used in mental model construction. Although still limited in number, studies have yielded important clues about the unique nature of L2 discourse processing, warranting further explorations and validations.

Jenkin and associates (Jenkin, Prior, Richard, Wainright-Sharp, & Bialystock, 1993), for example, compared mental representations emerging from L1 and L2 texts, using a framework proposed by Johnson-Laird and his colleagues (Ehrlich & Johnson-Laird, 1982; Mani & Johnson-Laird, 1982). The fundamental premise of the original study was that the formulation of distinct text representations requires different forms of information. The following examples may be helpful in conveying the core conception inherent in the premise:

(1) The spoon is behind the knife.
     The knife is to the right of the plate.
     The fork is to the left of the plate.
(2) The spoon is behind the knife.
     The knife is to the right of the plate.
     The fork is to the left of the knife.

Sentence cluster (1) is determinate in the sense that the relationships among all the objects described (spoon, knife, plate, and fork) are specified. In contrast, cluster (2) is indeterminate because it allows more than one interpretation of the fork location. The basic hypothesis here is that different forms of text information – in this instance, determinacy state – are needed to form varying levels of text representation. Specifically, propositional networks can be constructed on the basis of either determinate or indeterminate descriptions with equal facility. Inasmuch as the mental-situation model is analogous to the situation described in the text, its construction necessitates, in addition to object depictions, an interpretation of their relationships, thus requiring determinate descriptions.

In a replication study involving L2 readers, Jenkin et al. (1993) incorporated an additional factor: language familiarity. Assuming that two factors – determinacy state (determinate versus indeterminate) and language familiarity (L1 versus L2) – both affect the way text information is represented, they hypothesized that mental models can be formulated only when determinate descriptions appear in a familiar language. The hypothesis was tested through two post-reading measures: classification and statement recognition. In the classification task, participants were asked to determine whether a diagram was consistent with the description provided. In the recognition task, they were instructed to rank a sequence of sentences according to their similarity to the statements appearing in the description. The classification data indicated that, when reading in L1, participants performed better with determinate than with indeterminate information, but virtually no determinacy effect was found in reading L2 texts. In the statement-recognition task, moreover, participants made far more false-positive responses (i.e., erroneously accepting statements that did not appear in the description) in paraphrases than both L1 and L2 inference sentences. The researchers contended that, although participants were capable of forming both propositional networks and mental models in their L1, only propositional representations seemed to be possible in their L2. The findings thus suggest a strong language-familiarity effect on situation/mental-model building, and also explain differential determinacy impacts on mental representation building in L1 and L2. In effect, the outcomes paved the way to a promising new area of research by demonstrating that the content information is represented differently in text memory during L1 and L2 processing.

In another pioneer study, Horiba and associates (Horiba, van den Broek, & Fletcher, 1993) compared L1 and L2 English readers' use of text-structure information (e.g., causal chain status and story-grammar categories) during narrative text comprehension. Within the causal network framework (Trabasso & van den Broek, 1985), it was hypothesized that coherent text representations contain both content information about individual story events and actions and relational information connecting the story elements. Analyzing recall protocols, they found that relational cues were indeed incorporated in text representations among both L1 and L2 readers. Further analysis, however, revealed that relational information encoded in the recalls differed qualitatively among the two groups. Although global-coherence markers were represented more prominently in text memory among L1 readers, greater sensitivity to local coherence information was observed in L2 readers' recalls. In addition, L2 readers made extensive use of their knowledge of coherence markers in inferring the meaning of unknown words and phrases. Their findings are particularly important because the study is the first empirical demonstration that coherence building is an integral part of L2 text processing. Moreover, their findings corroborate Jenkin's research, suggesting a strong possibility that L1 and L2 text representations vary qualitatively.

In a subsequent study, Horiba (1996) examined the role of elaboration in achieving local coherence in L2 text representations. In keeping with the causal network framework, she hypothesized that readers' active involvement in encoding causal relations among text statements would increase coherence in text representations, resulting in better comprehension and retention. In the study, L2 learners of Japanese read a series of sentence pairs, with various degrees of semantic relatedness, and then, upon presentation of one sentence in each pair, recalled its corresponding statement. The read-and-recall performance was compared under two conditions: study and elaboration. In the study condition, participants were asked to memorize each pair, as a unit, by reciting them three times. In the elaboration condition, they were told to form a coherent, three-line story, by inventing and inserting a new sentence between each pair. The outcomes showed that the semantic relatedness among the sentences differentially affected recall performance in the two task conditions. Closely related sentence pairs were more easily recalled in the study condition, but the advantage virtually disappeared in the elaboration condition, implying that elaboration provides definitive facilitation in establishing causal connections, which, in turn, enhances text memory.

All in all, these pioneer studies have established a fresh arena of inquiry within contemporary frameworks. Cumulatively, the findings point the way to promising new directions in L2 discourse-processing research. Much benefit could derive from further, well-focused studies.

Text-coherence building among L2 readers

Here again, relatively few studies investigating text-coherence building, one of the most critical discourse-processing operations, are on record. In general, the results hint that there are individual differences in the ability to use connective devices, such as co-referential ties (e.g., Berkemeyer, 1994; Demel, 1990, 1994) and logical connectors (e.g., Geva, 1992; Goldman & Murray, 1992; McClure & Geva, 1983). In a well-structured study, for example, Geva (1992) assessed skills in using relational information conveyed by conjunctions, at three processing levels – intrasentential, intersentential, and discourse – among college ESL learners in Canada. Not surprisingly, L2 oral proficiency related strongly to an understanding of the logical implications inherent in English conjunctions. Further, Geva's data suggest that identifying logical relationships in local contexts (within and between sentences) is a necessary capacity, but in itself does not guarantee success in subsequent global-coherence building in extended discourse. Geva views these results as indicative of a developmental pyramid describing "the growing ability of L2 readers to use the logical meaning of conjunctions in texts as their L2 proficiency increases" (p. 744).

In another well-controlled study, Goldman and Murray (1992) compared qualitative and quantitative differences in the functional understanding of four connectors (additive, causal, adversative, and sequential) among L1 and L2 readers of English. Using the cloze procedure, they found that the groups' performance patterns were similar across conjunction types – that is, accuracy rates were higher with additive and causal connectors than with adversatives and sequentials. Further analysis, however, revealed two distinct, but related, sources of errors among L2 readers, one directly stemming from failure to understand intersentential relations and the other associated with a strong tendency to apply causal interpretations when inferring connection between two successive statements. These results clearly corroborate those from the Geva study, further suggesting that general comprehension skills – directly associated with L2 proficiency rather than specific connector knowledge – are responsible for observed differences in connector-use ability among L2 readers.

To sum up, these initial efforts have opened new vistas for further research in L2 text comprehension. Insofar as learning from texts is the dominant source of knowledge expansion among students, it would seem advantageous to determine how it can be nurtured. Exploring the elements facilitating knowledge acquisition through reading could yield valuable insights in perpetuating learning in a second language.

Roles of background knowledge in L2 text comprehension

Aside from the discourse-processing studies described above, significant efforts have concentrated on unraveling the roles of background knowledge in L2 text comprehension. The results further reinforced the strong relationship between background knowledge and effective comprehension in L2 reading (e.g., Carrell, 1983, 1984b, 1987; Carrell & Wallace, 1983). Building on earlier findings, current research has further probed issues regarding the specific impacts of knowledge – general, culture specific, and domain specific – on text understanding.

General knowledge

Several studies have examined diverse elements affecting the use of prior knowledge during L2 text comprehension, including L2 proficiency (Hammadou, 1991; Poissant, 1990; Ridgway, 1997), contextual support (e.g., Roller & Matambo, 1992), and perceived text difficulty (e.g., Peretz & Shoham, 1990). The main line of inquiry, however, has focused on ancillary factors, such as topic interest and gender, in efforts to explain the reported links between prior knowledge and comprehension (e.g., Bugel and Buunk, 1996; Carrell & Wise, 1998; Hammadou, 1991; LeLoup, 1993; Poissant, 1990; Ridgway, 1997). For example, in an attempt to further clarify the relationship between prior knowledge and comprehension, LeLoup (1993) hypothesized that the two are linked indirectly through an intervening factor – topic interest. Because we tend to be more attentive when reading something we are interested in, topic interest, logically, can increase or decrease content familiarity, which, in turn, affects text comprehension. By distinguishing topic familiarity and interest, LeLoup was able to compare their relative contributions to reading comprehension among American high school students studying Spanish. Her data indicated that topic interest accounted for a significant degree of comprehension variance over and above prior knowledge and L2 proficiency. She also found a significant gender effect, earmarking its probable role in explaining gender-based differences in topic interest and variations in prior knowledge.

The gender issue, it might be noted, also was investigated in a large-scale study involving nearly three thousand high school students in the Netherlands (Bugel & Buunk, 1996). Based on the premise that gender-based differences in topical interest give rise to obvious variations in prior knowledge among male and female L2 readers of English, researchers speculated that text topics would predict comprehension performance among male and female students. Their results confirmed that differences do exist in both topic interest and prior knowledge between genders. More critically, the differences were directly associated with gender-based performance variations in text comprehension. Based on these results, the researchers concluded that "sex differences in L2 reading comprehension are affected by the topic of the text" (p. 24). Given the large sample size, their findings appear definitive, but the core issue – regarding the relationship between gender and topical interest – remains inconclusive.

In a subsequent study, Carrell and Wise (1998) made a further attempt to disentangle some of the knots among topic interest, content familiarity, and gender as variables affecting comprehension among college ESL learners. Isolating the two key variables – prior knowledge and topic interest – empirically, the researchers posed two critical questions: Is there any empirical basis to support their relationship? And if so, how is the relationship affected by L2 proficiency and gender? Curiously, their data showed no systematic connection between prior knowledge and topic interest, thus affording no empirical verification of the uncontested assumption that topic interest is causally linked to differentially established knowledge bases. Although neither topic interest nor familiarity in themselves explained the variance in text comprehension, severe impairment was observed among those who lacked both. The data also revealed that comprehension performance among male and female participants was differentially affected by topic interest. Male students performed better on texts involving their topical interest, whereas females scored higher on texts of low topical interest. The researchers argue that each of the three key factors – prior knowledge, interest, and gender – may have differential impacts among readers with varying cognitive and linguistic capabilities. Presumably, the Carrell and Wise study implies that the relationship between prior knowledge and comprehension is mediated by other variables, and therefore is not as straightforward as it appears.

Culture-specific knowledge

Culture-specific knowledge has also attracted some attention among L2 reading researchers. In their classic study on cultural effects, Steffensen, Joag-Dev, and Anderson (1979), using two passages describing either Indian or American wedding ceremonies, compared recall performance among American and Asian-Indian college students. Both groups not only recalled more information when reading a culturally familiar text, but also evoked greater elaboration from texts describing their own cultural events. Moreover, greater distortion occurred in recall protocols based on culturally unfamiliar texts. Because language proficiency was not an issue among Indian students educated in English, the researchers attributed the performance patterns to differences in their cultural knowledge.

Similar findings occurred among college ESL learners. Johnson (1980), for example, found that, among Iranian ESL readers, cultural familiarity had a stronger impact on text recall than linguistic complexity. A subsequent study by Johnson (1982) also showed that cultural familiarity (i.e., knowledge about Halloween) was a more reliable predictor of recall performance than text-specific vocabulary knowledge among advanced ESL learners. In more recent studies, attention has focused on the precise ways culture-specific knowledge facilitates text-meaning construction. Kang (1992), for instance, asked Korean graduate students to think aloud when reading a culturally unfamiliar story in English. The resulting protocols demonstrated that Korean ESL readers, when inferring about unfamiliar words and expressions, relied heavily on their L1 cultural schema, causing Kang to suggest that L2 text information is filtered through L1 cultural knowledge for semantic interpretation.

From a somewhat different perspective, Steffensen, Goetz, & Cheng (1999) compared the quality and quantity of text-induced imagery and emotional reactions among Mandarin-speaking learners of English in a Chinese university. They listed and ranked their mental pictures and affective responses after reading either a Chinese text describing a trip in China or an English text describing a similar trip in the United States. Their data suggested that, although the participants' perceptions of the vividness of their mental images and the strength of their emotional reactions did not differ between the groups, a good deal more imagery and stronger emotional responses were reported by the group reading the Chinese (L1) text. These findings seem to lead to two tentative conclusions: (1) Mental images emerging from L2 texts are less vivacious than those emerging from L1 texts; (2) however restricted, imagery and affect can be formed in the absence of total understanding. It is not clear whether the limited imagery induced by the L2 text is entirely attributable to insufficient cultural sophistication. Because the L2 text required three times longer reading time, it may be that limited linguistic knowledge – or a combination of insufficient linguistic knowledge and cultural unfamiliarity – account for restricted imagery generation during L2 text processing. Future studies should elucidate the relative contributions to situation-model building of L2 linguistic and cultural knowledge.

Domain knowledge

In a widely cited study, Alderson and Urquhart (1985) compared the reading performance of college ESL students when reading texts in their area of specialization and those in other disciplines. Two findings are particularly noteworthy: Students' comprehension is far superior when reading texts in their areas of specialization, and L2 proficiency limitations often can be reduced when reading domain-relevant texts. In short, subject-matter sophistication enhances the comprehension of academic texts. More important, perhaps, the findings hint at two possible conditions under which L2 readers' knowledge compensates for limited linguistic sophistication: possessing high-level esoteric domain knowledge, and a text centered on a highly specialized topic. Corroborating findings were reported by Goldman and Duran (1988) in a study investigating the cognitive processes involved in reasoning during comprehension. Learners were asked to think aloud while answering post-reading questions in an introductory oceanography text. Through a careful analysis of the think-aloud protocols, the researchers found that knowledge base was a stronger predictor of text learning than language proficiency. Their contention was that ESL students with strong domain knowledge can activate relevant conceptual information, stored in long-term memory, to fill in the gaps created by limited linguistic sophistication.

In a more recent study, Chen and Donin (1997) directly examined the effects of domain knowledge on text processing among Chinese biology students in Canadian universities, using two types of recall procedures: online recall prompted during reading, and retrospective recall assessed after the text reading. Both procedures confirmed that domain knowledge and L2 proficiency significantly affect comprehension, but their relative contributions differ considerably at various processing levels. Whereas local-level processing relied predominantly on linguistic knowledge, virtually every aspect of higher-level conceptual operations involved content knowledge. The researchers concluded that the "results were consistent with theories of discourse comprehension that view processing of local lexical and syntactic information and processing of semantic and higher conceptual information as being both multilevel and modular" (p. 209).

All in all, then, the role of background knowledge is equally significant in L1 and L2 text comprehension. Outcomes from L2 studies consistently demonstrate that various knowledge sources differentially affect comprehension operations, thus suggesting that the ways in which conceptual knowledge affects comprehension are complex, interfacing, among other things, with L2 proficiency, text types, and L1 comprehension ability. It is hoped that future studies will address the factors encompassing each of the three critical elements – texts, tasks, and readers – in clarifying how knowledge facilitates L2 text comprehension.

Summary and future research suggestions

This chapter has provided a brief overview of the major conceptualizations emerging from discourse-processing research over the past three decades. Contemporary comprehension theories express the strong conviction that text information is encoded in multilevel representations, ranging from surface linguistic forms to propositional networks conveying underlying text meanings, and also to mental models representing corresponding real-life situations. Research on text-coherence building, in contrast, delineates explicit connective devices signaling text coherence at local and global levels. The ability to incorporate relational information conveyed by these devices is directly related to comprehension and retention. Inference, as well, is a critical process endemic to reading, serving as an implicit device for text-coherence building. Multiple factors, both text- and reader-related, affect inference generation. Because comprehension stems from the integration of text information and prior knowledge, the precise functions of knowledge in discourse understanding have also been a central concern in discourse-processing research. We now are beginning to recognize the specific paths through which disparate knowledge sources – general, domain, and formal – contribute to the disparate operations involved in text-meaning construction.

Although still limited in quantity, over the past decade researchers have probed issues at the heart of L2 text processing. Empirical studies currently are demonstrating a broad array of new insights: Sufficient L2 proficiency (although what constitutes "sufficiency" has yet to be clarified) is needed for text-coherence building; text information is represented differently in memory when reading in L1 and L2; and domain knowledge is a more powerful predictor of learning from academic texts than is L2 proficiency. These findings further attest to the constructive nature of L2 reading. It is legitimate, therefore, to suspect that the mental-model theories currently prevalent in L1 discourse research might also create a viable framework for adequately characterizing the unique nature of L2 text-information processing. In view of the comparative conceptual sophistication of L2 readers, two issues offer fertile promise for future L2 discourse research: the compensatory mechanisms of background knowledge and L2-specific constraints on inference generation.

Additional explorations of background knowledge, particularly its interplay with L2 proficiency during comprehension (more background knowledge offsets low proficiency), deserve further attention. As noted earlier, L1 theories generally postulate that surface–form analysis and propositional computation precede conceptual integration, thus allowing situation-model building to operate on solid textbases. However, because of their limited linguistic sophistication, L2 readers are likely to construct situation models on insufficient and/or inaccurate textbases. Thus, it is logical to speculate that nonlinguistic competencies compensate, somewhat, in one way or another, for insufficient linguistic knowledge. Although empirical findings indicate that domain knowledge, in certain types of text, relates more strongly to comprehension performance than L2 proficiency, little is known about the precise ways in which conceptual knowledge countervails restricted linguistic resources in achieving text understanding. Because both prior knowledge and L2 proficiency are complex aptitudes, theoretically, each must be dissected in order to determine which specific knowledge forms offset deficiency in which particular L2 proficiency aspects.

There also is evidence that inference ability is a crucial factor in successful L2 text comprehension. Oddly, there has been little effort to unveil, on a scientific basis, either the specific processes involved in inferential generation among L2 readers or the conditions affecting it. L1 research, in contrast, has reached several significant conclusions. During reading, for example, inference is used to overcome conceptual gaps in a text. Presumably, three capacities are essential: well-developed text information-extraction skills, rapid access to prior knowledge, and adept use of working-memory resources. Because L2 linguistic knowledge has a profound and decisive impact on each of these elements, there is an obvious need for more investigations that disassemble and dichotomize the precise ways each of the above-mentioned capabilities is constrained by limited linguistic sophistication. In short, we need heavy-duty inferences about the place of inference in L2 text comprehension.

8 *Text structure and comprehension*

To reiterate a point in the preceding chapter, good texts are not a collection of randomly assorted sentences. Rather, they are carefully structured to convey semantic relationships among their elements, as well as to signal the comparative importance of discrete ideas. Significant elements, for example, often are placed in prominent text locations to highlight their relative weight and are connected with other text segments in clearly detectable ways. Coherent texts, moreover, have distinct, easily identifiable structural characteristics. Meyer and Rice (1984) define text structure as the specific ways in which "ideas in a text are interrelated to convey a message to a reader" (p. 319). Logically, then, knowledge of text structure should enhance text-meaning construction in measurable ways. Inasmuch as information emphasized in disparate discourse genres differs as a natural consequence of the diversity in communicative functions and intent, text structure also varies from genre to genre. Consequently, systematic analyses of text structure across discourse genres yield significant cues on an additional requirement underlying successful text comprehension.

The primary objective in this chapter, consequently, is to elucidate the specific impact of text-structure variables on discourse comprehension. At the outset, two major text types – narrative and exposition – are described and cross-linguistic comparisons of distinct text-structure properties are examined. On the basis of empirical findings, the role of structural variables in L2 text comprehension is then examined.

Narrative texts

Narrative texts share many characteristics with face-to-face oral communication. To illustrate, typical social interactions often involve the exchange of personal experiences, recounting what happened and why. The depiction of commonly shared experiences is customary, and their centrality in narrative discourse has two important, interrelated implications: Narrative discourse appeals to readers' shared knowledge of the world, and therefore it is easier to understand and recall than other types of texts. Although understanding the structural properties of nonnarrative text genres, such as exposition and argumentation, generally requires considerable training, such formal training is not essential in reading narrative discourse. Empirical studies, in fact, demonstrate that even preschool children have little difficulty grasping event sequences described in stories and folktales (e.g., Scollon & Scollon, 1981; Stein & Glenn, 1979), and recall capability among adult readers generally is far superior in narrative, than in expository texts (e.g., Freedle & Halle, 1979; Graesser, 1981).

Characteristics of narratives

Although there is no clear consensus about the precise definition of narratives, researchers generally concur on one major characteristic: Narrative discourse is embedded in a communicative exchange between speaker/writer and listener/reader. Graesser, Golding, and Long (1991), for example, proposed a definition in which the communicative element is heavily emphasized:

Narratives are expressions of event-based experiences that (a) are either stored in memory or cognitively constructed, (b) are selected by the teller/writer to transmit to the audience/reader, and (c) are organized in knowledge structures that can be anticipated by the audience. (1991, p. 174)

Broad agreement also has been reached about the central components of narrative discourse, including characters (animate beings exhibiting clearly specified goals and motives for their achievement), setting (the particular time frame and spatial location where the events are unfolded), complications (problems or conflicts encountered by main characters), plots (sequences of events), affect patterns (elements soliciting emotional intrigue), and values (morals emphasized in text). Another significant characterization is that narratives allow emphasis on the author's perspective by maneuvering event presentation. A single chain of events can be described in a number of different ways, and the impact of individual events, therefore, can be manipulated through deliberate omission and elaboration. The chronology also can be altered to underscore a specific event by using flashbacks, flash forwards, and embeddings. Structural manipulations of this sort used to emphasize authors' viewpoints provide a fertile terrain for slanting convictions.

Analysis of narrative texts

Over the past three decades, serious attempts have been made to identify typical structural organizations in narrative discourse. Two different approaches emerging from the research – story grammars and causal-network approaches – are widely used in ongoing narrative-comprehension studies.

Story grammar

A story grammar refers to the initial outcome of attempts to construct a formal device for analyzing narrative texts. The ultimate purpose is to describe the reader's implicit and explicit knowledge about the structural properties of stories and how such knowledge guides comprehension of a particular class of narratives – that is, simple, well-formed stories prevalent in the oral tradition, such as fairy tales and folklore (e.g., Mandler, 1984; Mandler & Johnson, 1977; Stein & Glenn, 1979). Although story grammars vary in details, their basic elements are consistent, typically containing one character, a conflict confronting the character, a goal sought, a plot depicting the character's sequential attempts to accomplish the goal, and a summation of the ultimate outcome. Rooted in structural linguistics, story grammars involve a number of common formal components designed to impart obligatory fundamental regularities. Mandler's grammar (1987), for example, postulates a set of node categories and rewrite rules, as follows:

 (1) Story → setting + episode
 (2) Episode → beginning + complex reaction + coal path + ending
 (3) Complex reaction → simple reaction + goal
 (4) Goal path → attempt + outcomes
 (5) Beginning → an event that initiates the complex reaction
 (6) Simple reaction → an emotional or cognitive response
 (7) Goal → a state that a character wants to achieve
 (8) Attempt → an intentional action or plan of a character
 (9) Outcome → a consequence of the attempt, specifying whether the goal is achieved
(10) Ending → a reaction

   Although restricted in scope, the grammars offer reasonably systematic and objective ways to describe the structural properties of stories – that is, how well they are constructed and formatted. Once applied to a particular story, the grammars assign a hierarchical structure for depicting the information explicitly presented in the text. During story parsing, therefore, the explicit, or surface, text elements – phrases, clauses, and sentences – are first segmented and then assigned to terminal node categories, whose interconnections are represented in a single tree structure.

Through the hierarchical ordering, story grammars establish principled means of predicting story comprehension. Story grammars predicted, for example, that the structural hierarchy of explicit text statements equate with their relative importance – that is, superordinate information in the hierarchy is more prominently represented in text memory than is subordinate information. Because of the varying prominence of individual node categories, story grammars also predict whether more salient nodes, such as setting, initiating events, and consequences, are more memorable than others. Canonical order, in addition, has been known to affect story comprehension and memory. In short, story grammars provide reasonably accurate predictions about increased comprehension difficulty in direct ratio to the extent that the presentation of text statements deviates from the canonical order of node categories.

By generating sizable sets of empirically testable predictions, story grammars have stimulated a considerable body of research. Comprehension studies, for example, consistently show robust impacts of node-category salience on story recall across cultures and ages (e.g., Mandler, 1984; Mandler & Johnson, 1977; Stein & Glenn, 1979). Others provide empirical support for the predicted effect of canonical event-statement order on passage recall (e.g., Mandler & Goodman, 1982). Reading-time data also revealed that readers habitually spend more time on sentences marking the beginning and ending of an episode (e.g., Mandler & Goodman, 1982), suggesting that the episode may be the fundamental unit of processing in story comprehension. Somewhat surprisingly, however, to date predictions about the relative importance attached to information hierarchy (i.e., superordinate versus subordinate) have minimal substantiation (e.g., van den Broek & Trabasso, 1986).

As a text-comprehension model, however, story grammars suffer major shortcomings – namely, they describe neither the conceptual basis nor constraints necessary for explaining plot development (Graesser et al., 1991). For instance, structural analysis of node categories fails to offer adequate explanations of what caused an event to occur, how the outcome affected the main character's emotional state, and what prompted him or her to take subsequent actions. As a consequence, story grammars are incapable of describing or explaining the crucial constructive aspects of discourse comprehension – elaboration, reasoning, inference, and so on.

Causal networks

In an attempt to overcome these shortcomings, the subsequent, causal chain approach – a contrasting method of narrative text analysis – has evolved from two related premises. Narratives describe how objects and characters are changed as a result of events and actions, and therefore causal relations among connected events, actions, and states constitute the dominant mental representation components (e.g., Black & Bower, 1980; Omanson, 1982). The decisive factor underlying this claim is that the causal-chain status is a pivotal element in predicting text-recall performance. According to van den Broek (1994), causal-chain statements describe a chain of connected events, actions, and states that are directly relevant to main plot development. Causal-chain statements, because of their centrality, sustain text flow by moving the story forward coherently. These statements are a sharp contrast to the dead-end sentences, which offer little or nothing to plot development. The central hypothesis is that the two types of statements – causal-chain and dead-end – are differentially represented in text memory. The hypothesis has been tested through a variety of measures: text recall, summarization, text statement importance ratings, statement groupings, and text reading time (Graesser et al., 1991). The studies do indeed demonstrate that causal-chain statements appear most frequently in text summaries and also receive higher importance ratings than dead-end statements (e.g., Trabasso & van den Broek, 1985). Importantly, the causal-chain prominence remained, even when identical statements were presented either as a segment of the causal chain or as dead ends (e.g., Omanson, 1982; Wolman, 1991).

The approach, however, is limited in several important regards (van den Broek, 1994). A causal-chain analysis, for example, presumes that a single event or action has only one consequence, posing a major constraint because it prohibits the analysis from identifying shared causality when multiple events conjoin to explain an outcome or shared impact when a single event has multiple consequences. Given the frequency of occurrences involving multiple causes and consequences in both actual and fictional situations, the limitations constitute a serious impediment. Further, when analyzing causal relations, the causal-chain approach is heavily dependent on intuitive judgments rather than on objective criteria.

Responding to these limitations, more sophisticated network theories, explaining the causal structure of narrative texts, have been proposed (e.g., Graesser, 1981; Trabasso, Secco, & van den Broek, 1984; Trabasso & van den Broek, 1985). Unlike the single linear structure assumed in the causal-chain analysis, network models presume that

Sample Narrative

Story grammar category[a]	Statement number	Statement
S	1	One day, Brian was looking through the newspaper.
IE	2	He saw an ad for some fancy CD players.
IR	3	He really liked the way they looked.
G	4	Brian decided he wanted to buy one.
A	5	He called the store for the price of a nice model.
O	6	He did not have enough money.
G	7	He decided to work a paper route.
A	8	For months he got up early,
O	9	so that he had his afternoons free,
A	10	and delivered the newspapers.
O	11	He quickly earned the $300 that he needed.
A	12	On his first day off, he went to the store.
O	13	He bought the CD player that he had wanted for so long.
C	14	He was so happy that he immediately organized a party.

[a] Story grammar categories are labeled as follows: Setting (S), Initiating Event (IE), Internal Response (IR), Goal (G), Attempt (A), Outcome (O), Consequence (C).

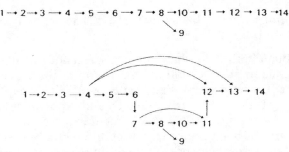

Figure 8.1   Causal-chain (top) and causal-network (bottom) representations of the sample narrative (reprinted from P. van den Broek, 1994, pp. 543, 545).

story events often stem from multiple causal antecedents, and also may have more than one consequence. Figure 8.1 contrasts the ways the two – chain and network – approaches graphically represent causal links in a text.

What is more, network models incorporate systematic procedures in identifying text causal relations. To wit, Trabasso, van den Broek, and Suh (1989) proposed judgment criteria consisting of two sequential elements: temporal order and necessity condition. Potential causes of an event are hypothesized provisionally. The two subcriteria are then applied sequentially: Are the possible causes *temporally prior* to the event in question, and are they *operative* at the point of occurrence? In the subsequent step, the potential causes are pitted against one another to determine which best explains, in the context of the story, why the target event occurred. Because of the multiple linkages assumed in causes and effects, network models predict that heavily connected event statements are more prominently represented in text memory. Empirical evidence, in fact, suggests that statements holding multiple causal connections are recalled more frequently, rated more important, and included more often in text summaries than those with fewer connections (e.g., Fletcher & Bloom, 1988; Trabasso & van den Broek, 1985; Wolman, 1991).

Another anticipation emanating from network models is that, aside from the statements themselves, their interrelationships also are encoded in the mental representation of a text. The models thus postulate that the strength of the causal connection between the antecedent and target statements is directly related to recall performance. The two sentence pairs below, taken from the Myers and Duffy 1990 study, are illustrative:

(1) Jimmy's big brother beat him up. The next day he was covered with bruises.
(2) Jimmy went to his friend's house. The next day he was covered with bruises.

Although both pairs share the target (second) sentence, they differ in the strength of the causal link between the antecedent and target sentences. The antecedent (first) sentence in pair (1) explains the cause of Jimmy's bruises much more directly and explicitly than that in pair (2). It can be foreseen, then, that if relational information is retained in memory, the two priming sentences differentially affect the memorability of the target sentence. The hypothesized effect was tested through a cued-recall task (Myers, Shinjo, & Duffy, 1987). Participants were asked to read a large set of sentence pairs and were then presented with one (antecedent) sentence from each pair. The task was to recall the accompanying (target) statement. The underlying logic was that, if the causal relationships were encoded in memory, there would be a perceptible difference in recall performance. Based on the network theory, the recall of statements in explicitly connected pairs, as in (1) above, was predicted to be superior to that in neutral pairs, as in (2). A follow-up instructional study (Myers & Duffy, 1990) yielded additional testimony to the significance of causal links in text representations.

Participants were given a series of analogous sentence pairs and asked to construct a causal connection, if it was not present, between two statements in each pair. The ensuing cued recall demonstrated that performance on the neutral pairs improved to the same level as the explicit pairs, intimating that the recognition of causal relations can perhaps be taught, and also that, in the event of their absence, reader deduction could improve text memory.

To recap, narrative texts have distinct structural characteristics, manifesting their mission of transmitting event-based experiences from author to audience. Serious efforts have been made to catalog these characteristics, together with their relation to narrative comprehension and memory. Whereas story grammars focus on simple, well-formed stories, more sophisticated network models explicate the causal structure of narrative texts. Studies suggest that the central components of mental representations in narrative text include connected events, actions, and states, as well as their causal relations.

Expository texts

Contrary to the defining nature of narratives – appealing to shared knowledge among readers – expositions essentially are informational, intended to induce new insights. As observed in the preceding chapter, much of the early research focused on formalizing the structural properties of expositions, and in so doing, highlighted the specific ways these variables affect text comprehension (e.g., Kintsch, 1974; Kintsch & van Dijk, 1978; Meyer, 1975; Miller & Kintsch, 1980). Two pioneer, widely used text analysis approaches, one proposed by Kintsch and his associates (e.g., Kintsch, 1974; Kintsch & van Dijk, 1978) and the other by Meyer and her colleagues (e.g., Meyer 1975; Meyer & Rice, 1984), deserve mentioning as a preface to exploring the cognitive processes involved in expository text comprehension within newer mental-model frameworks (e.g., Britton, 1994; Gernsbacher, 1990, 1996).

Propositional analysis: Kintsch's system

In the interests of cross-referencing, the Kintsch system uses propositions as the basic unit of analysis. Propositions, to recapitulate, represent the smallest text unit that can logically be falsified. A significant feature of propositions is their tendency to preserve text *meaning*, but not necessarily their surface linguistic forms. The Kintsch system assumes that texts can be broken down into propositions, which then can be linked together, on the basis of argument overlap so as to establish a network of propositions representing the underlying text meaning. As described in Chapter 7, although the text's microstructure is created by analyzing its surface form, the macrostructure is constructed through top-down operations by using summarization rules, such as deletion, generalization, and construction. The macrostructure thus can be seen as a strategically devised overall text organization, reflecting readers' responses to certain discourse cues signaling the relative importance of information. In short, the macrostructure is a separate organizational unit overlaying the propositional textbase rather than a summary layer derived from the text analysis.

The Kintsch system, despite its age, makes useful claims about text-structure impacts on comprehension. To wit, text elements appearing at higher levels of the structural hierarchy hold more prominent status in text memory than those relegated to lower levels. Higher-level information, therefore, is better retained and more easily accessed. The effects of the structural hierarchy on text memory have been extensively studied. The results indicate that content elements represented at the higher levels of the structural hierarchy were recalled more frequently and more accurately than those at the lower levels (e.g., Kintsch & Keenan, 1973; Kintsch, Kosminsky, Streby, McKoon, & Keenan, 1975; Manelis, 1980). Another finding was that the reader's ability to form macrostructures is a reliable indicator of reading ability. Macrostructure construction necessitates not only surface text analysis for proposition generation but also conceptual manipulations, such as generalization and synthesis, to reduce generated text-base propositions. Conceivably, then, both sets of skills discriminate good from poor readers. The possibilities have been substantiated by studies demonstrating that readers able to generate macrostructures extracted more information, with better retention, than those less sensitive to relative information significance (e.g., Kintsch, 1977; Kintsch & Vipond, 1979).

Text structure analysis: Meyer's system

Meyer's system also creates a hierarchical representation. Her approach, however, differs from the Kintsch system in several major ways. It utilizes the idea unit rather than the proposition as the basis of text-structure analysis. Idea units are similar to propositions in that they represent explicitly expressed text content. Unlike propositions, however, they also embody inferred relations inherent in text ideas. In the end, by converging these inferred relations, the system generates a monolithic, hierarchically organized representation of the text structure. In this regard, Meyer's top-level text structure corresponds to Kintsch's macrostructure even though the two evolve through completely different operations. Whereas the macrostructure is generated through a cognitive operator independent of text-based propositional analysis, the top-level structure is an outgrowth of such analysis. Meyer and Rice delineate five basic forms of top-level relationships:

(1) *An antecedent/consequent or covariance* rhetorical relationship shows a causal relationship between topics.
(2) A *response* rhetorical relationship includes the remark and reply, question and answer, and problem and solution formats.
(3) A *comparison* relationship points out differences and similarities between two or more topics.
(4) A *collection* relationship shows how ideas or events are related together into a group on the basis of some commonality.
(5) A *description* relationship gives more information about a topic by presenting attributes, specifics, explanations, or settings. (Meyer & Rice, 1984, pp. 326–327)

In their series of empirical studies, Meyer and colleagues confirmed that readers who recognize and utilize top-level structures remember more text ideas (e.g., Meyer, 1979, 1982; Meyer et al., 1980), top-level information is more likely to be recalled than lower-level items (Meyer, 1975, 1977), alternate top-level structures differentially affect text memory (Meyer & Freedle, 1984), and training in identifying top-level structures improves recall performance (Bartlett, 1978). Collectively, these findings make it plain that text-structure variables substantially affect how content information is represented in text memory.

Structure-building framework

The approaches just discussed focus mainly on text-structure variables and their connection with text memory. More recent models, however, emphasize the constructive nature of comprehension, attempting to explain the characteristics of mental text representation, as well as the processes used in its construction (e.g., Britton, 1994; Gernsbacher, 1990; Goldman, Varma, & Cote, 1996; Kintsch, 1994, 1998). The structure-building framework, proposed by Gernsbacher (1990), typifies one such endeavor. Its basic premise is that the goal of comprehension is to build coherent mental representations, referred to as "structure." The building blocks of structure are memory nodes. Three fundamental operations compose the critical components of structure building: foundation laying, structural mapping, and substructure progressing. When the reader encounters novel ideas, relevant information stored in long-term memory is activated. This initial activation constitutes laying a foundation. Once the foundation is laid, the next step is to develop a structure by incorporating incoming information cohering with previously introduced ideas. However, if the incoming information does not fit the current structure, the reader changes tactics, initiating a new structure.

The psychological reality of these central processes has been tested. Foundation laying, for example, is strongly supported by empirical results, showing that reading time is longer during the beginning segments of text chunks, such as the first word of a sentence and the first sentence of a paragraph (e.g., Aaronson & Ferres, 1983); sentences are better recalled when the content word appearing at the initial position is used as a cue (e.g., Bock & Irwin, 1980); and readers tend to regard the first sentence of a paragraph as its critical essence (e.g., Kieras, 1981). Empirical findings also support the practice of mapping by verifying that referentially coherent sentences are processed faster than those that lack coherence (e.g., Anderson, Garrod, & Sanford, 1983; Haviland & Clark, 1974). Finally, the process of structural shifting has been confirmed by the observation that the transitional elements of a text – words and sentences used to alter the topic or viewpoint – require considerably longer reading time and are more difficult to recall (e.g., Clements, 1979; Olson, Duffy, & Mack, 1984). In recent years, this and similar models have evoked renewed interest in text-information processing. It is because of them and more sophisticated kindred extensions that cognitive processes unique to expository text comprehension have been conceptually explored and empirically scrutinized.

Grammar of exposition

Within the structure-building framework, Britton (1994) proposed a grammar of exposition. In accordance with the framework's basic premises, he posits that the author of an expository text makes particular, characteristic moves for advancing the discourse, signaling how the structure can be reconstructed. If properly perceived, these moves can serve as instructions to guide readers through their structure-building processes. The governing contention is that expository texts are systematically coded for structural regularities, and therefore the grammar of exposition can be formulated as a set of rules to capture these regularities. In theory, consequently, the reader should be able to build the intended structure by following the author's directions. In actuality, authors do not always provide appropriate signals, and, as a result, structure-building instructions may be absent, incomplete, or ambiguous. Moreover, to follow cogent instructions, the reader must have an implicit understanding of the structural rules and their cues. Additionally, even when instructions are successfully interpreted, the reader is under no obligation to use them. In sum, successful expository text structure-building depends largely on the clarity and astuteness of the author's instructions, as well as on the reader's adeptness and diligence in following those instructions.

Britton's grammar consists of five fundamental mandates signaling the key moves: EXPAND, ENLARGE-ON, MOVE-ON, UNITIZE, and STOP. The first two, EXPAND and ENLARGE-ON, denote virtually the same function – expanding on the topic – which is the most basic step in expositions. When the topic to be enlarged is the overall text theme, EXPAND is used to indicate the operation occurring at the topmost discourse level. At all lower levels, however, the same move is denoted by ENLARGE-ON. At the middle levels, ENLARGE-ON means that the topic to be expanded is the text subsection. Expansion at the lowest level, also signaled by ENLARGE-ON, pertains to the newly introduced element in the previous sentence. Britton likens these moves to typical classroom teacher instruction: When students encounter difficulty grasping a point, teachers are likely to further explain the content through illustrations and examples to facilitate understanding. In similar fashion, authors use EXPAND with any text topic whenever they think it would be helpful to the reader. Theoretically, authors can continue EXPANDing to the limits of their knowledge, but they usually stop when they think the topic is sufficiently clear, or when there are space limitations. The topmost move, EXPAND, is then followed by operations such as UNITIZE (integrating the contents of active memory) and MOVE-ON (advancing to the next subtopic).

According to Britton, several other more implicit but equally useful clues also are used. Linguistic recurrence serves as an example. When a sentence contains a content word from the previous sentence, the reader can utilize lexical overlap to connect the two sentences. Typically, linguistic repetition informs the reader that the overlapped element usually is the enlarged-on target. A second form of implicit instructions is syntactic in nature, cueing the reader that a syntactically prominent element, say, the head of a noun phrase, is a possible topic for expansion. Yet another type of implicit clue lies in the way newly introduced information is displayed. The cue is important because new information is used to drive the discourse forward. When sentences contain more than one new element, however, problems can occur. The canonical positioning – placing the information to be enlarged near the end rather than at the beginning – helps the reader to determine which new element is most likely to be expanded in what follows.

For the structure-building instructions to function effectively, both readers and authors must be sensitive to the structural regularities in expository texts. Sensitivity of this sort varies widely. Insofar as authors of expository texts generally are experts in their fields, why incomplete and inaccurate instructions are so commonplace is puzzling. Ironically, author expertise sometimes cerates a liability in providing helpful instructions. Specialists sometimes underestimate the amount of explanation necessary to communicate effectively with novice readers. Britton, in fact, contends that "an important parameter determining the understandability of an expository text is the rate at which the author moves on" (1994, p. 663). Moreover, much of expert text processing is highly automated, adding further complications. Because of their ingrained automaticity, experts sometimes have difficulty reflecting on their own text-meaning construction processes, which may create impediments to their attention to a text's structural elements. As a result, they overlook essential structure-building instructions, thus requiring readers to construct the intended structure without explicit guidelines.

Learning from expository texts

The primary objective in reading an expository text is to gain insight on a given topic. Lonergan (1970) defines insight as enhanced understanding occurring when the reader senses either a new relationship among conceptual elements within a knowledge base or new conceptual relationships between multiple knowledge bases. According to Britton (1994), insight generation depends on two sequential operations: first building a mental structure, and then extracting a critical, or insight, proposition, which induces conceptual restructuring. Building on Britton's explications, what follows explores the formulation of insight-generating propositions. Consider the following statements as an illustration:

(1) Transferred L1 knowledge is a major source of interference in L2 learning.
(2) Transferred L1 knowledge has no impact on L2 learning.
(3) Transferred L1 knowledge can establish a basis for developing L2 knowledge.

For many readers in applied linguistics, these statements represent familiar concepts. When originally encountered, however, they represented novel concepts. In these sentences, for the reader to accept the underlying propositions as such, a set of basic premises must be either conveyed in the text or presumed to exist in the reader's prior knowledge. For example, statement (1) presumes that language and behaviors are acquired in similar fashion; language learning involves habit formation; and learning a new language necessitates the formation of new habits (L2), which eventually replace the old (L1). When these premises are connected logically, the intended insight stipulated in statement (1) occurs – that is, previously formed L1 habits interfere with the formation of new habits. In contrast, statement (2) cannot be accepted as valid unless the reader is convinced that L2 learning, like L1 acquisition, is governed by universal principles, and therefore L1 and L2 learning are essentially the same. Together, these convictions yield a critical insight: Transferred L1 knowledge plays no role in L2 learning. Neither set of premises underlying statements (1) and (2), however, is sufficient to justify statement (3). Behavioristic habit-formation conceptions provide little basis for assuming that the learner is actively involved in constructing the new system (L2). Similarly, the strong nativistic view negates the possibility that prior L1 learning experience contributes to L2 learning. Hence, for statement (3) to be convincing, the reader's conceptual foundation must first be reshaped through the incorporation of a special meaning into the pivotal concepts, such as language learning and knowledge acquisition, by either emphasizing or de-emphasizing particular aspects of the terms' original implication. Once appropriate conceptual reshaping has occurred, the resulting insight proposition establishes new links between the existing knowledge bases.

In statement (3), for example, the concept of language learning can be reshaped by emphasizing two aspects: The learning depends on *experience*, and its process is *constructive*. A newly shaped conception of language learning could then generate a novel insight that transferred L1 knowledge establishes a basis for developing another body of linguistic knowledge. Further, the additional acumen, stemming from the reconfiguration of existing conceptions, enables readers to reorganize their perceptions about existing relations among known conceptual elements by formulating altered conceptions about language transfer and linguistic knowledge formation. Such apperceptive restructuring also gives rise to subsequent corollary understanding – for example, "transferred L1 knowledge differentially facilitates L2 knowledge construction among learners with typologically diverse L1 backgrounds" – as well as "the transfer of non-language-specific competencies provides all L2 learners equal facilitation, regardless of their L1 backgrounds." Hence, the concept of conceptual restructuring explains, in part, why both degree and depth of text understanding differ widely among individuals with varying domain knowledge. Put another way, knowing more about the content means that each mental structure will have a larger number of nodes. When a new link is established between two or more well-developed knowledge bases, all constituent nodes in each structure also become connected. Hence, the more one knows about something, the more node connections expand exponentially.

To summarize, in addition to conveying content information, the objective of expository texts is to induce new insights. Through capitalizing on structural regularities, the goal of comprehension is to construct the text representations conveyed by the author, by following explicit and implicit devices signaling regularities. Early research focused on formalizing text-structure properties and the relatively static relationships between those properties and comprehension. More recent efforts, however, concentrate on the specific ways text-structure properties affect the processes involved in building coherent text representations. In the current aspirations, gaining new insights – the critical aspect of expository comprehension – is viewed as establishing new relationships among existing knowledge substructures. In due course, learning through reading demands two critical elements: the ability to construct text representations (comprehension) and solid conceptual bases (domain knowledge).

Cross-linguistic variations in text structure

Contrastive rhetoric

Cross-linguistic variations in discourse structure have been extensively studied from an entirely different, contrastive rhetoric, perspective (e.g., Connor & Kaplan, 1987; Kaplan, 1966; Purves, 1988). Rhetoric in this arena is defined as "the choice of linguistic and structural aspects of discourse – chosen to produce an effect on an audience" (Purves, 1988, p. 9). Inasmuch as cultural groups differ in their uses of written texts (e.g., Heath, 1983; Scribner & Cole, 1981), similar variations can be predicted in the way the concept of text itself is perceived. Purves (1988) asserted that two dimensions of text, content and form, constitute the surface manifestations of cultural differences. Both are also affected by two considerations reflecting culture-specific uses of literacy. The first relates to perceived functions of written text. In some cultures, the primary function of writing is basically referential, whereas in others it seems both cognitive and expressive. Consequently, the relative emphasis placed on a particular function within a cultural group shapes perceptions of both text content, and form appropriateness.

The second factor contributing to cultural variation stems from conceptions of writing, because they determine, in large measure, the degree to which the writer must invent either text content or form. If, for example, writing is regarded merely as speech transcription, the writer's main task is simply to transform what is said into print form, in which case little invention is required. However, if writing is conceived as the process whereby the writer's knowledge and beliefs are organized and presented, the task is far more complicated because it entails selecting appropriate forms as well as placing content in the designated format. Moreover, writing can also be viewed as the generation of content and, sometimes, forms. When this is the case, written discourse can be taken as an outgrowth of the writer's creative invention. In short, perceptions of discourse demands, cognitive as well as functional, are inherent in the literacy practices in a particular cultural context. Given that these perceptions strongly influence writers in shaping and organizing their ideas, it is hardly surprising that basic discourse patterns – content, organization, and explicit organization cues – vary across languages and cultures.

Cross-linguistic variations in written-discourse structure

In a series of influential publications, Kaplan (1966, 1987, 1988) propounds definitive ways in which rhetorical conventions vary across languages – for example, how the discourse topic is marked in a text and how it is developed through various rhetorical devices, such as definition, classification, and exemplification. His contentions have provoked considerable debate among researchers and fostered empirical examinations of cross-linguistic/cultural variations in text-structure elements. Kachru (1988), for instance, conducted an in-depth analysis of topic progression in two Hindi expository texts. She found parallel uses of contrasting topic development styles: English-like, straight linear progression, and nonlinear, circular development. Noting that there is no categorically definable topical-progression format in Hindi paragraphs, the researcher concluded that what can be identified as culture-specific may lie in the relative distribution of different paragraph structures.

Similarly, Bickner and Peyasantiwong (1988) compared reflective essays authored by Thai and American high school students. They found that the writings shared a number of similar structural properties, particularly in the prominence of a topic sentence, placement of supporting sentences, and the use of examples to illustrate dominant points. One notable difference, however, lay in the information used to support the topic sentence. American students accepted the terms defined in the task prompt at face value, rarely expanding on them in their essays. In contrast, nearly all Thai students outlined somewhat elaborate definitions of these terms. The researchers concluded that the emphasis on listed definitions reflected the commonly held conception among Thai writers that the primary function of an essay is to explain the issue under consideration by compiling and reporting all details.

By analyzing narrative texts written by American and Thai high school students, Indrasuta (1988) illustrated similarities and differences in narrative construction in the two cultures. Although some differences clearly were attributable to linguistic properties – morphosyntactic, in particular – she argued that cultural factors offer more coherent explanations of variations in the discourse structure. She observed, for example, that perceived narrative functions differed between the two groups; whereas American students characterized the dominant purposes of narratives as entertainment and information, their Thai counterparts viewed them primarily as a vehicle for exposition and instruction. Indrasuta contended, moreover, that the perception of narrative functions, molded in a particular culture, leads to expected teaching methods in writing instruction. This, perhaps, explains why high school writers in both cultures, in order to comply, planned their compositions by selecting culturally appropriate content and conventional rhetorical structure.

In an effort to identify a culture-specific rhetorical style in Japanese, Hinds (1987) described the traditional Japanese essay format, called "ki-shou-ten-ketsu," in which each of the four text segments represents a distinct function in topic progression. "Ki," for example, marks the beginning by introducing a problem or topic. It is followed by two steps: "shou" (developing the main theme) and "ten" (describing several loosely related subtopics, without overt connective devices or transition markers). "Ketsu," the concluding segment, connects all the ideas presented. The reader is expected to retain loosely connected ideas, as such, until the final segment, "ketsu," provides a conceptual base for linking them together. Hinds argued that traditional Japanese essays impose unique requirements stemming from their unique format. Eggington (1987) referenced similar style preferences in Korean essay writing, observing that the organization appears rather disjointed, lacking linear sequential progression as well as explicit clues for connecting text ideas. Interestingly, L1 Korean readers, he noted, generally find the traditional loosely connected idea presentation easier to understand than the English-like linear topical progression, again demonstrating that cultural conditioning has a strong impact on how text information is encoded and retained.

Within the contrastive-rhetoric framework, the universality of story grammars has been tested against folktales in non-Western cultures. Matsuyama (1983), for instance, contended that the story-grammar approach does not capture the structural properties of Japanese folk-tales, many of which are less goal oriented and plot focused than typical Western stories. Soter (1988) also found the story-grammar method ineffectual in analyzing personal narratives in English produced by non-Western L2 writers. Thus, in short, an impressive array of studies in contrastive rhetoric affirm that culture-specific uses of literacy have indisputable impacts on the notion of text, shaping the conception of what constitutes appropriate content and format.

Cross-linguistic variations in oral-discourse structure

In an attempt to identify cross-linguistic variations in preferred discourse organization, oral narrative structures have also been analyzed. In comparing story-retelling styles of native Greek and English speakers after viewing a film, Tannen (1980) found a variety of culture-specific choices in narrative presentation. For example, recounts by native English speakers contained detailed descriptions of actual events portrayed, as well as cinematographic techniques used in the film. In contrast, Greek viewers elaborated on the content, enriching it with additional events and lengthy comments on characters' motives and feelings. These findings suggest that culturally conditioned rhetorical expectations dictate story-retelling processes, particularly with respect to what should be included, and in what organizational format. It is of particular interest that distinct traditions evolve in a culture and eventually develop a life of their own through expected narrative presentation procedures, which, over time, give rise to culture-specific recounting patterns.

From a developmental perspective, Berman and Slobin (1994) compared the acquisition of oral narrative competence among children in typologically diverse languages. In examining the effects of grammatical typology on rhetorical style, the researchers, based on Talmy's classification (1985), distinguish satellite-framed and verb-framed languages. Talmy believes that languages allocate movement information, including motion, manner, and direction, between the main verb and supporting elements, referred to as "satellite," in two distinct ways. In satellite-framed languages, such as English and German, verbs merely indicate movement, occasionally specifying manner, as in "walk," "run," and "fall." Movement direction, however, is conveyed by satellites, as apparent in the English verb phrases "walk *out*," "run *down*," and "fall *in*." Satellite-framed languages thus can entail detailed descriptions of motion path, because the syntax allows for the accumulation of path satellites to a single verb, together with prepositional phrases, as is evident in (1) below. Contrastingly, in verb-framed languages, such as Spanish, Hebrew, and Turkish, directionality is conveyed by the main verb alone, as in Spanish *entrar* (enter) and *salir* (exit). In these languages, detailed elaboration of motion path and manner is optional, though it can be achieved with separate phrases, as shown in (2).

(1) The deer threw them off over a cliff into the water.
(2) El búho salió volando del agujero (the owl exited flying from the hole). (Berman & Slobin, 1994, p. 118)

The researchers clarify several stylistic consequences of this particular grammatical typology. To wit, a major characteristic of narrative style in satellite-framed languages, such as English, is "a great deal of dynamic path and manner description" (p. 119). They attribute this abundance to the typological tendency to present motion-path information outside the verb. In contrast, their analysis shows that path descriptions are far less embellished in verb-framed languages, such as Spanish. Instead, these languages use more elaborated locative descriptions. Further, the narrator in verb-framed languages is expected to provide sufficient scene-setting information to allow the movement trajectory to be inferred from context. Hence, stylistic characteristics in narrative discourse can be partially explained by language-specific stylistic preferences uniquely associated with grammatical typology.

In sum, studies in contrastive rhetoric make it plain that how discourse information is organized and presented varies widely across languages and cultures. Sources of such variations range from the very notion of text to conventional beliefs about reader/writer responsibilities, as well as stylistic preferences associated with grammatical typology. Although it is virtually certain that these variances have significant impacts on L2 text comprehension research, little has been explored as to the extent and manner in which incongruent L1 and L2 text-structure properties alter L2 text-information processing behaviors. Seemingly, a great deal could be gained from further research applying the current findings in writing and speaking to reading comprehension. The next section speculates about possible ways in which cross-linguistic structural variations could affect L2 text comprehension.

Cross-linguistic influences on L2 text comprehension

In view of the cross-linguistic/cultural variations in discourse construction, it is likely that both L1 and L2 text-structure knowledge play a distinct, but equally important, role in L2 text comprehension. Given the repeated evidence that L2 writers' reliance on L1 rhetorical schemas is sustained well after a high level of L2 proficiency has been achieved (e.g., Indrasuta, 1988; Soter, 1988), we can reasonably assume that L1 text-structure knowledge is also used during comprehension. Presumably, then, L2 mental-model construction could be influenced to some degree by both L1 and L2 rhetorical knowledge. Consequently, such possible reciprocation and meshing warrant serious in-depth examinations of cross-linguistic interactions during L2 text comprehension. Two factors are particularly pertinent: L1 and L2 rhetorical distance, and the reader's ability to exploit L2 text-structure information.

Rhetorical distance allows reliable estimates of the extent to which L1 text-structure schema facilitates L2 discourse processing. When the two languages share similar text-structure properties, L1 schema, presumably activated during L2 text comprehension, can provide parallel facilitative assistance in identifying key ideas and their semantic relations. Moreover, there is reason to believe that L1–L2 rhetorical distance may interact with L2 linguistic knowledge. The minimal level of L2 proficiency necessary for recognizing the rhetorical frame in an L2 text may increase as the distance widens. The distance thus can alter the minimum linguistic requirement for effective L2 discourse processing. If L1 and L2 texts share similar structural properties, L2 text processing could be guided by L1 text-structure insights even before a linguistic threshold is attained. Should this be the case, L1 text-structure knowledge could offset limited L2 linguistic sophistication. If, on the other hand, L1 and L2 discourse share only nominal organizational properties, similar L1 top-down facilitation cannot be expected. With only minimal structural guidance, readers must rely on their own properties of mind to determine the relative significance of individual ideas, inferring their relationships primarily from lexical and syntactic information. Thus, their L2 text processing entails somewhat more demanding problem solving, necessitating higher levels of L2 linguistic sophistication.

The ability to exploit text-structure information also relates to L2 text comprehension. To recapitulate, L1 studies consistently demonstrate that there are vast capability differences among L1 readers, and the capability is a facet of overall reading competence. It is reasonable to assume, therefore, that L2 readers are not uniformly adept at using discourse signals, even when they are reading their L1. Conceivably, then, those lacking competence in their L1 are unlikely to develop it in a new language. Thus, without proper interventions, the initial gap among L2 readers stemming from inability to use text-structure signals will remain, if not worsen, regardless of L2 proficiency gains.

In short, dual-language involvement, like other aspects of reading, should characterize discourse-processing behaviors among L2 readers. Examining the conjoint impacts of L1 and L2 text-structure knowledge, self-evidently, is an extremely tricky enterprise, both conceptually and methodologically. However, in view of their centrality to L2 text comprehension, empirical explorations of cross-linguistic issues in L2 discourse processing are of vital significance in gaining a better understanding of comprehension variance among L2 readers.

Studies on L2 text structure and comprehension

Cross-linguistic influences, as noted earlier, have attracted limited attention in the major corpus of L2 studies, primarily in deference to two other predominant lines of inquiries: the role of L2 text-structure knowledge in comprehension, and the effectiveness of text-structure instruction.

Role of text-structure knowledge in L2 text comprehension

The effects of text-structure knowledge, in the main, have been studied, by using Meyer's top-level structure classifications. Carrell (1984a), for example, examined the effects of rhetorical-structure knowledge on text comprehension among college-level ESL learners with mixed L1 backgrounds. Comparing recall performance on four types of expository texts – problem/solution, comparison, causation, and collection – she found considerable variation when producing recall protocols in ability to utilize the text's rhetorical organization information. Her data indicated that students using structural information recalled a considerably higher proportion of text concepts. Further, among the various L1 groups, the four text types disparately affected recall performance. Spanish ESL learners, for example, retained more information from the comparison, problem/solution, and causation texts than from the collection. Arabic-speaking participants, in contrast, performed best on comparison and worst on causation. Asian students (Korean and Chinese) exhibited yet another pattern, recalling twice as much information from the problem/solution and causation texts as from the other two. These results were partially replicated by Foo (1989), demonstrating that college-level L2 learners of English in Hong Kong had more information recalled from the problem-solution text than from the collection. This same "Asian" pattern, however, was not apparent in another study involving English learners in Singapore (Tian, 1990). Although the findings to date are somewhat inconclusive, they suggest the strong possibility that text type may have differential impacts on text memory among L2 readers with diverse L1 backgrounds.

The effects of L2 proficiency in exploiting text-structure information were explored in other studies. Horiba (1990) observed that high- and low-proficiency L2 learners of Japanese engaged in different levels of text processing. High-proficiency learners gave greater attention to global discourse features, whereas low-proficiency readers were more preoccupied with the extraction of local-text (lexical and morphosyntactic) information. This seemingly explains why low-proficiency learners are far less affected by text-structure variables than are their high-proficiency counterparts. Similarly, Chen and Donin (1997) found that L2 proficiency among Chinese ESL learners had a greater impact on lower-level lexical and syntactic operations than on higher-level discourse processing, at least in part intimating that L2 proficiency may determine the degree to which structure variables affect L2 text-information processing. A subsequent Horiba study (1993) involving L1 and L2 readers of Japanese, in fact, confirmed that the ability to recognize discourse coherence is a critical determinant separating L1 and L2 as well as high- and low-proficiency L2 readers. Her data demonstrated that L1 readers and advanced L2 learners sensed the significance of the structural variables in coherence building, and indeed incorporated them in their mental-model construction. Interestingly, however, similar sensitivity was not evident among intermediate learners. In a similar vein, Salager-Meyer (1994) determined that text-structure variables diversely affect comprehension among ESL learners with varying L2 proficiency when reading domain-specific, conceptually demanding texts. Viewed as a whole, the findings offer strong empirical support for the conviction that L2 linguistic sophistication is directly related to structural sensitivity, thus accounting for the diverse impacts of text-structure variables on comprehension among high- and low-proficiency L2 learners.

Effectiveness of text-structure instruction

Another line of research deals with the effectiveness of text-structure instruction. The rationale is as follows: L1 research suggests that the ability to use structural information is causally related to reading comprehension, and also that the ability is not universal. It follows, then, that explicit training on top-level text structure should benefit readers. L1 instructional studies, as noted earlier, offer convincing evidence supporting advantages of text-structure instruction. Although still limited in numbers, current studies investigating explicit L2 text-structure instruction generally demonstrate that such training engenders substantial comprehension gains, as well as improved recall of both expository (e.g., Carrell, 1985; Lee & Riley, 1990; Tang, 1992) and narrative texts (e.g., Amer, 1992; Kitajima, 1997).

Nonetheless, some caution is necessary, because there is considerable evidence suggesting that the effectiveness of text-structure training may be influenced by other factors. Raymond (1993), for example, concluded that structural training differentially affected comprehension performance in texts with disparate content familiarity. Introducing text-structure elements, in short, can be detrimental when the content is conceptually demanding or unfamiliar. Raymond further observed that learners with adequate structural awareness prior to the training exhibited virtually no ability gains in using top-level structural information, again hinting that such training may not benefit all L2 learners. Davis, Lang and Samuels (1988) offered additional caution. They determined that explicit text-structure instruction had a significant facilitative impact only when the text was organized in canonical format, and thus was compatible with the instruction. The training, however, was of little assistance when the text did not match the instructed structural patterns. Structural training appears to be more complex than has been assumed, entailing elements beyond text-structure knowledge. Consequently, additional investigations, clarifying how and when instruction provides facilitative benefits, are essential.

Summary and future research suggestions

The research on text structure has substantially advanced our understanding of the specific ways content information is organized in various text types. We now know that structural organization is explicitly signaled, and that text structure and organizational devices vary across genres within a single language, as well as across languages. Most critically, text-structure knowledge augments comprehension and memory. The related L2 studies hint that several additional factors – L2 proficiency, L1–L2 rhetorical distance, L1 reading ability – also must be considered in evaluating text-structure knowledge among L2 readers and its impact on text comprehension. Their findings generally suggest that notable differences in text-structure knowledge exist among L2 learners (e.g., Carrell, 1984a, 1992; Horiba, 1993; Salager-Meyer, 1991). The variance is directly linked both to L2 proficiency (e.g., Foo, 1989; Riley, 1993; Salager-Meyer, 1994) and to L1 reading ability (e.g., Benedetto, 1985). Further, the ability to perceive overall rhetorical organization is a strong predictor of text-recall performance (e.g., Carrell, 1984a; Foo, 1989; Horiba, 1993; Urquhart, 1984). Varying text types, as well, differentially affects text memory among L2 readers with various L1 backgrounds and proficiency levels (e.g., Carrell, 1984a; Foo, 1989; Riley, 1993; Salager-Meyer, 1991; Tian, 1990).

Although the research pool has generated interesting conceptualizations through careful replications of L1 studies, cross-linguistic issues, as indicated, have received far less attention than they deserve. In light of their potential contributions to understanding L2 reading's unique nature, several promising agendas are worth considering for future text-structure research in the L2 context. First, the perceptible systematicity with which text structure deviates across languages should allow us to form reasonably accurate estimates of L1–L2 rhetorical distance – that is, the extent to which L1 and L2 rhetorical structures share common properties. If clearly articulated and properly gauged, the notion of rhetorical distance can offer fruitful explanations of the reported interactions between text types and L1 backgrounds (e.g., Carrell, 1984a; Foo, 1989). By extension, it also predicts the relative difficulty of particular text types experienced by particular groups of L2 readers. Perhaps of greatest importance, however, methodical examinations of L1–L2 rhetorical distance will shed substantial light on cross-linguistic transfer during discourse processing. If, for example, aspects of L1 rhetorical schemas automatically activated during L2 discourse processing can successfully be identified, new insights may point the way to subsequent studies involving cross-linguistic interaction between transferred L1 rhetorical knowledge and L2 text-structure properties.

Second, although L2 text-structure knowledge is assumed to expand concomitantly with increased L2 linguistic sophistication – lexical and morphosyntactic knowledge, in particular – there is little support for the assumption. Their relationship has yet to be demonstrated on both conceptual and empirical grounds. Such skepticism stems from two significant factors. First, development linearity between L2 proficiency and text-structure knowledge is unlikely because their progressions can be altered by L1–L2 orthographic distance. Because research suggests that low-proficiency L2 learners lean heavily on local-information extraction, their reading processes may remain unaffected by text-structure variables, at least until their lower-level processing becomes sufficiently automated. In all likelihood, processing automaticity evolves at various rates among L2 readers with diverse L1 backgrounds. Other things being equal, the rapidity is determined, in large measure, by the degree to which their L1 and L2 orthographic systems share similar properties. Inasmuch as sensitivity to text-structure variables does not develop until they receive adequate direct attention, and such attentional shift does not occur until lower-level processing efficiency is achieved, we logically could conclude that L1–L2 orthographic distance may determine, at least in part, the extent to which L2 proficiency predicts the use of top-down text-structure schemas during L2 text processing. A single pattern of connections, therefore, cannot be assumed among L2 readers with divergent L1 orthographic backgrounds.

The second factor shedding doubt on the uniformity of the alliance between L2 proficiency and text-structure knowledge is L1–L2 rhetorical distance. Rhetorical structure, within any text genre, varies across languages, and we reasonably can posit that similarity in L1 and L2 text organization, as well as analogous rhetorical conventions, accelerates L2 text-structure knowledge acquisition. Here again, L2 proficiency is likely to be foreordained by the rhetorical distance between the two languages. In the aggregate, there is room to question whether L2 proficiency and text-structure knowledge develop simultaneously in uniform, linear fashion among learners with diverse L1 backgrounds.

Finally, the research makes it plain that text types entail different genre-specific processing requirements, necessitating information from multiple knowledge bases. Limited information is available, however, about how specific aspects of background knowledge interact with L2 linguistic sophistication. Learning from an expository text, for example, entails reconstructing the message intended by the author and the necessary restructuring of existing knowledge bases. Comprehension success, therefore, is determined in large measure by the abilities to activate appropriate knowledge bases and to assimilate new insights into relevant conceptions. Content-relevant domain knowledge, therefore, may well compensate for limited L2 linguistic and rhetorical sophistication in expository comprehension. One might even presume that the more specialized the text, the greater the degree of conceptual compensation. Narratives, on the other hand, impose an entirely different set of requirements. Recognizing causal relationships among events serves as an illustration. Content-relevant background knowledge obviously is important in narrative comprehension, but it does not substitute for event-specific information, supplied by the author, necessary for linking text elements. In short, in-depth analyses of genre-specific requirements, both linguistic and conceptual, should illuminate commonly observed intra-individual variations in comprehension across text genres.

PART III

LOOKING AT THE WHOLE

9 *Individual differences*

Why study individual differences? There is a simple answer: Virtually all reading competencies are subject to variation. Research on individual differences, therefore, can yield useful information for both reading theory and practice. On theoretical grounds, by dissecting basic competencies, the research can determine their specific contributions to reading capability, which in turn illuminates two fundamental puzzles: what constitutes successful reading and what precisely distinguishes strong from weak readers. In so doing, the research can help refine existing models of reading. On pedagogical grounds, individual-difference studies can yield critical information essential in ensuring instructional quality. For instruction to be efficacious, interventions must target skills that are causally related to reading performance. A clearer understanding of variations in competencies and their direct effect on reading performance can enable practitioners to identify which skills to emphasize with greater accuracy.

As illustrated in previous chapters, considerable data currently are available with respect to the ways readers vary in comprehension capacities: operations such as decoding, syntactic parsing, and coherence building. In the interests of exploring additional dimensions of reading ability, this chapter analyzes research on individual differences from both single-skills and integrative multiple-skills perspectives. The typology and tradition of single-skills studies are examined together with possible limitations of their implications. Newer approaches to analyzing multiple competencies in tandem are then described. As a preliminary observation, it should be stated that, although a wide variety of factors, such as motivation, home print environment, and community support, have been associated with individual differences in reading achievement, the consideration here is restricted to the cognitive and linguistic capabilities directly linked with text-information processing.

Traditions of individual-difference research

Individual-difference studies in L1 reading involve varying perspectives and a wide range of research methodologies. To evaluate the validity and utility of their collective findings, it is helpful to understand how the research evolved. Tracing developments from the early 1930s on, Spiro and Myers (1984) identified several distinct roots.

Heavily influenced by intelligence testing, the earliest efforts concentrated on general mental capacity as the predictor of reading acquisition. The logic was that, because intelligence tests reliably predict academic achievement and reading is an integral element in academic learning, intelligence tests should be able to distinguish those likely to become successful learners and readers. Although the rationale was clear in this research, reading and subject-matter learning were not separated. The IQ-based predictions were quickly replaced by a more rational notion of reading aptitude as a particular subset of mental abilities specifically related to reading. The intelligence-test approach, although short-lived, laid a solid methodological foundation by establishing a strong psychometric orientation for subsequent studies.

As a result of the research shift from general intelligence to reading aptitude, increasing attention was given to correlates of reading ability. Within the psychometric tradition, scores from large batteries of tasks were statistically reduced to a smaller set of functionally distinct ability clusters, based on their unique contributions to reading performance. The underlying rationale was straightforward: Insofar as potential causal factors can be extracted from many reading correlates, their successful identification sets the stage for subsequent hypothesis testing. This paradigm remains influential in the current reading research literature.

As a natural extension of the focus on reading correlates, succeeding studies compared skilled and less-skilled readers on a wide range of capabilities, presumably related to successful comprehension. By identifying specific capacities distinguishing the two ability groups, the research goal ripened into determining sources of reading problems. However, the correlational nature of the studies necessitated some discretion in interpreting the findings because not all discriminating factors were causally related to reading ability. For example, although skilled and less-skilled readers were found to differ in their eye-fixation duration, longer fixation in itself, although a symptom of visual processing difficulties, does not cause poor comprehension.

Another investigative cluster was grounded in information-processing theories. Although hypothesis testing in itself does not distinguish it from other approaches, the closer tie with cognitive theories sets it apart. The tested constructs were selected on the basis of well-refined, experimentally validated reading models. In the interest of scientific legitimacy, a selected construct was isolated for a carefully controlled experimental task. The intent was to establish a causal linkage between the hypothesized competency and reading ability with minimum procedural contamination. However, experimental tasks generally have little resemblance to real-life reading, which has evoked a growing concern about the generalizability of the findings to actual reading situations.

To summarize, three general tendencies characterize individual-difference research in L1 reading. First, research goals have shifted from inquisitive explorations to experimental validations of causal linkages between hypothesized variables and reading performance. Second, as the notion of reading ability has been progressively refined, investigative foci have shifted from general mental capacity as the core basis of reading ability to the specific cognitive structures supporting the requisite operations. Third, despite the shift in research goals and conceptual foundations, psychometric orientation by and large has remained prevalent.

Individual-difference studies can be earmarked by their unique strengths and limitations. Grounded in established cognitive theories, the research outcomes generally are interpretable through common conceptual frameworks, thereby facilitating their functional utility in knowledge synthesis and accumulation. Their strong psychometric orientation, moreover, ensures a certain level of objectivity, allowing cross-study comparisons of findings and implications. On the downside, however, because of the predominantly correlational nature of the research, there is a perennial risk of drawing unwarranted causal inferences beyond what the data permit. On occasion, such interpretive misdemeanors, in fact, have given rise to misguided practice. Many experimental tasks, moreover, do not replicate what people actually do in real-life reading. As a result, some skepticism exists about the validity and generalizability of using findings derived from contrived tasks, devoid of context, in predicting real-life reading performance.

Empirical findings from single-focus studies

Over a half-century span, single-focus studies have advanced our understanding of individual differences in requisite reading competencies. An abridgment of their findings, based on a synthesis by Daneman (1991) and a more recent report by the National Reading Panel (2000), is instructive.

Perceptual processing

Eye-movement studies consistently demonstrate that good and poor readers differ on virtually all indices of eye-movement behaviors, including fixation frequency, duration, and regression. Poor readers, for example, make two to three times more fixations and they are of considerably longer duration than those of good readers. They also backtrack more than skilled readers. Consistent variations between the ability groups clearly imply that eye movements are a reliable indicator of reading ability. If we assume that such behaviors are reflective of perceptual capability, the salient question is what accounts for their systematic variations. These observations led to a hypothesis that good readers cover larger text segments at each fixation.

The hypothesis was tested by comparing perceptual span. The findings, however, indicated that span size does not differ either among novice and experienced readers or among high- and low-achieving students, suggesting that visual span is not a probable factor in determining developmental or individual differences. Other studies, moreover, revealed a possible relationship between letter-identification efficiency and reading ability, but only when identification tasks required extraction of linguistic information from displayed letters. Collectively, these findings would seem to imply that variances in eye-movement indices are indicative of linguistic-information extraction competence rather than perceptual capabilities. Perceptual capacity in itself does not appear to engender reading-ability differences.

Word recognition

In contrast, researchers generally agree that word-recognition competence is a significant determinant of reading ability. Inasmuch as word recognition involves several discrete operations, as discussed in Chapter 3, the following research findings are summarized according to processing components.

Lexical access

Through simple tasks, such as physical matching, lexical judgement, and word naming, lexical-access studies measure how rapidly and accurately word information, whether visual, phonological, or semantic, is accessed in lexical memory. The tasks obviously necessitate efficiency in both visual processing and lexical-information extraction. The findings suggest that efficiency in lexical access is more closely allied with reading speed than with comprehension. The correlations between lexical-access speed and reading ability, furthermore, tend to be moderate at best. It is unlikely, therefore, that access speed alone explains individual differences in reading ability to any significant extent.

Phonological decoding

On the other hand, overwhelming evidence supports the high probability that phonological decoding is vital in early reading development. The findings consistently demonstrate that, of the two routes to accessing phonological code (grapheme-to-phoneme translation and word-information retrieval), grapheme-to-phoneme translation is most directly related to reading acquisition in alphabetic languages. Interestingly, phonological decoding skill also varies among older, more experienced readers. The important question, thus, is whether any systematic relationship between decoding variation and reading ability remains after students advance beyond the initial learning-to-read stage. Given that pseudoword naming is one of the most reliable measures differentiating strong and weak high school readers, the answer appears to be yes. One way of explaining the unwavering significance of phonological decoding, even among experienced readers, is that virtually all operations beyond word recognition – syntactic disambiguation, lexical inference, co-reference resolution, and so on – necessitate working memory. Because, as discussed in Chapter 3, phonologically encoded information is more durable than any other form of representation in working memory, decoding ability is mandatory for the efficient use of working-memory resources. It is no surprise, therefore, that decoding efficiency directly affects component operations in reading *at* and *beyond* the lexical level.

Contextual use

Top-down reading models were widely accepted in the 1970s, particularly their conviction that good readers rely on context to a greater extent than poor readers in anticipating forthcoming words. The assumption was that words are identified during the process of satisfying various constraints (e.g., semantic, syntactic, and contextual) rather than through an analysis of visual input. Put another way, good readers are adept at guessing what word should follow on the basis of the semantic and syntactic context in the preceding text. Ability to use contextual information during word recognition, therefore, was viewed as a critical factor explaining individual differences in reading ability. However, there is little empirical evidence supporting such guessing behaviors during lexical processing, particularly among good readers.

As noted in Chapter 3, good readers are superior at identifying words in and out of context, and the gap between good and poor readers narrows when word recognition takes place in context. Contrary to expectations, poor readers seemingly derive more benefit from context than good readers, using contextual information to compensate for their inefficient word-recognition skills. This obviously casts serious doubt on the central supposition that contextual information overrides incoming visual input from individual words in print. In brief, the ability to use contextual information during word recognition does not appear to be causally related either to lexical-processing competence or to general reading ability.

Vocabulary knowledge

It is well documented that good readers have larger vocabularies than poor readers. In fact, vocabulary knowledge correlates more highly with reading comprehension than any other variable. One might think such knowledge should be a significant yardstick of individual differences in reading ability. However, careful scrutiny suggests otherwise. For one thing, the reported connection between vocabulary and comprehension is essentially correlational, disallowing causal inferences; for another, not all types of vocabulary instruction generate measurable gains in comprehension, and not all readers benefit uniformly from vocabulary instruction. As described in Chapter 4, the emerging belief is that vocabulary and comprehension are indirectly linked through third constructs, presumably related to both, such as background knowledge, reasoning skill, and inference ability. In this regard, knowledge of individual word meanings is necessary for text-content understanding, but vocabulary size in itself does not appear to be causally linked to reading ability. Seemingly, the critical competencies underlying incidental word learning also support many of the major operations essential to reading comprehension. In sum, the relationship between reading and vocabulary is more complex than has been assumed in that it is neither unidirectional nor as straightforward as it may seem.

Comprehension ability

Although decoding is unique to visual-information processing, much of the comprehension ability is shared between reading and listening. In keeping with an observation in Chapter 2, the "simple view of reading" (Gough & Tunmer, 1986; Hoover & Gough, 1990) suggests that, although comprehension skills develop through oral interactions well before reading commences, they cannot be put to use until sufficient decoding competence develops. Gough and colleagues contend that, once the initial learning-to-read stage concludes, the degree of reading variance explained by decoding decreases. Conversely, they reason that, in the subsequent reading-to-learn stage, reading becomes increasingly dependent on the comprehension component. Hence, in this view, comprehension ability subsumes adequate decoding competence. However, when comprehension difficulty occurs, isolating the source of problems is a major challenge, because virtually every comprehension operation depends on outputs from lower-level operations. Although current understanding is far from complete, as delineated in Chapters 7 and 8, clearer pictures of text representations and their construction processes are beginning to emerge after three decades of explorations on discourse processing. The major research implications for individual differences can be synthesized as follows.

Coherence building

Integration of partially assembled information is central to text comprehension. Inasmuch as texts do not always provide the necessary clues for constructing coherent representations, text-based bridging inference is also viewed as an alternative form of information integration. Because integration procedures depend on other processing competencies, as noted earlier, problems are difficult to isolate. Poor inference performance, as an illustration, can be explained by any one of the following deficits, either singly or in combination: poor vocabulary, inefficient word recognition, ineffective syntactic parsing, or insufficient background knowledge. Moreover, it has been observed that variations in integration quality among strong and weak readers magnify as processing demands increase – for example, when information to be processed is embedded in more structurally complex sentences, and when segments to be integrated are separated by a greater distance.

Although little exploration has distinguished the component factors in comprehension, in recent models of text understanding, considerable efforts in incorporating individual differences in text-coherence building are notable. For example, as discussed in Chapter 7, Kintsch (1994, 1998), within his construction-integration model, explains that poor readers are more susceptible to incomplete understanding and misinterpretation, because their textbases are not solid enough to create sufficient constraints for deactivating irrelevant information during the integration process. Similarly, Gernsbacher (1996), within her structure-building framework, attributes poor comprehension performance among less-skilled readers to their faulty "suppression mechanism." As characterized in Chapter 8, the suppression mechanism supposedly dampens activation of memory nodes when incoming information does not cohere with the emerging interpretation of the text. If the mechanism does not function properly, however, irrelevant information inadvertently is incorporated into the ongoing structure, inhibiting the construction of coherent text representations.

Text-structure knowledge

Content information is differentially organized in distinct text types. Therefore, in detecting and isolating significant text ideas, text-structure knowledge plays a major role in comprehension and retention. Research further supports this probability by demonstrating that text-structure variables have a discernible impact on discourse processing: Text-structure knowledge varies widely among readers, and, more critically, training in the use of specific organizational mechanisms typically improves comprehension. Although it is evident that text-structure knowledge accounts for individual differences in reading ability, it also should be noted that the acquisition of this knowledge is an outgrowth of extensive reading experience. Hence, the causal impact of this capability is not as clear-cut as that of decoding and other lower-level processing competencies.

Background knowledge

Reading comprehension, as repeatedly noted, results from the integrative interaction between derived textual information and preexisting knowledge. What readers know essentially determines how much information can be extracted from the text. The knowledge, moreover, is heavily relied upon when reading between the lines. Because what individuals know, and how well they know it, varies widely, background knowledge can be a major factor explaining both quantitative and qualitative differences in comprehension outcomes. Here again, however, caution is necessary in determining causal directions, because the relationship between knowledge and comprehension is not likely to be unilateral. Insofar as reading is the primary medium of knowledge acquisition and expansion in the academic context, the two supposedly are developmentally reciprocal – that is, gains in one enhance the development of the other in cyclical fashion. This obviously makes it difficult to determine whether those who know more read better, or whether those who read better know more.

Trends in L2 single-focus studies

L1 single-focus studies have significantly influenced the way individual differences among L2 readers are conceptualized and examined. Although many L2 studies borrow investigative tactics from L1 research, clear distinctions remain. For example, developmental factors are of less concern in L2 studies, because they involve mainly individuals with substantial L1 literacy and schooling experience. Instead, L2 research incorporates a range of collateral factors associated with dual-language involvement: L1 reading ability, L2 linguistic knowledge, L1 and L2 linguistic distance, and so on. Currently, three dominant investigative areas are being pursued.

The primary research strand deals with the precise role of L2 proficiency in explaining information-processing performance variations. General patterns of correspondence between proficiency and processing levels are emerging from systematic comparisons of high- and low-proficiency L2 learners. Lexical-level processing, as a case in point, predominates among low-proficiency learners, whereas far heavier involvement in information integration and conceptual manipulations is typical in the reading behaviors of high-proficiency learners. Presumably, these differences explain why low-proficiency learners are sensitive to local linguistic elements but not to global text organizations. L2 proficiency is a dominant force in determining which aspects of text-information processing L2 readers engage in during comprehension at given points of their L2 development.

Another research strand elucidates the mechanisms through which L1 linguistic and cultural backgrounds affect L2 reading performance. Inasmuch as L1 knowledge and processing skills transfer across languages, conceivably L2 information processing can be constrained by preestablished L1 procedures. L2 studies indeed demonstrate that diversity in L1 linguistic and cultural experience helps explain how and why L2 readers differ in their processing behaviors. To illustrate, L2 readers with contrasting L1 backgrounds utilize noticeably distinct decoding procedures, reflecting the structural properties of their respective L1 writing systems. Although transfer research verifies that variations in prior literacy experience account for procedural differences in L2 processing, it has yet to determine whether such variations affect comprehension outcomes.

Under the assumption that L1 reading ability provides a solid base for developing an additional set of reading skills in a second language, a third research area examines the impact of L1 reading ability on L2 reading development. The evidence suggests that initial differences among beginning L2 readers with disparate L1 reading ability tend to widen during L2 reading development, simply because they begin their learning from an uneven footing. Empirical support for the presumption exists in consistently solid correlations between L1 and L2 reading abilities among bilingual school-aged children (e.g., Cummins, 1979, 1986, 1991; Legarretta, 1979; Troike, 1978), as well as in parallel strategies used by L2 learners in their L1 and L2 (e.g., Jimenez, Garcia, & Pearson, 1995; Pritchard, 1990). As already observed, however, efficient use of L1 strategies cannot occur until sufficient L2 proficiency has been achieved. The dominant speculation is that L1-based facilitation is mediated by L2 linguistic knowledge. Nonetheless, L1 reading ability constitutes yet another source of individual differences in L2 reading ability.

Alternative approaches in individual-difference studies

Despite impressive strides in clarifying the capabilities underlying successful reading performance, implications from single-focus studies are still somewhat insufficient because they rarely address interconnections among component competencies. For example, some abilities necessary for comprehension functionally depend on other component skills. Their true influences, therefore, cannot be determined in isolation. Similarly, a number of additional capabilities are linked with reading performance, but only indirectly through their respective mediating variables. Without incorporating these intermediary factors, correlational data only obscure whatever causal relationships exist. It is essential, therefore, that individual-difference research go beyond examinations of single skills separately. Systematic efforts in exploring the interconnections and interactions among competency components are under way.

Component skills approach

The component skills approach exemplifies efforts to find a viable method of disentangling intermingled components. The objective of the approach, as addressed in Chapter 2, is to identify specific individual differences in text-information processing. Conforming with the premise that reading is a complex information-processing system, consisting of a finite number of theoretically distinct and empirically separable mental operations (Carr et al., 1990), the approach aims at isolating distinct reading operations, exploring their functional interdependence, and in so doing determining their relative contributions to overall reading ability. The success of the approach depends on

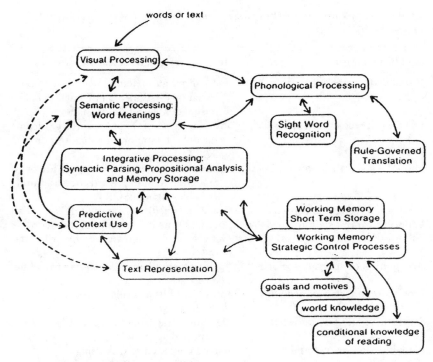

Figure 9.1   Model of the information-processing structure of the reading system to guide component skills analysis (reprinted from Carr et al., Vavrus, Evans, 1990, p. 8).

accurate construct identification within an accepted reading theory. At the same time, because of the explicit ties with a particular theory, the approach generates empirical data that can establish a solid basis for theory modifications and/or refinements. Hence, the approach allows theory construction and its validation to proceed hand in hand, thus safeguarding one another.

The approach has been implemented in a number of investigations. Carr et al. (1990), for example, conducted a study with young students in a university reading clinic. Participants were second- to ninth-grade readers with below-grade reading levels. Using a reading component model (Figure 9.1), the researchers devised a large battery of assessment tasks, as described in Table 9.1. At the outset, data were subjected to correlational analyses. The resulting correlational matrix was then converted into a distance metric through straightforward mathematical manipulations. Each correlation was squared to obtain the proportion of simple variance shared by any

Table 9.1. *Component skills assessment battery (reprinted from Carr et al., 1990, p. 13)*

Skill being tapped	Test or performance measure used
Visual code formation and evaluation	Same-different matching with differences based on cAsE mAtCh oR mIsMaTcH (visual configuration or shape)
Sight-word recognition accuracy	Pronunciation of familiar words graded for difl (Slosson oral reading test or SORT)
Phonological translation accuracy	Pronunciation of unfamiliar pseudowords matching to SORT words on structural variables (PseudoSORT)
Sight-word recognition speed	Speeded (timed) version of SORT
Phonological translation speed	Speeded (timed) version of pseudoword
Phonological awareness	Gates-McKillop knowledge of word parts test
Recognition of accurate spellings	Spelling test of Durrell analysis or reading difficulty
Production of accurate spellings	Iowa test of basic skills language skills spelling test
Semantic vocabulary knowledge	Definition test using SORT words identified accurately
Predictive context use and verification	Forced-choice cloze task using modified-version Stanford achievement test's comprehension test
Integrative processing	Listening comprehension test from Durrell reading-listening series
Working memory for item identities	Free-recall digit span
Working memory for item order	Serial-recall digit span
General pattern sensitivity	Raven's coloured progressive matrices
Intelligence	Standardized IQ test such as Wechsler Intelligence scales for children, revised
Overall reading comprehension efficiency	Accuracy per unit time in reading comprehension test for Durrell reading-listening series

two components. The reciprocal of the squared correlation was then calculated, producing a number between 1.0 and infinity, with the smaller numbers representing greater shared variances. The functional distance among the tested skills was then represented graphically in the form of a map, referred to as a cognitive skills map, as shown in Figure 9.2.

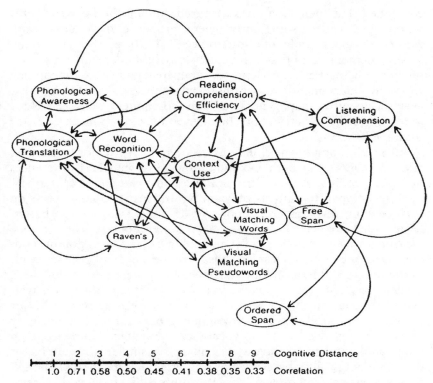

Figure 9.2 Cognitive skills map of individual differences in reading performance (reprinted from Carr et al., 1990, p. 27).

Based on the map, the researchers interpreted their data. They first identified two major competency clusters, one involving visual-processing capabilities and the other consisting of phonological decoding skills. Both were significant in explaining individual differences in overall comprehension performance. They concluded that the two partially overlapping clusters were in neighboring competency groups. Listening comprehension was independently related to reading comprehension; context use was also independent, but differed in that it sustained roughly equal distance from most other variables. Somewhat surprisingly, general intelligence was pushed to the periphery because of its weak correlation with reading comprehension.

On the basis of remarkably similar correlational patterns observed among school-aged children with grade-level reading proficiency (Levy & Hinchley, 1990), as well as older, more experienced readers (Cunningham, Stanovich, & Wilson, 1990), Carr and associates concluded that their "map has captured, among the below average school-aged readers, some fairly general properties of system organization relevant to individual differences" (1990, p. 30). The analysis thus demonstrates that comprehension ability depends on several distinct, but partially overlapping, competency clusters functioning relatively independently of one another. Of greatest significance, however, the cognitive map, generated by the component analysis, yielded a number of hypotheses about linkages among component skills for future validations.

All in all, component skills analysis has had a major impact on research concerning both individual and developmental differences in reading ability. To illustrate, Scanlon and Vellutino (1997) examined the comparative effects of cognitive and instructional factors on early reading development among at-risk kindergartners. Test batteries included five task clusters, each consisting of two to five cognitive measures: meaning construction, phonological and orthographic coding, verbal memory and learning, visual processing, and print concept. Participating children, initially diagnosed as potentially at-risk upon kindergarten entry, were divided into three ability groups (poor, average, and good) on the basis of their first-year reading scores. Major findings were as follows: The three ability groups differed significantly in word knowledge but not in vocabulary or syntactic knowledge. In the phonological and orthographic coding, the single significant factor discriminating ability-based groups was letter identification. Although poor readers encountered considerably more difficulty in verbal memory and new-word learning, there was little visual-memory difference. Finally, the average and good reader groups performed similarly on any of the cognitive measures. Because of poor readers' persistent problems with verbal-memory tasks, these results were interpreted as an indication that "there is an underlying common cause of difficulties in reading and verbal memory, namely, impaired phonological processing ability" (p. 211).

To sum up, the picture emerging from component skills analysis studies suggests that the complexity inherent in reading ability stems from the multiplicity of components and their functional interconnections. Seemingly, the key to dealing with the intricacies lies in dissecting and unraveling closely interwoven competency elements.

Implications of the component skills approach for L2 reading research

In view of the added complexity arising from dual-language involvement, the component skills approach should be equally, if not more,

suitable for examining individual differences in L2 reading development. Despite its potential utility, however, the procedure has yet to
be fully explored – a fact that is attributable both to the lack of a
viable L2 reading model and to the demanding requirements in constructing large task batteries in two languages. The potential merits of the approach in analyzing L2 reading ability nonetheless are
substantial.

To begin with, it could illuminate the place of L2 knowledge in
L2 reading comprehension. Although there is general agreement that
linguistic knowledge and reading ability are complex constructs, the
multidimensionality of neither has been adequately addressed in L2
reading research. Consolidating the abilities into single scores prohibits the analyses from telling us much about the specific linguistic requirements for particular processing operations. Insofar as L1
studies repeatedly demonstrate that different knowledge sources are
necessitated for varying text-information processing operations, and
also that L1 and L2 knowledge together play an important role in L2
comprehension, it is imperative to carry out detailed, finely grained
analyses to determine connection patterns between the two multidimensional constructs.

Moreover, initiating systematic comparisons of skills inventories in
two languages would make it possible to assess the relative facilitation benefits resulting from transferred L1 competencies in L2 reading
development. It is often speculated, though not empirically tested,
that transferred L1 skills contribute differentially to L2 comprehension among readers with diverse L1 backgrounds. More facilitation,
for example, is anticipated when L1 and L2 share similar structural
properties, because transferred L1 skills can be used, without major modifications, to process L2 input. By graphically representing
the functional overlap among L1 and L2 requisite skills in varying
source/target-language combinations, the analysis could yield useful
information about L1-based benefits during L2 comprehension.

Further, competence dissection could create large windows for investigating the specific impacts of yet another competence dimension
associated with L2 reading ability: restricted L2 linguistic sophistication. By comparing and contrasting ways in which component skills
contribute to reading performance in L1 and L2 within individual
readers, we should be able to pinpoint specific deficiencies attributable
to limited L2 linguistic sophistication. Furthermore, similar comparisons of individuals across proficiency levels could also allow us to
determine, with increased proficiency, which deficiencies are most easily overcome. Conceivably, developmental analyses of this sort could
yield useful insights on ways to diagnose early reading problems, and

thereby pave the way to effective intervention programs for beginning L2 readers.

Component analysis studies involving L2 readers

Currently, only a handful of L2 studies – although the number is increasing sharply – have explored the component approaches to investigate contributions of lower-level skills (e.g., August et al., 2000, 2001; Carlisle & Beeman, 2000; Verhoeven, 2000; Wade-Wooley & Geva, 2000). In a series of studies, Durgunoglu et al. (1993) traced factors influencing L2 word-reading competence development among first-grade students in Spanish-to-English transitional bilingual programs. Their task batteries involved word naming, pseudoword naming, spelling, receptive vocabulary, letter knowledge, phonological awareness, and oral language comprehension. Administering these tasks in Spanish (L1) and English (L2), they found that L1 phonological awareness and letter knowledge were closely related to realword and pseudoword naming in both Spanish and English. Their longitudinal data also revealed that bilingual children began to develop L2 basic word-recognition and spelling skills, presumably by borrowing from their L1 literacy skills, even before formal L2 literacy instruction commenced. Oral proficiency, however, was not a reliable predictor of early reading success in either language. The researchers concluded that L2 reading acquisition is facilitated by transferred L1 word-reading competence to a far greater extent than target-language oral proficiency.

Similarly, Gholamain and Geva (1999) scrutinized developmental differences in basic reading skills among L1-dominant school-aged bilingual children learning to read in English (L1) and Persian (L2). Their measures included working memory, letter knowledge, word recognition, and pseudoword naming. By administering these tests in the two languages, they identified diverse sources of individual differences in biliteracy development. Their findings demonstrated that performance on corresponding measures in L1 and L2 correlated significantly; working-memory capacity and letter-naming speed substantially affected performance variation in word-reading ability across languages and proficiency levels; and once Persian letters are mastered, Persian (L2) word recognition was achieved with the same efficiency as English (L1), despite far less exposure and processing experience. They reasoned that "individual differences in reading different alphabetic orthographies can be partially understood in terms of common underlying cognitive factors" (p. 208). Given that sound–symbol correspondence is considerably more regular in Persian than in English, their results apparently suggest that the development of

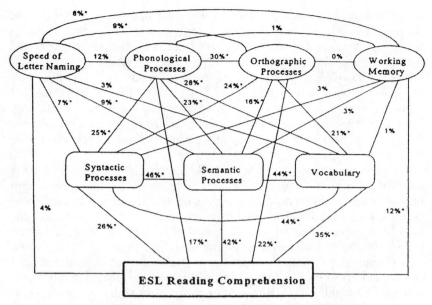

Figure 9.3   Schematic representation of the relationship between lower-level and higher-level language-processing skills (reprinted from Nassaji & Geva, 1999, p. 259).

word-reading skills is greatly facilitated by orthographic regularity. The study thus mandates that L2 reading skills development must consider both language-specific elements and common factors shared across languages.

Working with adult L2 readers, Nassaji and Geva (1999) compared the relative impact of higher- and lower-processing skills on reading comprehension among advanced ESL learners with Farsi L1 backgrounds. Large task batteries within the component analysis framework were developed. Lower-level processing tasks included homophone judgment, orthographic legality judgment, and letter naming, whereas the higher-level processing measures involved syntactic-violation detection and sentence verification (determining whether a given sentence makes sense). In addition, working-memory capacity and vocabulary knowledge were measured. Reading ability as well was assessed through three disparate measures: comprehension, silent-reading rate, and word reading. As evident in Figure 9.3, the data clearly indicated that higher-level processing skills correlated more highly with reading-test scores than lower-level processing skills. Subsequent regression analyses revealed that, although lexical-processing skills largely were subsumed in higher-level processing competence, they nonetheless explained a significant portion of reading comprehension variance. Consequently, the outcomes further support the conviction that lower-level processing skills contribute directly – and indirectly through higher-level operations – to successful reading performance among advanced L2 readers. The study sheds substantial light on two critical – not yet fully explored – issues in L2 reading: interconnections among lower- and higher-processing skills and the sustained impact of lower-level processing skills well beyond initial reading development.

To sum up, then, component skills analysis demonstrates strong promise as a viable tool for disentangling interwoven cognitive and linguistic variables in dual-language processing. Because lexical competence traditionally is viewed as a covariate of L2 knowledge, the analysis's capabilities to interpret and elucidate the role of lower-level processing skills in comprehension, independent of linguistic knowledge, is particularly important. It is commonly assumed that the contribution of word recognition diminishes once all symbols are learned. Through careful analyses of component skills, the studies just mentioned amply show that this is not the case. As demonstrated in Chapter 3, orthographic knowledge involves far more than simply knowing letter names. The studies of Durgunoglu et al. (1993) and Gholamain and Geva (1999) demonstrate that L2 decoding competence develops somewhat independently of L2 oral proficiency; additional factors, other than L2 lexical and morphosyntactic knowledge, contribute to its development. Similarly, the study of Nassaji and Geva (1999) suggests that lower-level processing competence plays a major role in L2 reading comprehension well after a high-level proficiency has been achieved. All in all, component skills analysis offers strong potential for unfolding a number of knotty issues in L2 reading by untangling heavily intertwined variables.

Working memory

Once extracted from print, lexical information must be consolidated into larger, meaningful chunks, such as phrases, sentences, and paragraphs. Working memory plays a pivotal role in this critical process. Beyond lexical access, virtually every operation in reading relies on working memory. Consistently high correlations between working-memory capacity and reading performance (e.g., Daneman & Carpenter, 1980, 1983; Daneman & Merikle, 1996) attest to the probability that the capacity is yet another dominant source of individual differences in reading ability.

Defining working-memory capacity

The premise of working memory as a shared cognitive resource holds strong implications for individual-differences research. Miyake and Friedman (1998) define working memory as "a computational arena or workspace, fueled by flexibly deployable, limited cognitive resources, or activation that support both the execution of various symbolic computations and the maintenance of intermediate products generated by these computations" (p. 341). This view reflects the active, dynamic nature of working memory, constituting a sharp contrast with the traditional conception of passive storage function. Because working-memory resources are restricted, its dual functions – storage and computation – compete for its limited capacity. In complex tasks, simultaneously activated operations impose a heavier computational burden, leaving little room for the storage function. To wit, it has been widely observed that, although performance on the digit-span test has no clear relation to reading test scores, the ability to report the digits in reverse order correlates significantly with reading performance. Daneman (1991) explains this apparent conundrum by pointing out that regular digit-span tests tap only the passive storage function, whereas reverse digit-span tests, because the reversal operation imposes additional processing demands, create a trade-off between the computation and storage functions. In point of fact, research suggests that working-memory capacity is particularly important in complex cognitive tasks, necessitating multistep operations such as ambiguity resolution (Miyake, Just, & Carpenter, 1994), syntactic parsing (King & Just, 1991), and inference generation (Singer & Ritchot, 1996).

Nonetheless, care still must be taken, because tasks used to measure working-memory capacity sometimes tap similar, if not identical, abilities underlying reading. To illustrate, the reading-span test, widely used in current research, requires participants to read a set of semantically unrelated sentences aloud and, upon conclusion, to indicate the last word in each sentence. By gradually increasing the number of sentences in each successive set (usually from two to six), the task demands increase, imposing cumulatively heavier burdens on the memory's storage function. As an index of working-memory capacity, the "reading span" is estimated on the basis of either the total number of correctly reported sentence-final words or the highest set size successfully completed. Daneman (1991) justifies the procedure's rationale as follows: "the comprehension processes used in reading the sentences would consume less of the working memory resources of the better readers; consequently, they should have more residual capacity to store the sentence-final words" (p. 528). Under this reasoning, the computational aspects of working-memory capacity and reading ability are not distinguished. Consequently, although useful, the cyclical nature of the logic sometimes complicates precise differentiation of the two constructs. Multiple accounts, in fact, have been offered to explain the high correlations between working-memory measures and complex tasks (e.g., Engle, Kane, & Tulhoski, 1999; Ericsson & Delaney, 1999; Stoltzfus et al., 1996; Waters & Caplan, 1996). Engle et al. (1999) believe that the intimate connection is indicative of the shared capability underlying the two – namely, the ability to readily shift attention between processing and storage functions. On the other hand, Ericsson and Delaney (1999) attribute performance variations in working-memory tasks to differences in encoding and retrieval competence, resulting from varying experience and expertise. Hence, it is somewhat uncertain what constitutes working-memory capacity and how it can best be measured.

Working-memory studies involving L2 readers

The concept of working memory as a shared cognitive resource also has had significant impact on L2 research. Miyake and Friedman (1998), for example, postulate that working memory may be a central component of language-learning aptitude, because major aptitude elements, such as structural analysis, memory, and phonological decoding, are all recognized as functionally connected with working memory. Additional studies, seeking to unveil the specific ways working memory influences L2 learning in general are under way.

With respect to adult L2 reading, consistently high correlations have been found between reading performance and working-memory capacity. Again, although only a handful of studies are on record, they raise issues uniquely pertinent to L2 reading. Harrington and Sawyer (1992) compared the extent to which working-memory capacity relates to reading ability and grammatical knowledge among L2 learners of English at a Japanese university. Using several measures of working-memory capacity, including reading span, digit span, and single-word span tests, the researchers concluded that reading span alone was correlated significantly with both L2 reading and grammar test scores. Given that the other span tests – digit and single-word – are designed to tap only storage function, their nonsignificant correlations with L2 reading performance appear to imply that comprehension necessitates an ability to store and process information simultaneously. Here, too, however, it is less than certain that reading-span tests measure a construct totally independent of reading ability.

Osaka and Osaka (1992) investigated the relationship between L1 and L2 working-memory capacity among Japanese college students majoring in English. Using English and Japanese versions of reading-span tests, the researchers found remarkably high correlations between L1 and L2 working-memory scores. They interpreted the outcomes as suggestive that working-memory resources in large part are shared across languages, and its capacity, therefore, is somewhat independent of linguistic knowledge.

Miyake and Friedman (1998) also studied the particular ways working memory influences L2 sentence comprehension among Japanese learners of English. They measured L1 and L2 working-memory capacity, sensitivity to L2 syntactic properties, and comprehension of syntactically complex L2 sentences. Once again, L1 and L2 working-memory capacity were highly correlated. L1 and L2 working-memory capacity, moreover, were systematically related to L2 sentence comprehension and L2 syntactic sensitivity. On the basis of these findings, Miyake surmised that working-memory capacity both directly and indirectly, through appropriate syntactic cue selection, affects complex sentence comprehension.

In another study, Fortkamp (1999) suggests that the impact of working-memory capacity may interact with the particular processing requirements of various cognitive tasks. Using multiple measures of working memory in L1 (Portuguese) and L2 (English), the study revealed a close relationship between L1 and L2 performance within each span test. In contrast, speaking and reading-span test scores correlated differentially with a variety of information-processing tasks. Although still inconclusive, the findings are suggestive of a possibility that working-memory capacity is modality specific. Furthermore, insofar as reading performance correlates only with the reading-span test, it is again unclear whether the capacity is task-domain specific or the observed correlation is merely a methodological artifact.

Viewed as a whole, it is clear that working memory as a shared cognitive resource is involved in virtually every aspect of reading subcomponent processes among both L1 and L2 readers. In all likelihood, then, working-memory capacity is a dominant factor distinguishing good and poor readers. The extent to which the capacity is independent of reading ability, however, is less certain. It is unclear, moreover, exactly what "working-memory capacity limitations" really means. The general consensus is that capacity limitations derive from multiple factors, such as processing-skills deficiency and attention-shifting ability. Miyake and Shah (1999), in fact, suggest that "the key issue is to identify which factors are operating under what circumstances and to specify how these different factors jointly contribute to the overall capacity limitations" (p. 448). Further clarification of these fundamental premises would seem imperative.

Summary and future research suggestions

Individual differences occur in all aspects of reading. Single-focus studies identify many competency clusters directly associated with successful comprehension. However, most are primarily correlates of reading ability, offering little direct explanation of reported performance variations. Phonological decoding, perhaps, is the major competence whose causal connection with early reading acquisition has been empirically supported. Although the studies have generated a copious stockpile of information, their implications are somewhat restricted, largely because their findings reveal little about developmental or functional interdependence among the component competencies. Recently, a growing number of studies have begun to explore such interconnections to determine their conjoint impacts on successful reading performance. The early research suggests that several distinct skill clusters – including orthographic processing, phonological decoding, and listening comprehension – contribute significantly, albeit differently, to individual variations in reading ability. Working memory is another research area exploring the bedrock of performance variation. Because it offers cognitive resources for integrating sequentially presented information, its function can influence virtually all aspects of comprehension. Consequently, the consistently high correlations found between working-memory capacity and reading ability are hardly surprising.

Several additional factors – for example, L2 proficiency and L1 reading ability – have now been incorporated in L2 individual-difference studies. Although systematic patterns are beginning to emerge, more is needed to clarify interconnections among component skills and between languages. Currently, limited but worthwhile efforts in a multi-dimensional analysis of L2 reading ability within the component skills framework are under way. Early findings generally suggest that individual differences in L2 reading can partially be accounted for by both language-specific capabilities and competencies shared across languages. A handful of studies have also pursued systematic examinations of the interstices between working memory and L2 reading comprehension, substantiating the conviction that working-memory capacity is strongly related to reading ability among L2 learners. Consistently high correlations between L1 and L2 working-memory capacity indices, moreover, suggest that working memory provides a shared cognitive resource across languages.

Promising findings arising from pioneering work clearly intimate that exploration of component skills analysis is a fertile avenue in expanding individual-difference studies. Two issues appear to be particularly pertinent. First, the generalizability of the current findings should be tested with L2 learners from a broader array of L1 backgrounds. Existing research is restricted to alphabetic learners learning a second alphabetic language. The extent to which the findings are applicable in cross-orthographic situations, involving either nonalphabetic learners of an alphabetic language or alphabetic learners of a nonalphabetic language, is inconclusive. L1 decoding competence, for example, has been found to be a powerful predictor of L2 word-reading ability among Spanish-speaking learners of English, but it hardly seems reasonable to expect the same degree of L1-based facilitation among ESL learners with nonalphabetic L1 backgrounds. Second, current studies tend to focus on lower-level processing skills. A careful analysis of higher-level competencies could almost certainly provide further illumination of the cognitive peculiarities among L2 learners with atypical combinations of conceptual sophistication and limited linguistic knowledge.

The significance of working memory in reading is firmly established. Indeed, studies show that working-memory capacity is an indispensable factor in successful comprehension. The complex nature of the construct, however, demands further clarifications. Inasmuch as the capacity is likely to be domain specific, the degree to which the construct is functionally independent of processing competencies is unresolved. In essence, the critical question is whether the construct alludes to differences in the working-memory resources themselves or to differences in the ability to use them efficiently. The distinction has major consequences for interpreting the reported variations in working-memory capacity. Prudent conceptual clarifications, bolstered by empirical validations, could greatly increase our understanding of the cognitive constraints on complex task performance.

10 *Developing strategic reading*

Accomplished readers continuously adjust their reading behaviors to accommodate text difficulty, task demands, and other contextual variables. Monitoring their reading process carefully, they take immediate steps when encountering comprehension problems. Aware of their own cognitive and linguistic resources, they are capable of directing their attention to the appropriate clues in anticipating, organizing, and retaining text information. These and similar behaviors, separating accomplished and less-accomplished readers, essentially characterize what is referred to as strategic reading. It is generally acknowledged that beyond information-processing skills, reading proficiency requires capabilities for exploiting cognitive and other resources to their maximum benefit. For these reasons, readers' real-time thoughts and actions – what they do and why – have attracted serious attention in both L1 and L2 reading research. Three issues are central: what behaviors are consciously initiated by readers to improve their ongoing comprehension, how such reader-initiated behaviors can be examined systematically with different groups of readers under varying conditions, and which reader-initiated actions are most efficacious in enhancing comprehension.

Several circumstances contribute to the popularity of this research. First, the significance of strategic reading has become widely recognized only relatively recently. Researchers now generally concur that strategic reading is vital in academic pursuits, where reading often is inseparable from learning, necessitating both understanding and retaining complex, often unfamiliar concepts. Second, recent advancements in research methodology now afford stable data on reader introspection, creating a window through which readers' own accounts of how a task is performed – and the ways they manage a wide range of cognitive activities – can be deciphered and analyzed. Third, inasmuch as strategy use is a deliberate, reader-initiated process, once understood it can be demonstrated for others. Put simply, having been identified, strategies used by good readers can be shared, through explicit

instruction and training, by those who do not use them. In short, findings from the research yield direct, functional implications for classroom practice.

This chapter centers on an in-depth overview of strategic reading –
its nature and development – beginning with the main concept of reading strategies, and then turning to the profound role of metacognition
in strategic reading. In passing, factors affecting L2 strategic reading
are also discussed in the context of recent empirical findings.

Strategic reading

Defining strategic reading

What exactly does it mean to read strategically? To respond to this
question, the base concept must first be defined. Weinstein and Mayer
(1986) suggest that "cognitive strategies" refers to a broad array of
actions that help govern behavior, emotion, motivation, communication, attention, and comprehension. Under a similar conceptual rubric,
Paris, Wasik, and Turner (1991) describe strategies as "actions selected
deliberately to achieve particular goals" (p. 692). These definitions
serve as a basis for identifying and classifying reading strategies in
subsequent studies (e.g., Anderson, 1991; Chamot & El-Dinary, 1999;
Cohen, 1996; Rubin, 1987). Rubin (1987), for example, views them
as "any set of operations, steps, plans, routines used by the learners
to facilitate the obtaining, storage, retrieval, and use of information"
(p. 19). Similarly, Anderson (1991) designates strategies as "deliberate,
cognitive steps that learners can take to assist in acquiring, storing, and
retrieving new information" (p. 460). In a more recent study, Chamot
and El-Dinary (1999) adopted a much broader definition: "mental
procedures that assist learning and that occasionally can be accompanied by overt activities" (p. 319). Coalesced with the earlier descriptions, reading strategies can be characterized by three core elements:
deliberate, goal/problem-oriented, and reader-initiated/controlled.

Why should we be concerned with reading strategies? The simplest
answer is that processing skills alone do not make readers proficient.
Several factors explain why we must look beyond processing competence. To begin with, reading is purposeful; we do not read merely for
the sake of reading. Readers have designated purposes – for example,
reading an interoffice memo to confirm a meeting time, reading a user
manual to find out how to set up a DVD, reading the latest issue of
a magazine to keep up with celebrity whereabouts, reading a journal article to acquire information about gene-altering technologies,
or reading a biology textbook to prepare for an examination. There

is considerable advantage, therefore, when readers have a clear notion of their specific purposes, recognizing that each entails a distinct mode of text-information processing. Consider the examples just mentioned as an illustration. The word *reading* in each statement can be replaced with a different verb, conveying a specific processing mode imposed by the purpose – *glancing at* an interoffice memo to confirm a meeting time, *scanning* a user manual to find out how to set up a DVD, *skimming* the latest issue of a magazine to keep up with celebrity whereabouts, *reviewing* a journal article to acquire information about gene-altering technologies, or *studying* a biology textbook to prepare for an examination.

Few beginning L1 readers understand the purposeful, goal-oriented nature of reading and, as a result, many rarely adjust their processing modes (e.g., Baker & Brown, 1984). Strategic reading thus depends on children's cumulative sophistication regarding what reading involves and who they are as a reader. In stressing the developmental interconnections among reading, learning, and cognition, Paris et al. (1991) suggested six reasons why strategic reading is critical in school learning:

1. Strategies allow readers to elaborate, organize, and evaluate information derived from text.
2. The acquisition of reading strategies coincides and overlaps with the development of multiple cognitive strategies to enhance attention, memory, communication, and learning.
3. Strategies are personal cognitive tools that can be used selectively and flexibly.
4. Strategic reading reflects metacognition and motivation because readers need to have both the knowledge and disposition to use strategies.
5. Strategies that foster reading and thinking can be taught directly by teachers.
6. Strategic reading can enhance learning throughout the curriculum. (1991, p. 609)

Beyond these, strategic reading obviously becomes a necessity for processing conceptually challenging contents. Regardless of proficiency and experience, every reader encounters comprehension obstacles of one sort or another. In fact, it is not uncommon even for skilled readers to experience comprehension breakdowns when reading abstruse, conceptually knotty materials. What differentiates successful from unsuccessful readers when confronted with demanding content is the willingness to counter the challenge by finding ways to circumvent the impediments. To overcome comprehension impairments, for example, readers must sense the nature of the problem, its possible solutions, and available resources to determine what works best.

Similarly, as readers ascend the educational ladder, progressively interfused tasks create yet another reason why a mastery of strategic reading is critical. In simple tasks such as locating a meeting room from a memo, sophisticated strategies are unnecessary. But, in demanding tasks, requiring information retention for further interrogations and reflections, as in essay writing or critical reviews, even a vague sense of the task objective provides indispensable guidance during both reading (e.g., how much information needs to be extracted from the text) and post-reading contemplation (e.g., how best to use extracted information in achieving the objective). Strategically savvy readers, therefore, consciously make efforts to sort and organize text information for later use.

Strategy classifications

The literature identifies a broad array of reading strategies. Although differences in the reported strategies are modest, deviations occur in the ways they are classified, as a consequence of researchers' own disparate views of reading processes and strategies.

Chamot and O'Mallety (1994) introduced three interrelated, function-based strategy clusters: *cognitive* (used for accomplishing a specific cognitive task during reading, such as inference and word-part analysis), *metacognitive* (used to regulate cognitive processing, as in comprehension monitoring and repairs), and *social and affective* (used when interacting cooperatively with others during reading, such as seeking outside assistance). The classification adopted by Anderson (1991), as shown in Table 10.1, includes five categories: *supervising* (used for monitoring progress in comprehension), *supporting* (used for regulating processing behaviors, such as skipping unknown words, or initiating dictionary use), *paraphrasing* (aiding local-information processing, through the use of cognates, word-part analysis), *establishing text coherence* (assisting global text-information processing), and *test taking* (used in accomplishing a particular task on a reading test). Paris et al. (1991) constructed yet another way of grouping strategies, based on time of use: *before*, *during*, and *after* reading. Pre-reading strategies mainly assist in the activation of prior knowledge relevant to the text to be read; during reading strategies primarily aid main-idea detection through inferences and cross-referencing; and post-reading strategies comprise activities for reviewing and pondering text content.

Two broad distinctions are common in these diverse categorizations: one distinguishing between cognitive and metacognitive strategies and the other differentiating local and global information-processing strategies. Studies indicate that these distinctions are useful in identifying

Table 10.1. *Categories of processing strategies (reprinted from N. J. Anderson, 1991, p. 463)*

I. Supervising strategies. The reader:
  1. refers to the experimental task;
  2. recognizes loss of concentration;
  3. states failure to understand a portion of the text;
  4. states success in understanding a portion of the text;
  5. adjusts reading rate in order to increase comprehension;
  6. formulates a question;
  7. makes a prediction about the meaning of a word or about text content;
  8. refers to lexical items that impede comprehension;
  9. confirms/disconfirms an inference;
  10. refers to the previous passage; or
  11. responds effectively to text content.
II. Support strategies. The reader:
  12. skips unknown words;
  13. expresses a need for a dictionary;
  14. skims reading material for a general understanding;
  15. scans reading material for a specific word or phrase; or
  16. visualizes.
III. Paraphrase strategies. The reader:
  17. uses cognates between L1 and L2 to comprehend;
  18. breaks lexical items into parts;
  19. paraphrases;
  20. translates a word or a phrase into the L1;

  21. extrapolates from information presented in the text; or
  22. speculates beyond the information presented in the text.
IV. Strategies for establishing coherence in text. The reader:
  23. rereads;
  24. uses context clues to interpret a word or phrase;
  25. reacts to author's style or text's surface structure;
  26. reads ahead;
  27. uses background knowledge;
  28. acknowledges lack of background knowledge; or
  29. relates the stimulus sentence to personal experiences.
V. Test-taking strategies. The reader:
  30. guesses without any particular considerations;
  31. looks for the answers in chronological order in the passage;
  32. selects an answer not because it was thought to be correct, but because the others did not seem reasonable, seemed similar, or were not understandable;
  33. selects an alternative through deductive reasoning;
  34. matches the stem and/or alternatives to a previous portion of the text;
  35. selects a response because it is stated in the text;
  36. selects a response based on understanding the material read;

Table 10.1 (*cont.*)

37. makes reference about time allocation;	43. expresses uncertaintly at correctness of an answer chosen;
38. reads the questions and options after reading the passage;	44. skips a questions and returns to it later;
39. reads the questions and options before reading the passage;	45. skips a question that is not understood and leaves the response blank;
40. changes an answer after having marked one;	46. marks answers without reading in order to fill the space; or
41. receives clues from answering one question that are helpful in answering another;	47. recognizes during the think-aloud protocol that an answer marked is incorrect.
42. stops reading the options after reaching the answer;	

differences in strategy use among readers. It has been found, for instance, that experienced L1 readers use global strategies to a greater extent than local strategies, whereas novice readers rely more heavily on local strategies (e.g., Myers & Paris, 1978; Paris & Jacobs, 1984). A similar tendency is noted in studies involving high- and low-proficiency L2 readers (e.g., Carrell, 1989; Chamot & El-Dinary, 1999; Young & Oxford, 1997). Moreover, recent research comparing the effectiveness of cognitive and metacognitive strategy training shows that explicit instruction on cognitive strategies yields small, short-term improvements in reading performance, whereas training on metacognitive strategies results in more stable, long-term comprehension gains (Carrell, 1998; Tang & Moore, 1992; Zhicheng, 1992).

Reading skills versus strategies

Although researchers generally agree that strategic reading and skillful reading differ, skills and strategies are not clearly distinguished in the literature. The two terms frequently are used interchangeably in references to a broad range of processing tasks, behaviors, and abilities. The confusion becomes particularly confounding when processing operations such as inference and cognate recognition are referred to as strategies in strategy studies and as skills in the reading literature (Alderson, 2000; Grabe, 1999). Although attempts have been made to differentiate the two, the distinction remains somewhat unclear. Paris and associates (1991), for example, argued that the manner in which actions are executed during comprehension is the defining element separating the two – that is, whereas skills are used *subconsciously*, strategies require *deliberate* activation. They maintain that the distinction is apparent in all operations ranging from grapheme–phoneme mapping to text summarization, regardless of processing levels or tasks. Their contention, in fact, is that a developing skill can be construed as a strategy whenever its use involves conscious activation, thereby suggesting that strategies, in fact, are "skills under consideration" (1991, p. 611). However, using activation manner as the defining factor can also be problematic, particularly in L2 reading, because the distinction becomes blurred when used in non-reader-initiated operations, requiring conscious execution, such as decoding familiar words in an unfamiliar writing system or parsing syntactically simple sentences in an unfamiliar language.

Although the discernment is not critical in describing what readers do, it becomes significant when the implications of reader actions are drawn. The following phenomenon serves as an example. During reading, low-proficiency readers are predominantly involved in decoding, whereas high-proficiency readers concentrate on conceptual processing, such as making inferences and hypothesizing (e.g., Chamot & El-Dinary, 1999; Cziko, 1980; Horiba, 1990; Vandergrift, 1997). If these behaviors are regarded as strategies, the variations can be viewed as the result of conscious decisions during reading. This obviously would imply that L2 readers deliberately alter their behaviors by shifting their attentional focus. This interpretation, therefore, creates a base for recommending that, through instruction and training, low-proficiency learners be encouraged to direct their attention to higher-level conceptual operations.

Alternatively, if the observed behaviors are considered skills rather than strategies, a completely different implication emerges – that is, the reported differences simply are a behavioral manifestation of divergent processing competence. Low-proficiency readers tend to engage more heavily in lower-level processing, possibly because their decoding skills are not yet sufficiently developed. This interpretation would then imply that readers' actions are symptomatic of their competence rather than their inclinations. Thus, requiring them to focus on something for which they are not yet ready would hardly improve their performance. Similarly, designing explicit strategy training based on what good readers do, without considering why they do it, is equally unlikely to yield significant benefits. To draw valid implications for classroom practice, it is imperative, first, to differentiate what readers *can* do from what they *intend* to do, and then conceptualize effective ways to provide explicit strategy instruction.

Perhaps one way to accomplish the differentiation would be to use intention rather than activation manner as the defining criterion. Reading actions, in short, can be interpreted as strategies when executed intentionally. Skills, in contrast, refer to what readers actually do to achieve their intended actions. Skill activation, therefore, may or may not be deliberate. Theoretically, readers are assumed to use strategies consciously, whereas skill activation can be either conscious or subconscious. Several benefits might be achieved through distinguishing the two in strategy research. It would sharpen the focus; in assessing skills, how successfully the operation is accomplished should be primary. Analyzing strategies, on the other hand, should fixate on what readers plan to do, and for what reason. Additionally, the distinction would compartmentalize the two throughout their evolution, allowing explorations of the impact of one, independent of the other, on comprehension performance.

Finally, the separation would facilitate analysis of the complex procedures necessitated in both skills and strategies. Lexical inference, as a case in point, is treated as a skill in some studies and as a strategy in others. Technically, it is neither. Based on this dissection, the reader's attempt to define an unfamiliar word rather than skipping it would be a strategic action. The intention alone, however, would be insufficient because its execution requires auxiliary skills: word segmentation, word-part analysis, contextual and word-internal information integration, and so on. By dissecting skills and strategies, we may gain a far better opportunity to understand how reader-initiated behaviors facilitate comprehension.

Roles of metacognition in strategic reading

Metacognition, or cognition of cognition, refers to learners' understanding and control of their own thinking and learning. Many theorists believe these capabilities are primarily responsible for readers' online decision making in regulating their actions. As a consequence, a rapid growth of interest in the effects of metacognition on strategic reading has developed. The general consensus is that efficacious uses of reading strategies evolve in progressive stages, coinciding with children's growing awareness of the connections among reading, learning, and their own cognitive capabilities. Many strategies are acquired between the ages of 7 and 13, but their spontaneous use usually does not materialize until somewhere around the age of 10 (Paris et al., 1991). These findings further corroborate the widespread observation that young children read nonstrategically, advancing through the text linearly from the beginning to the end, without any adjustments such as rereading, backtracking, or skimming (e.g., Garner, 1990).

Long ago, Flavell (1978) was convinced that metacognition has two basic facets: the ability to reflect on one's own cognition and the capacity to regulate one's own cognitive activities. In the reading literature, metacognitive research addresses issues inherent in these two capabilities (Baker & Brown, 1984). Research on the *reflective* aspect deals essentially with learners' understanding of their own cognitive resources, as well as operational perception of how the understanding can facilitate their comprehension. The underlying premise is that, if readers can reflect on their own cognitive processes and functions, they should be able to determine what it takes to improve performance, as well as what they need to do to make it happen. The *control* aspect of metacognition, in contrast, basically concerns the mechanisms for regulating efforts to increase performance efficiency. Such regulatory behaviors include initiating the appropriate corrections and adjustments, and then evaluating the benefits of the actions taken.

Reading specialists tend to concur that comprehension monitoring is the decisive metacognitive capability separating good from poor readers. They generally conclude that, compared with their less-competent counterparts, good readers evaluate their comprehension accurately (e.g., Myers & Paris, 1978), initiate self-correction during oral reading (e.g., Clay, 1973), and eliminate more of the meaning-distorting, rather than grammatical, errors (e.g., Kavale & Schreiner, 1979). Eye-movement studies further suggest that, when confronted with challenging passages, good readers make a greater number of eye-movement adjustments – for example, increased fixation frequency and duration, as well as additional backtracking (e.g., Gibson & Levin, 1975).

According to Baker and Brown (1984), developing compensatory strategies constitutes yet another metacognitive issue in reading. The logic is straightforward: If readers are metacognitively capable, they should have a clear sense of their own cognitive limitations. Knowing what they can and cannot do, metacognitively adroit readers are likely to develop their own sophisticated strategies to offset their shortcomings. Therefore, through systematic observations of reader-initiated behaviors in problematic situations, we may be able to gain further insights into another facet of metacognitive facilitation among cognitively mature, skilled readers – self-actualized correctives.

Finally, it should be noted that metacognitive capabilities become operative only in reading tasks perceived as hard but attainable. When the task offers minimal challenge, or is interpreted as unworkable, there is little incentive for readers to make extra efforts to manipulate their cognitive resources, because nothing will be gained.

Verbal reports and protocol analysis

In metacognitive research, reader-initiated behaviors are examined chiefly through introspective reports produced by readers themselves. Although soliciting people's thoughts has long been a staple in everyday discourse, Ericsson and Simon (1984) converted the general practice of thought sharing into "a useful form of scientific inquiry" (Afflerback, 2000, p. 163). Unlike traditional research paradigms – that is, making indirect inferences about readers' understanding of text through their response to a variety of post-reading tasks – thought sharing taps directly into ongoing cognitive activities as they occur. Because of its process orientation and potential allowance for point-blank access to reader introspection, this methodology, often referred to as verbal protocol analysis, has fundamentally altered the nature of questions researchers pose as well as the inferences they derive about reading processes (Baker & Brown, 1984). For purposes of explication, the scientific rationale underlying verbal protocol analysis and discussion of the advantages and disadvantages associated with this data elicitation technique follow.

Verbal protocol analysis rationale

Verbal reports are obtained when readers think aloud while engaging in reading. The rationale of this process was explained in detail by Ericsson and Simon (1984). Human cognition embodies information processing. As Ericsson and Simon put it, "a cognitive process can be seen as a sequence of internal states successively transformed by a series of information processes" (p. 10). The postulation presumes that outputs from various processes are stored in multiple memories with distinct capacities and access characteristics. For example, sensory (e.g., iconic and echoic) memories receive information directly from the sensory organs and retain it for a very short duration, whereas short-term working memory stores a relatively small amount of heeded information for an intermediate duration. Long-term memory (LTM), Ericsson and Simon suggest, can be characterized as a large collection of interrelated information stored on a more stable basis.

The verbalization procedures individuals are required to use have desirable impacts on the types of memory accessed. For example, because output information, from ongoing or recently completed

Table 10.2. *A classification of different types of verbalization procedures (reprinted from K. A. Ericsson & H. A. Simon, 1984, p. 12)*

| | | Relation between heeded and verbalized information | | |
| | | Intermediate processing | | |
Time of verbalization	Direct one to one	Many to one	Unclear	No relation
While information is attended	Talk aloud think aloud			
While information is still in short-term memory	Concurrent probing	Intermediate inference and generative processes		
After the completion of the task-directed processes	Retrospective probing	Requests for general reports	Probing hypothetical states	Probing general states

processing, remains active in working memory, it is directly accessible for verbal reporting. In contrast, LTM information must first be transferred into working memory before it can be reported. Critically, the transferred information can be subjected to intermediary processes in working memory, such as generalization and inference. The resulting verbalization, inevitably, can become a product of the intermediary processes. Hence, Ericsson and Simon contend that two distinctions are essential in classifying the type and quality of verbal reports (see Table 10.2). The timing of verbalization (lapse between the action occurrence and the onset of reporting) is one such distinction, because it determines whether the heeded information is active in working memory, or transferred from LTM. Another distinction should be made with respect to the reporting procedures. For example, "concurrent verbalization" reports thoughts that occur during the execution of the assigned task, whereas "retrospective reporting" elicits verbalization of thoughts that occur after task completion.

Building on the Ericsson and Simon model, Cohen (1987) identified several types of verbal reporting. Self-observation, for example, entails participants' reporting the specific, predetermined processes used in a particular reading task either during or immediately after reading, whereas self-revelation is "a stream of consciousness disclosure of thought processes while the information is being attended to" (p. 84).

Because of its immediacy, self-revelation is likely to yield a direct, unedited version of working-memory content. Information gathered through self-observation, however, may involve LTM and also is likely to be a somewhat generalized and partially edited version of reader thoughts and actions.

When reporting involves working memory, the cognitive activities to be reported, and the reporting itself, compete for its limited capacity. Conceivably, reading performance and reporting performance influence each other; at the same time, other factors affecting the two, including task requirements, text, and elapsed time before the reporting, can also affect the quality and quantity of verbal reports, making it difficult to achieve reliable accounts of reader thoughts and actions. To illustrate, a common phenomenon in empirical studies is that, when asked, good readers verbalize their reading processes far more than poor readers (e.g., Anderson, 1991; Block, 1986). Although the simplest and most straightforward interpretation would be that good readers use more strategies than poor readers, other explanations also are possible. Good readers may be more conscious of their actions as well as more adept at verbalizing them. Alternatively, the observed differences in verbalization quantity may simply have been a manifestation of good readers' greater attentional capacity for reporting. Each of these scenarios gives rise to the possibility that verbal protocol data produced by good readers may describe what all readers, not just good ones, do. By the same token, if poor readers lack the ability to verbalize their actions, their reports would also unveil little about their reading behaviors. For these assorted reasons, researchers warn that diligence and caution are critical in interpreting protocol data (e.g., Alderson, 2000; Anderson, 1991; Cohen, 1998).

Unique contributions

Despite its probable shortcomings, to repeat, verbal protocol analysis has become a widely used methodology in L2 reading and learning research. Its prevalence, perhaps, can best be explained by clarifying what the analysis can tell us about reading. Afflerback (2000) describes three specific advantages of verbal protocol analysis. First, the method, when used to examine reader behaviors in well-defined tasks, permits systematic explorations of reader–task interactions. By illustrating the complexity inherent in readers' thoughts and actions, protocol-analysis studies collectively yield detailed descriptions of task-induced reader behaviors. We can learn, for example, how a particular task is perceived by readers, how the perception affects their actions, and how the task–reader interactions are refined as higher developmental states are reached. Properly used, verbal protocol analysis can tell us what readers do, as well as why they do it. The latter information is especially pivotal in decompounding the essence of strategic reading. It is not readily available in quantitative studies, using aggregate group data, which tell us what readers do, but not why.

Second, verbal protocol analysis can also clarify many of the intricacies associated with organizing and coordinating the broad array of strategies spanning subcomponent processes. By focusing on strategy orchestration, for example, verbal report data can highlight the interconnections among strategies, their dynamic interactions, the specific benefits of metacognitive strategy management in escalating reading efficiency, and, perhaps, most critically, contextual influences on effective strategy use.

Third, verbal protocol analysis permits examination of an important, yet largely neglected, issue in reading: the affective dimensions of reader response. Although literary theory has a long tradition of analyzing reader–text interaction from noncognitive perspectives, for the most part, the affects have been overlooked in reading research. By probing reader reactions to literary texts, verbal protocol analysis could help disentangle the rich complexity of reader emotions evoked by texts. Put simply, the accumulated research evidence tells us little about how readers react when, for example, they like or dislike a text. In short, reader emotion would seem to be a promising, yet to be explored, area of inquiry, and verbal protocol analysis has potential as a useful tool in helping us understand how readers' affective states influence the ways they interact with texts and the resulting effects on comprehension.

Methodological concerns revisited

The shortcomings inherent in verbal protocol analysis aside, other concerns remain regarding the way it is used in some studies. To begin with, data-collection procedures are not always clearly described. Because simultaneous engagement in reading and thought sharing can overload limited working-memory capacity, a variety of factors influencing either or both can affect verbal reporting. To make reasonably accurate inferences about reader behaviors under normal circumstances, peculiarities attributable to study-specific variables need to be isolated. However, without explicit and detailed descriptions of data-collection procedures, it is futile to compare verbal report data across studies, thereby restricting the generalizability of composite study findings.

Another concern is that, although verbal reports can elicit complex thoughts during reading, the information in itself reveals little about the reader's actions. There is a growing tendency to treat verbal protocols as behavioral data without empirical verifications as to how closely the reported actions and actual actions coincide, or how successfully those actions, which indeed took place, were carried out. In instances, blatant claims of connections linking reader behaviors and competence are made solely on the basis of the report data. Several researchers (e.g., Afflerback, 2000; Magliano & Graesser, 1993) strongly advocate data triangulation, by incorporating multiple, sequentially implemented procedures, such as construct analysis, systematic observations across tasks and texts, and the use of behavioral measures.

Yet another concern has to do with insufficient descriptions regarding different – that is, concurrent and retrospective – reporting procedures. As indicated earlier, concurrent reporting can be characterized essentially as an online exposé of working-memory content, whereas the time lapse in the retrospective procedure permits LTM involvement, thus allowing participants to generalize their own, and sometimes editorialized, actions. Moreover, participants, less restrained by working-memory limitations, can engage in secondary reassessments and revisions of their conclusions. There is a good chance, consequently, that the two reporting procedures yield data reflecting qualitatively different realities. More critically, the two may occur simultaneously even in a single think-aloud session.

Strategic reading among L2 readers

Several conclusions can be drawn from strategy research involving L1 readers. Inasmuch as strategies are reader-initiated actions used to accomplish a given task, strategic reading cannot be accomplished without the readers' desire and intent to read more efficiently. The acquisition of strategic reading, moreover, depends on the corresponding development of cognitive and metacognitive capabilities. With a growing awareness that reading involves text-meaning construction, good reading behaviors gradually mature from their initial uncertainty to specific tactics. For such developmental transformations to occur, readers must be confronted with sufficient expectations requiring increased efficiency and prudent resource management.

With the greater complexity in L2 reading, a number of additional factors also must be considered in defining strategic reading among L2 readers. Because lower-level processing competence directly affects strategy utilization, factors affecting decoding efficiency in L2 print processing must be considered. Insofar as L2 readers, already literate in their L1, supposedly possess a wide range of reading strategies, it is likely that the successful L1 strategy transfer is responsible, at least in part, for individual differences in L2 strategic reading. In addition, readers' understanding of, and convictions about, reading, molded through L1 literacy, are likely to influence how they deploy L2 strategies. Because these conceptions are an outcome of literacy experience embedded in a particular cultural context, it is probable that readers with diverse cultural backgrounds develop distinct views of reading and act on different assumptions regarding good reading behaviors.

To date, these L2-specific concerns have attracted minimal attention. The great majority of current research closely emulates L1 pursuits, focusing on three major issues: identifying strategies directly bearing on comprehension, comparing strategy use across different reader groups, and examining the effects of strategy instruction on reading improvement.

Strategies enhancing L2 comprehension

An initial, exploratory cluster of studies has described strategies associated with comprehension performance. The findings demonstrate that the bulk of reported strategies generally parallel reading achievement, but systematic connections between particular sets of strategies and reading effectiveness have not yet emerged (e.g., Anderson, 1991; Rusciolelli, 1995). Anderson (1991), for example, compared self-reported actions among college ESL learners in an American university to determine whether strategies used in reading an academic text differed from those used in a multiple-choice standardized reading test. His data suggest that participants who verbalized more during self-reports generally performed better on the reading tests. No systematic relationship was found, however, between the number of distinct strategies and reading performance. In fact, readers with both high and low test scores used similar strategies. The data also indicated little quantitative differences in the number of strategies reported during test taking and academic reading. A subsequent qualitative analysis, furthermore, revealed that readers seemed to know which strategies to use but failed to use them successfully. Anderson concluded that what accounts for performance differences is not an awareness of which strategies to use, but rather competence in implementing and monitoring their applications. He suggests, in fact, that "knowing how to assess the success of given strategy and apply corrective feedback to its use may be a more important skill to develop" (1991, p. 469).

Similarly, in her widely cited study, Block (1986) compared native and nonnative English-speaking college students enrolled in a remedial reading program. The outcomes are illuminating; all participants mentioned a variety of strategies, but only a few were successful in using them to aid comprehension. Here again, the empirical data reaffirm that knowing which strategies to use is minimally sufficient, because knowledge alone neither discriminates between successful and less successful readers nor predicts effective strategy use. The researcher found that "awareness of what they were doing and what they understood allowed some of them to teach themselves" (1986, p. 488), once more reinforcing the critical role of metacognitive awareness.

Patterns of strategy use among L2 readers

Since Hosenfield, in her 1977 pioneering study, demonstrated that successful use of inference strategy was a key factor differentiating good from poor L2 readers, interest in reading strategies among L2 researchers has escalated. Recent investigations have focused mainly on patterns of strategy use among disparate groups of L2 readers. Chamot and El-Dinary (1999), for example, explored the quality and quantity of reading strategies among high- and low-achieving elementary school learners in French, Japanese, and Spanish immersion classrooms. Although the total number of reported strategies was similar between the two groups, there was an interesting contrast in the types of strategies. Half the strategies reported by low-achieving students were decoding, but most strategies used by high-achieving students were of a conceptual nature, including inferences, predictions, elaborations, and so on. Other studies involving older learners also reflected the dominance of local strategies among low-proficiency participants (e.g., Carrell, 1989; Chern, 1994; de Courcy & Birch, 1993; Young & Oxford, 1997). In a third research approach, analyzing questionnaire responses among two groups of college L2 readers, native English-speaking learners of Spanish and native Spanish-speaking learners of English, Carrell (1989) discovered disparities in perceived effectiveness of divergent strategies among high- and low-proficiency L2 learners. High-proficiency readers regarded local strategies as ineffective, but low-proficiency readers did not.

Similar patterns of strategy use also have appeared in research comparing strategic behaviors in L1 and L2 reading. Young and Oxford (1997) found that native English-speaking college students relied heavily on local strategies when reading L2 (Spanish) but reverted to more global strategies in their L1. In her comparison of strategy use among college L2 readers of English in a Taiwanese university, Chern

(1994) added another variable, L2 proficiency. When reading English, Taiwanese students, regardless of their proficiency, were severely confused by unfamiliar words. Lexical familiarity, however, had virtually no impact on their L1 reading performance. She also found that high-proficiency learners used distinct cues in L1 and L2 reading – that is, greater use of global cues in L1 and heavier reliance on local cues in L2. Because such differentiation was not observed among low-proficiency learners, the findings seem to intimate that the two key variables, L2 proficiency and language familiarity, affect strategy use somewhat independently.

Yet another line of research centered on cross-language reading-strategy transfer among bilingual cohorts in U.S. schools. The results generally imply that students tend to use similar strategies in reading L1 and L2 (e.g., Calero-Breckheimer & Goetz, 1993; Jimenez et al., 1995; Pritchard, 1990), but strategy transfer increases notably when readers perceive the two languages as similar (e.g., Garcia, 1991; Jimenez, Garcia, & Pearson, 1996). Strategy training in one language also increases strategy use in the other (e.g., Muniz-Swicegood, 1994; Padron, 1992). Viewed collectively, these findings confirm that strategies developed in one language generally are transferred to another. It is noteworthy, however, that participants in these studies were predominantly bilingual in two related languages, Spanish and English. The extent to which the implications are generalizable to L2 readers with unrelated L1 backgrounds is uncertain. A study by Hua (1997) comparing strategy use among Chinese ESL learners in their L1 and L2, however, does shed some light on the issue. The study demonstrated that bilingual readers with unrelated L1 and L2 also used virtually identical comprehension strategies in their two languages, again suggesting that reading strategies may transfer across languages, regardless of linguistic distance.

Effectiveness of reading strategy instruction

A third strand of L2 studies examines the benefits of strategy instruction. Generally, the training aims at improving the performance of poor readers by instilling a self-regulatory reading mode through explicit, step-by-step demonstrations of good reading behaviors. Three approaches are modeled: cognitive strategies (used during text-information processing), metacognitive strategies (used in monitoring and regulating the reading), and test-taking strategies. The research by and large implies that strategy instruction has consistent, albeit short-term, impacts on performance. The magnitude of the impacts, however, varies across strategies.

Tang and Moore (1992), for example, compared training effectiveness in cognitive and metacognitive strategies for improving comprehension among college ESL learners. Both yielded similar comprehension gains after instruction, but only the metacognitive training propagated long-term benefits in continuous progress. In a similar training study with college ESL learners, in addition to cognitive and metacognitive strategies, Zhicheng (1992) provided explicit instruction on test-taking strategies. Post-training reading performance indicated that, while cognitive and metacognitive strategy instruction improved comprehension, training on test-taking strategies offered no clear long-term benefits.

Although empirical findings suggest that instructional outcomes may vary across strategy types, why and how instructional effectiveness differs among disparate strategies remains uncertain. The extent to which instructional benefits are affected by other variables, such as reader characteristics (e.g., L1 background and literacy competency, L2 proficiency), text properties (e.g., length, linguistic complexity, and content familiarity), and task nature (e.g., multiple-choice questions, text summary, recall), is also unclear. Given the reported benefits, much could be gained by differentiating these and other related variables, which may affect strategy instruction effectiveness.

Summary and future research suggestions

Strategic reading, obviously, is an essential competence for anyone who reads for the sake of learning and thinking. Several factors explain why processing skills alone are insufficient. Reading is a purposeful activity requiring well-suited modes of processing. Catering to its goal-oriented nature, therefore, expedites the choice of the most appropriate processing mode for a given purpose. Conceptually demanding tasks, moreover, require particularly careful comprehension monitoring, because they necessitate subsequent reflection. Because strategic reading is an outcome of children's growing understanding of what reading is, and of their role as a reader, a widespread belief is that metacognition – the explicit understanding of one's own cognitive capabilities – plays a central role in their spontaneous use of strategies to regulate their reading behaviors during comprehension. In fact, metacognitive studies demonstrate that good readers usually are adept at accurately evaluating their comprehension, initiating self-corrections during oral reading, and adjusting eye movements during silent reading. These findings clearly reinforce the importance of online monitoring in successful comprehension.

222   *Looking at the whole*

Because of their close affiliation with instruction, reading strategies also have attracted considerable attention among L2 researchers. Although additional elements are presumed to influence strategy use among L2 learners, curiously, limited attention has been given to L2-specific concerns in reading-strategy studies. Ongoing research tends to focus on the general issues raised in L1 investigations. To date, L2 findings suggest that degree of strategy use generally correlates with reading performance: High- and low-proficiency L2 learners use qualitatively different strategies, and explicit strategy instruction generates modest, but detectable, comprehension gains. Despite the complexity involved in L2 strategic reading, we are beginning to categorize L2 reading strategies, but additional effort is needed to illuminate the factors that facilitate their effective use during comprehension. Further explorations of L2 reading strategies might be pursued in several ways.

Restricted strategy use is common among beginning readers in both L1 and L2. Different factors, however, may be responsible. Although underdeveloped metacognition prohibits inexperienced L1 readers from using a broad range of strategies, metacognitively mature adult L2 readers should be aware of strategies and their merits. There have been a number of speculations about forces inhibiting effective strategy use, but little has been investigated empirically. Research has focused on L2 readers' intentions, with relatively little attention to their behavior.

Although useful, studies on strategy usage reveal little about the specific effect of a particular strategy on comprehension. For instance, skipping words is a commonly reported strategy, but we have no way of knowing why readers skip words because multiple explanations are possible. For example, skipping words, in one interpretation, can be taken as an indication of reader confidence – that is, knowing that particular words do not convey critical information for text-meaning construction. Alternatively, skipping could imply reader incompetence – that is, not knowing how to deal with unfamiliar words. Frequency comparisons of reported strategy uses do not permit reliable causal inferences about linkages between particular strategies and reading competence. It would be extremely helpful if, in future studies, intra-individual variations in strategy use when reading texts with contrasting linguistic and conceptual complexity were documented.

Although, in general, research findings attribute modest, but consistent, comprehension gains to strategy instruction, little information is available about which specific aspects of instruction are actually responsible for the reported improvements. Such data would be significant, if only because there are multiple ways of explaining the realized gains. One possibility, for example, would be that instruction familiarized readers with strategies with which they were unaware. Another might be that, through explanations of how a particular strategy aids comprehension, instruction might have convinced readers of its functional utility. Or, repeated practice could have induced greater ease in strategy implementation. Without a clear sense of the specific training benefits, it will be extremely difficult to establish a solid base for designing and modifying instructional tactics. Ultimately, of course, instruction should center on sensitizing readers to the consummate importance of regulating their reading behaviors, and, in so doing, illustrate how self-regulation can materialize through the self-monitoring of their own reading progress.

PART IV

THEORY INTO PRACTICE

11　Comprehension assessment

To recap, reading is a complex, multifaceted pursuit requiring the continuous deployment and integration of multiple operations. A long-standing conviction holds that adept reading is a constellation of interfaced capabilities, ranging from mechanical mappings to more sophisticated conceptual manipulations, such as reasoning and inference. It is not surprising, consequently, that assessing something of such complexity requires a clear consensus – which continues to remain elusive – about what constitutes reading ability. Currently, contradictory conceptions of comprehension govern assessment designs, resulting in a variety of approaches.

In L2 assessment, moreover, additional factors compound the complexity. Traditionally, reading is viewed as an integral aspect of language proficiency, and thus assessment continuously mirrors the prevailing definition of L2 proficiency. Recently, for example, the core element in L2 proficiency has shifted from discrete, decontextualized linguistic knowledge to communicative competence. Parallel shifts reflecting this change have also occurred in L2 reading assessment. Earlier emphasis on linguistic variables (e.g., lexical and syntactic complexity and/or familiarity) as the critical determinants of comprehension difficulty has substantially diminished. Instead, factors bearing on communicative, meaning-making intent (e.g., reading purposes and text content) have gained considerable prominence.

To understand current practices, the fundamental principles underlying disparate assessment procedures need further clarification. This chapter elucidates the conceptual bases of widely used assessment approaches. Following a description of the contrasting views on reading comprehension, the chapter considers their implications for test design and development. Assessment models, implemented in various L1 and L2 instructional contexts, are then examined, and illustrative assessment techniques are analyzed. Finally, a critical review of the factors uniquely associated with L2 reading assessment is provided.

Conceptualizing reading comprehension

Measuring reading comprehension, as noted earlier, is far from simple because there are multifarious definitions of comprehension. Owing to the inherent complexity, divergent conceptions currently exist in the literature. Because these views serve as the basis for deciding what and how to measure, it is essential to clarify their variations within the assessment context.

Comprehension as process versus as product

The basic premise underlying most reading assessment is that comprehension is a *product* of the reader's interaction with a text (Johnston, 1983). In essence, the product view presumes that the outcomes of reading are stored in the reader's long-term memory and can be measured by persuading the reader to demonstrate portions of the stored text representation. Such assumptions are clearly evidenced in common assessment measures such as true-false and multiple-choice questions, constructive responses, and free recall. Given the nature of post-reading administration, this approach places the major emphasis on memory as the dominant factor underlying successful demonstration of comprehension. However, another important, somewhat covert, assumption underlying the product approach is that memory and comprehension are largely inseparable – namely, for all practical purposes, comprehension occurs only if text information is stored in memory, and content retention is possible only when it is adequately understood. Be this as it may, a major point of controversy lies in the possibility that any portion of performance variance in post-reading production tasks can be explained by memory alone, without comprehension. Critics have also raised another concern: the obvious lack of attention given to the process through which stored representation is formulated.

In a contrasting conjecture, comprehension is conceived of as the *process* of extracting information from print and integrating it into a coherent meaning. As a result, the process view emphasizes the importance of working memory, cautioning that a delay in measuring comprehension makes it difficult to distinguish what is being comprehended from what was already in long-term memory. This approach hinges on a clear distinction between the ability to comprehend and the ability to remember, thus contrasting sharply with the product view. To measure comprehension without confounding it with memory, therefore, process-based assessment is designated to capture ongoing processing behaviors as they occur during reading, before text information is conveyed to long-term memory. Online processing tasks, think-aloud verbal reports, and eye-movement tracking serve as examples. Obviously, the process-based approach yields additional insights, compensating for the inevitable limitations in product-based assessment procedures. However, on the downside, the approach can have serious disruptive consequences, because it usually entails an additional task during reading.

Comprehension as sum of parts versus as a whole

Distinctions also can be made with respect to the critical competencies constituting comprehension, as an indivisible whole versus a cluster of decomposable components. The fundamental rationale of the holistic view is that, inasmuch as reading essentially is reasoning, comprehension ability and verbal intelligence are not easily differentiated. The logic here is that poor comprehension stems from a conceptual deficiency rather than from a deficit in one or more component skills (e.g., Thorndike, 1974). From a pedagogical perspective, Goodman (1967, 1969) contended that learning to read is a natural process during the course of human development, because language is learned as a whole through communication, and communicative use of language is intrinsic in reading. Dissecting such a communicative act into its parts, therefore, counteracts the fundamental premise. Accordingly, it is unlikely that a clear understanding of comprehension ability can be achieved by measuring discrete component skills.

The component view, in contrast, postulates that reading is a complex, multidimensional operation. Therefore, it can be dissected into a series of theoretically distinct procedures, each requiring a wide range of skills. As discussed in Chapter 9, individual differences exist in virtually all facets of reading competence. Consequently, it is essential to determine which particular variations are causally related to comprehension performance. Toward that end, systematic comparisons of the relative impacts of component skills should provide clues for identifying commonplace deficiencies among poor readers and, in so doing, pinpoint sources of reading problems. In this case, the logic shifts. Lacking precise assessment, truly effective diagnostic interventions may not be possible.

Although the two perspectives may seem diametrically opposed, in reality, as in the contrast between product and process orientations, they are complementary. Research, at the risk of redundancy, identifies a number of integral skills. Comprehension, therefore, cannot be simply viewed as a by-product of reading as a whole. At the same time, however, it also cannot be taken as the sum of information generated by the component operations, because the reader–text interaction often alters the meaning of assembled text information. The assessment implication, consequently, is that the root competence on which comprehension depends can be captured only by integrating a gestalt of the parts and the whole in tandem.

Degrees of comprehension

However comprehension is conceptualized, there is uniform agreement that it is not an all-or-nothing process or product. Some *readers*, for example, extract more text information than others; some *texts* are more easily understood than others; and some *contexts* foster comprehension better than others. Comprehension, in sum, is a matter of degree. Consequently, in considering the factors affecting its assessment, we must first define what is meant by "comprehending better" by clarifying the different perspectives from which degrees of comprehension can be characterized and then distinguished. Three such perspectives have received significant attention: processing levels, task requirements, and reader purposes (Enright, Grabe, Koda, Mosenthal, Mulkahy-Ernt, & Schedl, 2000).

The processing perspective utilizes sequential operations in defining degrees of comprehension. As mentioned earlier, reading success by and large is determined by performance on three hierarchical operation clusters: low-level decoding (converting print into linguistic information), interim-level textbase construction (extracting and integrating textual information), and higher-level situation-model building (synthesizing text information with prior knowledge). The underlying rationale is that performing higher-level operations in the hierarchy depends on processing competence at lower levels. To illustrate, coherent textbases cannot be established without accurate information derived from decoding, and situation models cannot be created without adequate text-level representations. The base logic, obviously, is that processing competencies at each level yield reliable estimates of text-representation completeness.

The cognitive requirements of individual-assessment tasks also distinguish degrees of comprehension. For instance, post-reading comprehension questions requiring specific *text-explicit* information can be answered by locating a word or phrase. Questions probing *text-implicit* information, in contrast, necessitate deeper understanding because they involve inferencing, and become even more demanding when readers are expected to expand on text meaning – determining content validity, evaluating argument plausibility, and so on. Differential task demands, therefore, can be used to judge comprehension depth. Accordingly, the virtue of this approach is that correspondence between task demands and comprehension can be captured through systematic performance comparisons on tasks of varying processing complexity.

Reader purposes offer yet another means of evaluating levels of text understanding. According to Carver (1990, 1997, 2000), as referenced in Chapter 1, readers alter their approach to reading texts according to their purposes. The theory postulates five alternative reading "gears," representing various purpose-induced reading modes: lexical access (gear 5: scanning), local semantic integration (gear 4: skimming), sentence integration and main-idea retention (gear 3: "rauding," or basic comprehension), grasping unfamiliar concepts (gear 2: learning), and remembering content information (gear 1: memorizing). Carver (2000) contended that processing demands increase as the gear shifts downward, resulting in slower reading rates. College students, for example, can scan at a rate of roughly six hundred standard-length words per minute (wpm), whereas the memorizing gear proceeds at a rate of 138 wpm. Self-evidently, the higher gears process text information far more rapidly, but the resulting text representation is compromised, as in the case of speedy scanning and skimming. In the lower gears, however, more accurate and complete representation is achieved at the expense of reduced speed. Hence, in general, degree of text understanding can be estimated on the basis of the reading mode dictated by the reader's purpose.

Developmental stages, moreover, must be carefully considered when incorporating comprehension levels in reading assessment. To wit, the two major elements – learning to read and reading to learn – are developmentally and functionally discrete, each entailing different objectives. The interpretation of "comprehension," therefore, must consider their respective expectations. In learning to read, for example, readers must master adequate decoding skills, because at this stage, reading pertains to extracting meaning at the lexical level, and comprehension alludes only to uncovering familiar content. In the subsequent reading-to-learn stage, on the other hand, comprehension, reflecting its primary focus on obtaining new knowledge, implies constructing meaning from unfamiliar content. In sum, reading assessment must conform to the qualitatively different skills readers are developing at each distinct stage.

Assessment purposes

Reading assessment should include systematic samplings of reading behaviors that guide decisions about reading ability (Johnston, 1983). Because assessment outcomes are used for various purposes, information required to determine reading ability differs widely. Therefore, different kinds of reading samples also are needed in identifying, for example, the source of a given reading difficulty, and in comparing the effectiveness of two instructional programs. Consequently, it is critical to clarify how the assessment purposes and intended uses of assessment information should both guide and constrain task design. Three commonplace assessment functions are illustrative: administration, diagnosis, and classification.

Large-scale objective testing governs *administrative* decisions such as funding allocation and policy decisions. Accordingly, the assessment process collects information, which facilitates the evaluation of program outcomes or comparisons of educational achievement among particular subgroups, on the basis of factors such as race, gender, and socioeconomic status. The assessment, therefore, must include examinees with a full spectrum of reading abilities, as well as tasks eliciting a broad range of the behaviors inherent in the normal act of reading. Consequently, administrative assessment, by design, yields an overall picture of the reading characteristics of particular target groups, but not of either individual readers or specific component skills.

Another assessment purpose is *diagnostic*. The essential goal is to pinpoint sources of reading difficulties frequently experienced by underachieving readers. Unlike the relatively stable nature of administrative assessment, diagnostic testing reflects the dynamic nature of reading development and ongoing changes in both the manner and the rate of skills acquisition. For this reason, diagnostic assessment is responsive to individual differences and, unlike administrative assessment, does not necessitate group-based standardization. So long as the constructs to be measured are clearly specified, and based on solid theoretical foundations, the assessment can be criterion referenced, focusing only on skills considered potential factors in reading difficulty. Outcomes from such tightly regimented tests can inform and guide instructional decision making, particularly with respect to programs aimed at overcoming specific reading problems.

An additional assessment function is *classification*. By collecting information that creates a legitimate basis for individual comparisons, assessment data can be used to differentiate examinees. The test outcomes provide an infrastructure for decision making regarding such issues as college/university admissions, employment/promotion qualifications, appropriate academic-program placement, and course grades. Because the purpose of the assessment is to determine individual reading ability, whether relative to others or to specific criteria, capability must be compared on a common basis. However, this gives rise to a dilemma. Tests must contrast a wide variety of learners on a limited range of competencies, and therefore cannot profile specific individual differences; yet, the outcomes are used as a basis for making decisions about individuals.

Assessment models

Two distinct models currently are used in conjoining the three assessment purposes just described: objective assessment utilizing standardized tests, and informal assessment through direct observations of student performance (Calfee & Hiebert, 1991). Because the two models rely on completely different techniques for obtaining evidence on reading ability, their outcomes inevitably yield distinct reader profiles, whose implications for assessment utilization are as follows.

Standardized objective assessment

Administration and classification assessments typically are used to make high-stakes decisions. The general expectation, therefore, is that they provide stable information about students' reading ability. The major concerns in these large-scale assessments include time/cost efficiency, justification (legitimacy within accepted theories), objectivity, fairness, and aggregatability (adaptability to numerical consolidation).

The assessments predominantly rely on two standardized measures: norm-reference (NRT) and criterion-reference (CRT) tests. NRTs depict individual students' relative standing by using their peer group as the point of reference. CRTs, in contrast, are designed to indicate mastery of specific competencies by using an absolute performance level (e.g., percent correct, cutoff point) as the reference. CRTs are widely used to monitor externally developed curriculum and instructional achievement through the use of end-of-unit tests in commercially available reading texts and mandatory state/district competency tests.

Inasmuch as NRTs and CRTs are grounded in different conceptions and procedures, test features contrast in several critical aspects. For example, different criteria are used for NRT and CRT test-item selection. Whereas NRTs require a wide range of items covering the full spectrum of the target domain, CRTs rely on instruments that measure specific constructs alone. Item difficulty also is set differently. NRTs rely on performance variability to determine how well individual examinees perform on the test, and item difficulty typically is set at the 50% probability level to maximize the variance. CRTs, on the other hand, can rate individual test performance independently of how others score. Item difficulty, therefore, can be set at the 100% probability level in situations in which the target competence, presumably, has been mastered.

Despite their widespread use, both types of standardized tests have several shortcomings. As has been noted, reading modes by and large are determined by reading purposes, as well as by texts' genre-specific requirements. For example, a particular processing mode associated with "learning from expository texts for studying" does not always occur while browsing in informational texts – say, travel guides and cookbooks. Most commercially available tests, however, do not incorporate possible variations prompted by either reading purpose or text type.

Moreover, standardized test formats, such as multiple-choice, often have little relevance to real-life reading tasks. Yet, in many instances, their results can have major consequences on test takers' lives, as in the case of college admissions and hiring and promotion decisions. As a result, instruction tends to place a dominant emphasis on strategies that improve test performance rather than the essential competencies for effective reading. There is a good chance, therefore, that despite the close connection between instructional foci and standardized test performance, neither has any real bearing on how well students read in real-life situations.

Additionally, because standardized tests are designed to provide stable, but static, information about students' performance, they are not sensitive to intra-individual variations, such as dynamic developmental changes, and differing strategic operations across text types and reading purposes. Hence, the tests reveal little about individual readers' personal strengths and weaknesses in different reading modes and task conditions.

Furthermore, from an instructional standpoint, the utility of standardized tests is also somewhat limited. Because of the need to be curriculum independent, their outcomes cannot be used to guide instruction. To repeat, because standardized NRTs are not intended to measure any particular construct assumed to explain reading difficulty, test results do not indicate why examinees perform as they do, and yield little diagnostic insight. Finally, in keeping with the psychometric precepts, test reliability is the ultimate yardstick for standardized instruments (Calfee & Hiebert, 1991). This has major implications for the use of outcome information. Because psychometric testing presumes unidimensionality, any test item inducing systematically different responses is either replaced or eliminated. This creates the peculiar circumstance in which test performance can be more reflective of examinees' understanding of the test item's idiosyncrasies than of their reading ability (Johnston, 1983, 1984; Langer, 1987).

Similar concerns about the use of traditional NRTs exist in the L2 context. Many teachers and researchers, for example, suspect that the tests are incapable of capturing competencies essential for effective communication, as well as for participation in the target-language communities and workplaces. Carroll (1985), for instance, contends that, to obtain a more reliable measure of L2 proficiency, language tests should impose the same requirements on test takers as those necessary for language communication in real-life situations. Contemporary theory and research, in fact, suggest an alternative model, one grounded in the concept of communicative competence – the capacity to use language in its multiple forms as a tool for thinking, problem solving, and communication (Bachman, 1990; Canal, 1987).

Classroom-based performance assessment

As a result of the shortcomings associated with the standardized test paradigm, increased attention has been given to various forms of alternative assessment. In particular, a strong trend toward classroom-based authentic performance assessment has materialized. Several lines of development point to the importance of this movement. For example, instructional emphasis has shifted from discrete skills/knowledge elements to the competencies necessitated for accomplishing real-life reading tasks. From the growing conviction that knowing something, and how to use the knowledge in accomplishing a real-life task, are two distinct capabilities, substantial efforts have been initiated to establish performance standards for functional curricular attainments. Further, there is also an emerging consensus that valid assessment requires multiple sources of information (e.g., Bachman & Palmer, 1996; Hiebert, Valencia, & Afflerback, 1994).

Archbold and Newmann (1988) outline two critical factors in defining authentic assessment: utilizing tasks that approximate those used by experts, and having functional utility beyond evaluation. In language testing, Bachman (1990) defines authenticity as the extent to which the test replicates some specified real-world communication. Three additional interrelated notions further reinforce the conception of authenticity: viewing language ability as pragmatic ascription, using real-life performance as a criterion, and treating content relevance and predictive validity as acceptable bases for justifying test use.

The term "performance" also demands clarification. Hiebert et al. (1994) argued that performance, of necessity, demands demonstrations of acquired competence and knowledge through the creation of a product or a response. Almost two decades earlier, Clark (1978) contended that, in direct performance assessment, testing format and procedure should replicate, as closely as possible, authentic settings and task procedures in real-life situations where the competency in question is normally used.

The real strength of authentic performance assessment lies in its dynamic nature, in its sensitivity to students' shifting capabilities (Calfee & Hiebert, 1991). Although the goals overlap somewhat with standardized testing, the methods and strategies differ markedly in several important ways. The authentic performance approach requires a high level of professional knowledge, skill, and flexibility. If the ultimate goal of assessment is to guide instruction, assessment itself should offer ample opportunities for improving students' competence. Under this rubric, success on a given assessment task is interpreted against overall instructional goals, rather than treated as a yardstick of skill/knowledge mastery independent of the instruction. Conversely, failure on an assessment task is viewed as an indication that instructional changes may be in order. As in traditional standardized testing, validity and reliability are vital to the interpretation of assessment outcomes. Validity, in this context, involves the convergence of multiple sources of evidence on a hypothesized construct (Calfee & Hiebert, 1991). With respect to reliability, the chief issue is consistency of evidence over disparate tasks and situations.

In this approach, the cyclic nature of the feedback loop (i.e., initial observations result in interventions, which in turn are followed by the next round of observations) controls instructional decision making. Continuous reflection on students' overall achievement is the critical barometer in authentic performance assessment. Thus, effective classroom-based performance assessment must go beyond simply determining students' reading ability. And, given its close link with instruction, the bedrock principle in this approach to reading assessment is content validity. Because assessment outcomes are used to make critical instructional decisions, the assessment procedures themselves must be in sync with the curriculum itself.

Techniques in measuring reading comprehension

Further confirming the complexity of the construct of reading comprehension, there are diverse ways of conceptualizing how it can be best measured. Test users, consequently, must respect the basic assumptions underlying alternative assessment techniques.

Formal assessment techniques

Free recall

There is general agreement that free recall is the most straightforward procedure for assessing the outcome of reader–text interaction.

In this procedure, test takers typically are asked to describe everything they remember from the text read. Little time is required to prepare and administer the task, but scoring involves an extensive analysis of recall protocols. Research in the 1970s on discourse processing still provides useful guidance in analyzing recall protocols. For example, as described in Chapter 8, story grammar (e.g., Mandler & Johnson, 1977; Stein & Nezworski, 1978) permits systematic comparisons of how well text information is reconstructed in narratives based on essential story elements such as goal, setting, and outcome. Similarly, Meyer's (1975) recall scoring protocol is useful to compare the extent to which reproduced content information is coherent.

As noted above, however, recall protocol analysis is demanding. The construction of scoring templates, for example, is labor intensive, necessitating roughly 25 to 50 hours for a 250-word text (Bernhardt, 1991), and the scoring itself can take half an hour per protocol (Alderson, 2000). This in itself makes the procedure somewhat impractical for most assessment purposes. Further, although recall protocols reveal what has been stored and how (Bernhardt, 1991; Johnston, 1983), they offer no information on what is not recalled. It is virtually impossible to determine, for example, whether omission of certain text elements is attributable to lack of understanding, retention difficulty, or other factors. Moreover, recall performance is vulnerable to task conditions. For instance, there is evidence that recall protocols produced in L1 and L2 differ both qualitatively and quantitatively (Lee, 1986). Readers' perception of the task – that is, what they are asked to do – also affects what is recalled. Riley and Lee (1996) demonstrated that the instructions used in task administration are systematically related to the types of information recalled. When instructed to write a text summary, examinees produced considerably more main ideas than when simply asked to recall the passage.

In sum, free recall is intended to show, in the most direct way, what the reader remembers from reading without procedural contamination from additional task requirements. However, its strong reliance on memory makes it difficult to distinguish recalled elements extracted from the text and those retrieved from stored knowledge bases. Moreover, assessment outcomes offer little information about text content not included in recall protocols. Further, the demanding scoring procedure limits its utility in most instructional contexts.

Cued recall

In this technique, a series of questions requiring short answers are used. Constructed responses are then interpreted to determine the extent to which examinees understood the text. Because cued recall elicits specific information, unlike free recall, it does not require test takers to exhaust what they remember. Readers thus have a limited opportunity to demonstrate their comprehension. In addition, the method poses two significant challenges: generating effective questions and ensuring objective scoring. Question construction entails identifying the particular information most likely to reveal variations in text understanding. Question taxonomy, such as that in the following list (Garcia, 1991), often is used to guide this process.

- *textually explicit* questions: Question and answer are paraphrased or taken from a single sentence in the text.
- *textually implicit* questions: Question and answer are neither paraphrased nor found in a single sentence but appear in the passage.
- *scriptally implicit* questions: Only partial information, needed to answer the question, appears in the passage, thereby requiring examinees to use their script (or prior knowledge).

A taxonomy of this sort permits inferences about the cognitive processes underlying response construction. Even a simple taxonomy can yield reliable clues on cognitive operations during comprehension – for example, locating lexical information, integrating sentential information, and drawing on prior knowledge (e.g., Pearson & Johnson, 1978).

Ensuring scoring objectivity also requires precautions. Constructed responses, particularly those elicited by questions requiring implicit text information, cannot be scored on the basis of correct or incorrect. Objectivity, therefore, depends largely on a succinct, unabridged response key. Alderson (2000) notes that questions must be worded in ways that anticipate all possible answers. In actuality, however, it is unrealistic to assume that all possible responses can be divined in advance. Interpretations of unanticipated responses thus are highly susceptible to subjective judgments, posing further challenges.

Multiple-choice questions

Multiple choice is perhaps the most commonly used format in standardized reading comprehension tests. The procedure's advantages lie in the simplicity of its scoring procedure. Its mechanical nature not only ensures objectivity but also permits machine-mediated mass scoring. Beyond these, however, the technique has little additional benefit. Reading and testing specialists, in fact, have expressed a number of concerns about the legitimacy of multiple-choice questions as a valid method of assessing comprehension. Well-constructed distracters, for example, can alter stored information extracted from the text. Researchers have found that the presence of a plausible distracter is a strong predictor of question difficulty (Drum, Calfee, & Cook, 1981). Conceptual intrusion of this sort can cause learners to revise their text memory, biasing subsequent task performance.

Another shortcoming is the necessity for several task-specific operations, which normally do not occur in real-life reading. Matching serves as an example, because it requires students to match multiple-choice items with relevant text elements, in both their surface forms and their meanings. A potential complication arises, therefore, when distracters and corresponding text sentences are structurally congruent but semantically incongruent. To make correct selections, examinees not only must understand that semantic consistency is more vital than structural similarity, but also must have sufficient confidence to disregard surface linguistic resemblance (Johnston, 1983). Conceivably, then, similar sentence structures, sharing key words between distracters and text sentences, could be a critical determinant of item difficulty in multiple-choice questions.

What is more, in interpreting multiple-choice test results, considerable care must be taken because the problem-solving nature of the processing requirements gives rise to a significant risk – that is, performance variation could be more attributable to task-specific skills than to reading ability. More critically, because test-taking strategies are teachable, multiple-choice performance can be improved considerably through explicit training, without any progress in reading ability. Inasmuch as multiple choice is predominantly used in high-stakes assessment, it is all the more important that its implications be clearly understood when relying on its outcomes.

Cloze test

The cloze test involves completing blanks, created by deleting words systematically within a prespecified distance (say, every seventh word), from a selected text. The intent is to analyze what words the student chooses to substitute for each deletion. The underlying rationale is as follows: To substitute for the blanks, the reader must be sensitive to semantic and syntactic constraints in each local context. Cloze performance, therefore, can be taken as a reasonably accurate gauge of such sensitivity. Because text-information processing is guided by these constraints, the sensitivity can be regarded as a reliable indicator of reading ability.

Because of its relative ease in test construction, administration, and scoring, the cloze procedure, like multiple choice, is widely used. Here again, however, as in most other similar techniques, the procedure is not problem-free. To begin with, the test yields little information about why some blanks are not filled. Because of the test's production demands, more than one explanation of failed attempts is possible. For example, if a text segment is not understood, a blank obviously cannot be filled. And, even if it is understood, the slot may be left blank, if the deleted word is not in the examinee's productive vocabulary. A lack of morphosyntactic knowledge, moreover, can account for the generation of semantically appropriate but syntactically inappropriate responses. Research, in fact, indicated that grammatical knowledge correlates more highly with cloze performance than multiple-choice test scores (Koda, 1990a).

The cloze procedure appears to be more sensitive to surface linguistic forms than the underlying text meaning. For instance, totally different versions of a test can be constructed from the same text by simply altering the starting point of deletion. Put another way, depending on which word is deleted first, entirely different words require replacement. More critically, a study verifies that test performances of the same individuals differed considerably across alternative test versions created from the same text (Alderson, 2000). If, indeed, the cloze test is a valid measure of reading comprehension, this should not have occurred. The deviation clearly casts serious doubts about its construct validity.

The procedure's assessment capability, moreover, is generally limited to local understanding. Most deletion items are syntactically and semantically constrained within a single sentence, and an analysis of local segments immediately preceding and/or following the blank usually is sufficient for identifying either the deleted word or its synonym. Test performance, consequently, tells us little about global text-information processing competencies: sensitivity to discourse-level constraints, intersentential information integration, and so on.

Further, the cloze procedure, as in multiple choice, requires operations incongruous with those necessitated in the normal course of reading. To fill in blanks, for example, the periodically occurring empty slots must be retained in short-term memory until the meaning of the local sentential context is established. Theoretically, then, assessment outcomes can be more reflective of this and other task-specific capabilities than of reading ability, thereby prohibiting accurate inferences about normal reading behaviors.

Finally, scoring procedures as well can alter assessment outcomes. To illustrate, the strict criterion, allowing only the exact replacement of the original word, could underestimate actual text understanding, especially among good readers. Inasmuch as good readers have more extensive vocabulary knowledge, they are more likely to use synonyms, which in turn makes them more susceptible to penalization stemming from exact scoring. Again, research shows that cloze scores, based on a lenient criterion – allowing contextually appropriate synonyms – correlates more highly with other comprehension and L2 proficiency measures than those derived from exact-scoring methods (e.g., Shohamy, 1983).

In view of these concerns, alternative formats have been proposed. Rational cloze is one such variant. In lieu of using the fixed ratio (i.e., every, say, fifth word), a prespecified category of words (e.g., content words versus function words versus conjunctions) are deleted to test a specific facet of reading ability. For instance, by deleting the proportion of content words, text-meaning understanding can be estimated more accurately. In contrast, by deleting function words, the same text can be used to estimate grammatical control ability. The deletion of conjunctions can serve as a measure of relational understanding – namely, grasping semantic relations between clauses.

Abraham and Chapelle (1992) made it clear that different factors affect test difficulty in the standard fixed-ratio deletion and rational-deletion formats. The number of deleted content words in the standard format was the only text-intrinsic variable significantly influencing test difficulty. In the rational cloze, contrastingly, performance related inversely to the amount of context needed to restore the deleted content words, thus suggesting the importance of contextual support availability. Although it remains unclear what the standard format really measures, the rational cloze holds strong promise as a research tool for examining different reading ability components – such as grammatical sophistication, content knowledge, use of contextual clues, and information integration – by systematically manipulating deletion-word sampling. Some might argue that because the rational cloze violates the basic premise underlying cloze test construction – that is, random, unbiased word deletion – it should not be considered a true variant of the cloze procedure. In any event, much can be gained from further studies examining the extent and processes through which deletion procedures affect construct validity.

Summary

Summary tasks are commonly administered as an aspect of formal classroom assessment. Examinees are instructed to read a text, and then are asked to summarize its main ideas and supporting details. The virtue of the task lies in its close approximation of real-life activities – that is, communicating the gist of one's reading. The underlying rationale is that summarization and comprehension share two critical operations: identifying a text's main theme, and judging the relative importance of text elements based on their relevance to the theme. Moreover, both task construction and administration are simple.

The downside includes potential scoring subjectivity and additional processing requirements. A clear consensus as to what constitutes a good summary remains open to question. Therefore, summary quality ratings are prone to subjective judgments, particularly regarding what distinguishes good from poor summaries. Summary construction, moreover, entails much more than comprehension. Beyond retention, for example, it requires sorting and organizing extracted information for subsequent production. Here, too, when a summary must be written in the target language, the task mandates a much higher level of proficiency than that necessitated for comprehension. Poor summaries, therefore, can result from deficiencies in any of the skills noted in the preceding discussion. Successful summary performance, unquestionably, ensures successful comprehension, but what accounts for less-successful performance remains highly uncertain.

Informal classroom assessment techniques

In addition to formal assessment procedures, several informal techniques also are widely used in classrooms. The advantage of classroom assessment lies in the rich data derived from the broad picture of reading behaviors sampled during their development. Systematic observations provide multiple sources of information, which, when scrutinized, yield reliable estimates of how well a particular student can read a particular text under a particular condition. As previously observed, informal assessment often captures subtle changes in students' progress, which may fall through the cracks in formal procedures. Two widely used informal assessment techniques serve as illustrations.

Oral miscue analysis

Miscue analysis involves coding errors committed during oral text reading. The underlying premises are twofold: The ultimate goal of reading is meaning construction, and the goal is accomplished with three dominant cue systems: syntax, semantics, and graphophonics

(Goodman, 1969). Goodman maintained that because reading errors, or miscues, do not occur randomly, their systematic comparisons should generate individual students' developmental profiles. In a text explaining habitations, for example, graphophonic miscues (e.g., "habits" for "habitat") and semantic miscues (e.g., "house" for "habitat") signal fundamentally different processing behaviors. He and colleagues argue that it is the quality, and not the quantity, of miscues that distinguishes levels of reading ability (Goodman & Burke, 1972; Goodman & Gollasch, 1980).

Despite its popularity, miscue too is not entirely problem-free. It focuses on only a single aspect of reading behavior – oral reading errors – to infer comprehension ability in silent reading. Oral and silent reading impose various processing requirements (e.g., Mosenthal, 1978), and attempts to use such inferences as instructional guidelines for improving comprehension can easily be fallible. Likewise, oral reading behaviors are affected by elements other than reading ability. Text difficulty, topic familiarity, and reading purposes can also alter patterns of oral reading miscues (e.g., Christie & Alonso, 1980; Schwartz & Stanovich, 1981). It would be a mistake, therefore, to assume that the procedure invariably elicits optimum student behavior from a given text in a particular situation. Merely analyzing oral reading miscues alone, with little regard for textual and contextual constituents, is not likely to reflect reading ability or developmental profile accurately. Finally, current research strongly suggests that successful text comprehension necessitates far more than graphophonic, syntactic, and semantic clues: For example, other cue systems, such as discourse organization markers and coherence-signaling devices, are also essential. In short, relying on limited miscue samples can lead to a piecemeal explanation of reading ability.

Observation survey

In standardized NRTs, as mentioned earlier, individual reading ability is estimated only from group data, irrespective of contextual variables. The observational survey (Clay, 1989, 1991, 1993) contrasts sharply with such group-based objective assessment, providing a good example of what informal assessment can offer. Its goal is to obtain a deeper understanding of what happens to students in conjunction with the instructional context. The major strength of the approach lies in its solid theoretical base underlying the selection and/or construction of observational tasks. To illustrate, based on the assumption that learning to read requires simultaneous development of multiple competencies, Clay's observation inventory includes tasks measuring various capabilities known as requisites for early reading development:

• Command of oral language and control of sentence structures and inflections
• Reading of connected text
• Letter knowledge
• Reading vocabulary
• Writing vocabulary
• Concepts of print
• Discriminating word sounds
• Linking sounds and letters

Presuming that students progress on several fronts at the same time, there is general consensus that measuring one area of competency is insufficient for making accurate inferences about students' developmental stages and their reading ability. Teachers need to know how the learning of each competence occurs. Systematic observations of what students can and cannot do at a given point in time enable teachers to adjust their teaching to particular students to expedite progress.

Although often inclined to use informal classroom-based assessments, teachers' actual implementation is somewhat restricted. Two reasons explain the limited utilization. First, successful use of observation surveys depends heavily on the teacher's understanding of precisely what each task indicates about reading ability. Because survey tasks are construct referenced, their results provide very specific, but strongly limited, information about the construct at issue. Accordingly, without a clear sense of the reading model used in constructing the survey tasks, accurate interpretation of the observation data is unlikely. In sum, rigorous teacher grounding in the theoretical and technical insights is mandatory. Second, survey implementation is extremely labor intensive, involving a long series of tasks, administered on a one-to-one basis, requiring an extensive time commitment. Such demands patently warrant some kind of workable structure, which provides teachers with adequate time and resources to implement and benefit from finely honed observation techniques.

Roles of assessment in reading research and teaching

Roles of assessment in research

Functionally, reading research and assessment are interdependent. The best characterization of their relationship, perhaps, is that they are symbiotic: Research demands valid and reliable information on individuals' reading capabilities derived from assessment, and assessment depends on research to construe, delineate, and operationalize the constructs that define reading ability. Their respective objectives also reflect this mutual dependency; assessment aims at differentiating individuals on the basis of their reading skills, and research seeks principled ways to explain these differences. To benefit from this reciprocity, experts in reading research and assessment must have a clear understanding of how the two are complementary.

Assessment specialists obviously must keep pace with continually evolving theories. Text, for example, was once viewed simply as a transcription of spoken language. Reading was seen as the process of translating print into spoken language. Decoding skills, consequently, were considered the primary objective in acquiring comprehension competence. More recent postulations, however, emphasize active involvement of readers in text-meaning construction, placing equal importance on decoding and background knowledge. Clearly, such diverse, shifting views have major impacts on assessment design and task construction, prompting a reconsideration of what skills to measure and in what ways.

Conversely, reading researchers must stay informed about the specific task demands in differing assessment procedures in order to achieve accurate outcome interpretations. In particular, when research seeks a causal linkage between a hypothesized factor and reading performance, it is critical that the conception of reading ability remain internally consistent between the dependent (reading test scores) and independent (hypothesized factor) variables. If, for example, the independent variable in question is "global text-coherence building skill," using the cloze test to estimate reading ability (dependent variable) may undermine the predictive power of the independent variable. Because the cloze procedure is purported to measure local text understanding, its performance does not necessitate global text-coherence building. Using it to test the connection between these variables creates a serious threat to internal validity owing to the inconsistency between the research intent and the tool. Such conceptual disparity is even more problematic in applied instructional studies. When examining the effectiveness of explicit training in a particular skill known to promote reading comprehension, dependent measures (reading tasks) that actually utilize the skill must be selected. If the task can be accomplished without the skill, the outcome data will not yield reliable information on the expected instructional benefits. In short, the symbiosis between reading research and assessment requires sustained interaction between the two knowledge bases.

Roles of assessment in instruction

Instruction and assessment should enhance each other in cyclical fashion. Assessment outcomes, therefore, must inform instruction, and instruction in turn should guide assessment design. Such cyclical enhancement, however, does not routinely occur for several reasons. Reading assessment depends heavily on standardized norm-referenced procedures. Assessment tasks, by design, measure specific, externally determined aspects of reading ability. Hence, using standardized tests presumably mandates a curriculum specifically configured to test performance improvement, regardless of students' reading problems and disparate instructional goals. Moreover, the test results provide little insight into significant classroom factors: effectiveness of the instructional methods and objectives, correct skill utilization in the right way at the right time, and, of greatest importance, the particular impediments of individual students. Test scores, for example, may provide indices of relative performance, but they do not clarify what is infinitely more important – learning impediments and the corresponding alleviative actions that bring about improvement.

For assessment to guide instruction, targeted skills must be causally related to comprehension and trainable so that instruction and practice facilitate subsequent improvements. If skills are not carefully defined within accepted reading models, neither assessment nor instruction can propagate long-term gains in ability. Assessment outcomes shape instruction most forcefully when they pinpoint the specific reading problems of individual students. When teaching and assessment are closely intertwined, however, an obvious risk is that instruction may emphasize test-taking strategies if the assessment goals themselves are not grounded in authentic reading competencies.

Concerns specific to L2 reading assessment

In the L2 context, reading is generally regarded as an integral aspect of language proficiency, and, as a consequence, gauging L2 linguistic sophistication by observing reading behaviors is a relatively common practice. Hence, L2 reading assessment, by design, has dual functions: measuring both reading skills and language ability. As a result, L2 assessment issues center mainly on this functional duality, because blurred distinctions between the two can often obscure the assessment objectives. For example, determining whether test instructions should be given in L1 or L2 poses a problem, because it is hard to ascertain whether difficulties are attributable to limited reading ability or to a faulty understanding of the task itself. Because of their direct bearing on outcome interpretations, it is worthwhile considering these and other related concerns unique to L2 reading assessment.

L2 reading competence: Reading ability or language proficiency?

Despite its seeming functional duality, L2 reading assessment traditionally places much more weight on linguistic elements – for example, text length, syntactic complexity, and lexical familiarity – as stronger determinants of comprehension difficulty than nonlinguistic factors, such as background knowledge and conceptual complexity. As a case in point, American Council for the Teaching of Foreign Languages (ACTFL) proficiency guidelines define reading proficiency on the basis of text types and reading skills associated with each type (Alderson, 2000). Lee and Musumeci (1988) contend that two basic assumptions underlie reading proficiency. As shown in Table 11.1, L2 reading development spans progressive stages from simple enumerative texts to increasingly complex evaluative/projective texts, and text type by and large determines linguistic demands, which in turn mandate skills, ranging from somewhat mechanical procedures, such as visual recognition of learned elements to more sophisticated conceptual/reflective operations, involving content analysis and verification. Accordingly, two corresponding, developmental continua, one based on text type and the other based on reading skill, are used as benchmarks. Therefore, ACTFL reading proficiency guidelines, reflecting their primary emphasis on classifying learners according to language-manipulation capability, assign a prominent role to linguistic complexity implicit in text type.

The guidelines yield conflicting results with respect to their predictive validity. Several researchers have expressed strong skepticism, arguing that reading performance is influenced by a number of factors other than linguistic variables. Therefore, text characteristics alone are an insufficient base for discriminating L2 learners' reading ability (e.g., Allen, Bernhardt, Berry, & Demel, 1988; Lee & Musumeci, 1988). The Allen et al. study (1988), in fact, demonstrated that different text types selected from the ACTFL guidelines did not differentiate high- and low-proficiency high school learners of European languages. Edwards (1996), conversely, found that the text-type hierarchy underlying the ACTFL guidelines accurately predicted comprehension performance among L2 learners with various proficiency levels. Seemingly, then, the text-type hierarchy corresponds to some, but not all, dimensions of L2 reading proficiency.

Table 11.1. *Reading levels associated with text types and processing skills (reprinted from Lee and Musumeci, 1988, p. 174)*

Level	Text type	Sample texts	Reading skill
0/0+	Enumerative	Numbers, names, street signs, money denomination, office/shop designations, addresses	Recognize memorized elements
1	Orientated	Travel and registration forms, plane and train schedules, TV/radio program guides, menus, memos, newspaper headlines, tables of contents, messages	Skim, scan
2	Instructive	Ads and labels, newspaper accounts, instructions and directions, factual reports, formulaic requests on forms, invitations, introductory and concluding paragraphs	Decode, classify
3	Evaluative	Editorials, analyses, apologia, certain literary texts, biography with critical interpretation	Infer, guess, hypothesize, interpret
4	Projective	Critiques of art or theater performances, literary texts, philosophical discourse, technical papers, argumentation	Analyze, verify, extend, hypothesize

Language selection for administration and response construction

Language selection, as already observed, also is a unique concern in L2 reading assessment. Learners' understanding of task goals and procedures seriously affects their test performance, and language selection, whether L1 or L2, for nontext elements such as test administration, task instructions, and post-reading questions, similarly influences assessment outcomes. When L2 is used for task instructions, for example, there is always a likelihood that some examinees may pursue the task without understanding what they are to do. From a *language*-assessment perspective, a clear grasp of the task can be taken as a valid indication of L2 proficiency. From a *reading* perspective, however, text comprehension may not always reflect a similar command of other, nontext language skills (e.g., understanding procedures, questions, and prompts). Reading assessment aims at eliciting particular reading behaviors whose variations provide a basis for discriminating examinees' reading ability. Consequently, when performance is weakened by task misconceptions, the validity of the results can be seriously compromised. In a study involving Spanish-speaking fifth- and sixth-grade ESL learners in American public schools (Garcia, 1991), some students responded incorrectly to multiple-choice questions, not out of text misunderstanding but because they misconstrued multiple-choice items presented in L2. Post-test debriefing interviews disclosed that, when questioned in Spanish, many who performed poorly on the test described the text content correctly. Contamination of this sort, arising from nontext obstacles rather than comprehension limitation, is a hazard, particularly when the goal is assessing content understanding.

Selecting language for response construction is also an important concern because comprehension and production impose qualitatively and quantitatively different demands. Language-production skills generally lag behind comprehension capabilities, and task performance, if required in L2, can be seriously constrained by production, rather than comprehension, liabilities. In one study cited earlier, American college students studying Spanish produced, on average, longer and more accurate protocols in their L1 (Lee, 1986) than a comparable group who conveyed their recall in L2 (Carrell, 1983). Post-reading response construction subsumes comprehension, and it stands to reason that successful achievement can be a reliable indicator of comprehension competence. Unsuccessful performance, on the other hand, reveals little about comprehension per se, because failed efforts can be attributed either to comprehension or to production limitations. In the aggregate, language selection for auxiliary nontext elements is a unique problem in L2 reading assessment, particularly when the intent is gauging comprehension rather than language proficiency.

Lexical scaffolding

The use of lexical scaffolding via dictionaries and glossaries is not a unique issue in L2 assessment. Its implications, however, vary widely in L1 and L2 reading, because the relationship between vocabulary and conceptual knowledge differs among L1 and L2 readers. Reading is the primary means of knowledge acquisition among L1 readers, and it is plausible to assume that their written vocabulary mirrors their conceptual knowledge. Moreover, vocabulary size also can be a reasonably reliable indicator of text-meaning extraction capacity.

As suggested in Chapter 4, text comprehension and contextual word learning share similar skills, which explains, in part, their consistently high correlations. Logic suggests, then, that their affiliation perhaps justifies the avoidance of lexical scaffolding in L1 reading assessment when texts have conceptual and linguistic appropriateness.

Still, there are persuasive reasons to suspect that the assumed connection between vocabulary and conceptual knowledge does not always hold among L2 readers, especially those who acquire their L2 through formal instruction. In classroom instruction, L2 vocabulary generally is learned by linking new (L2) lexical labels with concepts already known through L1 labels. L2 vocabulary size, therefore, can be considered a manifestation of L2 proficiency, although not necessarily of conceptual knowledge or meaning-extraction ability. If the L2 reading assessment purpose is estimating L2 proficiency, lexical scaffolding may hamper accurate performance interpretations. On the other hand, if the major goal is measuring content understanding, lexical scaffolding, by facilitating ready access to conceptual storage, may reduce the risk of underestimating information-extraction and meaning-construction capabilities in conceptually familiar but linguistically unfamiliar texts.

Lexical scaffolding also can offset inequitable L1 facilitation stemming from differential degrees of lexical commonality between the two languages. Cognates, or shared lexical items, presumably facilitate lexical processing during L2 text comprehension, and performance differences can be explained, at least in part, by the extent to which the two languages share cognates, orthographically and semantically similar lexical items. We can safely postulate, therefore, that lexical scaffolding, by providing equal footing for learners with related and unrelated L1 backgrounds, can diminish unintentional variance stemming from L1–L2 lexical distance.

Further, when authentic texts designed for native-speaking audiences are used in assessment, L2 readers can be seriously handicapped by limited knowledge of words that convey culture-specific concepts. When using specialized words, unlikely to be known to intended audiences, authors typically make conscious efforts to provide clarification by including definitions or brief explanations. Problems may occur, however, when author suppositions and reader knowledge are not in sync, as in the case of L2 readers struggling with culturally loaded expressions. In such instances, the absence of lexical scaffolding may make assessment outcomes more reflective of cultural knowledge than of reading ability. For these assorted reasons, lexical scaffolding in L2 reading assessment appears to do more good than harm.

Measuring reading fluency

Despite the general consensus that reading comprehension depends on skilled decoding, efficiency measures rarely are incorporated in reading assessment (Fuchs, Fuchs, Hosp, & Jenkins, 2001). Most tests entail accurate word recognition and main-idea detection in short passages with generous time allowances. Short-text comprehension is an important aspect of reading ability, but processing efficiency is equally, if not more, critical. Carver (1993, 1997, 2000) views comprehension as a two-dimensional competence, manifesting itself in the interface between interpretive depth and processing speed. His basic contention is that processing efficiency is one of the core dimensions of reading ability. Contemporary reading theories, in somewhat the same vein, underscore the importance of going beyond the customary focus on accuracy. In the words of the National Reading Panel (2000, p. 3–5), the capability to "read a text quickly, accurately, and with proper expression" characterizes skillful reading. Recent assessment studies, in fact, suggest that fluency-based measures are better discriminators than accuracy-based measures, offering stronger correlations with general reading competence (e.g., Fuchs & Fuchs, 1999; Good, Simmons, & Kame'enui, 2001; Pinnell, Lyons, Deford, Bryk, & Seltzer, 1994). The implication is that the incorporation of additional fluency indices in reading assessment is warranted.

In L2 assessment, nonetheless, caution must be taken, because the cross-linguistic nature of L2 reading may not allow a presumption that effective processing consistently equates with reading ability among L2 learners with different L1 backgrounds. Orthographic systems share their properties with the target-language system in varying degrees, and, conceivably, L2 decoding efficiency differences could be explained by orthographic distance to a greater extent than by reading proficiency. The odds are good, therefore, that the connection between decoding and reading comprehension differs among L2 readers with disparate L1 backgrounds. In point of fact, processing efficiency, particularly phonological decoding, is differentially related among L2 readers of English with alphabetic and logographic L1 backgrounds (e.g., Koda, 1998, 1999).

Considering that phonological decoding in alphabetic and logographic orthographies entails different procedures, and that L1 processing patterns are transferred to L2 reading, it is likely that transferred skills continuously undergo adjustments to accommodate L2 orthographic peculiarities. Prior literacy experience provides substantial facilitation when the two languages are closely related, because transferred skills require minimal modifications. In the absence of similar facilitation, L2 decoding skill among learners with unrelated L1 backgrounds lags. More critically, it is also probable that connections between decoding and L2 proficiency, as well as between decoding and L2 comprehension, can vary systematically across L1 language groups. Again, the intimation is that even though fluency measures are desirable, care must be exercised, because L2 processing efficiency does not always portray L2 reading capacity.

Summary and future research suggestions

Despite the mixed conceptions about reading comprehension, there is broad consensus that it is not an all-or-nothing phenomenon. There are different perspectives through which degrees of comprehension are distinguished: processing levels, task nature, reader purposes, and so on. No single assessment task can reflect all distinctions separating good and poor comprehension. A large array of testing procedures currently are used to measure comprehension. In keeping with the diversity of assessment utilization, moreover, tasks are constructed and administered in two disparate formats: standardized objective tests and informal classroom-based observations.

Several additional issues are inherent in L2 reading assessment. Reading is considered an integral aspect of language proficiency, and its assessment often has dual goals: measuring reading skills and language facility simultaneously. Assessment concerns, therefore, stem primarily from a blurred distinction between the two goals. For example, using the target language for task administration and test instruction has different consequences when the focus is either on comprehension or on language capability. Further, discretion is needed in incorporating efficiency measures. Contemporary theories stress the significance of decoding efficiency in comprehension, but L2 research suggests that decoding skills develop disparately among L2 readers with different L1 orthographic backgrounds. The obvious conclusion is that cross-linguistic variations, arising from different L1 backgrounds, cannot be avoided. It is essential, therefore, that assessment designs anticipate and provide for possible liabilities.

Currently, the prevailing tendency in L2 assessment places more weight on language proficiency than on reading. Little effort, in fact, has been devoted to constructing pure measures of L2 reading ability. Several circumstances are responsible for the paucity. First and foremost, viable L2 reading models have yet to emerge. Lacking tested theoretical foundations, the major constituents of L2 reading ability remain uncertain. Second, early L2 reading studies were heavily influenced by the "universal" view of reading, contending that the requisite skills are universal across languages. The view, apparently, has now led to the widely held belief that all difficulties L2 readers experience are attributable to inadequate linguistic knowledge. Third, contemporary SLA theories conceive of language proficiency as competence in communicating in the target language. Because understanding texts written in the target language constitutes a critical dimension of such capability, the current approach mandates little provision for distinguishing reading ability from language proficiency.

Nonetheless, much of reading is both conceptual and linguistic, necessitating reasoning and other analytic capacities. Language-based L2 reading assessment, however, tends to measure information extraction and integration only in conceptually neutral texts, requiring meaning construction of familiar content alone. Unfortunately, these skills in themselves constitute only a partial base for assimilating new ideas in conceptually unfamiliar texts. Despite its significance, learning-through-reading capacity rarely is incorporated in the mainstream L2 reading assessment. Because this capacity is a fundamental in academic pursuits at all educational levels, it would seem useful, in future research, to consider redefining the basic functions of L2 reading assessment by reevaluating the current reading-as-language assessment models and incorporating more conceptually grounded skills, critical in learning from unfamiliar texts.

12 *Comprehension instruction*

The intent of the closing chapter is to provide overall summaries of comprehension research, and, in the process, discuss key considerations in drawing functional implications for L2 reading instruction. The hope is that, through insightful analyses and rational speculations, it should be possible to flesh out far better ways of consolidating theory and practice.

What we know about comprehension

As has been evident throughout this volume, decades of effort to uncloak the mysteries of comprehension have yielded massive amounts of information. Our only recourse would be to plow through the data stockpiles one by one. To clarify matters so as to extract significant insights that may improve the ways we go about instruction, the following sections point up major research findings directly relevant to comprehension enhancement.

Decoding

As repeatedly noted, comprehension is a meaning-construction process, involving integral interaction between text and reader. Extracting phonological information from individual words constitutes one of the first and most important steps in this endeavor. The ability is critical because most words in beginning reader texts already are in children's oral vocabulary, and therefore usable phonological information mediates access to meanings not yet familiar in their visual forms. However, what matters most in learning to read is the child's emerging conception of how print relates to speech, because it conveys regularities in the writing system, however reliable, in mapping phonological information onto graphic symbols. Such sensitivity enables children to read new words through analogy and inference rather than by rote memory, thus promoting analytic approaches to word learning and processing.

Critically, the procedural systematicity in symbol–sound mappings induces a gradual increase in the decoding efficiency so essential to comprehension. The importance of efficiency stems largely from the processing constraints imposed by limited working-memory capacity. Working memory's two major functions – computation and temporary information storage – compete for its limited capacity, and overtaxing one function hampers the other. Because word information, once extracted, must be retained in working memory until it is consolidated into larger, meaningful units, when word-information extraction skills are underdeveloped, the memory's computational function is overly strained, leaving little room for storage and subsequent information integration.

The logical implication would be that direct decoding-skill training should enhance reading comprehension. A recent review of instructional research, however, suggests that training beginning L1 readers to achieve decoding efficiency at the level of automaticity does not always augment reading performance (Pressley, 2000). Obviously, the ability to merely sound out words in isolation is insufficient for successful comprehension. In fact, when a word is misread, competent readers tend to recognize the error, because it does not make sense in context. Competent reading thus requires adequate attention to a word's meaning while focusing on its sound. Three elements appear to be mandatory in effective decoding instruction: (1) Students must acquire an explicit understanding of how their writing system works – namely, how phonological information is mapped onto individual symbols; (2) meaning extraction must be incorporated as an integral part of decoding training; and (3) symbol-to-sound mappings should be practiced in meaningful context.

In this regard, oral reading fluency, as noted in Chapter 11, has attracted considerable attention as a potentially reliable indicator of reading competence (e.g., Kame'enui & Simmons, 2001). Viewed as a "seemingly effortless recognition of words in connected text" (Good et al., 2001, p. 261), reading fluency represents capacities well beyond word-recognition accuracy to significantly aid comprehension. Moreover, fluency can be promoted through instruction (National Reading Panel, 2000). Interventions emphasizing the primacy of repeated practice have yielded a consistent and positive impact on both word recognition and comprehension of the practiced items (e.g., Faulkner & Levy, 1999; Lemoine, Levy, & Hutchinson, 1993; Stoddard, Valcante, Sindlear, O'Shea, & Algozzine, 1993). Currently, however, the extent to which such practice benefits are transferred to unpracticed texts, as well as whether fluency instruction in itself raises reading achievement, is somewhat uncertain.

Decoding is equally, if not more, important for L2 readers. Decoding efficiency, in fact, is one of the primary characteristics distinguishing strong and weak L2 learners. Several factors complicate the interplay between decoding and comprehension among L2 learners. L2 decoding efficiency is related both to L2 print-processing experience and to L1–L2 orthographic distance. Because L1 skills are transferred in L2 decoding regardless of orthographic distance, cross-language transfer explains, in large measure, the qualitative differences among learners from disparate L1 backgrounds in their methods of extracting word information from L2 visual input. Considering that well-developed decoding skills are a precondition for L2 comprehension, the importance of decoding training in L2 reading instruction is beyond dispute. To date, however, there has been relatively little exploration of how decoding development among L2 readers is best facilitated through teaching. Inasmuch as decoding efficiency develops at disparate rates, as well as in diverse manners, among L2 learners, the bottom line of the quandary is that no single training method is equally effective for all learners with divergent cognitive and linguistic dispositions.

Vocabulary knowledge

Text-meaning construction is virtually impossible without functional knowledge of the words appearing in the text. Although the close connection between vocabulary knowledge and comprehension is well established in reading research, the nature of their relationship is not as straightforward as it may seem. The two are developmentally interdependent, although comprehension necessitates adequate word knowledge, it is acquired primarily through extensive reading. Moreover, they are linked indirectly through their common underlying competencies. Vocabulary and comprehension both reflect conceptual knowledge and information-manipulation capabilities – for example, inference and contextual information integration. Their indirect connection, however, further adds to the intricacy.

The clear implication of these varied factors is that a distinction must be made between teaching *words* (direct vocabulary instruction) and teaching *how to learn words* (indirect vocabulary instruction). The two involve distinct techniques and have markedly different impacts on both vocabulary learning and comprehension development. Instructional studies clearly suggest that the direct teaching of vocabulary increases comprehension gains (e.g., Koury, 1996; Ryder & Graves, 1994) and that such instruction is even more efficacious when it incorporates conceptual scaffolding for subsequent text-content understanding (e.g., Medo & Ryder, 1993; Wixson, 1986), as well as when it provides multiple exposures in a variety of contexts (e.g., Beck, Perfetti & McKeown, 1982; McKeown et al., 1985).

Because vocabulary learning involves a number of related competencies, care must be exercised in designing instructional interventions. A recent meta-analysis suggests that the effectiveness of vocabulary instruction is seriously affected by levels of reading ability and age (National Reading Panel, 2000). High-ability middle-grade students, for example, derive far more benefit from instruction emphasizing incidental word learning through repetitive exposure than their low-ability counterparts (e.g., Nicholson & Whyte, 1992). In contrast, the keyword mnemonic method (associative memorization technique, as described in Chapter 4) facilitates word learning and retention to a much greater extent among low-ability students than among their higher-ability counterparts (e.g., McGivern & Levin, 1983).

Although systematic explorations have yet to be initiated, a similar ability-instruction interface appears to be likely among L2 learners. Developmental constraints associated with young L1 readers are not a serious concern among L2 learners, but other factors specifically related to L2 reading ability, such as L2 linguistic knowledge, L2 decoding capability, L1 reading competence, and L1–L2 lexical distance, need to be incorporated in designing L2 vocabulary instruction. Training focusing on word-part analysis, for example, may not be beneficial until learners have achieved a basic understanding of word formation and adequate morphological control in the target language. L2 studies generally support the effectiveness of explicit instruction on vocabulary expansion (e.g., Fraser, 1999; Paribakht & Wesche, 1997; Qian, 1999). Therefore, it could be essential to determine whether similar interventions can also lead to comprehension improvement.

Vocabulary knowledge, understandably, is closely interwoven with comprehension. In principle, instruction designed to increase vocabulary knowledge should also enhance comprehension. In actuality, however, the complexity of their relationship does not justify such face validity as a legitimate basis for unidirectional interventions. Providing text-word definitions may suffice for short-term gains. For long-term benefits, however, vocabulary instruction should aim at simultaneous enhancement of both vocabulary learning and comprehension, through training emphasizing their bottom-line, indispensable competencies. As Sternberg (1987) put it, teaching thousands of words through explicit instruction is hardly feasible, but it is possible to teach students how to teach themselves.

Syntactic processing

As discussed in Chapter 6, word information, once recognized, must be incrementally integrated to determine overall sentence meanings. Despite syntactic processing's centrality in comprehension, L1 reading research pays it little attention relative to most other operations. The reason is that basic syntactic knowledge is presumed to have been acquired by beginning L1 readers by the time reading instruction commences. However, this does not hold true in L2 reading. Many L2 readers begin reading before adequate L2 linguistic sophistication has been achieved. Obviously, syntactic knowledge is a major element, explaining performance differences in L2 reading, and can cause serious comprehension problems.

Several factors may clarify how syntactic knowledge, or the lack of it, gives rise to reading difficulties. Inadequate command of L2 syntactic knowledge, for example, necessitates other information sources, such as background knowledge, to integrate individual word meanings, often resulting in slower and less accurate sentence processing. Similarly, syntactic features, uncommon in L1, may also create processing difficulties, because unfamiliar features can inhibit smooth, linear progressions in case-role assignments, thus restricting efficient incremental information integration. And syntactic complexity – such as lack of structural transparency, violation of prototypicality, and ambiguity – also generates comprehension problems. Syntactically complex sentences often do not permit linear parsing, and sentential segments must be held in working memory until they can be integrated. Such demands are not unique to L2 reading, but it is likely that sentence processing is more severely disrupted by structural complexity in L2 than in L1, because inefficient decoding among L2 readers may also strain limited working-memory capacity.

Because of the systematicity inherent in syntactic processing, efficiency increase gradually transpires as decoding skills become automated. Automated parsing facilitates not only text-meaning construction, but economic use of working-memory resources in higher-level conceptual manipulations as well. The clear implication is that, if properly implemented, focused training on syntactic processing, in all probability, will strengthen reading comprehension among L2 readers. As in decoding development, practice is primary in prompting syntactic fluency. Based on the research evidence, several additional instructional targets should also be included in the training: syntactic knowledge assessment – particularly those aspects essential in comprehension; explicit instruction on mandatory, yet unacquired, syntactic properties; scaffolding exercises in sentence processing with structurally controlled texts; and transfer practice, progressively shifting from modified to authentic texts. Unlike decoding, syntactic processing is not limited to visual communication, and, therefore, the incorporation of multimedia materials, such as audio and video clips, should also be explored as alternative approaches to increasing L2 syntactic processing efficiency during reading comprehension.

Text-structure knowledge

Inasmuch as content information is differentially organized into distinct text types, text-structure knowledge heavily contributes to comprehension. However, everyone neither possesses this knowledge nor uses it effectively in global-information synthesis. Text-structure instruction is intended to reduce gaps in knowledge, and its use, among L1 readers. Explicit demonstrations of story content and organization generally improve narrative text comprehension and memory (e.g., Baumann & Bergeron, 1993; Buss, Ratliff, & Irion, 1985). With respect to L2 reading, we can safely assume that there is even greater variance in text-structure knowledge because structural variables, such as organizational principles, coherence signals, and connective devices, vary across languages. It is even more essential to include clear illustrations of genre-specific text structures. As a rule, studies on L2 instruction indicate that lucid structure-awareness training engenders comprehension gains in both expository (e.g., Carrell, 1985; Lee & Riley, 1990; Tang, 1992) and narrative texts (e.g., Amer, 1992; Kitajima, 1997).

A caution is imperative, however, because certain preconditions must be met for such structural sensitivity to mature. The ability to construct local text meanings, for example, usually precedes the development of structural awareness. The primary function of this knowledge is facilitating text-information organization for discourse-level integration, and knowledge cannot evolve before the reader is capable of assembling local information. Automated lower-level processing procedures, especially decoding and syntactic parsing, are another requisite. As noted earlier, underdeveloped information-extraction skills overtax working-memory capacity, diminishing attention space for global text features. Until these compulsory demands are met, text-structure instruction is not likely to yield the desired outcomes.

Main-idea detection

In many ways, main-idea detection is the very essence of text comprehension, necessitating abilities to differentiate key text concepts and identify their logical connections. As with text-structure knowledge, it cannot be assumed that students will intuitively know how to engage in the requisite operations for main-idea detection. Step-by-step demonstrations of the procedure, involving sorting, selecting, and integrating information, can provide substantial assistance in detecting critical text ideas. Currently, direct comprehension instruction focuses on three dominant objectives: bypassing unimportant information, using explicit text devices (pointers, for example) to identify significant ideas and their relationships, and visualizing the relationships through the use of graphic devices. A broad array of instructional methods have been field-tested. Hierarchical summary training, for example, proposed by Taylor and colleagues (Taylor, 1982; Taylor & Beach, 1984), directs students' attention to text-organization clues, including headings, subheadings, and paragraph topics, as well as ways of using them in text summaries. On the premise that visualization of text organization enhances text memory, the benefits of graphic-aids instruction also have been extensively studied with flowcharts (Geva, 1983), conceptual networking (Long & Aldersley, 1984), and conceptual mapping (Armbruster & Anderson, 1980, 1985). Consistently positive results from these and related studies clearly indicate that virtually any effort to direct students' attention to explicit text cues, highlighting key information, substantially facilitates main-idea detection and retention.

Inasmuch as training in main-idea detection involves global text analysis, premature implementation, as in text-structure instruction, can have negative impacts on L2 learners. Similar preconditions also apply. Lacking well-developed L2 decoding competence, for example, sufficient attentional capacity for information integration beyond sentence levels cannot be expected. Low-proficiency students, still preoccupied with decoding, are easily baffled by instructional interventions that require heavy attention to global text features. Moreover, introducing idea linkage across sentences to learners still struggling with word-meaning extraction also may induce frustration and confusion. In point of fact, timely implementation is vital in virtually all interventions focusing on higher-level operations, whose execution depends on multiple, previously acquired competencies.

Background knowledge

Background knowledge affects the almost all aspects of text-information processing. Texts, unfortunately, do not uniformly provide all necessary information for meaning construction, and a fair number of gaps, both conceptual and relational, are likely to occur.

To close these gaps through inferences, prior knowledge is necessary. Another determinant function of background knowledge is conceptual scaffolding, guiding readers in interpreting unfamiliar content. These functions demonstrate why text comprehension often is defined as the "integrative text–reader interaction" and explain why a reader's content-relevant knowledge forecasts how well the text will be understood. Knowledge and comprehension thus go hand in hand in determining what is extracted from the text and how it is assimilated.

However vital, teaching background knowledge in isolation is hardly practical, but instruction can assist students in using knowledge effectively during comprehension. Consequently, demonstrating how to activate content-relevant knowledge and conjoin new text information with the existing knowledge base can reap clear-cut benefits (e.g., Dole, Valencia, Greer, & Wardrop, 1991; Spires, Gallini, & Riggsbee, 1992). Providing students with practice in predicting story events based on personal experience, before reading, was found effective in improving story comprehension, particularly among poor readers (e.g., Hansen & Pearson, 1983). Story preview, where brief bits of forthcoming plot development are orally presented prior to reading to stimulate students' discussion, has also been reported to be beneficial (e.g., Graves, Cooke, & LaBerge, 1983; Neuman, 1988). The most widely used technique is known as question-generation and answering. Students are asked to create a series of "why" questions during their reading and to generate answers based on their prior knowledge as they read through the text. Multiple studies have shown consistently that self-questioning greatly enhances comprehension of factually dense texts (e.g., King, 1990, 1992; Martin & Pressley, 1991; Wood, Pressley, & Winne, 1990). Pressley (2000) attributed the reported benefits to the students' conscious effort to link prior knowledge to text content, and, in so doing, make the text "more sensible, and hence, more comprehensible and memorable" (p. 553).

Matters differ among L2 readers already literate in their L1. We can safely assume that, in most instances, they have learned, through prior literacy training, to draw on their knowledge during comprehension. Inadequate knowledge activation, however, is explained by other factors. Once again, working memory's limited capacity restricts effective knowledge use during L2 text comprehension. To recapitulate, beginning L2 readers often expend their attentional capacity on local information extraction without reserving sufficient resources for knowledge incorporation (e.g., Anderson, 1991; Horiba, 1990). Texts relying on extensive cultural knowledge for their interpretation, as explained in Chapters 4 and 7, also can compound L2 comprehension

262   *Theory into practice*

difficulty, particularly when they lack explanations of culture-specific events and other information, which, the authors presumed, would be general knowledge among their L1 audiences. L2 learners, for obvious reasons, do not necessarily possess the assumed knowledge.

These conditions patently do not warrant routine replications of L1 knowledge-use training. It is unlikely that uncertainty about ways to incorporate relevant knowledge is the major obstacle in L2 reading. Excessive emphasis on prior knowledge could instill the false notion that diligent attention to text information is unnecessary. Overreliance on previous knowledge, as suggested in Chapter 7, diminishes the knowledge-acquisition benefits of reading. There is no question that a lack of relevant content knowledge is problematic. Nonetheless, furnishing the missing information through force-feeding is counterintuitive, because the ultimate goal of reading instruction is teaching how to derive conceptual understanding through effective text-information processing.

Comprehension strategies

Accomplished readers consciously use a flexible reading approach to accommodate text difficulty, task demands, and other contextual challenges. They routinely monitor their comprehension processes, taking alternative steps when encountering blockages. Aware of their own cognitive resources, they continuously adjust their attention to focus on the right clues for anticipating, organizing, and integrating information. These behaviors, characterized as strategic reading in Chapter 10, generally are not observable among less-accomplished readers. Comprehension strategy instruction, therefore, aims at teaching good reading behaviors to those who need them.

In such instruction, monitoring is central. Although teaching comprehension monitoring in itself does not yield substantial gains (National Reading Panel, 2000), all strategic manipulations depend on the reader's self-perception of how well the text is being understood. In recent times, the dominant instructional emphasis has shifted from single to multiple strategies, focusing on their simultaneous adaptation and coordination. The newer approach is framed within sophisticated models of critical thinking, emphasizing the importance of self-regulation through core strategies – prediction, self-questioning, clarification, and summarization. The major objective, obviously, is to teach students how to draw on these conceptual tools as an aid to comprehension (e.g., Levin & Pressley, 1981; Palincsar & Brown, 1984). Put simply, the approach promotes self-regulated strategy use as a path to independent reading and thinking.

Because L1 strategy instruction is closely aligned with children's growing sensitivity to reading, learning, and cognition, its major premises are not entirely applicable to more mature learners. In adapting the training principles to L2 reading instruction, therefore, they must be modified to accommodate developmental differences among school-aged L1 readers and adult L2 learners. Recognizing that many L2 learners read strategically in their L1 but function like nonstrategic readers in L2 (e.g., Clarke, 1980; Wirotanan, 2002), it may be sensible to assume that the lack of strategy use among beginning L1 and adult L2 readers could be attributable to fundamentally different problems. Inasmuch as many of the comprehension strategies are directly linked to local text-meaning construction, inadequate L2 knowledge (vocabulary and grammar, in particular) and information-extraction skills almost certainly inhibit the use of strategies promoting global understanding. As discussed in Chapter 10, divergent conceptions of good reading behaviors, stemming from different cultural beliefs, may also cause L2 readers to select strategies based on L1 norms that contradict L2 expectations. Without adequate allowance of these "nondevelopmental" factors, direct adaptation of L1 instructional tactics is not likely to produce desired outcomes.

Finally, strategy training should address reading purposes. A major benefit of strategic reading lies in its flexible use of multiple strategies. The flexibility is critical because the reader must adjust a processing mode based on the reading purpose. Strategy training focusing on a particular mode of reading is effective only when the chosen strategy is congruent with what students use in their real-life reading. For example, teaching strategic approaches to informational texts may not be useful for college students required to read highly technical materials. In short, strategy instruction must include ways of selecting the approaches that are most efficacious and congruent with students' needs and intent.

Research interpretation and instructional applications

Based on the preceding discussion, it seems legitimate to conclude that three conditions are essential in designing explicit comprehension training: The training must emphasize skills causally related to reading performance; the target skills must allow modifications arising from practice; and the trainees must be developmentally ready for incorporating the target skills in their reading processes.

Although countless studies have produced an enormous body of information on the nature of reading and its development, such information alone, without considering these conditions, does not constitute effective instruction. Translating research findings into practice is hardly simplistic, because not all insights brought to light in empirical studies can be taught directly, or even have direct utility in improving comprehension. Therefore, practitioners must be both adroit and discerning in determining what should be incorporated in instruction and how. Several kinds of studies are especially relevant in considering research interpretations for practice: single-focus investigations identifying the competencies underlying successful reading; group-comparison studies describing the specific elements constituting effective reading behaviors; and psycholinguistic experimentation illuminating real-time information processing during comprehension. The sections that follow consider the potential problems and possible correctives in drawing pedagogical implications from the research findings.

Deriving implications from single-focus studies

Most single-focus studies are correlational in nature, and therefore do not permit direct causal inferences. Nonetheless, treating correlates as causal factors is a common misdemeanor in interpreting research outcomes. There is a widespread misconception, for example, that comprehension improvement can occur through training focusing on a particular correlate. Vocabulary knowledge serves as an illustration. The consistently high correlations between vocabulary and reading scores have given rise to the fallacy that poor comprehension ability stems from inadequate text word-meaning knowledge. In turn, this has led to the misguided belief that comprehension ability can be increased by teaching text-word definitions. But vocabulary knowledge and comprehension are related primarily through their common underlying competencies. Consequently, it is highly improbable that significant gains in comprehension competence can be achieved merely by providing text word meanings. Logically, their benefits are limited to the particular reading material used for instruction, as well as to students who already possess adequate comprehension capability.

Another inherent difficulty in interpreting research findings from single-focus studies, as referred to in Chapter 9, is that functional interdependence among competencies is generally disregarded. When a particular component skill is found to be a strong predictor of comprehension performance, once again, the commonsensical logic would be to promote reading ability through the training of this particular skill. In actuality, however, the complex interconnections among the component skills prohibit such simplistic reasoning. Consider lexical inference: The ability to infer context-appropriate word meanings depends on a number of other capabilities, including decoding, syntactic parsing, word-part analysis, content-relevant background knowledge, and so on. Therefore, training in lexical inference, however skillfully designed, will be of limited benefit to those who have not yet developed the requisite, corollary competencies.

Deriving implications from group-comparison studies

Comparing the behaviors of good and poor readers and their respective competencies is widely used in determining the factors essential to successful comprehension. The research, generating a long list of discriminating variables, generally describes how the groups differ, without explaining why. Therefore, we must recognize that not all behavioral indicators can be taken as causal factors explaining comprehension variance. Some characteristics differentiating strong from weak readers are causally related to reading ability. Others, however, are symptomatic of particular skill deficiencies – in which case, any instructional attempt in correcting poor behaviors will be futile. For example, although poor readers read more slowly, reading speed is not a cause, but a symptom of problems associated with text-information processing. Simply telling poor readers to read faster, therefore, is of no avail.

Similarly, strong and weak readers differ markedly on most indices of eye movement: fixation frequency, duration, backtracking, and so on. The problem, then, is how best to deal with the observed differences. Would it be legitimate to interpret the differences as indicating that comprehension depends on specific eye movement patterns? If so, could we improve the comprehension by teaching weak readers how to move their eyes? Inasmuch as eye-movement patterns are behavioral manifestations of print-information extraction efficiency, rather than sources of their ability differences, teaching eye-movement patterns will not ameliorate either decoding efficiency or comprehension problems among poor readers.

Verbal protocol-analysis studies also probe differences in reader abilities, using readers' own perceptions of what occurs during comprehension. Protocol analysis, however, reveals little about what actually transpires during reading. As discussed in Chapter 10, without behavioral data showing which action preceded, and which followed, a reported behavior – say, skipping words – it is impossible to determine whether the word skipping is a sign of reader *competence* (knowing which words to skip) or *incompetence* (not knowing how to deal with unfamiliar words). Despite the limitations, verbal protocols often are treated as behavioral data, resulting in unwarranted identifications of good reading behaviors to be modeled in strategy training. Nonetheless, awareness of such behaviors clearly is distinct from their actual execution. Consequently, instructional interventions, disregarding the distinction, are likely to be ineffective.

Deriving implications from psycholinguistic studies

Psycholinguistic experimentation provides a glimpse of real-time text-information processing. Because the operations, in large measure, are automated, they cannot be analyzed either by asking readers to describe what they do or by observing ongoing behaviors during comprehension. We know, for example, that illegally combined letter strings are more easily rejected as a possible word than are legally constructed strings, and we know that the decision speed with legal and illegal strings is greater among skilled than among less-skilled readers. What does this intimate about ability differences? First, skilled readers are more sensitive to the constraints on letter distributions (i.e., knowing which letter combinations are permitted); second, this sensitivity plays a decisive role in reading development.

The major pedagogical question is which of the two – distributional sensitivity or reading achievement – takes precedence? Logically, if one does precede the other, the sensible thing would be to teach the preceding competence first in order to facilitate the second. This seemingly straightforward question is not simple, however, because the relationship between the two is neither linear nor unidirectional; rather, they are reciprocal in that gains in one enhance growth in the other. This being the case, acquiring distributional sensitivity requires ample exposure to visual input in the target language. Conversely, reading efficiency evolves from the reader's attempt to exploit structural regularities implicit in the input. Sensitivity to such regularities thus heavily facilitates reading skills development. In this case, practice yields greater benefits than explicit explanations. To sum up, research information of considerable value in understanding reading development cannot always be incorporated in teaching without first probing instructional utility – and, one might add, it is important that instruction be consonant with the research implications.

Basic principles of comprehension instruction

The literature on instructional studies in L1 reading suggests four major principles used in designing instruction and implementing direct teaching of comprehension skills and strategies:

- *Commitment*: Learners must recognize that acquired skills have lasting utility.
- *Step-by-step sequential demonstration*: Learners need to know not only what should be done but also how it is best done.
- *Sustained incremental practice*: Learners need to be provided with ample opportunities to practice instructed skills with simplified training materials, followed by authentic texts.
- *Timely implementation*: Learners must master prerequisite competencies before instruction in target skills.

The following discussion describes effective approaches to comprehension instruction through synopses of widely used instructional tactics, reflecting the aforementioned principles.

A triad of declarative, procedural, and conditional knowledge generally is suggested as the important bases for fostering students' metacognitive understanding (Paris, Lipson, & Wixson, 1983). *Declarative knowledge* deals with knowing what learning and practice involve. In "lexical inference" training, for example, declarative knowledge refers to an understanding of how educated guessing through context information can lead to word meaning. *Procedural knowledge*, in contrast, refers to knowing how. Using inference again as an example, procedural knowledge implies a systematic delineation of the process used in inferring context-appropriate meanings of unknown words. Finally, *conditional knowledge* refers to knowing why and when it is useful to infer word meanings. Commonly used instructional tactics, almost without exception, incorporate components specifically requiring volitional applications of instructed strategies. The following descriptions explain how each tactic reflects the instructional principles listed above.

Instructional tactics

Direct explanations

Once familiarized with a reading strategy, students may or may not use it on their own accord in real-life reading situations. To ensure sustained utilization, after training, students must not only become adept in using a strategy but also must sense the benefits it affords. There is considerable evidence that students' beliefs serve as a filter through which their instructional experience is interpreted and absorbed (e.g., Nist & Simpson, 2000), and it would be extremely advantageous to incorporate explicit explanations of precisely how the strategy at hand advances their reading progress. If students are not convinced that the strategy is beneficial, declarative knowledge itself may not initiate productive changes in their reading patterns. The rationale's logic has been tested empirically in two kinds of investigations: intervention studies measuring the effectiveness of direct explanations on strategy use (e.g., Paris, Cross, & Lipson, 1984; Paris & Oka, 1986), and teacher-preparation studies tracing the impact of teacher training on subsequent instructional quality (e.g., Duffy, Roehler, Meloth, Vavrus, Book, & Putnam, 1986; Duffey, Roehler, & Putnam, 1987; Roehler & Duffy, 1984). Although both interventions yielded noticeable increases in students' metacognitive awareness and strategic manipulation, no measurable gains occurred in their standardized reading test scores. Future research exploring the approach's long-term benefits would be useful in advancing the importance of faith in a strategy's value.

Teacher modeling

Struggling students frequently find it difficult to understand teacher explanations through words alone. Modeling offers students additional assistance in grasping what it means to comprehend a text, and how the emerging comprehension can be monitored (e.g., Pearson & Gallagher, 1983). For example, the teacher can think aloud to demonstrate how understanding materializes from the text, and talk aloud to show how various comprehension-enhancing actions, such as raising questions, answering them, and generating predictions, can be initiated. Students thus are encouraged to apply what has been demonstrated by imitation or adaptation in teacher-guided exercises, and then are given ample opportunities to use the procedures in independent practice. The gradual transition of responsibility from the teacher to the student is the key factor in attaining the ultimate goal: developing self-regulated reading.

Cooperative learning

Cooperative leaning is defined as "any pattern of classroom organization that allows students to work together to achieve their individual goals" (Harris & Hodges, 1995, p. 45). It provides opportunities for students to model, discuss, and evaluate the usefulness of comprehension strategies as they read. A wide variety of activities, specifically designed to heighten strategy awareness and improve strategic manipulations – such as cognitive modeling, oral reading, peer tutoring, peer editing, and composition revising – should be included.

The approach offers several obvious advantages. Small-group collaborations create a less threatening, low-anxiety learning environment. Students actively engage in either reading itself or in reflecting on what has been read. Discussions of both the reading processes and content promote metacognitive dialogues among students. Moreover, studies show that cooperative learning is effective in increasing motivation, time on task, and overall academic achievement (e.g., Bramlett, 1994; Guthrie et al., 1996; Klinger, Vaughn, & Schumm, 1998).

Reciprocal teaching

Reciprocal teaching, proposed by Palincsar and Brown (1984), is perhaps the most prominent, widely cited method of teaching multiple comprehension strategies. The technique, like cooperative learning, involves small-group discussions, but differs in its rigid sequence of events. After a portion of a text is read, the student leader, designated by either the teacher or the group members, poses a question. The members respond, and the leader presents a summary of the group reactions. The group then participates in a roundtable conversation, asking clarification questions or discussing predictions about the upcoming text content. The sequence is specifically designed to promote core comprehension strategies – question generation, clarification, prediction, and summarization – one at a time in each phase of the sequence. The great strength of the approach lies in its capacity to foster multiple strategy use while engaging students in content understanding. Because of its heavy reliance on metacognitive sophistication, this approach generally is more successful with older and high-ability students (e.g., National Reading Panel, 2000), as well as when accompanied by explicit strategy explanations (e.g., Pressley, 2000).

L2 instructional approaches

Current practices

Reflecting the commonly held belief that reading competence is an integral dimension of language proficiency, L2 instructional intentions and methods tend to fluctuate between improving language proficiency and enlarging reading capabilities. Bamford and Day (1998) described four dominant techniques for teaching L2 reading: grammar translation, post-reading comprehension questioning, skills/strategies training, and extensive reading. According to Bamford and Day, grammar translation and post-reading questioning are traditional approaches widely used in preparing students for the foreign language examinations required for college admissions and similar screening purposes. Despite their heavy utilization, their effectiveness rarely has been tested directly. In most instances, they serve as a control, in treatment studies, to be compared with the target instructional outcome.

In contrast, skills/strategies training and extensive reading derive from L1 reading instruction and focus primarily on reading-ability improvement. Heavily influenced by Elley and Mangbuhai's 1983 publication, "The impact of reading on second language learning," extensive reading has been broadly advocated (e.g., Anderson, 1993; Bamford & Day, 1998; Yu, 1993) and its merits evaluated (e.g., Lituanas, Jacobs, & Renandya, 1999; Yu, 1999). Although skills/strategies enhancement activities are commonly incorporated in many L2 reading texts, many techniques are based on L1 instructional methods used in teaching reading/study skills to monolingual, native-speaking students (Silberstein, 1987). L2 instructional studies routinely show positive results, supporting the instructed skills and/or strategies tested. However, the studies used incompatible conceptual and methodological bases, thereby prohibiting direct comparisons. Consequently, it would be advantageous to establish a common base in L2 instructional research to determine legitimate working principles in designing/adapting teaching tactics for L2 readers, in lieu of endorsing study-specific algorithms. Toward this end, what follows is a consideration of important precautions in adapting L1 teaching methods to L2 instruction.

Factors involving the adaptation of L1 instructional tactics

L1 borrowing, as noted, is the most widely exercised approach in L2 instructional development. However, fundamental differences in students must be considered in such adaptations. Unlike beginning L1 readers, for example, L2 readers have more diversity in learning objectives, are metacognitively more sophisticated, and differ widely in prior literacy experiences. Because of these circumstances, their unfamiliarity with some strategies and different processing behaviors cannot be interpreted simply as knowledge or skill deficiencies. For example, when L2 procedural variations arise from the automatic activation of prior L1 skills, L2 readers may not have conscious awareness. Hence, their procedural variations cannot be easily modified through instruction designed to emulate native-like processing behaviors. These factors are elaborated below.

Reading purposes and aims are the central elements in orchestrating L2 instruction. L2 reading texts vary considerably in content, genre, and linguistic complexity, because L2 readers have disparate reading goals. To repeat, reading intent, in large measure, dictates how text information is processed. Moreover, because different processing modes entail distinct strategies, instruction should be mode specific, reflecting the dominant reading objectives (e.g., informational versus procedural versus pleasurable). For example, for American businessmen learning Chinese, in anticipation of temporary relocation to Beijing, informational reading may suffice. On the other hand, American students pursuing graduate degrees in Chinese universities must accumulate highly specialized knowledge, primarily through reading in Chinese. Obviously, the two groups need very different strategic approaches.

L1–L2 distance is another important element to be considered. Instructional approaches adapted from L1 may be beneficial for one group of L2 readers but unusable with another group that has different profiles. If decoding competence, for instance, is required for the execution of a particular strategy, the efficacy of the strategy instruction is totally dependent on the learner's L2 decoding capability. Moreover, because L1–L2 orthographic distance is largely responsible for differences in L2 decoding success, learners with similar and dissimilar L1 orthographic backgrounds are likely to deviate in decoding efficiency at any given point in their L2 development. Therefore, those with dissimilar backgrounds, resulting in lagging decoding development, likely will be handicapped in mastering the strategy at hand.

Finally, but of equal importance, in adopting L1 instructional approaches, careful attention must be given to the linguistic knowledge presumed to have been acquired by native-speaking students before formal reading instruction. Because the same presumption cannot hold for most L2 readers, instruction, dependent on linguistic capabilities yet to be acquired, obviously cannot succeed. In adopting L1 instructional procedures, therefore, it is essential to ensure that the prerequisite knowledge has been acquired.

Thoughts on further instructional research and practice

Continuing efforts to resolve ongoing issues in L2 reading have highlighted the complexity inherent in consolidating multiple variables. Promising new conceptualizations are emerging from the current theoretical postulations: Reading involves a number of subcomponent processes; each necessitates distinct competencies; individuals differ considerably in their ways of assimilating the component operations; necessary competencies deviate across languages; and L1 language-specific competencies often transfer to L2 reading. With these postulations as basic premises, we can speculate about promising future steps in dealing with the complexity in advancing L2 instructional research and practice. Much might be gained, for example, if we could find ways to consider these new insights in tandem, both to reduce practitioner overload and to unify the improvement efforts. Converting theory into practice is most productive when a few related ideas are combined into chunks and explored as a whole, rather than pursued in individual tidbits. If nothing else, it would substantially enhance the ongoing professional currency of instructors.

Considering the intricacy inherent in L2 reading, it is predictable that instructional effectiveness depends largely on teachers' knowledge of reading processes, skills in incorporating the knowledge in their instruction, and flexibility in accommodating students' diverse needs. In brief, L2 learning is greatly augmented when teachers know what students bring, linguistically and conceptually, to the instruction, how students' dispositions vary, and how these variations affect the instructional tactics teachers intend to use. Inasmuch as these insights do not routinely emanate as a matter of course from classroom experience, rigorous, sustained upgrading in enriched methods of monitoring students' linguistic, cognitive, and metacognitive growth is of great import.

Dual-language involvement patently is a major factor in the complexity of L2 reading instruction. Although it is generally acknowledged that L1 reading experience heavily influences L2 text processing, it is virtually impossible for teachers to understand, let alone cope with, every possible L1-based variation among their linguistically heterogeneous students. Still, such awareness is central in accommodating the disparate needs of students with divergent L1 backgrounds. If instruction is based entirely on native, monolingual speakers' processing behaviors, disregarding the impediments that arise when L2 learners must simultaneously cope with two languages, disparities are almost certain to occur between the unilingual norms assumed in the instruction and students' encumbrances stemming from multilingual processing.

Theoretically, one way to assist teachers would be to provide readily accessible information describing the structural properties likely to evoke blockages in common L1s. It would be helpful, for example, for teachers to know the meaning-construction devices in specific languages, and how they are represented graphically. The information would help teachers be more astute observers, analyze behavioral differences among students with different prior literacy experiences, and, of greatest importance, develop suitable coping mechanisms.

In view of the large variance among L2 readers, future instructional research might capitalize on new opportunities to individualize reading instruction in manageable, but more sophisticated, fashion. The enhanced capabilities of advanced computer technology – including speech recognition, multimedia presentations, interactive features, and instant linkages to other relevant information – hold strong promise for major breakthroughs in L2 reading instruction. To be sure, advances in technology-enhanced language instruction have increased exponentially; the technology, to date, has focused predominantly on the cosmetic updating of instructional delivery and presentation formats (e.g., Al Seghayer, 2003; Conrad, 1996). Regrettably, not enough has been done to explore rational approaches to incorporating cutting-edge technological capabilities in L2 reading curriculum. Classroom-based applied instructional research could yield valuable insights in how computer technology can best be integrated to help overcome cross-linguistic impediments. Although constant technological changes seemingly make it difficult to establish sustained research programs, in actuality, through cooperative alliances, it is far from impossible. As Kamil, Intrator, & Kim (2000) suggested, technological updates occur almost yearly, but the fundamental instructional issues do not. State-of-the-art technological applications, with the potential for overcoming linguistic barriers to reading development, can be achieved only through continuous collaborations among reading researchers, teachers, and technology specialists.

To recap, research and instruction are symbiotic. Properly coalesced, they enhance each other in several productive ways. The instructional approach, for example, can unearth various problems associated with learning to read, and research can give birth to possible solutions. Research identifies impediments, and instruction introduces new ways to overcome the hindrances. Research can also elicit unsuspected, usable competencies, further augmenting reading proficiency. It is only through committed instruction that hypothesized benefits and suspected obstacles can be tested. Put another way, research discovers the darkness that clouds reading difficulties, and exploratory instruction may shed new light. Their unrealized symbiosis, however, has yet to be tested in L2 studies. It is for these reasons that long-term integrated research programs, incorporating clearly articulated linkages with practice, warrant such explorations. Conjoined efforts of this sort could substantially help eliminate some of the complexities in the existing muddle and unveil new ways of guiding reading development.

References

Aaronson, D., & Ferres, S. (1983). Lexical categories and reading tasks. *Journal of Experimental Psychology: Human Perception and Performance*, 9, 675–699.

Abraham, R. G., & Chapelle, C. A. (1992). The meaning of cloze test scores: An item difficulty perspective. *Modern Language Journal*, 76, 468–479.

Abu Rabia, S. (1995). Learning to read in Arabic: Reading, syntactic, orthographic and working memory skills in normally achieving and poor Arabic readers. *Reading Psychology*, 16, 351–394.

Adams, M. J. (1990). *Beginning to read.* Cambridge: MIT Press.

Adams, M. J. (1994). Modeling the connections between word recognition and reading. In R. B. Ruddell, M. R. Ruddell, & H. Singer (Eds.), *Theoretical models and processes of reading* (4th ed.; pp. 830–863). Newark, DE: International Reading Association.

Afflerback, P. (2000). Verbal reports and protocol analysis. In M. L. Kamil, P. B. Mosenthal, P. D. Pearson, & R. Barr (Eds.), *Handbook of reading research* (Vol. 3; pp. 163–180). Mahwah, NJ: Erlbaum.

Aitchison, J. (1994). *Words in the mind* (2nd ed.). Oxford: Blackwell.

Akamatsu, N. (1999). The effects of first language orthographic features on word recognition processing in English as a second language. *Reading and Writing*, 11(4), 381–403.

Albert, M. L., & Obler, L. K. (1978). *The bilingual brain.* New York: Academic Press.

Alderson, J. C. (1984). Reading in a foreign language: A reading problem or a language problem? In J. C. Alderson & A. H. Urquhart (Eds.), *Reading in a foreign language* (pp. 1–24). London: Longman.

Alderson, J. C. (2000). *Assessing reading.* Cambridge, UK: Cambridge University Press.

Alderson, J. C., & Urquhart, A. H. (1985). This test is unfair: I'm not an economist. In P. Haupman, R. LeBlanc, & M. B. Wesche (Eds.), *Second language performance testing/L'Évaluation de la 'performance' en langue seconde* (pp. 25–44). Ottawa: University of Ottawa Press.

Allen, E. D., Bernhardt, E. B., Berry, M. T., & Demel, M. (1988). Comprehension and text genre: An analysis of secondary school foreign languages readers. *Modern Language Journal*, 72, 163–172.

Allington, R. L., & Fleming, J. T. (1978). The misreading of high frequency words. *Journal of Special Education, 12*, 417–421.

Al Seghayer, K. (2003). The impact of the presence of some organizational devices on the construction of a coherent mental representation of hypertext content exhibited by intermediate ESL readers. Unpublished doctoral dissertation, University of Pittsburgh.

Amer, A. A. (1992). The effect of story grammar instruction on EFL students' comprehension of narrative text. *Reading in a Foreign Language, 8*, 711–720.

Anderson, A., Garrod, S. C., & Sanford, A. J. (1983). The accessibility of pronominal antecedents as a function of episodic shifts in narrative text. *Quarterly Journal of Experimental Psychology, 35*, 427–440.

Anderson, J. R. (1983). *The architecture of cognition.* Cambridge: Harvard University Press.

Anderson, N. J. (1991). Individual differences in strategy use in second language reading and testing. *Modern Language Journal, 75*, 460–472.

Anderson, N. J. (1993). Repeated reading. In R. R. Day (Ed.), New ways in teaching reading. Alexandria, VA: TESOL, 190–191.

Anderson, R. C., & Davison, A. (1988). Conceptual and empirical bases of readability formulas. In A. Davison & G. M. Green (Eds.), *Linguistic complexity and text comprehension* (pp. 23–54). Hillsdale, NJ: Erlbaum.

Anderson, R. C., & Freebody, P. (1983). Reading comprehension and the assessment and acquisition of word knowledge. In B. Hutson (Ed.), *Advances in reading/language research: A research annual* (pp. 231–56). Greenwich, CT: JAI Press.

Anderson, R. C., & Nagy, W. E. (1991). Word meaning. In R. Barr, M. L. Kamil, P. Mosenthal, & P. D. Pearson (Eds.), *Handbook of reading research* (Vol. 2; pp. 512–538). New York: Longman.

Anderson, R. C., & Pearson, P. D. (1984). A schema-theoretic view of reading comprehension. In P. D. Pearson (Ed.), *Handbook of reading research* (pp. 255–291). New York: Longman.

Anderson, R. C., Reynolds, R. E., Schallert, D. L., & Goetz, E. T. (1977). Frameworks for comprehending discourse. *American Educational Research Journal, 14*, 367–382.

Andrews, S. (1992). Frequency and neighborhood effects on lexical access: Lexical similarity or orthographic redundancy? *Journal of Experimental Psychology: Learning, Memory, and Cognition, 18*, 234–254.

Archbold, D. A., & Newmann, F. M. (1988). *Beyond standardized testing.* Reston, VA: National Association of Secondary School Principals.

Armbruster, B. B., & Anderson, T. H. (1980). *The effect of mapping on the free recall of expository text* (Tech. Rep. No. 160). Urbana, IL: University of Illinois, Center for the Study of Reading.

Armbruster, B. B., & Anderson, T. H. (1985). Frames: Structures for informative text. In D. H. Jonassen (Ed.), *The technology of text* (Vol. 2, pp. 90–104). Englewood Cliff, NJ: Educational Technology Publications.

August, D., Calderon, M., & Carlo, M. (2000). *Transfer of skills from Spanish to English: A study of young learners.* Report for practitioners, parents, and policy makers. (ED-98-CO-0071).

August, D., Calderon, M., & Carlo, M. (2001). *Transfer of skills from Spanish to English: A study of young learners.* Updated review of current literature relevant to the technical issues in the implementation of the study. Washington, DC: Center for Applied Linguistics.

Bach, E., Brown, C., & Marslen-Wilson, W. D. (1986). Crossed and nested dependencies in German and Dutch: A psycholinguistic study. *Language and Cognitive Processes, 1,* 249–262.

Bachman, L. F. (1990). *Fundamental considerations in language testing.* Oxford: Oxford University Press.

Bachman, L. F., & Palmer, A. S. (1996). *Language testing in practice: Designing and developing useful language tests.* Oxford: Oxford University Press.

Baker, L., & Brown, A. L. (1984). Metacognitive skills and reading. In P. D. Pearson (Ed.), *Handbook of reading research* (pp. 353–394). New York: Longman.

Balota, D. (1994). Visual word recognition: The journey from features to meaning. In M. A. Gernsbacher (Ed.), *Handbook of psycholinguistics* (pp. 303–358). San Diego: Academic Press.

Balota, D., Pollasek, A., & Rayner, K. (1985). The interaction of contextual constraints and parafoveal visual information in reading. *Cognitive Psychology, 17,* 364–390.

Bamford, J., & Day, R. R. (1998). Teaching reading. *Annual Review of Applied Linguistics, 18,* 124–141.

Barker, K., Torgesen, J. K., & Wagner, R. K. (1992). The role of orthographic processing skills on five different reading tasks. *Reading Research Quarterly, 27,* 334–345.

Bartlett, B. J. (1978). Top-level structure as an organizational strategy for recall of classroom text. Unpublished doctoral dissertation, Arizona State University, Tempe.

Bates, E., & MacWhinney, B. (1987). Competition, variation, and language learning. In B. MacWhinney (Ed.), *Mechanisms of language acquisition* (pp. 157–194). Hillsdale, NJ: Erlbaum.

Bates, E., & MacWhinney, B. (1989). Functionalism and the competition model. In B. MacWhinney & E. Bates (Eds.), *The cross-linguistic study of sentence processing* (pp. 3–73). Cambridge: Cambridge University Press.

Bates, E., McNew, S., MacWhinney, B., Devescovi, A., & Smith, S. (1982). Functional constraints on sentence processing: A cross-linguistic study. *Cognition, 11,* 245–299.

Baumann, J. F., & Bergeron, B. S. (1993). Story map instruction using children's literature: Effects on first graders' comprehension of central narrative elements. *Journal of Reading Behavior, 25,* 407–437.

Beck, I. L., & Dole, J. A. (1992). Reading and thinking with history and science text. In C. Collins & J. M. Mangieri (Eds.), *Teaching thinking: An agenda for the twenty-first century* (pp. 1–22). Hillsdale, NJ: Erlbaum.

Beck, I. L., Perfetti, C. A., & McKeown, M. G. (1982). Effects of long-term vocabulary instruction on lexical access and reading comprehension. *Journal of Educational Psychology, 74*, 506–521.

Becker, C. A. (1985). What do we really know about semantic context during reading? In D. Besner, T. Waller, & G. MacKinnon (Eds.), *Reading research: Advances in theory and practice* (Vol. 5; pp. 125–166). New York: Academic Press.

Benedetto, R. A. (1985). Language ability and the use of top-level organizational strategies. Paper presented at the annual meeting of the National Reading Conference, San Diego. ERIC Document Reproduction Service No. ED 266 437.

Bensoussan, M., Sim, D., & Weiss, R. (1984). Lexical guessing in context in EFL reading comprehension. *Journal of Research in Reading, 2*, 15–32.

Bereiter, C. (1991). Implications of connectionism for thinking about rules. *Educational Researcher, 20*, 10–16.

Berkemeyer, V. C. (1994). Anaphoric resolution and text comprehension for readers of German. *Unterrichtspraxis, 27*, 15–22.

Berlin, B., & Kay, P. (1969). *Basic color terms: Their universality and evolution.* Berkeley: University of California Press.

Berman, R. A. (1984). Syntactic components of the foreign language reading process. In C. J. Alderson & A. H. Urquhart (Eds.), *Reading in a foreign language* (pp. 13–159). London: Longman.

Berman, R. A. (1986). A cross-linguistic perspective: Morphology and syntax. In P. Fletcher & M. Garman (Eds.), *Language acquisition: Studies in first language development* (2d ed.; pp. 429–448). New York: Cambridge University Press.

Berman, R. A., & Slobin, D. I. (1994). *Relating events in narrative: A crosslinguistic developmental study.* Hillsdale, NJ: Erlbaum.

Bernhardt, E. B. (1987). Cognitive processes in L2: An examination of reading behaviors. In J. Lantolf & A. Labarca (Eds.), *Delaware symposium on language studies: Research on second language acquisition in the classroom setting* (pp. 37–50). Norwood, NJ: Ablex.

Bernhardt, E. B. (1991). *Reading development in a second language.* Norwood, NJ: Ablex.

Bernhardt, E. B., & Kamil, M. L. (1995). Interpreting relationships between L1 and L2 reading: Consolidating the linguistic threshold and the linguistic interdependence hypotheses. *Applied Linguistics, 16*, 15–34.

Bialystock, E. (1988). Levels of bilingualism and levels of language awareness. *Developmental Psychology, 24*, 560–567.

Bialystock, E. (2001). *Bilingualism in development.* Cambridge: Cambridge University Press.

Biber, D. (1988). *Variation across speech and writing.* New York: Cambridge University Press.

Bickner, R., & Peyasantiwong, P. (1988). Cultural variation in reflective writing. In A. C. Purves (Ed.), *Writing across languages and cultures: Issues in contrastive rhetoric* (pp. 160–176). Newbury Park, CA: Sage.

Biemiller, A. (1979). Changes in the use of graphic and contextual information as functions of passage difficulty and reading achievement level. *Journal of Reading Behavior, 11*, 307–319.

Blachman, B. A. (1991). Phonological awareness: Implications for prereading and early reading instruction. In S. A. Brady & D. P. Shankweiler (Eds.), *Phonological processing in literacy* (pp. 9–36). Hillsdale, NJ: Erlbaum.

Black, J. B., & Bower, G. H. (1980). Story understanding as problem solving. *Poetics, 9*, 223–250.

Blau, E. K. (1982). The effects of syntax on readability for ESL students in Puerto Rico. *TESOL Quarterly, 16*, 517–528.

Bley-Vroman, R. (1989). What is the logical problem of foreign language learning? In S. M. Gass, & J. Schachter (Eds.), *Linguistic perspectives on second language acquisition* (pp. 41–68). New York: Cambridge University Press.

Block, E. (1986). The comprehension strategies of second language readers. *TESOL Quarterly, 20*, 463–494.

Bock, J. K., & Irwin, D. E. (1980). Syntactic effects of information availability in sentence production. *Journal of Verbal Learning and Verbal Behavior, 19*, 467–484.

Boland, J. E., Tanenhaus, M. K., & Garnsey, S. M. (1990). Evidence for the immediate use of verb control information in sentence processing. *Journal of Memory and Language, 29*, 413–432.

Bossers, B. (1991). On thresholds, ceilings and short-circuits: The relation between L1 reading, L2 reading and L2 knowledge. *AILA Review, 8*, 45–60.

Bowers, P., Golden, J., Kennedy, A., & Young, A. (1994). Limits upon orthographic knowledge due to processes indexed by naming speed. In V. W. Berninger (Ed.), *The varieties of orthographic knowledge I: Theoretical and developmental issues* (pp. 173–218). Dordrecht, the Netherlands: Kluwer.

Bowey, J. A., & Francis, J. (1991). Phonological analysis as a function of age and exposure to reading instruction. *Applied Psycholinguistics, 12*, 91–121.

Bradley, L. (1988). Rhyme recognition and reading and spelling in young children. In R. L. Masland & M. W. Masland (Eds.), *Pre-school prevention of reading failure* (pp. 143–152). Parkton, MD: York Press.

Bradley, L., & Bryant, P. (1991). Phonological skills before and after learning to read. In S. A. Brady & D. P. Shankweiler (Eds.), *Phonological processing in literacy* (pp. 37–45). Hillsdale, NJ: Erlbaum.

Bramlett, R. K. (1994). Implementing cooperative learning: A field study evaluating issues for school-based consultants. *Journal of School Psychology, 32*, 67–84.

Bransford, J. D. (1983). Schema activation – schema acquisition. In R. C. Anderson, J. Osborn, & R. C. Tierney (Eds.), *Learning to read in American schools*. Hillsdale, NJ: Erlbaum.

Bransford, J. D., Barclay, J. R., & Franks, J. J. (1972). Sentence memory: A constructive versus interpretive approach. *Cognitive Psychology, 3,* 193–209.

Bransford, J. D., & Franks, J. J. (1972). The abstraction of linguistic ideas: A review. *Cognition, 1,* 211–249.

Bransford, J. D., & Johnson, M. K. (1972). Contextual prerequisites for understanding: Some investigations of comprehension and recall. *Journal of Verbal Learning and Verbal Behavior, 11,* 717–726.

Bransford, J. D., & McCarrell, N. A. (1977). A sketch of a cognitive approach to comprehension: Some thoughts about understanding what it means to comprehend. In P. Johnson-Laird & P. Wason (Eds.), *Thinking: Reading in cognitive science* (pp. 191–212). Cambridge: Cambridge University Press.

Britton, B. (1994). Understanding expository text: Building mental structures to induce insights. In M. A. Gernsbacher (Ed.), *Handbook of psycholinguistics* (pp. 641–674). San Diego: Academic Press.

Brown, T., & Haynes, M. (1985). Literacy background and reading development in a second language. In T. H. Carr (Ed.), *The development of reading skills* (pp. 19–34). San Francisco: Jossey-Bass.

Bryant, P., MacLean, M., & Bradley, L. (1990). Rhyme, language, and children's reading. *Applied Psycholinguistics, 11,* 237–252.

Brysbaert, M. (1998). Word recognition in bilinguals: Evidence against the existence of two seperate lexicons. *Psychologica Belgica, 38,* 163–175.

Bugel, K., & Buunk, B. P. (1996). Sex differences in foreign language text comprehension: The role of interests and prior knowledge. *Modern Language Journal, 80,* 15–31.

Buss, R. R., Ratlliff, J. L., & Irion, J. C. (1985). Effects of instruction on the use of story structure in comprehension of narrative discourse. *National Reading Conference Yearbook, 34,* 55–58.

Calero-Breckheimer, A., & Goetz, E. T. (1993). Reading strategies of biliterate children for English and Spanish texts. *Reading Psychology, 14,* 177–204.

Calfee, R., & Hiebert, E. (1991). Classroom assessment of reading. In R. Barr, M. Kamil, P. Mosenthal, & P. D. Pearson (Eds.), *Handbook of reading research II* (pp. 246–280). New York: Longman.

Canal, M. (1987). The measurement of communicative competence. *Annual Review of Applied Linguistics, 8,* 67–84.

Carlisle, J. F. (1988). Knowledge of derivational morphology and spelling ability in fourth, sixth, and eighth graders. *Applied Psycholinguistics, 14,* 177–195.

Carlisle, J. F., (1995). Morphological awareness and early reading achievement. In L. Feldman (Ed.), *Morphological aspects of language processing* (pp. 189–209). Hillsdale, NJ: Erlbaum.

Carlisle, J. F., & Beeman, M. M. (2000). The effects of language of instruction on the reading and writing achievement of first-grade Hispanic children. *Scientific Studies of Reading, 4,* 331–353.

Carpenter, P. A., Miyake, A., & Just, M. A. (1994). Working memory constraints in comprehension: Evidence from individual differences, aphasia, and aging. In M. A. Gernsbacher (Ed.), *Handbook of psycholinguistics* (pp. 1075–1122). New York: Academic Press.

Carpenter, P. A., Miyake, A., & Just, M. A. (1995). Language comprehension: Sentence and discourse processing. *Annual Review of Psychology, 46,* 91–120.

Carr, T. H., Brown, T. L., Vavrus, L. G., & Evans, M. A. (1990). Cognitive skill maps and cognitive skill profiles: Componential analysis of individual differences in children's reading efficiency. In T. H. Carr & B. A. Levy (Eds.), *Reading and its development: Component skills approaches* (pp. 1–55). San Diego: Academic Press.

Carr, T. H., & Levy, B. A. (Eds.). (1990). *Reading and its development: Component skills approaches.* San Diego: Academic Press.

Carrell, P. L. (1983). Three components of background knowledge in reading comprehension. *Language Learning, 33,* 183–207.

Carrell, P. L. (1984a). The effects of rhetorical organization on ESL readers. *TESOL Quarterly, 18,* 441–469.

Carrell, P. L. (1984b). Inferencing in ESL: Presuppositions and implications of factive and implicative predicates. *Language Learning, 34,* 87–112.

Carrell, P. L. (1985). Facilitating ESL reading by teaching text structure. *TESOL Quarterly, 19,* 727–752.

Carrell, P. L. (1987). Content and formal schemata in ESL reading. *TESOL Quarterly, 21,* 461–481.

Carrell, P. L. (1988). Some causes of text-boundedness and schema interference in ESL reading. In P. L. Carrell, J. Devine, & D. Eskey (Eds.), *Interactive approaches to second language reading* (pp. 101–113). New York: Cambridge University Press.

Carrell, P. L. (1989). Metacognitive awareness and second language reading. *Modern Language Journal, 73,* 121–134.

Carrell, P. L. (1991). Second language reading: Reading ability or language proficiency? *Applied Linguistics, 12,* 159–179.

Carrell, P. L. (1992). Awareness of text structure: Effects on recall. *Language Learning, 42,* 1–20.

Carrell, P. L. (1998). Can reading strategies be successfully taught? *Australian Review of Applied Linguistics, 21,* 1–20.

Carrell, P. L., & Wallace, B. (1983). Background knowledge: Context and familiarity in reading comprehension. In M. A. Clarke & J. Handscome (Eds.), *On TESOL '82* (pp. 245–308). Washington, DC: TESOL.

Carrell, P. L., & Wise, T. E. (1998). The relationship between prior knowledge and topic interest in second language reading. *Studies in Second Language Acquisition, 20,* 285–309.

Carroll, J. B. (1971). Development of native language skills beyond the early years. In C. Reed (Ed.), *The learning of language* (pp. 97–156). New York: Appleton-Century-Crofts.

Carroll, J. B. (1985). LT + 25, and beyond? Comments. *Language Testing, 3*, 123–129.

Carver, R. P. (1990). *Reading rate: A review of research and theory.* New York: Academic Press.

Carver, R. P. (1993). Merging the simple view of reading with Rauding theory. *Journal of Reading Behavior, 4*, 439–454.

Carver, R. P. (1994). Percentage of unknown vocabulary words in text as a function of the relative difficulty of the text: Implications for instruction. *Journal of Reading Behavior, 26*, 413–437.

Carver, R. P. (1997). Reading for one second, one minute, or one year from the perspective of Rauding theory. *Scientific Studies of Reading, 1*, 3–45.

Carver, R. P. (2000). *The cause of high and low reading achievement.* Mahwah, NJ: Erlbaum.

Chafe, W. L., & Danielewicz, J. (1986). Properties of spoken and written languages. In R. Horowitz & S. J. Samuels (Eds.), *Comprehending oral and written language* (pp. 83–112). New York: Academic Press.

Chamot, A. U., & El-Dinary, P. B. (1999). Children's learning strategies in language immersion classrooms. *Modern Language Journal, 83*, 319–338.

Chamot, A. U., & O'Malley, J. M. (1994). Instructional approaches and teaching procedures. In K. Spangenberg-Urbschat & R. Pritchard (Eds.), *Kids come in all languages: Reading instruction for ESL students* (pp. 82–107). Newark, DE: International Reading Association.

Chaudron, C. (1983). Simplification of input: Topic restatements and their effects on L2 learners' recognition and recall. *TESOL Quarterly, 17*, 437–458.

Chaudron, C., & Richards J. (1986) The effect of discourse markers on the comprehension of lectures. *Applied Linguistics, 7*, 113–127.

Chen, H.-C., & Leung, Y.-S. (1989). Patterns of lexical processing in a nonnative language. *Journal of Experimental Psychology: Learning, Memory, and Cognition, 15*, 316–325.

Chen, Q., & Donin, J. (1997). Discourse processing of first and second language biology texts: Effects of language proficiency and domain-specific knowledge. *Modern Language Journal, 81*, 209–227.

Chen, Y. P., & Allport, D. A. (1995). Attention and lexical decomposition in Chinese word recognition: Conjunctions of form and position guide selective attention. *Visual Cognition, 2*, 235–268.

Chen, Y. P., Allport, D. A., & Marshall, J. C. (1996). What are the functional orthographic units in Chinese word recognition: The stroke or the stroke pattern? *Quarterly Journal of Experimental Psychology, 49*(A), 1024–1043.

Chern, C.-I. (1992, December). The psychological reality of Chinese characters – native vs. non-native Chinese readers' judgments of graphic similarity. Paper presented at the Eighth ILE International Conference, Hong Kong.

Chern, C.-I. (1994). Chinese readers' metacognitive awareness in reading Chinese and English. Paper presented at the annual meeting of International Language in Education Conference, Hong Kong. ERIC Document Reproduction Service No. ED 386 060.

Chilant, D., & Caramazza, A. (1995). Where is morphology and how is it processed? The case of written word recognition. In L. B. Feldman (Ed.), *Morphological aspects of language processing* (pp. 55–76). Hillsdale, NJ: Erlbaum.

Christie, J. F., & Alonso, P. A. (1980). Effects of passage difficulty on primary-grade children's oral reading error patterns. *Educational Research Quarterly, 5*, 41–49.

Cirilo, R. K. (1981). Referential coherence and text structure in story comprehension. *Verbal Learning and Verbal Behavior, 20*, 358–367.

Clark, H. H., & Clark, E. V. (1977). *Psychology and language.* New York: Harcourt Brace Jovanovich.

Clark, J. L. D. (1978). Interview testing research at Educational Testing Service. In J. L. D. Clark (Ed.), *Direct testing of spoken proficiency: Theory and application.* Princeton, NJ: Educational Testing Service.

Clarke, M. A. (1980). The short circuit hypothesis of ESL reading: Or when language competence interferes with reading performance. *Modern Language Journal, 64*, 203–209.

Clarke, M. A. (1988). The short circuit hypothesis of ESL reading: Or when language competence interferes with reading performance. In P. L. Carrell, J. Devine, & D. E. Eskey (Eds.), *Interactive approaches to second language reading* (pp. 114–124). New York: Cambridge University Press.

Clay, M. M. (1973). *Reading: The patterning of complex behavior.* Auckland, New Zealand: Heinemann.

Clay, M. M. (1989). Concept about print: In English and other languages. *Reading Teacher, 42*, 268–277.

Clay, M. M. (1991). *Becoming literate: The construction of inner control.* Auckland, New Zealand: Heinemann.

Clay, M. M. (1993). *Reading recovery: A guidebook for teachers in training.* Portsmouth, NH: Heinemann.

Clements, P. (1979). The effects of staging on recall from prose. In R. O. Freedle (Ed.), *New directions in discourse processing*, vol. 2, *Advances in discourse processes* (pp. 287–330). Norwood, NJ: Ablex.

Coady, J. (1979). A psycholinguistic model of the ESL reader. In R. Mackay, B. Barkman, & R. R. Jordan (Eds.), *Reading in a second language* (pp. 5–12). Rowley, MA: Newbury House.

Cohen, A. D. (1987). Student processing of feedback on their composition. In A. Wenden & J. Rubin (Eds.), *Leaner strategies in language learning* (pp. 57–69). Englewood Cliffs, NJ: Prentice Hall.

Cohen, A. D. (1996). Verbal reports as a source of insights into second language learner strategies. *Applied Language Learning, 7*, 5–24.

Cohen, A. D. (1998). *Strategies in learning and using a second language.* London: Longman.

Cohen, A. D., Olshtain, E., & Rosenstein, D. S. (1986). Advanced EFL apologies: What remains to be learned? *International Journal of the Sociology of Language, 62*, 51–74.

Connor, U., & Kaplan, R. B. (1987). Introduction. In U. Connor & R. B. Kaplan (Eds.), *Writing across languages: Analysis of L2 text* (pp. 1–5). Reading, MA: Addison-Wesley.

Conrad, K. B. (1996). CALL-Non-English L2 instruction. *Annual Review of Applied Linguistics, 16*, 158–181.

Cormier, P., & Kelson, S. (2000). The roles of phonological and syntactic awareness in the use of plural morphemes among children in French immersion. *Scientific Studies of Reading, 4*, 267–294.

Crain, S., & Nakayama, M. (1987). Structural dependence in grammar formation. *Language, 63*, 522–543.

Crain, S., & Shankweiler, D. (1988). Syntactic complexity and reading acquisition. In A. Davison & G. M. Green (Eds.), *Linguistic complexity and text comprehension* (pp. 167–192). Hillsdale, NJ: Erlbaum.

Cuetos, F., & Mitchell, D. C. (1988). Cross-linguistic differences in parsing: Restrictions on the use of the Late Closure strategy in Spanish. *Cognition, 30*, 73–105.

Cummins, J. (1979). Linguistic interdependence and educational development of bilingual children. *Review of Educational Research, 49*, 222–251.

Cummins, J. (1984). Implications of bilingual proficiency for the education of minority language students In P. Allen, M. Swain, & C. Brumfit (Eds.), *Language issues and education policies: Exploring Canada's multilingual resources*. Oxford: Pergamon Press.

Cummins, J. (1986). Empowering minority students: A framework for intervention. *Harvard Educational Review, 56*, 18–36.

Cummins, J. (1991). Interdependence of first- and second-language proficiency in bilingual children. In E. Bialystok (Ed.), *Language processing in bilingual children* (pp. 70–89). New York: Cambridge University Press.

Cummins, J., & Mulcahy, R. (1978). Orientation to language in Ukrainian-English bilingual children. *Child Development, 49*, 1239–1242.

Cummins, J., Swain, M., Nakajima, K., Handscombe, J., & Green, D. (1981). *Linguistic interdependence in Japanese and Vietnamese students*. Report prepared for the Inter-America Research Associates, June. Toronto: Ontario Institute for Studies in Education.

Cunningham, A. E., Stanovich, K. E., & Wilson, M. R. (1990). Cognitive variation in adult college students differing in reading ability. In T. H. Carr & B. A. Levy (Eds.), *Reading and its development: Component skills approaches* (pp. 129–160). San Diego: Academic Press.

Cziko, G. A. (1980). Language competence and reading strategies: A comparison of first- and second-language oral reading errors. *Language Learning, 30*, 101–114.

Da Fontoura, H. A., & Siegel, L. S. (1995). Reading syntactic and memory skills of Portuguese-English Canadian children. *Reading and Writing: An International Journal, 7*, 139–153.

Daneman, M. (1991). Individual differences in reading skills. In R. Barr, M. L. Kamil, P. Mosenthal, & P. D. Pearson (Eds.), *Handbook of reading research* (Vol. 2, pp. 512–538). New York: Longman.

Daneman, M., & Carpenter, P. A. (1980). Individual differences in working memory and reading. *Journal of Verbal Learning and Verbal Behavior, 19,* 450–466.

Daneman, M., & Carpenter, P. A. (1983). Individual differences in integrating information between and within sentences. *Journal of Experimental Psychology: Learning, Memory, and Cognition, 9,* 561–583.

Daneman, M., & Merikle, P. M. (1996). Working memory and language comprehension: A meta-analysis. *Psychonomic Bulletin and Review, 3,* 422–433.

Danner, F. W. (1976). Children's understanding of intersentence organization in the recall of short descriptive passages. *Journal of Educational Psychology, 68,* 174–183.

Davis, F. B. (1968). Research in comprehension in reading. *Reading Research Quarterly, 3,* 499–545.

Davis, J. N., Lange, D. L., Samuels, S. J. (1988). Effects of text structure instruction on foreign language readers' recall of a scientific journal article. *Journal of Reading Behavior, 20,* 203–214.

Davison, A., Wilson, P., & Hermon, G. (1985). *Effects of syntactic connectives and organizing cues on text comprehension.* Champaign, IL: Center for the Study of Reading.

de Courcy, M., & Birch, G. (1993). *Reading and writing strategies used in a Japanese immersion program.* Victoria, Australia: University of Melbourne. ERIC Document Reproduction Service No. ED 388 097.

DeFrancis, J. (1989). *Visible speech: The diverse oneness of writing systems.* Honolulu: University of Hawaii Press.

Demel, M. C. (1990). The relationship between overall comprehension and comprehension of coreferential ties for second language readers of English. *TESOL Quarterly, 24,* 267–292.

Demel, M. C. (1994). The relationship between overall comprehension and coreferential tie comprehension for second language readers of Spanish literature. *Linguistics and Education, 6,* 289–311.

Derwing, B. L., Smith, M. L., & Wiebe, G. E. (1995). On the role of spelling in morpheme recognition: Experimental studies with children and adults. In L. B. Feldman (Ed.), *Morphological aspects of language processing* (pp. 3–28). Hillsdale, NJ: Erlbaum.

Devine, J. (1987). General language competence and adult second language reading. In J. Devine, P. L. Carrell, & D. E. Eskey (Eds.), *Research on reading English as a second language* (pp. 73–86). Washington, DC: TESOL.

Devine, J. (1988). A case study of two readers: Models of reading and reading performance. In J. Devine, P. L. Carrell, & D. E. Eskey (Eds.), *Interactive approach to second language reading* (pp. 127–130). New York: Cambridge University Press.

Dewaele, J.-M., & Pavlenko, A. (2002). Emotion vocabulary in interlanguage. *Language Learning, 52,* 263–322.

Dijkstra, T., & van Heuven, W. J. B. (1998). The BIA model and bilingual word recognition. In J. Grainger & A. M. Jacobs (Eds.), *Localist connectionist approaches to human cognition* (pp. 189–225). Mahwah, NJ: Erlbaum.

Dijkstra, T., Van Jaarsveld, H., & Ten Brinke, S. (1998). Interlingual homograph recognition: Effects of task demands and language intermixing. *Bilingualism: Language and Cognition, 1,* 51–66.

Dole, J. A., Valencia, S. W., Greer, E. A., & Wardrop, J. L. (1991). Effects of two types of prereading instruction on the comprehension of narrative and expository text. *Reading Research Quarterly, 26,* 142–159.

Dooling, D. J., & Mullet, R. L. (1973). Locus of thematic effects in retention of prose. *Journal of Experimental Psychology, 97,* 404–406.

Drum, P. A., Calfee, R. C., & Cook, L. K. (1981). The effects of surface structure variables on performance in reading comprehension tests. *Reading Research Quarterly, 16,* 486–514.

Drum, P. A., & Konopak, B. C. (1987). Learning word meanings from written context. In M. G. McKeown & M. E. Curtis (Eds.), *The nature of vocabulary acquisition* (pp. 73–88). Hillsdale, NJ: Erlbaum.

Duffy, S. A. (1986). Role of expectations in sentence integration. *Journal of Experimental Psychology: Learning, Memory, and Cognition, 12,* 208–219.

Duffy, G. G., Roehler, L. R., Meloth, M. S., Vavrus, L. G., Book, C., Putnam, J., & Wesselman, R. (1986). The relationship between explicit verbal explanation during reading skill instruciton and student awareness and achievement: A study of reading teacher effects. *Reading Research Quarterly, 21,* 237–368.

Duffy, G. G., Roehler, L. R., & Putnam, J. (1987). Putting the teacher in control: Basal reading textbooks and instructional decision making. *Elementary School Journal, 87,* 357–366.

Dupuy, B., & Krashen, S. (1993). Incidental vacabulary acquisition in French as a foreign language. *Applied Language Learning, 4,* 55–63.

Duques, S. L. (1989). Grammatical deficiencies in writing: An investigation of learning disabled college students. *Reading and Writing, 1,* 309–325.

Durgunoglu, A. Y. (1998). Acquiring literacy in English and Spanish in the United States. In A. Y. Durgunoglu & L. Verhoeven (Eds.), *Literacy development in a multilingual context: Cross-cultural perspectives* (pp. 135–145). Mahwah, NJ: Erlbaum.

Durgunoglu, A. Y., Nagy, W. E., & Hancin, B. J. (1993). Cross-language transfer of phonemic awareness. *Journal of Educational Psychology, 85,* 453–465.

Durkin, D. (1979). What classroom observations reveal about reading comprehension instruction. *Reading Research Quarterly, 14,* 481–533.

Durso, F. T., & Shore, W. J. (1998). Partial knowledge of word meanings. *Journal of Experimental Psychology: General, 120,* 190–202.

Dwyer, E. S. (1997). Getting started the right way: An investigation into the introduction of Kanji study to neophyte Japanese learners. Unpublished doctoral dissertation, University of Texas at Austin.

Edwards, A. L. (1996). Reading proficiency assessment and the ILR/ACTFL typology: A reevaluation. *Modern Language Journal, 80*, 350–361.

Eggington, W. G. (1987). Written academic discourse in Korean: Implications for effective communication. In U. Connor & R. B. Kaplan (Eds.), *Writing across languages: Analysis of L2 text* (pp. 153–168). Reading, MA: Addison-Wesley.

Ehri, L. C. (1984). How orthography alters spoken language competencies in children learning to read and spell. In J. Downing & R. Valtin (Eds.), *Language awareness and learning to read* (pp. 119–147). New York: Springer-Verlag.

Ehri, L. C. (1994). Development of the ability to read words: Update. In R. Ruddell, M. R. Ruddell, & H. Singer (Eds.), *Theoretical models and processes of reading*, 4th ed. (pp. 323–358). Newark, DE International Reading Association.

Ehri, L. C. (1998). Grapheme-phoneme knowledge is essential to learning to read words in English. In J. L. Metsala & L. C. Ehri (Eds.), *Word recognition in beginning literacy* (pp. 3–40). Mahwah, NJ: Erlbaum.

Ehri, L. C., & Wilce, L. S. (1980). The influence of orthography on readers' conceptualization of the phonemic structure of words. *Applied Psycholinguistics, 1*, 371–385.

Ehrlich, K., & Johnson-Laird, P. N. (1982). Spatial descriptions and referential continuity. *Journal of Verbal Leaning and Verbal Behavior, 22*, 75–87.

Elley, W. B., & Mangbuhai, F. (1983). The impact of reading on second language learning. *Reading Research Quarterly, 19*, 53–67.

Ellis, N. C. (1994). Vocabulary acquisition: The implicit ins and outs of explicit cognitive mediation. In N. C. Ellis (Ed.), *Implicit and explicit learning of language* (pp. 211–282). London: Academic Press.

Ellis, N. C. (2002). Frequency effects in language processing: A review with implications for theories of implicit and explicit language acquisition. *Studies in Second Language Acquisition, 24*, 143–188.

Ellis, N. C., & Beaton, A. (1993). Psycholinguistic determinants of foreign language vocabulary learning. *Language Learning, 43*, 559–617.

Engle, R. W., Kane, M. J., & Tuholski, S. W. (1999). Individual differences in working memory capacity and what they tell us about controlled attention, general fluid intelligence, and functions of the prefrontal cortex. In A. Miyake & P. Shah (Eds.), *Models of working memory* (pp. 102–134). New York: Cambridge University Press.

Enright, M., Grabe, W., Koda, K., Mosenthal, P., Mulkahy-Ernt, P., & Schedl, M. (2000). TOEFL 2000 reading framework: A working paper. *TOEFL Monogram Series*, MS-17. Princeton, NJ: Educational Testing Service.

Ericsson, K. A., & Delaney, P. F. (1999). Long-term working memory as an alternative to capacity models of working memory in everyday skilled performance. In A. Miyake & P. Shah (Eds.), *Models of working memory* (pp. 257–297). New York: Cambridge University Press.

Ericsson, K. A., & Simon, H. A. (1984). *Protocol analysis: Verbal reports as data*. Cambridge: MIT Press.

Ervin, S. M., & Osgood, C. E. (1954). Second language learning and bilingualism. *Journal of Abnormal and Social Psychology, 49*, 139–146.

Everson, M. E. (1998). Word recognition among learners of Chinese as a foreign language: Investigating the relationship between naming and knowing. *Modern Language Journal, 82*, 194–204.

Everson, M. E., & Ke, C. (1997). An inquiry into the reading strategies of intermediate and advanced learners of Chinese as a foreign language. *Journal of the Chinese Language Teacher Association, 32*, 1–20.

Faulkner, H. J., & Levy, B. A. (1999). Fluent and nonfluent forms of transfer in reading: Words and their message. *Psychonomic Bulletin and Review, 6*, 111–116.

Favreau, M., & Segalowitz, N. (1982). Second language reading in fluent bilinguals. *Applied Psycholinguistics, 3*, 329–341.

Favreau, M., & Segalowitz, N. (1983). Automatic and controlled processes in the first- and second-language reading of fluent bilinguals. *Memory and Cognition, 11*, 565–574.

Feldman, L. B., & Bentin, S. (1994). Morphological analysis of disrupted morphemes: Evidence from Hebrew. *Quarterly Journal of Experimental Psychology, 47*, 407–435.

Fender, M. (2003). English word recognition and word integration skills of native Arabic- and Japanese-speaking learners of English as a second language. *Applied Psycholinguistics, 24*, 289–316.

Ferreira, F., & Clifton, C., Jr. (1986). The independence of syntactic processing. *Journal of Memory and Language, 25*, 348–368.

Ferreira, F., & Henderson, J. M. (1990). The use of verb information in syntactic parsing: Evidence from eye movements and word-by-word self-paced reading. *Journal of Experimental Psychology: Language, Memory, and Cognition, 16*, 555–568.

Ferreira, F., & Henderson, J. M. (1995). Eye movement control during syntactic analysis and reanalysis. In J. M. Henderson, M. Singer, & F. Ferreira (Eds.), *Reading and language processing* (pp. 119–147). Mahwah, NJ: Erlbaum.

Flavell (1978). Metacognitive development. In J. M. Scandura & C. J. Brainerd (Eds.), *Structural/process theories of complex human behavior*. Alphen a. d. Rijn, the Netherlands: Sijthoff & Noordhoff.

Fletcher, C. R., & Bloom, C. P. (1988). Causal reasoning in the comprehension of simple narrative texts. *Journal of Memory and Language, 27*, 235–244.

Flynn, S. (1987a). Contrast and construction in a parameter-setting model of L2 acquisition. *Language Learning, 37*, 19–62.

Flynn, S. (1987b). *A parameter-setting model of L2 acquisition*. Hingham, MA: Kluwer Academic Publishing.

Flynn, S. (1989). The role of the head-initial/head-final parameter in the acquisition of English relative clauses by adult Spanish and Japanese speakers.

In S. M. Gass & J. Schachter (Eds.), *Linguistic perspectives on second language acquisition* (pp. 89–108). New York: Cambridge University Press.

Flynn, S., & Espinal, I. (1985). Head-initial/head-final parameter in adult Chinese L2 acquisition of English. *Second Language Research*, 1, 93–117.

Foo, R. W. K. (1989). A reading experiment with L2 readers of English in Hong Kong: Effects of the rhetorical structure of expository texts on reading comprehension. *Hong Kong Papers in Linguistics and Language Teaching*, 12, 49–62.

Ford, M., Bresnan, J. W., & Kaplan, R. M. (1982). A competence based theory of syntactic closure. In J. W. Bresnan (Ed.), *The mental representation of grammatical relations* (pp. 727–796). Cambridge: MIT Press.

Fortkamp, M. B. M. (1999). Working memory capacity and aspects of L2 speech production. *Communication and Cognition*, 32, 259–295.

Fowler, A. E., & Liberman, I. Y. (1995). The role of phonology and orthography in morphological awareness. In L. B. Feldman (Ed.), *Morphological aspects of language processing* (pp. 157–188). Hillsdale, NJ: Erlbaum.

Fowler, C. A., Napps, S. E., & Feldman, L. B. (1985). Relations among regular and irregular morphologically related words in the lexicon as revealed by repetition priming. *Memory and Cognition*, 13, 241–255.

Fraser, C. (1999). Lexical processing strategy use and vocabulary learning through reading. *Studies in Second Language Acquisition*, 21, 225–242.

Frazier, L. (1978). On comprehending sentences: Syntactic parsing strategies. Unpublished doctoral dissertation, University of Connecticut, Storrs.

Frazier, L. (1990). Parsing modifiers: Special purpose routines in the human sentence processing mechanism? In D. A. Balota, G. B. Flores d'Arcais, & K. Rainer (Eds.), *Comprehension processes in reading* (pp. 303–330). Hillsdale, NJ: Erlbaum.

Frazier, L., & Flores d'Arcais, G. B. (1989). Filler-driven parsing: A study of gap filling in Dutch. *Journal of Memory and Language*, 28, 331–344.

Freedle, R. O., & Halle, G. (1979). Acquisition of new comprehension schemata for expository prose by transfer of a narrative schema. In R. O. Freedle (Ed.), *New directions in discourse processing* (pp. 121–135). Norwood, NJ: Ablex.

Frost, R., Katz, L., & Bentin, S. (1987). Strategies for visual word recognition and orthographic depth: A multilingual comparison. *Journal of Experimental Psychology: Human Perception and Performance*, 13, 104–115.

Fuchs, L. S., & Fuchs, D. (1999). Monitoring student progress toward the development of reading competence: A review of three forms of classroom-based assessment. *School Psychology Review*, 28, 659–671.

Fuchs, L. S., Fuchs, D., Hosp, M. K., & Jenkins, J. R. (2001). Oral reading fluency as an indicator of reading competence: A theoretical, empirical, and historical analysis. *Scientific Studies of Reading*, 5, 239–256.

Gairns, B. (1992). Cognitive processing in ESL reading. Unpublished Master's thesis, Ohio University, Athens.

Garcia, G. E. (1991). Factors influencing the English reading test performance of Spanish-speaking Hispanic children. *Reading Research Quarterly, 26,* 371–393.

Garner, R. (1990). When children and students do not use learning strategies: Toward a theory of settings. *Review of Educational Research, 60,* 517–529.

Garner, R., Alexander, P., Slater, W., Hare, V. C., Smith, T., & Reis, R. (1986). Children's knowledge of structural properties of expository text. *Journal of Educational Psychology, 78,* 411–416.

Garrod, S. C., & Sanford, A. J. (1994). Resolving sentences in a discourse context: How discourse representation affects language understanding. In M. A. Gernsbacher (Ed.), *Handbook of psycholinguistics* (pp. 675–698). San Diego: Academic Press.

Gass, S. M. (1983). Language transfer and universal grammatical relations. In S. M. Gass & L. Selinker (Eds.), *Language transfer in language learning* (pp. 69–82). Rowley, MA: Newbury House.

Gass, S. M. (1987). The resolution of conflicts among competing systems: A bidirectional perspective. *Applied Psycholinguistics, 8,* 329–350.

Gass, S. M. (1989). How do learners resolve linguistic conflict? In S. M. Gass & J. Schachter (Eds.), *Linguistic perspectives on second language acquisition* (pp. 183–202). New York: Cambridge University Press.

Gass, S. M. (1999). Discussion: Incidental vocabulary learning. *Studies in Second Language Acquisition, 21,* 319–334.

Gass, S. M., & Schachter, J. (Eds.). (1989). *Linguistic perspectives on second language acquisition.* New York: Cambridge University Press.

Gass, S. M. & Selinker, L. (Eds.). (1983). *Language transfer in language learning.* Rowley, MA: Newbury House.

Gathecole, S., & Baddeley, D. (1993). *Working memory and language.* Hove, UK: Erlbaum.

Gernsbacher, M. A. (1990). *Language comprehension as structure building.* Hillsdale, NJ: Erlbaum.

Gernsbacher, M. A. (1996). The structure-building framework: What is it, what it might also be, and why? In B. K. Britton & A. C. Graesser (Eds.), *Models of understanding text* (pp. 289–312). Mahwah, NJ: Erlbaum.

Geva, E. (1983). Facilitating reading comprehension through flowcharting. *Reading Research Quarterly, 15,* 384–405.

Geva, E. (1992). The role of conjunctions in L2 text comprehension. *TESOL Quarterly, 26,* 731–747.

Geva, E. (1999). Learning to read in a second language. In T. Nunes & P. Bryant (Eds.), *Integrating literacy, research and practice.* Amsterdam: Springer-Verlag.

Geva, E., & Siegel, L. S. (2000). Orthographic and cognitive factors in the concurrent development of basic reading skills in two languages. *Reading and Writing, 12,* 1–30.

Gholamain, M., & Geva, E. (1999). Orthographic and cognitive factors in the concurrent development of basic reading skills in English and Persian. *Language Learning, 49,* 183–217.

Gibson, E. J., & Levin, H. (1975). *The psychology of reading*. Cambridge: MIT Press.

Gleitman, L. R. (1985). Orthographic resources affect reading acquisition – if they are used. *Remedial and Special Education, 6*, 24–36.

Gleitman, L. R., & Rozin, P. (1978). The structure and acquisition of reading I: Relation between orthographies and the structure of language. In A. S. Reber & D. L. Scarborough (Eds.), *Towards a psychology of reading: The proceedings of the CUNY conference* (pp. 1–54). Hillsdale, NJ: Erlbaum.

Glenberg, A. M., Meyer, M., & Lindem, K. (1987). Mental models contribute to foregrounding during text comprehension. *Journal of Memory and Language, 26*, 69–83.

Goetz, E. T. (1979). Inferring from text: Some factors influencing which inferences will be made. *Discourse Processes, 2*, 179–195.

Goldman, S. R., Cote, N. C., & Saul, E. U. (1995). Paragraphing, reading, and task effects on discourse comprehension. *Discourse Processing, 20*, 273–305.

Goldman, S. R., & Duran, R. P. (1988). Answering questions for oceanography texts: Learner, task and text characteristics. *Discourse Processing, 11*, 373–412.

Goldman, S. R., & Murray, J. D. (1992). Knowledge of connectors as cohesion devices in text: A comparative study of native-English and English-as-a-second-language speakers. *Journal of Educational Psychology, 84*, 504–519.

Goldman, S. R., & Rakestraw, J. A., Jr. (2000). Structural aspects of constructing meaning from text. In M. L. Kamil, P. Mosenthal, P. D. Pearson, & R. Barr (Eds.), *Handbook of reading research* (Vol. 3; pp. 311–336). Mahwah, NJ: Erlbaum.

Goldman, S. R., Varma, S., & Cote, N. (1996). Extending capacity-constrained construction integration: Toward "smarter" and flexible models of text comprehension. In B. K. Britton & A. C. Graesser (Eds.), *Models of understanding text* (pp. 73–113). Mahwah, NJ: Erlbaum.

Good, R. H., III, Simmons, D. C., & Kame'enui, E. J. (2001). The importance and decision-making utility of a continuum of fluency-based indicators of foundational reading skills for third-grade high-stakes outcomes. *Scientific Studies of Reading, 5*, 257–288.

Goodman, K. S. (1967). Reading: A psycholinguistic guessing game. *Journal of the Reading Specialist, 6*, 126–135.

Goodman, K. S. (1969). Analysis of oral language miscues: Applied psycholinguistics. *Reading Research Quarterly, 5*, 9–30.

Goodman, K. S. (1973). Psycholinguistic universals of the reading process. In F. Smith (Ed.), *Psycholinguistics and reading* (pp. 21–29). New York: Holt, Rinehart and Winston.

Goodman, K. S., & Gollasch, F. V. (1980). Word omissions: Deliberate and non-deliberate. *Reading Research Quarterly, 16*, 6–13.

Goodman, Y. M., & Burke, C. L. (1972). *Reading miscue inventory: Procedures for diagnosis and evaluation*. New York: Macmillan.

Goswami, U., & Bryant, P. (1992). Rhyme, analogy, and children's reading. In P. B. Gough, L. C. Ehri, & R. Treiman (Eds.), *Reading acquisition* (pp. 49–64). Hillsdale, NJ: Erlbaum.

Gottardo, A., Siegel, L. S., Yan, B., & Wade-Woolley, L. (2001). Factors related to English reading performance in children with Chinese as a first language: More evidence of cross-language transfer of phonological processing. *Journal of Educational Psychology, 93,* 530–542.

Gough, P., & Tunmer, W. (1986). Decoding, reading, and reading disability. *RASE: Remedial and Special Education, 7,* 6–10.

Grabe, W. (1999). Developments in reading research and their implications for computer-adaptive reading assessment. In M. Chalhoub-Deville (Ed.), *Issues in computer-adaptive tests of reading* (pp. 11–48). New York: Cambridge University Press.

Graesser, A. C. (1981). *Prose comprehension beyond the word.* New York: Springer-Verlag.

Graesser, A. C., Golding, J. M., & Long, D. L. (1991). Narrative representation and comprehension. In R. Barr, M. L. Kamil, P. Mosenthal, & P. D. Pearson (Eds.), *Handbook of reading research* (Vol. 2, pp. 171–205). New York: Longman.

Graham, C. R., Hamblin, A. W., & Feldstein, S. (2001). Recognition of emotion in English voices by speakers of Japanese, Spanish and English. *International Review of Applied Linguistics, 39,* 19–37.

Graves, M. F. (1986). Vocabulary learning and instruction. In E. Z. Rothkopf (Ed.), *Review of research in education* (pp. 49–89). Washington, DC: American Educational Research Association.

Graves, M. F., Cooke, C. L., & LaBerge, M. J. (1983). Effects of previewing difficult short stories on low ability junior high school students' comprehension, recall, and attitudes. *Reading Research Quarterly, 28,* 262–276.

Gray, W. S. (1960). The major aspects of reading. In J. Robinson (Ed.), *Sequential development of reading abilities* (Vol. 22, pp. 8–24). Chicago: University of Chicago Press.

Green, D. W., & Meara, P. (1987). The effects of script on visual search. *Second Language Research, 3,* 102–117.

Griffin, G., & Harley, T. A. (1998). List learning of second language vocabulary. *Applied Psycholinguistics, 17,* 443–460.

Gu, Y., & Johnson, R. K. (1996). Vocabulary learning strategies and language learning outcomes. *Language Learning, 46,* 643–679.

Gundel, J. K., & Tarone, E. E. (1983). Language transfer and the acquisition of pronominal anaphora. In S. M. Gass & L. Selinker (Eds.), *Language transfer in language learning* (pp. 281–296). Rowley, MA: Newbury House.

Guthrie, J. T., Van Meter, P., McCann, A. D., Wigfield, A., Bennett, L., Poundstone, C. C., Rice, M. E., Faibisch, F. M., Hunt, B., & Mitchell, A. M. (1996). Growth of literacy engagement: Changes in motivations and strategies during concept-oriented reading instruction. *Reading Research Quarterly, 31,* 306–332.

Haenggi, D., Gernsbacher, M. A., & Bollinger, C. M. (1993). Individual differences in situation-based inferencing during narrative text comprehension. In J. van Oostendorp & R. A. Zwaan (Eds.), *Naturalistic text comprehension: Advances in discourse processing* (pp. 79–96). Norwood, NJ: Ablex.

Hakuta, K. (1976). A case study of a Japanese child learning English as a second language. *Language Learning, 26*, 321–351.

Hakuta, K. (1982). Interaction between particles and word order in the comprehension and production of simple sentences in Japanese children. *Developmental Psychology, 18*, 62–76.

Halliday, M. A. K., & Hasan, R. (1976). *Cohesion in English*. London: Longman.

Hamburger, H., & Crain, S. (1982). Relative acquisition. In S. Kuczaj II (Ed.), *Language development: Syntax and semantics* (pp. 245–274). Hillsdale, NJ: Erlbaum.

Hammadou, J. (1991). Interrelationships among prior knowledge, inference, and language. *Modern Language Journal, 75*, 27–38.

Hancin-Bhatt, B., & Nagy, W. (1994). Lexical transfer and second language morphological development. *Applied Psycholinguistics, 15* (3), 289–310.

Hancin-Bhatt, B., & Bhatt, R. M. (1997). Optimal L2 Syllables: Interactions of Transfer and Developmental Effects. *Studies in Second Language Acquisition, 19*, 331–78.

Harrington, M. (1987). Processing transfer: Language-specific processing strategies as a source of interlanguage variation. *Applied Psycholinguistics, 8*, 351–377.

Harrington, M., & Sawyer, M. (1992). L2 working memory and L2 reading skill. *Studies in Second Language Acquisition, 14*, 25–38.

Harris, T. L., & Hodges, R. E. (Eds.). (1995). *The literacy dictionary: The vocabulary of reading and writing*. Newark, DE: International Reading Association.

Hatch, E., Polin, P., & Part, S. (1974). Acoustic scanning and syntactic processing: Three reading experiments – first and second language learners. *Journal of Reading Behavior, 6*, 275–285.

Haviland, S. E., & Clark, H. H. (1974). What's new? Acquiring new information as a process in comprehension. *Journal of Verbal Learning and Verbal Behavior, 13*, 512–521.

Hayashi, M., Ulatowska, H. K., & Sasanuma, S. (1985). Subcortical aphasia with deep dyslexia: A case study of a Japanese patient. *Brain and Language, 25*, 293–313.

Haynes, M., & Baker, I. (1993). American and Chinese readers learning from lexical familiarization in English texts. In T. Huckin, M. Haynes, & J. Coady (Eds.), *Second language reading and vocabulary acquisition* (pp. 153–180). Norwood, NJ: Ablex.

Haynes, M., & Carr, T. H. (1990). Writing system background and second language reading: A component skills analysis of English reading by native-speaking readers of Chinese. In T. H. Carr & B. A. Levy (Eds.),

Reading and its development: Component skills approaches (pp. 375–421). San Diego: Academic Press.

Hayth-Roth, B., & Thorndyke, P. W. (1979). Integration of knowledge from text. *Journal of Verbal Learning and Verbal Behavior, 18*, 91–108.

Heath, S. B. (1983). *Ways with words*. New York: Cambridge University Press.

Henriksen, B. (1999). Three dimensions of vocabulary development. *Studies in Second Language Acquisition, 21*, 303–318.

Hiebert, E. H., Valencia, S. W., & Afflerbach, P. P. (1994). Definitions and perspectives. In S. W. Valencia, E. H. Hiebert, & P. P. Afflerback (Eds.), *Authentic reading assessment* (pp. 6–21). Newark, DE: International Reading Association.

Hinds, J. (1987). Reader versus writer responsibility: A new typology. In U. Connor & R. B. Kaplan (Eds.), *Writing across languages: Analysis of L2 text* (pp. 141–152). Reading, MA: Addison-Wesley.

Hintzman, D. L. (1986). "Schema abstraction" in a multiple-trace memory model. *Psychological Review, 93*, 411–428.

Ho, C. S.-H., & Bryant, P. (1999). Different visual skills are important in learning to read English and Chinese. *Educational and Child Psychology, 16*, 4–14.

Hogaboam, T. W., & Perfetti, C. A. (1978). Reading skill and the role of verbal experience in decoding. *Journal of Educational Psychology, 70*, 717–729.

Holmes, V. M. (1984). Parsing strategies and discourse context. *Journal of Psycholinguistic Research, 13*, 237–257.

Hoover, W. A., & Gough, P. B. (1990). The simple view of reading. *Reading and Writing: An Interdisciplinary Journal, 2*, 127–160.

Horiba, Y. (1990). Narrative comprehension processes: A study of native and non-native readers of Japanese. *Modern Language Journal, 74*, 188–202.

Horiba, Y. (1993). The role of causal reasoning and language competence in narrative comprehension. *Studies in Second Language Acquisition, 15*, 49–81.

Horiba, Y. (1996). The role of elaborations in L2 text memory: The effect of encoding task on recall of causally related sentences. *Modern Language Journal, 80*, 151–164.

Horiba, Y., van den Broek, P. W., & Fletcher, C. R. (1993). Second language readers' memory for narrative texts: Evidence for structure-preserving top-down processing. *Language Learning, 43*, 345–372.

Hosenfeld, C. (1977). Learning about learning: Discovering our students' strategies. *Foreign Language Annals, 9*, 117–129.

Hu, M., and Nation, I. S. P. (2000). Unknown vocabulary density and reading comprehension. *Reading in a Foreign Language, 13*, 403–430.

Hua, T. (1997). The relationship between reading comprehension processes in L1 and L2. *Reading Psychology, 18*, 249–301.

Hulstijin, J. H. (1997). Mnemonic methods in foreign language vocabulary learning: Theoretical considerations and pedagogical implications. In

J. Coady & T. Huckin (Eds.), *Second language vocabulary acquisition* (pp. 203–224). New York: Cambridge University Press.

Hutchins, E. (1980). *Culture and inference.* Cambridge: Harvard University Press.

Inagaki, S. (2001). Motion verbs with goal PPs in the L2 acquisition of English and Japanese. *Studies in Second Language Acquisition, 23,* 153–170.

Indrasuta, C. (1988). Narrative styles in the writing of Thai and American students. In A. C. Purves (Ed.), *Writing across languages and cultures: Issues in contrastive rhetoric* (pp. 206–226). Newbury Park, CA: Sage.

Inoue, A., & Fodor, J. D. (1995). Information-paced parsing of Japanese. In R. Mazuka & N. Nagai (Eds.), *Japanese sentence processing* (pp. 9–64). Hillsdale, NJ: Erlbaum.

Irujo, S. (1986). Don't put your leg in your mouth: Transfer in the acquisition of idioms on a second language. *TESOL Quarterly, 20,* 287–304.

Irwin, J. W., & Pulver, C. J. (1984). Effects of explicitness, clause order and reversibility on children's comprehension of causal relationships. *Journal of Educational Psychology, 76,* 399–407.

Issidorides, D. C., & Hulstijin, J. H. (1992). Comprehension of grammatically modified and nonmodified sentences by second language learners. *Applied Psycholinguistic, 13,* 147–171.

Jakobovits, L. A., & Lambert, W. E. (1961). Semantic satiation among bilinguals. *Journal of Experimental Psychology, 62,* 576–582.

Jenkin, H., Prior, S., Richard, R., Wainwright-Sharp, A., & Bialystok, E. (1993). Understanding text in a second language: A psychological approach to an SLA problem. *Second Language Research, 9,* 118–139.

Jiang, N. (2002). Form-meaning mapping in vocabulary acquisition in a second language. *Studies in Second Language Acquisition, 24,* 617–638.

Jimenez, R. T., Garcia, G. E., & Pearson, P. D. (1995). Three children, two languages, and strategic reading: Case studies in bilingual/monolingual reading. *American Educational Research Journal, 32,* 31–61.

Jimenez, R. T., Garcia, G. E., & Pearson, P. D. (1996). The reading strategies of bilingual Latina/o students who are successful English readers: Opportunities and obstacles. *Reading Research Quarterly, 31,* 90–112.

Johnson, P. (1980). The effects of the language complexity and the culturally determined background of the text on the reading comprehension of Iranian students in ESL. Doctoral dissertation, University of Illinois. *Dissertation Abstracts International, 41,* 2482-A.

Johnston, P. (1982). Effects on reading comprehension of building background knowledge. *TESOL Quarterly, 16,* 503–516.

Johnston, P. (1983). *Reading comprehension assessment: A cognitive basis.* Newark, DE: International Reading Association.

Johnston, P. (1984). Assessment in reading. In P. D. Pearson (Ed.), *Handbook of reading research* (pp. 147–184). New York: Longman.

Johnson-Laird, P. N. (1983). *Mental model.* Cambridge: Harvard University Press.

Juel, C. (1988). Learning to read and write: A longitudinal study of fifty-four children from first through fourth grade. *Journal of Educational Psychology, 80,* 437–447.

Juel, C., Griffith, P. L., & Gough, P. B. (1986). Acquisition of literacy: A longitudinal study of children in first and second grade. *Journal of Educational Psychology, 78,* 243–255.

Juffs, A. (1998). Main verb versus reduced relative clauses ambiguity resolution in L2 sentence processing. *Language Learning, 48,* 107–147.

Juffs, A., & Harrington, M. (1996). Garden path sentences and error data in second language sentence processing. *Language Learning, 46,* 283–326.

Just, M. A., & Carpenter, P. A. (1980). A theory of reading: From eye fixation to comprehension. *Psychological Review, 87,* 329–354.

Just, M. A., & Carpenter, P. A. (1987). *The psychology of reading and language comprehension.* Boston: Allyn & Bacon.

Kachru, Y. (1988). Writers in Hindi and English. In A. C. Purves (Ed.), *Writing across languages and cultures: Issues in contrastive rhetoric* (pp. 109–137). Newbury Park, CA: Sage.

Kail, M. (1989). Cue validity, cue cost, and processing types in sentence comprehension in French and Spanish. In B. MacWhinney & E. Bates (Eds.), *The cross-linguistic study of sentence processing* (pp. 77–117). New York: Cambridge University Press.

Kame'enui, E. J., & Simmons, D. C. (2001). The DNA of reading fluency. *Scientific Studies of Reading, 5,* 203–210.

Kamil, M. L., Intrator, S. M., & Kim, H. S. (2000). The effects of other technologies on literacy and literacy learning. In M. L. Kamil, P. B. Mothenthal, P. D. Pearson, & R. Barr (Eds.), *Handbook of reading research* (Vol. 3, pp. 771–790). Mahwah, NJ: Erlbaum.

Kang, H. W. (1992). Cultural inference in second language reading. *International Journal of Applied Linguistics, 2,* 95–119.

Kaplan, R. B. (1966). Cultural thought patterns in intercultural education. *Language Learning, 16,* 1–20.

Kaplan, R. B. (1987). Cultural thought patterns revisited. In U. Connor & R. B. Kaplan (Eds.), *Writing across languages: Analysis of L2 text* (pp. 9–22). Reading, MA: Addison-Wesley.

Kaplan, R. B. (1988). Contrastive rhetoric and second language learning: Notes towards a theory of contrastive rhetoric. In A. C. Purves (Ed.), *Writing across languages and cultures: Issues in contrastive rhetoric* (pp. 275–304). Newbury Park, CA: Sage.

Katz, L., & Frost, R. (1992). Reading in different orthographies: The orthographic depth hypothesis. In R. Frost & L. Katz (Eds.), *Orthography, phonology, morphology, and meaning* (pp. 67–84). Amsterdam: Elsevier.

Katz, L., Rexer, K., & Lukatela, G. (1991). The processing of inflected words. *Psychological Research, 53,* 25–32.

Katz, N., Baker, E., & MacNamara, J. (1974). What's in a name? A study of how children learn common and proper nouns. *Child Development, 65,* 469–473.

Katz, R. B., Shankweiler, D., & Liberman, I. Y. (1981). Memory for item order and phonetic recoding in the beginning reader. *Journal of Experimental Child Psychology, 32,* 474–484.

Kavale, K., & Schreiner, R. (1979). The reading processes of above average and average readers: A comparison of the use of reasoning strategies in responding to standardized comprehension measures. *Reading Research Quarterly, 15,* 102–128.

Ke, C. (1998). Effects of language background on the learning of Chinese characters among foreign language students. *Foreign Language Annals, 31,* 91–100.

Keenan, J. M., Baillet, S. D., & Brown, P. (1984). The effects of causal cohesion on comprehension and memory. *Journal of Verbal Learning and Verbal Behavior, 23,* 115–126.

Kelch, K. (1985). Modified input as an aid to comprehension. *Studies in Second Language Acquisition, 7,* 81–90.

Kellerman, E. (1983). Now you see it, now you don't. In S. M. Gass & L. Selinker (Eds.), *Language transfer in language learning* (pp. 112–134). Rowley, MA: Newbury House.

Kellerman, E., & Sharwood Smith, M. (Eds.). (1986). *Crosslinguistic influence in second language acquisition.* Oxford: Pergamon Press.

Kelliher, S., & Henderson, L. (1990). Morphologically based frequency effects in the recognition of irregularly inflected words in auditory word recognition. *British Journal of Experimental Psychology, 81,* 527–539.

Kennedy, A., Murray, W., Jennings, F., & Reid, C. (1989). Parsing complements: Comments on the generality of the principle of minimal attachment. *Language and Cognitive Processes, 4,* 51–76.

Kieras, D. E. (1981). Component processes in the comprehension of simple prose. *Journal of Verbal Learning and Verbal Behavior, 20,* 1–23.

Kilborn, K., & Ito, T. (1989). Sentence processing strategies in adult bilinguals. In B. MacWhinney & E. Bates (Eds.), *The cross-linguistic study of sentence processing* (pp. 256–291). New York: Cambridge University Press.

King, A. (1990). Improving lecture comprehension: Effects of a metacognitive strategy. *Applied Educational Psychology, 29,* 331–346.

King, A. (1992). Comparison of self-questioning, summarizing, and note-taking review as strategies for learning from lectures. *American Educational Research Journal, 29,* 303–325.

King. J., & Just, M. A. (1991). Individual differences in syntactic processing: The role of working memory. *Journal of Memory and Language, 30,* 580–602.

Kintsch, W. (1974). *The representation of meaning in memory.* New York: Erlbaum.

Kintsch, W. (1977). On comprehending stories. In M. A. Just & P. Carpenter (Eds.), *Cognitive processes in comprehension* (pp. 33–61). Hillsdale, NJ: Erlbaum.

Kintsch, W. (1988). The use of knowledge in discourse processing: A construction-integration model. *Psychological Review, 95,* 163–182.

Kintsch, W. (1992). A cognitive architecture for comprehension. In H. L. Pick, P. van den Broek, & D. C. Knill (Eds.), *The study of cognition: Conceptual and methodological issues* (pp. 143–164). Washington, DC: American Psychological Association.

Kintsch, W. (1994). The psychology of discourse processing. In M. A. Gernsbacher (Ed.), *Handbook of psycholinguistics* (pp. 721–739). San Diego: Academic Press.

Kintsch, W. (1998). *Comprehension: A paradigm for cognition.* New York: Cambridge University Press.

Kintsch, W., & Keenan, J. M. (1973). Reading rate and retention as a function of the number of propositions in the base structure of sentences. *Cognitive Psychology, 5,* 257–279.

Kintsch, W., Kosminsky, E., Streby, W. J., McKoon, G., & Keenan, J. M. (1975). Comprehension and recall as a function of content variables. *Journal of Verbal Learning and Verbal Behavior, 14,* 196–214.

Kintsch, W., & van Dijk, T. A. (1978). Towards a model of text comprehension and production. *Psychological Review, 85,* 363–394.

Kintsch, W., & Vipond, D. (1979). Reading comprehension and readability in educational practice and psychological theory. In L. G. Nelson (Ed.), *Perspectives of memory research* (pp. 325–366). Hillsdale, NJ: Erlbaum.

Kintsch, W., & Welsch, D. M. (1991). The construction-integration model: A framework for studying memory for text. In W. E. Hockley & S. Lewandowsky (Eds.), *Relating theory and data: Essays on human memory in honor of Bennett B. Murdock* (pp. 367–385). Hillsdale, NJ: Erlbaum.

Kitajima, R. (1997). Referential strategy training for second language reading comprehension of Japanese texts. *Foreign Language Annals, 30,* 84–97.

Kitayama, S., & Markus, H. R. (Eds.). (1994). *Emotion and culture: Empirical studies of mutual influence.* Washington, DC: American Psychological Association.

Kleiman, G. M. (1975). Speech recording in reading. *Journal of Verbal Learning and Verbal Behavior, 14,* 323–339.

Klinger, J. K., Vaughn, S., & Schumm, J. S. (1998). Collaborative strategic reading during social studies in heterogeneous fourth-grade classrooms. *Elementary School Journal, 99,* 3–22.

Knight, S. (1994). Dictionary use while reading: The effects on comprehension and vocabulary acquisition for students of different verbal abilities. *Modern Language Journal, 78,* 285–299.

Koda, K. (1988). Cognitive process in second language reading: Transfer of L1 reading skills and strategies. *Second Language Research, 4,* 133–156.

Koda, K. (1989). The effects of transferred vocabulary knowledge on the development of L2 reading proficiency. *Foreign Language Annals, 22,* 529–542.

Koda, K. (1990a). Factors affecting second language text comprehension. In J. Zutell & S. McCormick (Eds.), *Literacy theory and research: Analyses from multiple paradigms* [39th Yearbook of the National Reading Conference] (pp. 419–427). Chicago: National Reading Conference.

Koda, K. (1990b). The use of L1 reading strategies in L2 reading. *Studies in Second Language Acquisition, 12*, 393–410.

Koda, K. (1992). The effects of lower-level processing skills on the development of second language reading. *Modern Language Journal, 76*, 502–512.

Koda, K. (1993). Transferred L1 strategies and L2 syntactic structure during L2 sentence comprehension. *Modern Language Journal, 77*, 490–500.

Koda, K. (1998). The role of phonemic awareness in L2 reading. *Second Language Research, 14*, 194–215.

Koda, K. (1999). Development of L2 intraword structural sensitivity and decoding skills. *Modern Language Journal, 83*, 51–64.

Koda, K. (2000a). Cross-linguistic interactions in the development of L2 intraword awareness: Effects of logographic processing experience. *Psychologia, 43*, 26–46.

Koda, K. (2000b). Cross-linguistic variations in L2 morphological awareness. *Applied Psycholinguistics, 21*, 297–320.

Koda, K. (2002). Writing systems and learning to read in a second language. In W. Li, J. S. Gaffiney, & J. L. Packard (Eds.), *Chinese children's reading acquisition: Theoretical and pedagogical issues* (pp. 225–248). Boston: Kluwer Academic.

Koda, K., Takahashi, E., & Fender, M. (1998). Effects of L1 processing experience on L2 morphological awareness. *Ilha do Desterro, 35*, 59–87.

Koda, K., & Takahashi, T. (2004). Role of radical awareness in lexical inference in Kanji. Manuscript submitted for publication.

Koury, K. A. (1996). The impact of preteaching science content vocabulary using integrated media or knowledge acquisition in a collaborative classroom. *Journal of Computing in Childhood Education, 7*, 179–197.

Krashen, S. (1983). Newmark's "ignorance hypothesis" and current second language acquisition theory. In S. M. Gass & L. Selinker (Eds.), *Language transfer in language learning* (pp. 135–156). Rowley, MA: Newbury House.

Kroll, J. F., & Curley, J. (1988). Lexical memory in novice bilinguals: The role of concepts in retrieving second language words. In M. Gruneberg, P. Morris, & R. Sykes (Eds.), *Practical aspects of memory* (Vol. 2; pp. 389–395). London: John Wiley and Sons.

Kroll, J. F., & Sholl, A. (1992). Lexical and conceptual memory in fluent and nonfluent bilinguals. In R. J. Harris (Ed.), *Cognitive processing in bilinguals* (pp. 191–204). Amsterdam: Elsevier.

Kroll, J. F., & Stewart, E. (1994). Category inference in translation and picture naming: Evidence for asymmetric connections between bilingual memory representations. *Journal of Memory and Language, 33*, 149–174.

Kroll, J. F., & Sunderman, G. (2003). Cognitive processes in second language acquisition. In C. Doughty & M. Long (Eds.), *Handbook of second language acquisition*. Cambridge, MA: Blackwell Publishers.

Kuhara-Kojima, K., Hatano, G., Saito, H., & Haebara, T. (1996). Vocalization latencies of skilled and less skilled comprehenders for words written in Hiragana and Kanji. *Reading Research Quarterly, 31*, 158–171.

LaBerge, P., & Samuels, S. J. (1974). Toward a theory of automatic information processing in reading. *Cognitive Psychology, 6*, 293–323.

Lambert, W. E. (1969). Psychological studies of interdependencies of the bilingual's two languages. In J. Puhvel (Ed.), *Substance and structure of language* (pp. 99–126). Los Angeles: University of California Press.

Langer, J. A. (1987). The construction of meaning and the assessment of comprehension: An analysis of reader performance on standardized test items. In R. Q. Freedle & R. P. Duran (Eds.), *Cognitive and linguistic analyses of test performance* (pp. 225–244). Norwood, NJ: Ablex.

Laufer, B. (1997). The lexical plight in second language reading: Words you don't know, words you think you know, and words you can't guess. In J. Coady & T. Huckin (Eds.), *Second language vocabulary acquisition* (pp. 20–34). New York: Cambridge University Press.

Laufer, B., & Patribakht, S. T. (1998). The relationship between passive and active vocabularies: Effects of language learning context. *Language Learning, 48*, 365–391.

Leck, K. J., Weekes, B. S., & Chen, M. J. (1995). Visual and phonological pathways to the lexicon: Evidence from Chinese readers. *Memory and Cognition, 23*, 468–476.

Lee, C. D., & Gasser, M. (1992). Where do underlying representations come from?: A connectionist approach to the acquisition of phonological rules. In J. Dinsmore (Ed.), *The symbolic and connectionist paradigms: Closing the gap* (pp. 179–207). Hillsdale, NJ: Erlbaum.

Lee, J. F. (1986). On the use of the recall task to measure L2 reading comprehension. *Studies in Second Language Acquisition, 8*, 83–93.

Lee, J. F., & Musumeci, D. (1988). On hierarchies of reading skills and text types. *Modern Language Journal, 72*, 173–187.

Lee, J. F., & Riley, G. L. (1990). The effects of prereading, rhetorically oriented frameworks on the recall of two structurally different expository texts. *Studies in Second Language Acquisition, 12*, 25–41.

Legarreta, D. (1979). The effects of program models on language acquisition of Spanish speaking children. *TESOL Quarterly, 13*, 521–534.

LeLoup, J. W. (1993). The effect of interest level in selected text topics on second language reading comprehension. *Dissertation Abstracts International, 54*, 1709-A.

Lemoine, H. E., Levy, B. A., & Hutchinson, A. (1993). Increasing the naming speed of poor readers: Representations formed across repetitions. *Journal of Experimental Child Psychology, 55*, 297–328.

Leong, C. K. (1989). Productive knowledge of derivational rules in poor readers. *Annals of Dyslexia, 39*, 94–115.

Levelt, W. J. M. (1989). *Speaking: From intention to articulation.* Cambridge: MIT Press.

Levin, J. R., Levin, M. E., Glashman, L. D., & Nordwall, M. B. (1992). Mnemonic vocabulary instruction: Additional effectiveness evidence. *Contemporary Educational Psychology, 17,* 156–174.

Levin, J. R., & Pressley, M., (1981). Improving children's prose comprehension: Selected strategies that seem to succeed. In G. M. Santa & B. L. Hayes (Eds.), *Children's prose comprehension: Research and practice* (pp. 44–71). Newark, DE: International Reading Association.

Levy, B. A. (1975). Vocalization and suppression effects in sentence memory. *Journal of Verbal Learning and Verbal Behavior, 14,* 304–316.

Levy, B. A., & Hinchley, J. (1990). Individual and developmental differences in the acquisition of reading skills. In T. H. Carr & B. A. Levy (Eds.), *Reading and its development: Component skills approaches* (pp. 81–128). San Diego: Academic Press.

Li, W., Anderson, R. C., Nagy, W., & Zhang, H. (2002). Facets of metalinguistic awareness that contribute to Chinese literacy. In W. Li, J. S. Gaffiney, & J. L. Packard (Eds.), *Chinese children's reading acquisition: Theoretical and pedagogical issues* (pp. 87–106). Boston: Kluwer Academic.

Liberman, I. Y., Mann, V. A., Shankweiler, D., & Werfelman, M. (1982). Children's memory for recurring linguistic and non-linguistic material in relation to reading ability. *Cortex, 18,* 367–375.

Liberman, I. Y., Shankweiler, D., Fischer, F. W., & Carter, B. (1974). Explicitly syllable and phone segmentation in the young child. *Journal of Experimental Child Psychology, 18,* 201–212.

Liberman, I. Y., Shankweiler, D., & Liberman, A. M. (1989). The alphabetic principle and learning to read. In D. Shankweiler & I. Y. Liberman (Eds.), *Phonology and reading disability: Solving the reading puzzle* (pp. 1–33). International Academy of Research on Learning Disabilities Monograph Series. Ann Arbor: University of Michigan Press.

Liberman, I. Y., Shankweiler, D., Liberman, A. M., Fischer, F. W., & Fowler, C. (1977). Phonetic segmentation and recoding in the beginning reader. In A. S. Reber & D. Scarborough (Eds.), *Toward a psychology of reading* (pp. 207–225). Hillsdale, NJ: Erlbaum.

Lituanas, P. M., Jacobs, G. M., & Renandya, W. A. (1999). A study of extensive reading with remedial reading students. In Y. M. Cheah & M. N. Seok (Eds.), *Language instructional issues in Asian classrooms* (pp. 91–104). Newark, DE: International Reading Association.

Logan, G. D. (1988). Toward an instance theory of automatization. *Psychological Review, 95,* 492–527.

Lonergan, B. (1970). *Insight.* New York: Philosophical Library.

Long, D. L., Seely, M. R., Oppy, B. J., & Golding, J. M. (1996). The role of inferential processing in reading ability. In B. K. Britton & A. C. Graesser (Eds.), *Models of understanding text* (pp. 189–214). Mahwah, NJ: Erlbaum.

Long, G., & Aldersley, S. (1984). Networking: Application with hearing-impaired students. In C. D. Holley, & D. F. Dansereau (Eds.), *Spatial learning strategies: Techniques, applications, and related issues* (pp. 109–125). New York: Academic Press.

Long, M. H. (1985). Input and second language acquisition theory. In S. M. Gass & C. G. Madden (Eds.), *Input in second language acquisition* (pp. 377–393). Rowley, MA: Newbury House.

Lorch, R. F., Jr. (1989). Text signaling devices and their effects on reading and memory processes. *Educational Psychology Review, 1,* 209–234.

MacDonald, M. C., Just, M. A., & Carpenter, P. A. (1992). Working memory constraints on the processing of syntactic ambiguity. *Cognitive Psychology, 24,* 56–98.

Macnamara, J. (1970). Comparative studies of reading and problem-solving in two languages. *TESOL Quarterly, 4,* 107–116.

MacWhinney, B. (1987). Applying the competition model to bilingualism. *Applied Psycholinguistics, 8,* 315–327.

MacWhinney, B. (1992). Transfer and competition in second language learning. In R. J. Harris (Ed.), *Cognitive processing in bilinguals* (pp. 371–390). Amsterdam: Elsevier Science Publications.

MacWhinney, B., & Bates, E. (Eds.). (1989). *The cross-linguistic study of sentence processing.* New York: Cambridge University Press.

MacWhinney, B., Bates, E., & Kliegl, R. (1984). Cue validity and sentence interpretation in English, German, and Italian. *Journal of Verbal Learning and Verbal Behavior, 23,* 127–150.

Magliano, J., & Graesser, A. (1993). A three-pronged method for studying inference generation in literacy text. *Poetics, 20,* 193–232.

Mandler, J. M. (1984). *Stories, scripts, and scenes: Aspects of schema theory.* Hillsdale, NJ: Erlbaum.

Mandler, J. M. (1987). On the psychological reality of story structure. *Discourse Processes, 10,* 1–29.

Mandler, J. M., & Goodman, M. S. (1982). On the psychological reality of story structure. *Journal of Verbal Learning and Verbal Behavior, 21,* 507–523.

Mandler, J. M., & Johnson, N. S. (1977). Remembering of things parsed: Story structure and recall. *Cognitive Psychology, 9,* 111–151.

Manelis, L. (1980). Determinants of processing for propositional structures. *Memory and Cognition, 8,* 49–57.

Mani, K., & Johnson-Laird, P. N. (1982). The mental representation of spatial descriptions. *Memory and Cognition, 10,* 181–187.

Mann, V. A. (1985). A cross-linguistic perspective on the relation between temporary memory skills and early reading ability. *Remedial and Special Education, 6,* 37–42.

Mann, V. A., Shankweiler, D., & Smith, S. T. (1984). The association between comprehension of spoken sentences and early reading ability: The role of phonetic representation. *Journal of Child Language, 11,* 627–643.

Martin, V. L., & Pressley, M. (1991). Elaborative-interrogation effects depend on the nature of the question. *Journal of Educational Psychology, 83,* 113–119.

Matsuyama, U. K. (1983). Can story grammar speak Japanese? *Reading Teacher, 36,* 666–669.

Mazuka, R. (1991). Processing of empty category in Japanese. *Journal of Psycholinguistic Research, 20,* 215–232.

Mazuka, R. (2000). *The development of language processing strategies: A cross-linguistic study between Japanese and English.* Hillsdale, NJ: Erlbaum.

Mazuka, R., & Itoh, K. (1995). Can Japanese speakers be led down the garden path? In R. Mazuka & N. Nagai (Eds.), *Japanese sentence processing* (pp. 295–330). Hillsdale, NJ: Erlbaum.

Mazuka, R., & Lust, B. (1990). On parameter setting and parsing: Predictions from cross-linguistic differences in adult and child processing. In L. Frazier & J. de Villiers (Eds.), *Language processing and language acquisition* (pp. 163–206) Dordrecht, the Netherlands: Kluwer.

Mazuka, R., & Nagai, N. (1995). Japanese sentence processing: An interdisciplinary approach. In R. Mazuka & N. Nagai (Eds.), *Japanese sentence processing* (pp. 1–8). Hillsdale, NJ: Erlbaum.

McClelland, J. L., & Rumelhart, D. E. (1985). Distributed memory and the representation of general and specific information. *Journal of Experimental Psychology: General, 114,* 159–188.

McClelland, J. L., St. John, M., & Taraban, R. (1989). Sentence comprehension: A parallel distributed processing approach. *Language and Cognitive Processes, 4,* 287–335.

McClure, E., & Geva, E. (1983). The development of the cohesive use of adversative conjunctions in discourse. *Discourse Processes, 6,* 411–432.

McConkie, G. W., & Zola, D. (1981). Language constraints and the functional stimulus in reading. In A. M. Lesgold & C. A. Perfetti (Eds.), *Interactive process in reading* (pp. 155–175). Hillsdale, NJ: Elrbaum.

McDonald, J. (1987). Sentence interpretation in bilingual speakers of English and Dutch. *Applied Psycholinguistics, 8,* 379–413.

McGinnis, S. (1995). Student attitudes and approaches in the learning of written Chinese. Paper presented at the annual conference of the American Association for Applied Linguistics, Long Beach, CA.

McGivern, J. E., & Levin, J. R. (1983). The keyword method and children's vocabulary learning: An interaction with vocabulary knowledge. *Contemporary Educational Psychology, 8,* 46–54.

McKeown, M. G. (1993). Creating effective definitions for young word learners. *Reading Research Quarterly, 28,* 16–31.

McKeown, M. G., Beck, I., Omanson, R., & Pople, M. (1985). Some effects of the nature and frequency of vocabulary instruction on the knowledge and use of words. *Reading Research Quarterly, 20,* 522–535.

McKoon, G., & Ratcliff, R. (1989). Semantic association and elaborative inferences. *Journal of Experimental Psychology: Learning, Memory and Cognition, 15,* 326–338.

Meara, P. (1996). The dimensions of lexical competence. In G. Brown, K. Malmkjaer, & J. Williams (Eds.), *Performance and competence in second language acquisition*. Cambridge: Cambridge University Press.

Meara, P., & Jones, G. (1988). Vocabulary size as a placement indicator. In P. Grunwell (Ed.), *Applied linguistics in society. British Studies in Applied Linguistics 3*. London: Center for Information in Language Teaching and Research.

Meara, P., & Jones, G. (1990). *Eurocentres vocabulary size test 10KA*. Zurich: Eurocentres Learning Service.

Medo, M. A., & Ryder, R. J. (1993). The effects of vocabulary instruction on readers' ability to make causal connections. *Reading Research and Instruction, 33*, 119–134.

Meyer, B. J. F. (1975). *The organization of prose and its effects on memory*. Amsterdam: North-Holland.

Meyer, B. J. F. (1977). The structure of prose: Effects on learning and memory and implications for educational practice. In R. C. Anderson, R. J. Spiro, & W. E. Montague (Eds.), *Schooling and the acquisition of knowledge* (pp. 179–200). Hillsdale, NJ: Erlbaum.

Meyer, B. J. F. (1979). Organizational patterns in prose and their use in reading. In M. L. Kamil & A. J. Moe (Eds.), *Reading research: Studies and applications*. Clemson, SC: National Reading Conference.

Meyer, B. J. F. (1982). Reading research and the composition teacher: The importance of plans. *College Composition and Communication, 33*, 37–49.

Meyer, B. J. F., Brandt, D. M., & Bluth, G. J. (1980). Use of top-level structure in text: Key for reading comprehension of ninth-grade students. *Reading Research Quarterly, 16*, 72–103.

Meyer, B. J. F., & Freedle, R. O. (1984). Effects of discourse types on recall. *American Educational Research Journal, 21*, 121–143.

Meyer, B. J. F., & Rice, G. E. (1984). The structure of text. In P. D. Pearson (Ed.), *Handbook of reading research* (Vol. 1; pp. 319–352). New York: Longman.

Miller, G. A. (1988). The challenge of universal literacy. *Science, 241*, 1293–1299.

Miller, G. A., & Gildea, P. M. (1987). How children learn words. *Scientific American, 257*(3), 94–99.

Miller, J. R., & Kintsch, W. (1980). Readability and recall of short prose passages: A theoretical analysis. *Journal of Experimental Psychology: Human Learning and Memory, 6*, 335–354.

Minsky, M. (1975). A framework for representing knowledge. In P. Winston (Ed.), *The psychology of computer vision* (pp. 211–277). New York: Winston.

Mitchell, D. C. (1994). Sentence parsing. In M. A. Gernsbacher (Ed.), *Handbook of psycholinguistics* (pp. 375–410). New York: Academic Press.

Mitchell, D. C., & Holmes, V. M. (1985). The role of specific information about the verb in parsing sentences with local structural ambiguity. *Journal of Memory and Language, 24*, 542–559.

Miyake, A., & Friedman, N. P. (1998). Individual differences in second language proficiency: Working memory as language aptitude. In A. F. Healy & L. E. Bourne Jr. (Eds.), *Foreign language learning: Psycholinguistic studies on training and retention* (pp. 339–364). Mahwah, NJ: Erlbaum.

Miyake, A., Just, M. A., & Carpenter, P. A. (1994). Working memory constraints on the resolution of lexical ambiguity: Maintaining multiple interpretations in neutral context. *Journal of Memory and Language, 33,* 175–202.

Miyake, A., & Shah, P. (1999). Towards unified theories of working memory: Emerging general consensus, unresolved theoretical issues, and future research directions. In A. Miyake & P. Shah (Eds.), *Models of working memory* (pp. 442–482). New York: Cambridge University Press.

Montrul, S. (2001). Agentive verbs of manner of motion in Spanish and English as second languages. *Studies in Second Language Acquisition, 23,* 171–206.

Moravcsik, J. E., & Kintsch, W. (1995). Writing quality, reading skills, and domain knowledge. In J. M. Henderson, M. Singer, & F. Ferreira (Eds.), *Reading and language processing* (pp. 232–246). Mahwah, NJ: Erlbaum.

Mori, Y., & Nagy, W. (1999). Integration of information from context and word elements in interpreting novel Kanji compounds. *Reading Research Quarterly, 34,* 80–101.

Mosenthal, P. (1978). The new and given in children's comprehension of presuppositive negatives in two modes of processing. *Journal of Reading Behavior, 10,* 267–278.

Mou, L. C., & Anderson, N. S. (1981). Graphemic and phonemic codings of Chinese characters in short-term retention. *Bulletin of the Psychonomic Society, 17,* 255–258.

Muljani, M., Koda, K., & Moates, D. (1998). Development of L2 word recognition: A connectionist approach. *Applied Psycholinguistics, 19,* 99–114.

Muniz-Swicegood, M. (1994). The effects of metacognitive strategy training on the reading performance and fluent reading analysis strategies of third grade bilingual students. *Bilingual Research Journal, 18,* 83–97.

Myers, J. L., & Duffy, S. A. (1990). Causal inferences and text memory. In A. C. Graesser & G. H. Bower (Eds.), *The psychology of learning and motivation: Inferences and text comprehension* (Vol. 25; pp. 159–173). San Diego: Academic Press.

Myers, J. L., Shinjo, M., & Duffy, S. A. (1987). Degree of causal relatedness and memory. *Journal of Memory and Language, 26,* 453–465.

Myers, M., & Paris, S. G. (1978). Children's metacognitive knowledge about reading. *Journal of Educational Psychology, 70,* 680–690.

Nagy, E. W. (1997). On the role of context in first- and second-language vocabulary learning. In N. Schmitt & M. McCarthy (Eds.), *Vocabulary: Description, acquisition and pedagogy* (pp. 64–83). Cambridge: Cambridge University Press.

Nagy, W. E., & Anderson, R. C. (1984). How many words are there in printed school English? *Reading Research Quarterly, 19,* 304–330.

Nagy, W. E., & Anderson, R. C. (1998). Metalinguistic awareness and literacy acquisition in different languages. In D. Wagner, R. Venezky, & B. Street (Eds.), *Literacy: An international handbook* (pp. 155–160). Boulder, CO: Westview Press.

Nagy, W. E., Anderson, R. C., & Herman, P. A. (1987). Learning word meanings from context during normal reading. *American Educational Research Journal, 24,* 237–270.

Nagy, W. E., & Gentner, D. (1990). Semantic constraints on lexical categories. *Language and Cognitive Processes, 5,* 169–201.

Nagy, W. E., & Herman, P. A. (1987). Breadth and depth of vocabulary knowledge: Implications for acquisition and instruction. In M. G. McKeown & M. E. Curtis (Eds.), *The nature of vocabulary acquisition* (pp. 73–87). Hillsdale, NJ: Erlbaum.

Nagy, W. E., Herman, P. A., & Anderson, R. C. (1985). Learning words from context. *Reading Research Quarterly, 20,* 233–253.

Nagy, W. E., & Scott, J. A. (2000). Vocabulary processes. In M. L. Kamil, P. B. Mothenthal, P. D. Pearson, & R. Barr (Eds.), *Handbook of reading research* (Vol. 3; pp. 269–284). Mahwah, NJ: Erlbaum.

Naigles, L. G. (1990). Children use syntax to learn verb meanings. *Journal of Child Language, 17,* 357–374.

Naigres, L. (1990). Children use syntax to learn verb meanings. *Journal of Child Language, 17,* 357–374.

Nassaji, H., & Geva, E. (1999). The contribution of phonological and orthographic processing skills to adult ESL reading: Evidence from native speakers of Farsi. *Applied Psycholinguistics, 20,* 241–267.

Nation, I. S. P. (1990). *Teaching and learning vocabulary.* Rowley, MA: Newbury House.

Nation, I. S. P. (2001). *Learning vocabulary in another language.* Cambridge: Cambridge University Press.

Nation, P., & Newton, J. (1997). Teaching vocabulary. In J. Coady & T. Huckin (Eds.), *Second language vocabulary acquisition* (pp. 238–254). New York: Cambridge University Press.

National Reading Panel. (2000). *Teaching children to read: An evidence-based assessment of the scientific research on reading and its development for reading instruction.* Washington, DC: National Institute of Child Health and Human Development.

Neuman, S. B. (1988). Enhancing children's comprehension through previewing. *National Reading Conference Yearbook, 37,* 219–224.

Nicholson, T., & White, B. (1992). Matthew effects in learning new words while listening to stories. In C. K. Kinzer & D. J. Leu (Eds.), *Literacy research, theory, and, practice: Views from many perspectives: Forty-first Yearbook of the National Reading Conference* (pp. 499–503). Chicago, IL: The National Reading Conference.

Nist, S. L., & Simpson, M. L. (2000). College studying. In M. L. Kamil, P. B. Mothenthal, P. D. Pearson, & R. Barr (Eds.), *Handbook of reading research* (Vol. 3, pp. 645–666). Mahwah, NJ: Erlbaum.

Odlin, T. (1989). *Language transfer: Cross-linguistic influence in language learning.* New York: Cambridge University Press.

Oller, J. W., Jr. (1972). Assessing competence in ESL reading. *TESOL Quarterly, 4,* 107–116.

Oller, J. W., Jr., & Tullius, J. (1973). Reading skills of non-native speakers of English. *IRAL, 11,* 69–80.

Olshtain, E. (1983). Sociocultural competence and language transfer: The case of apology. In S. M. Gass & L. Selinker (Eds.), *Language transfer in language learning* (pp. 232–249). Rowley, MA: Newbury House.

Olson, G. M., Duffy, S. A., & Mack, R. L. (1984). Thinking-out-loud as a method for studying real-time comprehension processes. In D. E. Kieras & M. A. Just (Eds.), *New methods in reading comprehension research* (pp. 253–286). Hillsdale, NJ: Erlbaum.

Omanson, R. C. (1982). An analysis of narratives: Identifying central, supportive, and distracting content. *Discourse Processes, 5,* 195–224.

Osaka, M., & Osaka, N. (1992). Language-independent working memory as measured by Japanese and English reading span tests. *Bulletin of the Psychonomic Society, 30,* 287–289.

Packard, J. L. (2000). *The morphology of Chinese: A linguistic and cognitive approach.* New York: Cambridge University Press.

Padron, Y. (1992). The effect of strategy instruction on bilingual students' cognitive strategy use in reading. *Bilingual Research Journal, 16,* 35–52.

Palincsar, A. S., & Brown, A. L. (1984). Reciprocal teaching of comprehension-fostering and monitoring activities. *Cognition and Instruction, 1,* 117–175.

Paribakht T. S., & Wesche, M. (1993). The relationship between reading comprehension and second language development in a comprehension-based ESL program. *TESL Canada Journal, 11,* 9–29.

Paribakht T. S., & Wesche, M. (1997). Vocabulary enhancement activities and reading for meaning in second language vocabulary acquisition. In J. Coady & T. Huckin (Eds.), *Second language vocabulary acquisition* (pp. 174–200). New York: Cambridge University Press.

Paribakht T. S., & Wesche, M. (1999). Reading and incidental L2 vocabulary acquisition: An introspective study of lexical inferencing. *Studies in Second Language Acquisition, 21,* 195–224.

Paris, S. G., Cross, D. R., & Lipson, M. Y. (1984). Informed strategies for learning: A program to improve children's reading awareness and comprehension. *Journal of Educational Psychology, 76,* 1239–1252.

Paris, S. G., & Jacobs, J. E. (1984). The benefits of informed instruction for children's reading awareness and comprehension skills. *Child Development, 55,* 2083–2093.

Paris, S. G., Lipson, M. Y., & Wixson, K. K. (1983). Becoming a strategic reader. *Contemporary Educational Psychlology, 8,* 293–316.

Paris, S. G., & Oka, E. R. (1986). Children's reading strategies, metacognition, and motivation. *Developmental Review, 6,* 25–56.

Paris, S. G., Wasik, B. A., & Turner, J. C. (1991). The development of strategic reading. In R. Barr, M. L. Kamil, P. B. Mosenthal, & P. D. Pearson (Eds.), *Handbook of reading research* (Vol. 2; pp. 609–640). New York: Longman.

Parker, K., & Chaudron, C. (1987). The effects of linguistic simplification and elaborative modification on L2 comprehension. *University of Hawaii Working Papers in ESL, 6,* 107–133.

Pearlmutter, N. J., & MacDonald, M. C. (1995). Individual differences and probabilistic constraints in syntactic ambiguity resolution. *Journal of Memory & Language, 34,* 521–542.

Pearson, P. D. (1975). The effects of grammatical complexity on children's comprehension, recall, and conception of certain semantic relations. *Reading Research Quarterly, 10,* 155–192.

Pearson, P. D., & Fielding, L. (1991). Comprehension instruction. In R. Barr, M. L. Kamil, P. Mosenthal, & P. D. Pearson (Eds.), *Handbook of reading research* (Vol. 2; pp. 815–860). New York: Longman.

Pearson, P. D., & Gallagher, M. C. (1983). The instruction of reading comprehension. *Contemporary Educational Psychology, 8,* 317–344.

Pearson, P. D., & Johnson, D. D. (1978). *Teaching reading comprehension.* New York: Holt, Rinehart and Winston.

Peng, D. L., Yang, H., & Chen, Y. (1994). Consistency and phonetic independency effects in naming task of Chinese phonograms. In Q. Jing, H. Zhang, & D. Peng (Eds.), *Information processing of Chinese language* (pp. 26–41). Beijing: Beijing Normal University.

Peretz, A. S., & Shoham, N. (1990). Testing reading comprehension in LSP: Does topic familiarity affect assessed difficulty and actual performance? *Reading in a Foreign Language, 7,* 447–455.

Perfetti, C. A. (1985). *Reading ability.* New York: Oxford University Press.

Perfetti, C. A. (1990). The cooperative language processors: Semantic influences in an autonomous syntax. In D. A. Balota, G. B. Flores d'Arcais, & K. Rainer (Eds.), *Comprehension processes in reading* (pp. 205–230). Hillsdale, NJ: Erlbaum.

Perfetti, C. A. (1994). Psycholinguistics and reading ability. In M. A. Gernsbacher (Ed.), *Handbook of psycholinguistics* (pp. 849–894). New York: Academic Press.

Perfetti, C. A., Beck, I., Bell, L. C., & Hughes, C. (1987). Phonemic knowledge and learning to read are reciprocal: A longitudinal study of first grade children. *Merrill-Palmer Quarterly, 33,* 283–319.

Perfetti, C. A., & Lesgold, A. M. (1977). Discourse comprehension and source of individual differences. In M. A. Just & P. A. Carpenter (Eds.), *Cognitive process in comprehension* (pp. 141–184). Hillsdale, NJ: Erlbaum.

Perfetti, C. A., & Lesgold, A. M. (1979). Coding and comprehension in skilled reading and implications for reading instruction. In L. B. Resnick & P. Weaver (Eds.), *Theory and practice of early reading* (pp. 57–84). Hillsdale, NJ: Erlbaum.

Perfetti, C. A., & Zhang, S. (1995). Very early phonological activation in Chinese reading. *Journal of Experimental Psychology: Learning, Memory, and Cognition*, 21, 24–33.

Perfetti, C. A., Zhang, S., & Berent, I. (1992). Reading in English and Chinese: Evidence for a "universal" phonological principle. In R. Frost & L. Katz (Eds.), *Orthography, phonology, morphology, and meaning* (pp. 227–248). Amsterdam: North-Holland.

Perrig, W., & Kintsch, W. (1985). Propositional and situational representations of text. *Journal of Memory and Language*, 24, 503–518.

Phinney, M. (1987). The pro-drop parameter in second language acquisition. In T. Roeper & E. Williams (Eds.), *Parameter setting* (pp. 221–246). Boston: D. Reide Publishing.

Pica, T., Doughty, C., & Young, R. (1986). Making input comprehensible: Do interactional modifications help? *ITL Review of Applied Linguistics*, 72, 1–25.

Pinnell, G. S., Lyons, C. A., Deford, D. E., Bryk, A. S., & Seltzer, M. (1994). Comparing instructional models for the literacy education of high-risk first graders. *Reading Research Quarterly*, 29, 8–39.

Pitts, M., White, H., & Krashen, S. (1989). Acquiring second language vocabulary through reading: A replication of the Clockwork Orange study using second language acquirers. *Reading in a Foreign Language*, 5, 271–275.

Poissant, H. (1990). Linguistic and cultural factors in text comprehension. Paper presented at the World Congress on Reading, Stockholm, Sweden. ERIC Document Reproduction Service No. ED 340 010.

Potter, M. C., So, K. F., Von Eckardt, B., & Feldman, L. B. (1984). Lexical and conceptual representation in beginning and more proficient bilinguals. *Journal of Verbal Learning and Verbal Behavior*, 23, 23–38.

Pressley, M. (2000). What should comprehension instruction be the instruction on? In M. L. Kamil, P. B. Mothenthal, P. D. Pearson, & R. Barr (Eds.), *Handbook of reading research* (Vol. 3, pp. 545–562). Mahwah, NJ: Erlbaum.

Pressley, M., Levin, J. R., & McDaniel, M. A. (1987). Remembering versus inferring what a word means: Mnemonic and contextual approaches. In M. G. McKeown & M. E. Curtis (Eds.), *The nature of vocabulary acquisition* (pp. 107–128). Hillsdale, NJ: Erlbaum.

Pring, L., & Snowling, M. (1986). Developmental changes in word recognition: An information-processing account. *Quarterly Journal of Experimental Psychology*, 38, 395–418.

Pritchard, R. (1990). The effects of cultural schemata on reading processing strategies. *Reading Research Quarterly*, 25, 273–296.

Purves, A. C. (1988). Introduction. In A. Purves (Ed.), *Writing across languages and cultures: Issues in contrastive rhetoric* (pp. 9–24). Newbury Park, CA: Sage.

Qian, D. D. (1999). Assessing the roles of depth and breath of vocabulary knowledge in reading comprehension, *Canadian Modern Language*

Review, 56, 282–307. Unpublished doctoral dissertation, University of Toronto.

Rainer, K., Carlson, M., & Frazier, L. (1983). The interaction of syntax and semantics during sentence processing: Eye movements in the analysis of semantically biased sentences. *Journal of Verbal Learning and Verbal Behavior, 22*, 358–374.

Raymond, P. M. (1993). The effects of structure strategy training on the recall of expository prose for university students reading French as a second language. *Modern Language Journal, 77*, 445–458.

Rayner, K., & Bertera, J. H. (1979). Reading without a fovea. *Science, 206*, 468–469.

Read, J. (1993). The development of a new measure of L2 vocabulary knowledge. *Language Testing, 10*, 355–371.

Read, J. (1997). Vocabulary and testing. In N. Schmitt & M. McCarthy (Eds.), *Vocabulary: Description, acquisition and pedagogy* (pp. 303–320). Cambridge: Cambridge University Press.

Read, J. (2000). *Assessing vocabulary*. Cambridge: Cambridge University Press.

Recht, D. R., & Leslie, L. (1988). Effect of prior knowledge on good and poor readers. *Journal of Educational Psychology, 80*, 16–20.

Richard, J. C. (1976). The role of vocabulary teaching. *TESOL Quarterly, 10*, 77–189.

Ridgway, T. (1997). Thresholds of the background knowledge effect in foreign language reading. *Reading in a Foreign Language, 11*, 151–175.

Rigg, P. (1977). The miscue ESL project. In H. D. Brown, C. A. Yorio, & R. H. Crymes (Eds.), *On TESOL '77* (pp. 106–118). Washington, DC: TESOL.

Riley, G. L. (1993). A story approach to narrative text comprehension. *Modern Language Journal, 77*, 417–432.

Riley, G. L., & Lee, J. F. (1996). A comparison of recall and summary protocols as measures of second-language reading comprehension. *Language Testing, 13*, 173–189.

Rintell, E. M. (1984). But how did you feel about that? The learner's perception of emotion in speech. *Applied Linguistics, 5*, 255–264.

Roehler, L. R., & Duffy, G. G. (1984). Direct explanation of comprehension processes. In G. G. Duffy, L. R. Roehler, & J. Mason (Eds.), *Comprehension instruction: Perspectives and suggestions* (pp. 265–280). New York: Longman.

Roller, C. M., & Matambo, A. R. (1992). Bilingual readers' use of background knowledge in learning from text. *TESOL Quarterly, 26*, 129–141.

Roser, N., & Juel, C. (1982). Effects of vocabulary instruction on reading comprehension. In J. Niles & L. Harris (Eds.), *New inquiries in reading research and instruction* (pp. 110–118). Chicago: National Reading Conference.

Rubin, H. (1991). Morphological knowledge and writing ability. In R. M. Joshi (Ed.), *Written language disorders* (pp. 43–69). New York: Kluwer Academic.

Rubin, J. (1987). Learner strategies: Theoretical assumption, research history. In A. Wenden & J. Rubin (Eds.), *Learner strategies in language learning* (pp. 15–30). London: Prentice Hall International.

Ruddel, M. R. (1994). Vocabulary knowledge and comprehension: A comprehension process view of complex literary relationships. In R. Ruddel, M. R. Ruddel, & H. Singer (Eds.), *Theoretical models and processes of reading* (4th ed.; pp. 414–447). Newark, DE: International Reading Association.

Ruke-Dravina, V. (1971). Word associations in monolingual and multilingual individuals. *Linguistics, 74*, 66–84.

Rusciolelli, J. (1995). Student responses to reading strategies instruction. *Foreign Language Annals, 28*, 262–273.

Rutherford, W. E. (1983). Language typology and language transfer. In S. M. Gass & L. Selinker (Eds.), *Language transfer in language learning* (pp. 358–370). Rowley, MA: Newbury House.

Ryder, R. J., & Graves, M. F. (1994). Vocabulary instruction presented prior to reading in two basal readers. *Elementary School Journal, 95*, 139–153.

Ryan, A., & Meara, P. (1991). The case of invisible vowels: Arabic speakers reading English words. *Reading in a Foreign Language, 7*, 531–540.

Saito, H. (1981). Use of graphemic and phonemic encoding in reading Kanji and Kana. *Japanese Journal of Psychology, 52*, 266–273.

Saito, H., Inoue, M., & Nomura, Y. (1979). Information processing of Kanji (Chinese characters) and Kana (Japanese characters): The close relationship among graphemic, phonemic, and semantic aspects. *Psychologia, 22*, 195–206.

Saito, H., Masuda, H., & Kawakami, M. (1999). Subword activation in reading Japanese single Kanji character words. *Brain and Language, 68*, 75–81.

Saito, Y. (1989, December). The effects of article deletion in English on the cognitive processes reflected in the eye movements and metacognitive awareness of native readers and Japanese readers of English: An eye-tracking study. Paper presented at the annual meeting of National Reading Conference, Austin, TX.

Sakamoto, T. (1995). Transparency between parser and grammar: On the processing of empty subjects in Japanese. In R. Mazuka & N. Nagai (Eds.), *Japanese sentence processing* (pp. 275–294). Hillsdale, NJ: Erlbaum.

Salager-Meyer, F. (1991). Reading expository prose at the post-secondary level: The influence of textual variables on L2 reading comprehension: A genre-based approach. *Reading in a Foreign Language, 8*, 645–662.

Salager-Meyer, F. (1994). Reading medical English abstracts: A genre study of the interaction between structural variables and the reader's linguistic-conceptual competence. *Journal of Research in Reading, 17*, 120–146.

Sanders, T. J. M., Spooren, W. P. M., & Noordman, L. G. M. (1992). Toward a taxonomy of coherence relations. *Discourse Processes, 15*, 1–35.

Sanford, A. J., & Garrod, S. C. (1981). *Understanding written language.* Chichester: John Wiley & Sons.

Sasaki, Y. (1991). English and Japanese interlanguage comprehension strategies: An analysis based on the competition model. *Applied Psycholinguistics, 12,* 47–73.

Sasaki, Y. (1993). Paths of processing strategy transfer in learning Japanese and English as foreign languages: A competition model approach. *Studies in Second Language Acquisition, 16,* 43–72.

Sasanuma, S. (1975). Kana and Kanji processing in Japanese aphasics. *Brain and Language, 2,* 369–383.

Sasanuma, S. (1984). Can surface dyslexia occur in Japanese? In L. Henderson (Ed.), *Orthographies and reading: Perspectives from cognitive psychology, neuropsychology and linguistics* (pp. 43–56). Hillsdale, NJ: Erlbaum.

Scanlon, D. M., & Vellutino, F. R. (1997). A comparison of the instructional backgrounds and cognitive profiles of poor, average, and good readers who were initially identified as at risk for reading failure. *Scientific Studies of Reading, 1,* 191–215.

Scarcella, R. C. (1983). Discourse accent in second language performance. In S. M. Gass & L. Selinker (Eds.), *Language transfer in language learning* (pp. 306–326). Rowley, MA: Newbury House.

Schachter, J. (1988). Second language acquisition and its relationship to universal grammar. *Applied Linguistics, 9,* 219–235.

Schank, R. C., & Abelson, R. (1977). *Plans, scripts, goals and understanding.* Hillsdale, NJ: Erlbaum.

Schmitt, N. (1998). Tracking the incremental acquisition of second language vocabulary: A longitudinal study. *Language Learning, 48,* 281–317.

Schneider W., & Shiffrin, R. M. (1977). Controlled and automatic human information processing: Detection, search, and attention. *Psychological Review, 84,* 1–66.

Schwanenflugel, P. J., Blout, B. J., & Lin, P.-J. (1991). Cross-cultural aspects of word meaning. In P. J. Schwanenflugel (Ed.), *The psychology of word meanings* (pp. 74–90). Hillsdale, NJ: Erlbaum.

Schwartz, R. M., & Stanovich, K. E. (1981). Flexibility in the use of graphic and contextual information by good and poor readers. *Journal of Reading Behavior, 13,* 263–269.

Scollon, R., & Scollon, S. B. K. (1981). *Narrative, literacy and face in interethnic communication.* Norwood, NJ: Ablex.

Scott, J., & Nagy, W. (1997). Understanding the definitions of unfamiliar verbs. *Reading Research Quarterly, 32,* 184–200.

Scribner, S., & Cole, M. (1981). *The psychology of literacy.* Cambridge: Harvard University Press.

Segalowitz, N. S. (1986). Skilled reading in the second language. In J. Vaid (Ed.), *Language processing in bilinguals: Psycholinguistic and neurological perspectives* (pp. 3–19). Hillsdale, NJ: Erlbaum.

Segalowitz, N. S., Poulsen, C., & Komoda, M. (1991). Lower level components or reading skill in higher level bilinguals: Implications for reading instruction. *AILA Review, 8,* 15–30.

Segalowitz, N. S., & Segalowitz, S. J. (1993). Skilled performance, practice, and the differentiation of speed-up from automatization effects: Evidence from second language word recognition. *Applied Psycholinguistics, 14,* 369–385.

Seidenberg, M. S., & McClelland, J. L. (1989). A distributed, developmental model of word recognition and naming. *Psychological Review, 96,* 523–568.

Seidenberg, M. S., Tanenhaus, M. K., Leiman, J. M., & Bienkowski, M. (1982). Automatic access of the meanings of ambiguous words in context: Some limitations of knowledge-based processing. *Cognitive Psychology, 14,* 489–537.

Shankweiler, D., & Liberman, I. Y. (1972). Misreading: A search for causes. In J. F. Kavanaugh & I. G. Mattingly (Eds.), *Language by eye and by ear* (pp. 293–317). Cambridge: MIT Press.

Share, D., & Stanovich, K. E. (1995). Cognitive processes in early reading development: Accommodating individual differences into a model of acquisition. In J. S. Carlson (Ed.), *Issues in education: Contributions from psychology* (Vol. 1; pp. 1–57). Greenwich, CT: JAI Press.

Sharwood Smith, M. (1991). Language modules and bilingual processing. In E. Bialystok (Ed.), *Language processing in bilingual children* (pp. 10–24). New York: Cambridge University Press.

Shohamy, E. (1983). Interrater and intrarater reliability of the oral interview and concurrent validity with cloze procedure in Hebrew. In J. W. Oller (Ed.), *Issues in language testing research* (pp. 229–236). Rowley, MA: Newbury House.

Shu, H., & Anderson, R. C. (1997). Role of radical awareness in the character and word acquisition of Chinese children. *Reading Research Quarterly, 32,* 78–89.

Shu, H., & Anderson, R. C. (1999). Learning to read Chinese: The development of metalinguistic awareness. In A. Inhuff, J. Wang, & H. C. Chen (Eds.), *Reading Chinese scripts: A cognitive analysis* (pp. 1–18). Mahwah, NJ: Erlbaum.

Shu, H., Anderson, R. C., & Zhang, H. (1995). Incidental learning of word meanings while reading: A Chinese and American cross-cultural study. *Reading Research Quarterly, 30,* 76–95.

Siegel, L. S., & Ryan, E. B. (1988). Development of grammatical sensitivity, phonological, and short-term memory in normally achieving and learning disabled children. *Developmental Psychology, 24,* 28–37.

Silberstein, S. (1987). Let's take another look at reading: Twenty-five years of reading instruction. *English Teaching Forum, 25,* 28–35.

Singer, M. (1982). Comparing memory for natural and laboratory reading. *Journal of Experimental Psychology: General, 111,* 331–347.

Singer, M. (1994). Discourse inference processes. In M. A. Gernsbacher (Ed.), *Handbook of psycholinguistics* (pp. 479–516). San Diego: Academic Press.

Singer, M., Halldorson, M., Lear, J. C., & Andrusiak, P. (1992). Validation of causal bridging inferences in discourse understanding. *Journal of Memory and Language, 31*, 507–524.

Singer, M., & Ritchot, K. F. M. (1996). The role of working memory capacity and knowledge access in text inference processing. *Memory and Cognition, 24*, 733–742.

Skutnabb-Kangass, T., & Toukomaa, P. (1976). *Teaching migrant children's mother tongue and learning the language of the host country in the context of socio-cultural situation of the migrant family.* Helsinki: Finnish National Commission for UNESCO.

Slobin, D. I. (Ed.) (1985). *The crosslinguistic study of language acquisition* (Vol. 2). Hillsdale, NJ: Erlbaum.

Slobin, D. I., & Bever, T. G. (1982). Children's use of canonical sentence schemas: A crosslinguistic study of word order and inflections. *Cognition, 12*, 229–265.

Snow, C. E., Burns, M. S., & Griffin, P. (Eds.) (1998). *Preventing reading difficulties in young children.* Washington, DC: National Research Council.

Snow, C. E., & Hoefnagel-Hohle, M. (1978). The critical period of language acquisition: Evidence from second language learning. *Child Development, 49*, 1114–1128.

So, D., & Siegel, L. S. (1997). Learning to read Chinese: Semantic, syntactic, phonological and short-term memory skills in normally achieving and poor Chinese readers. *Reading and Writing: An International Journal, 9*, 1–21.

Soter, A. O. (1988). The second language learner and cultural transfer in narration. In A. C. Purves (Ed.), *Writing across languages and cultures: Issues in contrastive rhetoric* (pp. 177–205). Newbury Park, CA: Sage.

Speidel, G., Tharp, R., & Kobayashi, L. (1985). Is there a comprehension problem for children who speak nonstandard English? A study of children with Hawaiian-English backgrounds. *Applied Psycholinguistics, 6*, 83–96.

Spires, H. A., Gallini, J., & Riggsbee, J. (1992). Effects of schema-based and text structure-based cues on expository prose comprehension in fourth graders. *Journal of Experimental Education, 60*, 307–320.

Spiro, R. J., & Myers, A. (1984). Individual differences and underlying cognitive processes. In R. Barr, M. L. Kamil, & P. Mosenthal (Eds.), *Handbook of reading research* (pp. 471–504). New York: Longman.

Spivey-Knowlton, M. J., Tueswell, J. C., & Tanenhaus, M. K. (1994). Context effects in syntactic ambiguity resolution: Discourse and semantic influence in parsing reduced relative clauses. In J. M. Henderson, M. Singer, & F. Ferreira (Eds.), *Reading and language processing* (pp. 148–181). Mahwah, NJ: Erlbaum.

Stahl, S. A., & Fairbanks, M. M. (1986). The effects of vocabulary instruction: A model-based meta-analysis. *Review of Educational Research, 56*, 72–110.

Stahl, S. A., & Murray, B. A. (1994). Defining phonological awareness and its relationship to early reading. *Journal of Educational Psychology, 86,* 221–234.

Stanovich, K. E. (1986). Matthew effects in reading: Some consequences of individual difference in the acquisition of literacy. *Reading Research Quarterly, 21,* 360–406.

Stanovich, K. E. (1988). The language code: Issues in word recognition. In S. R. Yussen and M. C. Smith (Eds.), *Reading across the life span.* New York: Springer-Verlag.

Stanovich, K. E. (1991). Changing models of reading and acquisition. In L. Rieben & C. A. Perfetti (Eds.), *Learning to read* (pp. 19–32). Hillsdale, NJ: Erlbaum.

Stanovich, K. E. (2000). *Progress in understanding reading: Scientific foundations and new frontiers.* New York: Guilford Press.

Stanovich, K. E., Cunningham, A. E., & Cramer, B. B. (1984). Assessing phonological awareness of kindergarten children: Issues of task comparability. *Journal of Experimental Psychology, 38,* 175–190.

Stanovich, K. E., & West, R. F. (1989). Exposure to print and orthographic processing. *Reading Research Quarterly, 24,* 402–433.

Steffensen, M. S., Goetz, E. T., & Cheng, X. (1999). A cross-linguistic perspective on imagery and affect: Dual coding in Chinese and English. *Journal of Literacy Research, 31,* 293–319.

Steffensen, M. S., Joag-Dev, C., & Anderson, R. C. (1979). A cross-cultural perspective on reading comprehension. *Reading Research Quarterly, 15,* 10–29.

Stein, N. L., & Glenn, C. F. (1979). An analysis of story comprehension in elementary school children. In R. O. Freedle (Ed.), *New directions in discourse processing,* vol. 2, *Advances in discourse processes* (pp. 53–120). Norwood, NJ: Ablex.

Stein, N. L., & Nezworski, T. (1978). The effect of organization and instructional set on story memory. *Discourse Processes, 1,* 177–193.

Sternberg, R. J. (1987). Most vocabulary is learned from context. In M. G. McKeown & M. E. Curtis (Eds.), *The nature of vocabulary acquisition* (pp. 89–103). Hillsdale, NJ: Erlbaum.

Stoddard, K., Valcante, G., Sindlear, P., O'Shea, L., & Algozzine, B. (1993). Reading rate and comprehension: The effects of repeated readings, sentence segmentation, and intonation training. *Reading Research and Instruction, 32,* 53–65.

Stolz, J. A., & Feldman, L. B. (1995). The role of orthographic and semantic transparency of the base morpheme in morphological processing. In L. B. Feldman (Ed.), *Morphological aspects of language processing* (pp. 109–129). Hillsdale, NJ: Erlbaum.

Stoltzfus, E. R., Hasher, L., & Zacks, R. T. (1996). Working memory and aging: Current status of the inhibitory view. In J. T. E. Richardson, R. W. Engle, L. Hasher, R. H. Logie, E. R. Stoltzfus, & R. T. Zacks (Eds.), *Working memory and human cognition* (pp. 66–88). New York: Oxford University Press.

Swan, M. (1997). The influence of the mother tongue on second language vocabulary acquisition and use. In N. Schmitt & M. McCarthy (Eds.), *Vocabulary: Description, acquisition and pedagogy* (pp. 156–180). Cambridge: Cambridge University Press.

Tabossi, P., Spivey-Knowlton, M., McRae. K., & Tanenhaus, M. (1993). Semantic effects on syntactic ambiguity resolution: Evidence for a constraint-based resolution process. In C. Umilta & M. Moscovitch (Eds.), *Attention and performance XV* (pp. 589–615) Cambridge: MIT Press.

Taft, M. (1991). *Reading and the mental lexicon.* Hillsdale, NJ: Erlbaum.

Taft, M., & Zhu, X. P. (1995). The representation of bound morphemes in the lexicon: A Chinese study. In L. B. Feldman (Ed.), *Morphological aspects of language processing* (pp. 109–129). Hillsdale, NJ: Erlbaum.

Taillefer, G. F. (1996). L2 reading ability: Further insight into the short-circuit hypothesis. *Modern Language Journal, 80,* 461–477.

Talmy, L. (1985). Lexicalization patterns: Semantic structures in lexical forms. In S. Shopen (Ed.), *Language typology and syntactic description,* vol. 3, *Grammatical categories and the lexicon* (pp. 36–149). Cambridge: Cambridge University Press.

Tang, G. (1992). The effect of graphic representation of knowledge structures on ESL reading comprehension. *Studies in Second Language Acquisition, 14,* 177–195.

Tang, H. N., & Moore, D. W. (1992). Effects of cognitive and metacognitive pre-reading activities on the reading comprehension of ESL learners. *Educational Psychology, 12,* 315–331.

Tannen, D. (1980). A comparative analysis of oral narrative strategies: Athenian Greek and American English. In W. L. Chafe (Ed.), *The pear stories* (pp. 51–87). Norwood, NJ: Ablex.

Taylor, B. M. (1982). Text structure and children's comprehension and memory for expository material. *Journal of Educational Psychology, 74,* 323–340.

Taylor, B. M., & Beach, R. W. (1984). The effects of text structure instruction on middle-grade students' comprehension and production of expository text. *Reading Research Quarterly, 19,* 134–146.

Taylor, I., & Olson, D. R. (Eds.). (1995). *Scripts and literacy: Reading and learning to read alphabets, syllabaries and characters.* Dordrecht, the Netherlands: Kluwer.

Taylor, I., & Taylor M. M. (1995). *Writing and literacy in Chinese, Korean, and Japanese.* Philadelphia: John Benjamins.

Tian, G. S. (1990). The effects of rhetorical organization in expository prose on ESL readers in Singapore. *RELC Journal: A Journal of Language Teaching and Research in Southeast Asia, 21,* 1–13.

Thorndike, R. L. (1974). Reading as reasoning. *Reading Research Quarterly, 9,* 135–147.

Torgesen, J. K., & Burgess, S. R. (1998). In J. L. Metsala & L. C. Ehri (Eds.), *Word recognition in beginning literacy* (p. 3–40). Mahwah, NJ: Erlbaum.

Trabasso, T., Secco, T., & van den Broek, P. W. (1984). Causal cohesion and story coherence. In H. Mandl, N. L. Stein, & T. Trabasso (Eds.), *Learning and comprehension of text* (pp. 83–111). Hillsdale, NJ: Erlbaum.

Trabasso, T., & van den Broek, P. W. (1985). Causal thinking and the representation of narrative events. *Journal of Memory and Language, 24,* 612–630.

Trabasso, T., van den Broek, P. W., & Suh, S. Y. (1989). Logical necessity and transitivity of causal relations in stories. *Discourse Processes, 12,* 1–25.

Treiman, R., & Zukowski, A. (1991). Levels of phonological awareness. In S. A. Brady & D. P. Shankweiler (Eds.), *Phonological processes in literacy* (pp. 67–83). Hillsdale, NJ: Erlbaum.

Troike, R. C. (1978). Research evidence for the effectiveness of bilingual education. *NABE Journal, 3,* 13–24.

Tyler, A., & Nagy, W. (1989). The acquisition of English derivational morphology. *Journal of Memory and Language, 28,* 649–667.

Tyler, A., & Nagy, W. (1990). Use of derivational morphology during reading. *Cognition, 36,* 17–34.

Tzeng, O. J. L., & Wang, W. S.-Y. (1983). The first two R's: The way different languages reduce speech to script affects how visual information is processed in the brain. *American Scientist, 71,* 238–243.

Ulijin, J. M., & Strother, J. B. (1990). The effects of syntactic simplification on reading EST texts as L1 and L2. *Journal of Research in Reading, 13,* 38–54.

Urquhart, A. H. (1984). The effect of rhetorical ordering on readability. In J. C. Alderson & A. H. Urquhart (Eds.), *Reading in a foreign language* (pp. 160–175). London: Longman.

Vaid, J. (1995). Effect of reading and writing directions on nonlinguistic perception and performance: Hindi and Urdu data. In I. Taylor & D. R. Olson (Eds.), *Scripts and literacy: Reading and learning to read the world's scripts* (pp. 295–310). Dordrecht, the Netherlands: Kluwer Academic.

van den Broek, P. (1994). Comprehension and memory of narrative texts: Inferences and coherence. In M. A. Gernsbacher (Ed.), *Handbook of psycholinguistics* (pp. 539–588). San Diego: Academic Press.

van den Broek, P., & Trabasso, T. (1986). Causal network vs. goal hierarchies in summarizing text. *Discourse Processes, 9,* 1–15.

Vandergrift, L. (1997). The comprehension strategies of second language (French) listeners: A descriptive study. *Foreign Language Annals, 30,* 387–409.

van Dijk, T. A., & Kintsch, W. (1983). *Strategies of discourse comprehension.* New York: Academic Press.

Van Heuven, W. J. B., Dijkstra, T., & Grainger, J. (1998). Orthographic neighborhood effects in bilingual word recognition. *Journal of Memory and Language, 39,* 458–483.

Vellutino, F. R., Scanlon, D. M. (1987). Phonological coding, phonological awareness, and reading ability: Evidence from a longitudinal and experimental study. *Merrill-Palmer Quarterly, 33,* 321–363.

Vellutino, F. R., Scanlon, D. M., Sipay, E., Small, S., Pratt, A., Chen, R., & Denckla, M. (1996). Cognitive profiles of difficult to remediate and readily remediated poor readers: Early intervention as a vehicle for distinguishing between cognitive and experimental as basic causes of specific reading disability. *Journal of Educational Psychology, 88,* 601–638.

Verhoeven, L. (2000). Components in early second language reading and spelling, *Scientific Studies of Reading, 4,* 313–330.

Voss, J. F. (1972). On the relationship of associative and organizational processes. In E. Tulving & W. Donaldson (Eds.), *Organization of memory* (pp. 167–194). New York: Academic Press.

Wade-Woolley, L., & Geva, E. (2000). Processing novel phonemic contrasts in the acquisition of L2 word reading. *Scientific Studies of Reading, 4,* 295–311.

Wagner, R. K., Torgesen, J. K., & Rashotte, C. A. (1994). The development of reading-related phonological processing abilities: New evidence of bi-directional causality from a latent variable longitudinal study. *Developmental Psychology, 30,* 73–87.

Walker, C. H., & Meyer, B. J. F. (1980). Integrating different types of information in text. *Journal of Verbal Learning and Verbal Behavior, 19,* 263–275.

Wang, A. Y., Thomas, M. H., & Ouellette, J. A. (1992). Keyword mnemonic and retention of second-language vocabulary words. *Journal of Educational Psychology, 84,* 520–528.

Wang, M., Koda, K., & Perfetti, C. A. (2003). Alphabetic and non-alphabetic L1 effects in English semantic processing: A comparison of Korean and Chinese English L2 learners. *Cognition, 87,* 129–149.

Waters, G. S., & Caplan, D. (1996). The measurement of verbal working memory capacity and its relation to reading comprehension. *Quarterly Journal of Experimental Psychology, 49A,* 51–79.

Weinberg, A. (1995). Licensing constraints and the theory of language processing. In R. Mazuka & N. Nagai (Eds.), *Japanese sentence processing* (pp. 235–256). Hillsdale, NJ: Erlbaum.

Weinstein, C. E., & Mayer, R. E. (1986). The teaching of learning strategies. In M. R. Wittrock (Ed.), *Handbook of research on teaching* (3d ed.; pp. 315–27). New York: Macmillan.

White, L. (1989). *Universal grammar and second language acquisition.* Philadelphia: John Benjamins.

Wierzbicka, A. (1995). Emotion and facial expression: A semantic perspective. *Culture and Psychology, 1,* 227–258.

Wierzbicka, A. (1999). *Emotion across cultures.* Oxford: Oxford University Press.

Wirotanan, J. (2002). Reading strategies of university EFL Thai readers in reading Thai and English expository texts. Doctoral dissertation, University of Pittsburgh. *Dissertation Abstracts International, 63,* 05A.

Wixson, K. K. (1986). Vocabulary, instruction and children's comprehension of basal stories. *Reading Research Quarterly, 21,* 317–329.

Wolman, C. (1991). Sensitivity to causal cohesion in stories by children with mild mental retardation, children with learning disabilities, and children without disabilities. *Journal of Special Education, 25*, 135–154.

Wood, E. G., Pressley, M., & Winne, P. H. (1990). Elaborative interrogation effects on children's learning of factual content. *Journal of Educational Psychology, 82*, 741–748.

Yanco, J. J. (1985). Language contact and grammatical interference: Hausa and Zarma in Niamey, Niger. *Studies in African Linguistics, 9*, 318–322.

Yano, Y., Long, M. H., & Ross, S. (1994). The effects of simplified and elaborated texts on foreign language reading comprehension. *Language Learning, 44*, 189–219.

Yik, W. F. (1978). The effect of visual and acoustic similarity on short-term memory for Chinese words. *Quarterly Journal of Experimental Psychology, 30*, 386–494.

Yopp, H. K. (1988). The validity and reliability of phonemic awareness tests. *Reading Research Quarterly, 23*, 159–177.

Yorio, C. A. (1971). Some sources of reading problems in foreign language learners. *Language Learning, 21*, 107–115.

Young, D. (1999). Linguistic simplification of SL reading material: Effective instructional practice? *Modern Language Journal, 83*, 350–366.

Young, D. J., & Oxford, R. (1997). A gender-related analysis of strategies used to process written input in the native language and a foreign language. *Applied Language Learning, 8*, 43–73.

Yu, V. (1993). Extensive reading programs – how can they best benefit the teaching and learning of english? *TESL Reporter, 26*, 1–9.

Yu, W. V. (1999). Promoting second language development and reading habits through an extensive reading scheme. In Y. M. Cheah & M. N. Seok (Eds.), *Language instructional issues in Asian classrooms* (pp. 59–74). Newark, DE: International Reading Association.

Zhang, G., & Simon, H. A. (1985). STM capacity for Chinese words and idioms: Chunking and acoustical loop hypothesis. *Memory and Cognition, 13*, 193–201.

Zhang, H. C. (1994). Some studies on the recognition of Chinese characters. In Q. Jing, H. Zhang, & D. Peng (Eds.), *Information processing of Chinese language* (pp. 1–11). Beijing: Beijing Normal University.

Zhang, S., & Perfetti, C. A. (1993). The tongue-twister effect in reading Chinese. *Journal of Experimental Psychology: Learning, Memory, and Cognition, 19*, 1–12.

Zhicheng, Z. (1992). The effects of teaching reading strategies on improving reading comprehension for ESL learners. Paper presented at the annual meeting of the Mid-South Education Association, Knoxv-11c, TN, ERIC Document Reproduction Service No. ED 356 643.

Zhou, X., & Marslen-Wilson, W. (1994). Words, morphemes, and syllables in the Chinese mental lexicon. *Language and Cognitive Processes, 9*, 393–422.

Zhou, Y. G. (1978). To what degree are the "phonetics" of present-day Chinese characters still phonetic? *Zhougguo Yuwen, 146,* 172–177.

Zimmerman, C. B. (1997). Historical trends in second language vocabulary instruction. In J. Coady & T. Huckin (Eds.), *Second language vocabulary acquisition* (pp. 5–19). New York: Cambridge University Press.

Zwaan, R. A., & Radvansky, G. A. (1998). Situation models in language comprehension and memory. *Psychological Bulletin, 123,* 162–185.